T0345017

Aging Issues in the United States and Japan

A National Bureau
of Economic Research
Conference Report

Aging Issues in the United States and Japan

Edited by Seiritsu Ogura, Toshiaki Tachibanaki, and David A. Wise

The University of Chicago Press

Chicago and London

SEIRITSU OGURA is professor of economics at Hosei University.
TOSHIAKI TACHIBANAKI is professor of economics at the Kyoto
Institute of Economic Research, Kyoto University. DAVID A. WISE
is the John F. Stambaugh Professor of Political Economy at the
John F. Kennedy School of Government, Harvard University, and
the director for Health and Retirement Programs at the National
Bureau of Economic Research.

The University of Chicago Press, Chicago 60637
The University of Chicago Press, Ltd., London
© 2001 by the National Bureau of Economic Research
All rights reserved. Published 2001
Printed in the United States of America
10 09 08 07 06 05 04 03 02 01   1 2 3 4 5
ISBN: 0-226-62081-6 (cloth)

Library of Congress Cataloging-in-Publication Data

Aging issues in the United States and Japan / edited by Seiritsu
Ogura, Toshiaki Tachibanaki, and David A. Wise
        p.   cm. — (National Bureau of Economic Research
conference report)
    Includes bibliographical references and index. ·
    ISBN 0-226-62081-6 (alk. paper)
    1. Aged—United States—Economic conditions—
Congresses.   2. Aged—Japan—Economic conditions—
Congresses.   3. Age distribution (Demography)—Economic
aspects—United States—Congresses.   4. Age distribution
(Demography)—Economic aspects—Japan—Congresses.
    I. Ogura, Seiritsu.   II. Tachibanaki, Toshiaki, 1943–   III. Wise,
David A.   IV. Series.
HQ1064.U5 A63476   2001
305.26'0952—dc21   2001017450

Contents

Preface

This volume consists of papers presented at a joint Japan Center for Economic Research–National Bureau of Economic Research conference held in Kyoto, Japan, in May 1997. Financial support from the Department of Health and Human Services, National Institute on Aging (grants P01-AG05842 and P20-AG12810) and the Japan Center for Global Partnership, is gratefully acknowledged. Any other funding sources are noted in individual papers.

Any opinions expressed in this volume are those of the respective authors and do not necessarily reflect the views of the National Bureau of Economic Research, the Japan Center for Economic Research, or the sponsoring organizations.

Introduction

David A. Wise

The Japan Center for Economic Research and the National Bureau of Economic Research have been engaged in joint projects on the economics of aging and related areas for several years. Two prior conference volumes reporting the results of these studies have been published: Aging in the United States and Japan in 1994, and The Economic Effects of Aging in the United States and Japan in 1997. This volume contains papers presented in Kyoto, Japan, in May 1997. The papers are focused on four topics: (a) saving, wealth, and asset allocation over the life cycle, (b) health care and health care reform, (c) incentives for early retirement, as well as labor market incentives over the working life, and (d) population projections. In all but the fourth category, papers from both Japan and the United States are included. While the papers in the volume from the two countries are not strictly comparable, when considering the larger body of evidence in Japan and the United states, the evidence from one country can be contrasted with similar evidence from the other. The following summary draws heavily on the wording of the authors themselves.

Saving, Wealth, and Asset Allocation

In the United States

As the retired population grows relative to the working population, the prospects for public financing of support in retirement have generated in-

David A. Wise is the John F. Stambaugh Professor of Political Economy at the John F. Kennedy School of Government, Harvard University, and the director for health and retirement programs at the National Bureau of Economic Research.

creasing public and private concern. Yet a large fraction of Americans depend almost entirely on Social Security for support in retirement, and most Americans now reaching retirement age have accumulated very little in personal saving. Others have accumulated substantial saving. Why do some households have substantial wealth at retirement while others have very little? Indeed, why do some households with given lifetime earnings have substantial wealth at retirement, while other households with the same lifetime earnings accumulate very little wealth? In their paper on "Choice, Chance, and Wealth Dispersion at Retirement," Steven F. Venti and David A. Wise conclude that most of the dispersion in wealth, given similar lifetime earnings, must be attributed to the choice of whether to save at younger ages.

People accumulate different amounts of wealth in part because they have different earnings. We essentially set that dispersion aside by considering persons with similar lifetime earnings. Thus the discussion here is about the dispersion of asset accumulation among persons with the same lifetime earnings. Given lifetime earnings, Venti and Wise consider the importance of "chance" events versus the choice to save in determining asset accumulation.

Whether accumulated wealth is attributable to the choice to save rather than to chance can have significant implications for government policy. Many policies impose ex post taxes on accumulated assets. For example, elderly Americans who have saved when young and thus have higher capital incomes when older pay higher taxes on Social Security benefits. Shoven and Wise (1997, 1998) show that those who save too much in pension plans in particular face very large "success" tax penalties when pension benefits are withdrawn. In addition, pension assets left as a bequest can be virtually confiscated through the tax system. The spend-down Medicaid provision is another example. The belief—perhaps unstated—that chance events determine the dispersion in wealth may weigh in favor of such taxes in the legislative voting that imposes them.

If, on the other hand, the dispersion of wealth among the elderly reflects conscious lifetime spending versus saving decisions—rather than differences in lifetime resources—these higher taxes may be harder to justify and appear to penalize savers who spend less when they are young. From an economic perspective, if wealth accumulation is random, taxing saving has no incentive effects. On the other hand, if wealth accumulation results from conscious decisions to save versus spend, penalizing savers may have substantial incentive effects, discouraging individuals from saving for their own retirement and limiting aggregate economic growth. It is important to understand that this paper is about the dispersion in the accumulation of assets of persons with similar lifetime incomes. The issue raised here is not about progressive taxation, but rather about differences in tax imposed on persons who spend tomorrow versus today, given the same after-tax lifetime earnings.

In 1953 Milton Friedman wrote a paper he called "Choice, Chance, and the Personal Distribution of Income." In this paper he says,

Differences among individuals or families in the amount of income received are generally regarded as reflecting either circumstances largely outside the control of the individuals concerned, such as unavoidable chance occurrences and differences in natural endowment and inherited wealth. . . . The way that individual choice can affect the distribution of income has been less frequently noticed. The alternatives open to an individual differ, among other respects, in the probability distribution of income they promise. Hence his choice among them depends in part on his taste for risk. . . . The foregoing analysis is exceedingly tentative. . . . Yet I think it goes far enough to demonstrate that one cannot rule out the possibility that a large part of the existing inequality of wealth can be regarded as produced by men to satisfy their tastes and preferences.

Now, over forty years later, "people earn just enough to get by" is a phrase often used to explain the low personal saving rate in the United States. The implicit presumption is that households simply do not earn enough to pay for current needs and to save. Yet in other developed countries the saving rate at all income levels is much higher than in the United States. Even in Canada—in many respects similar to the United States—the personal saving rate is almost twice as high as that in the United States. Such international comparisons alone suggest that saving depends on much more than lifetime earnings.

Venti and Wise show in this paper that at all levels of lifetime earnings there is an enormous dispersion in the accumulated wealth of families approaching retirement. In the United States it is not only households with low incomes that save little. A significant proportion of high-income households also saves very little. And, not all low-income households are nonsavers. Indeed, a substantial proportion of low-income households saves a great deal. The authors then consider the extent to which differences in household lifetime financial resources explain the wide dispersion in wealth, given lifetime earnings. They find that very little of this dispersion can be explained by chance differences in individual circumstances—"largely outside the control of the individuals"—that might limit the resources from which saving might plausibly be made. We conclude that the bulk of the dispersion must be attributed to differences in the amounts that households choose to save. Choices vary enormously across households. Some choose to save more and spend less over their working lives, whereas others choose to save little and spend more while working. Wide dispersion in saving is evident at all levels of lifetime earnings, from the lowest to the highest. The differences in saving choices among households with similar lifetime earnings lead to vastly different levels of asset accumulation by the time retirement age approaches.

Perhaps more closely related to the choice of risk that Friedman emphasized, Venti and Wise also considered how much of the dispersion in wealth might be accounted for by different investment choices of savers—some more risky, some less risky—again given lifetime earnings. The authors find that investment choice matters but is not a major determinant of the dispersion in asset accumulation. It matters about as much as chance events that limit the available resources of households with the same lifetime earnings. Thus, although investment choices make a difference, the overwhelming determinant of the accumulation of wealth at retirement is simply the choice to save.

As a benchmark Venti and Wise also considered the assets that the Health and Retirement Survey (HRS) respondents would have accumulated had they saved given amounts over their working lives and earned given returns on their saving. Saving 10 percent of earnings and earning the average annual S&P 500 return (which has been 12.2 percent since 1926) would have led to accumulated assets much greater than the typical financial assets of HRS households at the time of the survey.

Perhaps based on the presumption—contrary to Friedman's conjecture—that differences in wealth can be attributed more to differences across households in adverse circumstances that limit saving than to explicit individual choices, government policy often penalizes persons who have saved over their lifetimes. For example, persons with the same lifetime earnings will face very different tax rates on Social Security benefits: Those who saved will pay higher taxes, while those who did not will pay lower taxes. Shoven and Wise (1997, 1998) show that persons who save too much through personal or employer-provided pensions face enormous tax penalties when they use these accumulated assets for retirement support. The evidence that differences in retirement wealth are due largely to saving choice while younger brings into question this tendency in tax policy. Although the distribution of the tax burden will inevitably be based on many factors, most observers believe that the extent to which older persons with more assets are taxed should depend in part on how they acquired the assets. Chance accumulation may weigh on the side of heavier taxes on those who have accumulated. On the other hand, accumulation by choosing to consume less when young, while others choose to consume more when young, weights against heavier taxes on those who accumulate assets for retirement. As emphasized at the outset, this paper is about the dispersion in the accumulation of assets of persons with similar lifetime earnings. The issue raised here is not about progressive income taxation, but rather—given the same after-tax earnings—about differences in the tax imposed on persons who save today in order to spend more tomorrow, versus those who spend everything today. The authors' analysis suggests that a very large proportion of the variation in the wealth of older households can be attributed to household saving choices while younger rather than to chance events that may have limited the resources available for saving. To the extent that most asset accumulation is due to choice rather than chance, the authors' results also suggest that ex ante taxing of saving may have more serious consequences for saving than may previously have been thought.

Finally, Venti and Wise explored the relationship between household saving and information about household saving that was obtained through two experimental saving modules administered in the third wave of the HRS. In general, the experimental module responses were consistent with household realized asset accumulation. About three-fourths of respondents said they had saved too little over the past twenty or thirty years, and the authors found a strong relationship between a household percentile level of assets, given lifetime earnings, and whether respondents thought they had saved enough. The accumulation of retirement assets is very strongly related to the age at which persons began to save for retirement. In addition, persons who accumulated more retirement assets tended to have a saving target or plan, and the plan typically included saving a portion of each paycheck. Those who accumulated little were more likely to say that they just couldn't get caught up on their bills or that they had a hard time sticking to a saving plan. Low saving rates seem to be only weakly related to an expectation that Social Security or employer pension plans would take care of retirement income, even among households with low lifetime earnings. The potential cost of health care is an important concern of a large fraction of households, and this concern appears to be unrelated to asset accumulation. On the other hand, there appears to be relatively little concern about job loss, support of children or parents, or financial market collapse. The results from the HRS experimental saving modules suggests that this type of information collection might fruitfully be pursued in more depth.

While Venti and Wise consider the reasons for wealth dispersion at retirement, James M. Poterba and Andrew A. Samwick examine changes in the ways people save over their lifetimes. This issue has become increasingly important as a larger fraction of saving for retirement is through personal retirement accounts, such as 401(k) plans, Individual Retirement Accounts, and others. Including employer-provided non-401(k)-defined contribution plans, over 76 percent of contributions are to plans controlled in large measure by individuals—who make participation, contribution, withdrawal, and asset allocation decisions. In "Household Portfolio Allocation over the Life Cycle," Poterba and Samwick analyze the relationship between age and portfolio structure of U.S. households. They find important differences in whether people own assets and portfolio shares over the life cycle. In addition, they find important differences by birth cohort.

The authors motivate their analysis by emphasizing that recent and prospective aging of the populations in developed countries has attracted attention in many nations. The potential effects of population aging on social security systems and the level of private and national saving have drawn the most interest from both academics and policy analysts. In the United States particular attention has focused on the adequacy of the baby boom generation's level of retirement saving. The way households allocate their accumulated saving across different assets—such as stocks, bonds, and real estate—has attracted less discussion, even though future economic security can depend as much on the way assets are invested as on the level of those assets. Asset allocation is also essential for understanding the behavior of individuals in the increasingly popular defined contribution pension plans that allow participants some discretion in their investment choices and for analyzing recent proposals for Social Security reform that call for mandatory saving accounts, with investment responsibility delegated to individuals.

Although there is little empirical work on asset allocation, there is a theoretical literature on the optimal portfolio behavior of individuals at different ages. This work is characterized by some controversy, in part between academics and practical financial advisers. In the standard portfolio choice paradigm that underlies most of financial economics, the only factor that should explain age-related differences in portfolio structure is differential risk aversion. In this setting, if a household is endowed with a time-invariant risk tolerance, then there should be no age-related patterns of portfolio allocation. Conditional on a household's risk aversion, there are strong predictions regarding the mix of risky and riskless assets that a household should hold. Moreover, regardless of their risk aversion, all households should hold risky assets in the same proportions within their risky asset portfolios.

This paper complements the substantial theoretical discussion of age-related patterns in asset allocation. It presents systematic empirical evidence on the basic patterns of household asset allocation over the life cycle. This information can help to evaluate competing models of household portfolio behavior, and more generally to assess proposals for greater reliance on household choices in retirement preparation. Using multiple waves of the Surveys of Consumer Finances, the authors control for systematic differences across birth cohorts in the age-specific pattern of asset ownership. Poterba and Samwick provide two broad conclusions. First, there are important differences across asset classes in both the age-specific probabilities of asset ownership and in the portfolio shares of different assets at different ages. The notion that all assets can be treated as identical from the standpoint of analyzing household wealth accumulation is not supported by the data. Institutional factors, asset liquidity, and evolving investor tastes must be recognized in modeling asset demand. These factors could affect analyses of overall household saving as well as the composition of this saving. Second, there are evident differences in the asset ownership probabilities of different birth cohorts. Older households were more likely to hold corporate stock, and less likely to hold tax-exempt bonds, than were younger households, at any given age. Recognizing these differences across cohorts is important when analyzing asset accumulation profiles.

The authors emphasize that empirical evidence on the structure of household portfolios bears on a variety of questions in financial economics and public finance. One question that the results address is the degree to which the standard life cycle framework of asset accumulation can be applied to different components of wealth. The life cycle model posits a hump-shaped pattern of asset accumulation as households age: They accumulate assets during their working years and spend down those assets during their retirement years. The results in the paper by Poterba and Samwick suggest that the hump-shaped pattern is not uniform across all assets. For example, as a percentage of total assets, financial assets show just the opposite pattern; they decline as households age, and then begin to increase at advanced ages. Investment real estate and equity in privately held businesses do display a hump-shaped pattern, as in the life cycle model, but owner-occupied housing does not, since there is no evident decline in its ownership at older ages.

The standard life cycle model does not distinguish between various types of assets. Yet when assets exhibit different degrees of liquidity (e.g., with financial assets more liquid than business net worth or other real estate assets), the age pattern of asset holdings may contain important clues for evaluating competing theories of saving behavior. Precautionary saving models suggest that households should seek assets that can be liquidated in the event of a financial need. The different age profiles that we identify should therefore provide grist for future research on motives for saving.

A second issue that their findings address is the importance of cohort-specific factors, such as experience with historical returns on different assets or exposure to financial advertisements, in shaping portfolio patterns. Baby boomers show roughly the average propensity to hold taxable equity and the average portfolio share of taxable equity. Younger cohorts show greater investment in taxable bonds, tax-exempt bonds, and tax-deferred accounts than do older cohorts. They show lower investments in bank accounts and other financial assets. Compared with previous cohorts, the baby boom generation appears to be more willing to take advantage of the more sophisticated financial instruments that have become available over the past twenty years.

Younger cohorts have also leveraged their assets to a greater extent than older cohorts. This suggests that greater use of debt may also be the result of liberalization of financial markets over the last two decades. Nonetheless, the burden of servicing this debt will reduce the extent to which the baby boomers can use their assets to support consumption in retirement. Their results suggest that borrowing behavior should receive attention, along with asset accumulation, in studies of financial preparation for retirement.

The authors point out that the important cohort patterns they identify suggest that it is essential to distinguish between the saving and asset accumulation of various cohorts as they approach retirement. The experience of one cohort as it approaches retirement may not translate to other, younger cohorts. These results provide a warrant for the type of research now being undertaken, in many contexts, on the retirement planning and preparation of the baby boom cohort in the United States.

In Japan

The United States has a long history of analyses of the relationship between promised social security benefits and private personal saving. The weight of the evidence is that increased social security promises reduce personal saving. Seki Asano finds that in Japan a reduction in social security benefits increased private saving. In his paper titled "The Social Security System and the Demand for Personal Annuity and Life Insurance: An Analysis of Japanese Microdata, 1990 and 1994," Asano examines the effect of changes in the public social security system on the private life insurance and annuity holdings of Japanese households.

The household surveys used in the analysis were collected in 1990 and 1994. During this time period, the Japanese economy experienced two important changes that are relevant for household saving. The first was the increase in the normal retirement age for social security from sixty to sixty-five. (See the summary of the paper by Yukiko Abe, which considers the labor supply incentive effects of other reforms to the social security system.) The second was a 40 percent decline in the value of marketable assets such as real estate and corporate stock. Both of these changes should have increased the need for households to accumulate additional personal wealth.

The analysis in this paper proceeds in three stages. The first involves the careful calculation of the expected values of the annuity and life insurance payments from the public pension system, both before and after the reforms. The second stage of the paper sets up a model of wealth accumulation based on the households' needs to provide both annuities and life insurance. In this model, public and personal saving are perfect substitutes. As a result, households are predicted to reduce their own saving in proportion to how much they are promised by the public systems. The last stage is an econometric test of the model.

The main results are that private annuity saving increased by more than enough to offset the effects of the government reform during this period. There was also some evidence that the increase was concentrated among the younger generations, who were most affected by the reforms. Life insurance holdings were less affected by the reforms. Overall, the results suggest a model of saving in which households have target levels of annuities and bequests and will save rapidly if necessary in order to achieve them.

In Japan and the United States

Many factors determine the intergenerational distribution of consumption. Perhaps foremost among these is economic growth. A high rate of economic growth enables each new generation to have higher levels of both consumption and lifetime income than were attainable by previous generations. In most economies experiencing rapid economic growth, the younger generations share some of their gains through public pension schemes that redistribute consumption from the young or middle-aged to the less well-off older generation. As long as growth continues and the dependency ratio (of retired to nonretired persons) remains low, such programs are little burden to younger generations. However, as the population begins to age and economic growth slows, these intergenerational transfer schemes can have significant adverse effects on the consumption of the young. In Japan, as in the United States and other countries, there is a serious concern that existing social welfare programs excessively favor the current older generation at great cost to younger generations. In "An Empirical Investigation of Intergenerational Consumption Distribution: A Comparison among Japan, the United States, and the United Kingdom," Makoto Saito considers how the gains from economic growth have been distributed among generations over the past thirty years in these three countries.

The analysis focuses on how both consumption and lifetime income have evolved for different generations of workers in Japan, the United States, and the United Kingdom. The analysis is based on age-classified consumption data for each country, spanning the years 1959–94 for Japan, 1972–94 for the United States, and 1971–91 for the United Kingdom.

Direct tabulations of these data reveal that in both the United States and Japan, per capita consumption has declined substantially over time for younger age groups, while consumption among the old has increased dramatically. In contrast, the young in the United Kingdom have fared better over time. This pattern raises the possibility that intergenerational transfers from the young to the old are of much larger scale in the United States and Japan than in the United Kingdom.

The paper next develops a theoretical framework to understand the consumption of different age groups over time. Observed consumption at a point in time combines age effects (e.g., the middle-aged consume more than the old) and cohort effects (e.g., older generation has higher post transfer lifetime income than younger generation). The cohort effects, which represent each generation's lifetime income available for consumption, may differ across generations. They represent the net effect of the complex interaction among economic growth, population aging, and the scale of intergenerational transfer programs. Each of these factors may vary both over time and across countries.

Age and cohort effects are estimated using the time series of age-classified consumption data. The empirical results are quite striking. In Japan lifetime income available for consumption peaked for the cohort born between 1932 and 1936. In the United States lifetime income peaked for the generation born between 1947 and 1951. Thus, in both countries younger generations fare worse than older generations. In contrast, lifetime incomes are higher for successively younger cohorts in the United Kingdom. Thus it appears that the interactions among slower economic growth, population aging, and government transfer policy have produced a quite different intergenerational distribution of consumption in the United Kingdom than in either Japan or the United States.

In addition to the principal finding regarding consumption trends in the three countries, several other results emerge as well. First, the results reject dynastic models based on altruism as explanations for consumption behavior in all three countries. Such models predict consumption smoothing across generations. The prediction is not supported by the data. Second, although the lifetime income may be falling for younger cohorts in the United States and Japan, it does not necessarily follow that the standard of living has decreased for these recent cohorts. The reason for this is that the real prices of goods fall in a growing economy. Indeed, the author calculates that based on the estimation results, the U.S. economy need grow at an annual rate of only 1.3 percent over the next two decades for the younger generation to keep up with the middle-aged generation. Finally, the estimated specification tested for liquidity constraints as an explanation for intergenerational differences in consumption by including the change in labor income as a determinant of the change in consumption. For most age intervals in all three countries, liquidity constraints are not an important source of differences in intergenerational consumption.

Health Care

In the United States and Other Countries

Health care is of particular importance to older persons, and the rising cost of health care is an important concern in almost all industrialized countries. In his paper titled "The Third Wave in Health Care Reform," David Cutler comments on a wave of health care reform that he believes will emphasize the efficiency of medical care. He draws attention to what he foresees in Organization for Economic Cooperation and Development (OECD) countries in general, including the United States and Japan.

The title of Cutler's paper refers to a forecast about coming trends in health care reform. He believes that a third wave of health care reform, focusing on improving the efficiency of medical care provision, will become common in the OECD in the next five to ten years.

The first wave of health care reform, Cutler assumes, was from the early 1950s until the early 1980s. In this era, most OECD countries built their health insurance systems. Universal coverage was guaranteed, and benefits were quite generous. There were few restrictions on the provision of services. As a result, medical spending consumed an increasing part of the economies of all OECD countries.

The growing cost of medical care led to the second wave of reform: a focus on cost containment. The most obvious way to limit medical spending is simply to limit the total amount of resources the medical sector can consume. Since governments in the OECD typically paid for most, if not all, of medical care spending, the government could easily limit overall spending. Furthermore, overall spending limits did not conflict with the goal of universal insurance coverage to a generous set of benefits. Thus, the 1980s saw the advent of wide-scale limits on medical spending in aggregate: global budgets for hospitals, volume reductions on physicians, and spending limits in institutions in the public sector.

However, limiting spending without altering the underlying demand or supply relations, Cutler emphasizes, does not necessarily lead to efficient medical care provision. In many countries, tight budget constraints have lead to inefficient provision of services and a growing role for the public sector. Some countries have concluded—and the author believes more will follow—that they need additional reforms to provide more of a market role in medical care provision. He refers to this incipient trend as the third wave of healthcare reform.

In this paper, Cutler documents the trends in OECD medical systems over the past fifty years. The world's medical systems have been in flux for most of the past fifty years. At first, countries built up their medical care system. Coverage was made universal, and benefits were generous. There was little demand- or supply-side cost sharing.

In the early 1980s, countries realized the unaffordability of generous demand incentives with no control over medical care supply. The typical response was to limit the total amount of services that could be provided. Given the commitment to universal insurance and low cost sharing that most countries had, this was the logical response. And this response saved money: The 1980s were characterized by much lower growth of medical costs than were the previous twenty years.

However, the strains in this approach ultimately became apparent. Excess demand with limits on the supply side led to waiting lists, nonpricing rationing, and the incentive to seek services out of the public sector. As a result, concern is shifting to the efficiency aspects of the market as well as the overall cost of the system.

A focus on efficiency, Cutler forecasts, is likely to involve two reforms, which he characterizes as the third wave of health care reform: increased competition for services, either at the level of the provider or at the level of the insurer; and increased patient cost sharing. Neither of these are easy reforms to undertake. Increased competition increases the incentives for adverse selection; increased cost sharing is more burdensome for the poor than for the rich. However, countries are finding, or are likely to find, that they have no alternative but to try these reforms.

As countries undertake a new round of health reform, it is important to keep one point in mind, says Cutler. To some extent, most countries are prisoners of what is done in the United States. When medical technology advances in the United States, it must ultimately advance around the world. Countries can make their systems more or less efficient and can speed up or delay the use of these technologies, but they are unlikely to postpone them forever. In this sense, stable medical reform around the world is likely to await stable medical reform in the United States.

In Japan

As in the United States, there are large differences in health care expenditures by geographic region. In their paper titled "Concentration and Persistence of Health Care Costs for the Aged," Seiritsu Ogura and Reiko Suzuki examine differences in health care costs for the elderly among municipalities in Japan.

The Ministry of Health and Welfare (MHW) releases data on regional differences in healthcare expenditure yearly. According to this data, looking at average per capita expenditure of those enrolled in the National Health Insurance Plan, expenditure ranged from the lowest in Okinawa to the highest in Hokkaido, where 1.97 times the Okinawa amount was spent on health care. Regional differences in health care expenditure are a phenomenon not unique to Japan, but can be seen in many other countries. They are a much larger issue in the United States, where the health care system is more market oriented, than in Japan. Although these regional discrepancies in Japan have been declining gradually, they still attract considerable attention in Japan. In particular, health care for the elderly takes up such a large share of total health care costs that it can alter the entire makeup of health care spending. Thus, in this study Suzuki and Ogura analyze the regional variation in elderly health care costs.

Probably the major reason for regional differences in health care expenditure, the authors conclude, lies in the oversupply of such health care facilities as staff, beds, and physicians. Recently, there has been speculation that the introduction of high-priced medical testing equipment such as computed axial tomography (CAT) scan and magnetic resonance imaging (MRI) equipment has caused advanced medical technology to become more widespread, thereby raising health care costs as well.

The first objective of the paper is to determine the factors behind the regional differences in health care expenditure, and to see how much of these discrepancies could be narrowed through equalizing the allocation of health care facilities and staff. Then, focusing on the government's transfers, which in effect transfer resources to areas with a high share of elderly, or with low income, the second objective is to see if it is important to attempt to close this gap, and if so, to clarify which features of expenditure might most appropriately be equalized.

In an effort to control healthcare costs, the MHW chooses about 150 municipalities (cities, towns, and villages) and requests that they make efforts to reduce health care expenditures. Municipalities are the smallest administrative units and are the insurance agents of the National Health Insurance Plan. The guidance to the municipalities is intended to encourage them to restrain wasteful healthcare spending on their enrollees (the residents in their municipalities). The authors emphasize that it is difficult for such small governmental units to bear large insurance risks, and they in fact receive large subsidies from the central government to pay the difference between their revenue and outlays.

The variation across municipalities in health care expenditures for the elderly is greater than the variation across larger geographical units such as prefectures. Intensity of health care supply works to increase these discrepancies, while the concentration of patients works to decrease them. The authors say, however, that even if it were possible to decrease the intensity of health care supply and patient density, and reduce differences across municipalities, this would not work to close the gaps, because the variation in expenditures is much greater than can be explained by the medical resources and patient density.

Since the elderly in low-income municipalities have longer hospital stays, health care expenditure is much higher than that in high-income municipalities. This is because low-income households do not have the capacity to care for the elderly in their homes, and hospitals take over the function of nursing homes. In addition, in low-income areas the revenue from insurance premiums is quite low, and these municipalities receive subsidies from the central government to pay for health care. In the present situation in which nursing care services are far from adequate, forcing the municipalities with high health care expenditures to lower their expenditures would mean that the channels for income transfer would be narrowed, and the income gap between the low- and high-income areas would widen, the authors say.

The smaller the population in the municipality, the greater the variation in their expenditure on health care. Municipalities with fewer than 1,000 people account for 25 percent of the cities, towns, and villages in this survey in eleven prefectures. The smaller municipalities are more likely to bear the risk of fluctuating health care expenditures. When considering these municipalities as insurers, the smaller they are, the higher the insurance risk. Among insurers there is a reinsurance system against high health care expenditures, and this covers these risks. Although this reinsurance system is effective, the authors argue that it would be better to expand the insurance base so that the risk is lowered. It is not, they say, rational to divide Japan into 3,251 separate insurance zones.

Satoshi Nakanishi and Noriyoshi Nakayama analyze the effects of demographic change on medical expenditures in Japan in their paper titled "The Effects of Demographic Change on Health and Medical Expenditures: A Simulation Analysis."

The goal of this study is to analyze the effect of demographic change on the health sector and the larger economy. The authors develop a simulation model with three sectors: (a) demand for medical services, (b) production of medical services, and (c) the general economy. Demand for medical services deals with patient behavior, and production of medical services deals with the behavior of hospitals and clinics. General economy models production of consumer goods other than health services and capital goods.

The share of GDP accounted for by medical expenditures will reach 11.3 percent by 2015. From 1960 to 1994, medical expenditures grew an average of 12.3 percent annually, greater than the 10.1 percent annual growth of GDP in the same period. As a result, medical expenditures as a percentage of GDP doubled from 2.5 percent in 1960 to 5.4 percent in 1994. From 1980 to 1994, medical expenditures grew at a slower rate, 5.5 percent per annum, after the Japanese government adopted a cost containment strategy aimed at limiting reimbursement rates while increasing the self-payment rate.

The results of the authors' simulation suggest that under the present health care system, the demand for medical care will grow at 2.7 percent per annum from 1991 to 2010. The share of GPD accounted for by medical expenditure will reach 11.3 percent by 2015 and thereafter will gradually decline. Although medical care expenditure will increase, the authors conclude that population aging will depress the health status of the typical elderly person. The authors find that it will be difficult to maintain the present level of health status in the 21st century. The authors also say that government cost containment strategies will mean that individuals will have to pay more for their own health care. In addition, the authors foresee a fall in national health status.

In the United States

In the United States, choice among health care plans has become an accepted goal of both employer-provided and public health care programs. Choice, however, brings with it the potential of adverse selection of high-cost users of medical care into generous and higher-cost plans. In "Choice among Employer-Provided Insurance Plans," Matthew J. Eichner considers the choice of plans by employees in a firm that offers three plans, which vary in generosity and in their cost to employees. Perhaps the central conclusion is that employees are reluctant to choose high-deductible plans—with greater risk of out-of-pocket costs—even though the lower premium for such plans would seemingly leave employees better off financially. While Eichner's analysis is based on the choices of employed persons, the ideas are equally applicable to older persons choosing among health care plans.

More choice has emerged as a politically palatable alternative to fundamental health reform in the United States. After several decades of rapid increases in the cost of providing coverage to employees, the elderly and the indigent, there was widespread anticipation of some governmental reform of the health care market. But even before it became clear that such reform would not materialize, and with increasing momentum afterward, firms sought to induce their employees to choose alternatives to the traditional fee-for-service plans, which presented the insured, their providers, or both with better incentives to control costs.

The incentives offered by firms to accept these new alternatives typically include expanded coverage and lower monthly premiums collected in the form of payroll deductions. Many employees now choose between a traditional fee-for-service plan with cost sharing and comparatively high payroll deductions, and one or more health maintenance organizations (HMOs) with no cost sharing and dramatically lower monthly payroll deductions. The HMOs use administrative or supply-side mechanisms to control the costs of providing care.

The federal government, too, has seized on choice as a means to lower health care costs. The Medicare program has allowed a number of HMOs to sign up the elderly. In return for accepting administrative controls over provision of services, the elderly are offered an expanded basket of services (typically including such things as pharmaceuticals and well-care) and freed from the bother of applying and then waiting for reimbursement from the Medicare system.

While HMOs have been in the forefront of the health care reform movement, other alternatives to traditional fee-for-service coverage have also emerged. The Health Insurance Access and Portability Act of 1996, known also as the Kennedy-Kassebaum bill, authorizes a limited trial of catastrophic insurance. Instead of seeking to implement cost control through administrative mechanisms and essentially eliminating coinsurance, catastrophic insurance aims to make individuals behave as if they are spending their own money. To provide the necessary liquidity to satisfy deductibles that might be several thousand dollars, the Kennedy-Kassebaum bill also provides for a tax-favored savings account from which expenditures below the level of the deductible are paid. This eliminates the tax advantages of low-deductible, high-premium insurance plans.

Under such a system, the question of how individuals make choices about insurance is critical. There are two fundamental questions, the answers to which will determine the long-term prospects of a system incorporating a high degree of choice among insurance alternatives. First, adverse selection of sicker individuals into the more generous coverage options is of concern. The initial estimates of cost saving from managed care and other alternative arrangements surely is at least in part due to the fact that these schemes attract the healthiest segments of the covered population. There is reason to suspect therefore that the cost savings will disappear or at least diminish as the number of people covered under the new alternatives—and the number of comparatively unhealthy people in particular—increases. Equally important is employee responsiveness to the pricing of the various insurance options. For example, how much lower must premiums be before large numbers of covered individuals will accept greater levels of risk bearing.

The Eichner paper presents some basic evidence on how employees choose health insurance coverage from a menu of options. (There is some evidence that they hesitate to choose low deductible plans, even though these may be offered at a discounted price that might leave them indifferent to the high deductible plan and other more generous coverage options.) This conclusion, however, is based on adherence to a standard expected utility approach, which might prove an inadequate framework for evaluating employee willingness to bear risk. In addition, the conclusions are no doubt sensitive to how one views the likelihood of persistent losses over a comparatively long time period. Applying this technique to the issue of plan choice is a future goal of this work.

In addition, the paper examines evidence concerning those employees who change plans voluntarily. This group consists disproportionately of larger family groupings that tend to move between two more-generous coverage options. Movement between plans seems to be associated with higher expenditures both before and after the move.

Labor Market Incentives

In Japan

Populations in almost all countries are aging rapidly, and life expectancies are increasing. Indeed, there is growing evidence that in the United States the health status of persons at retirement ages is increasing as well. Yet in almost countries persons are leaving the labor force at younger and younger ages. Perhaps Japan is an exception. Not only has the decline in labor force participation been modest in Japan, but even that modest decline has been met with changes in social security provisions, in an attempt to reverse the trend. Among industrialized countries, the fall in labor force participation of men between the ages of sixty and sixty-four has been much smaller in Japan than in other countries. Since 1990, the labor force participation of men in this age group in Japan has increased. An apparent reason for the increase was a series of changes in the provisions of the Japanese social security system, which was intended to reduce the incentive to retire early. In "Employees' Pension Benefits and the Labor Supply of Older Japanese Workers, 1980s–1990s," Yukiko Abe considers the effects of the disincentive in the system prior to the reform, as well as the potential effects of the reforms.

There are three major public pensions in Japan. The Employees' Pension insurance (EP) covers workers in the private sector and their spouses and is the largest public pension system in Japan. Public sector employees and private school personnel are covered by mutual aid associations (MAA) of several different types. Self-employed workers are covered by the National Pension (NP). Here, the focus is on the institutional structure relevant to the benefit structure for those who are covered by EP and are subject to provisions for working beneficiaries.

Currently, EP participants are eligible to receive benefits at age sixty (whereas the NP eligibility starts at age sixty-five). The starting age for EP eligibility is scheduled to increase gradually from 2001 to 2013. That is, before the eligibility age, EP participants aged sixty to sixty-four will receive only the benefit portion that is proportional to their lifetime EP contributions and will not receive the base benefits that the plan provides. Prior changes starting in the late 1980s were also intended to reduce early retirement incentives. However, even under the current system, work disincentives still exist, according to Abe.

In her paper, Abe examines the effects of EP benefit rules on labor supply. Although Abe's estimates suggest that the increase in labor supply of older persons in the early 1990s cannot be attributed in large part to the reforms she analyzes, several other reforms occurred concurrently and may have contributed to the increase in labor force participation: The mandatory retirement age was increased; subsidies were provided for hiring older workers; and the maximum number of hours worked was reduced.

In the United States

In the United States, there are also strong incentives to leave the labor force early. In "The Motivations for Business Retirement Policies," Richard Woodbury examines the reasons for early retirement incentives in employer-provided pension plans in the United States. Unlike most analyses of incentive effects of pension plans, his analysis is based on extensive interviews with corporate executives. He concludes that even though the retirement incentives are strong—as demonstrated by other authors—the wish to encourage older employees to leave the workforce is "typically not a central motivation for the policy design" (331).

Most traditionally defined benefit pension plans in the United States encourage older workers to retire. For long-service employees, the financial incentive to retire often begins as young as age fifty-five. By age sixty-five, essentially all pension plans encourage retirement. The financial incentives in pension plans and their significant effects on retirement have been the subject of a growing literature in economics (see, e.g., Lumsdaine and Wise 1994). Absent from the literature, however, is any clear analysis of why firms have designed pension plans this way. To the extent that firm motivations are addressed, the common theoretical assumption is that the incentives are deliberate business policy decisions designed to induce retirement among older workers who are paid more for their productive value.[1] But this assumption is made without any evidence from the companies that have implemented the plans. It may also be true, as suggested tangentially by Kotlikoff and Wise (1989), that firms are largely unaware of the complex financial incentives in their pension plans. It may be that firms have designed their plans for completely different reasons. Woodbury's study sets out to understand better the motivations of firms in designing pension plans, as well as why these motivations have resulted in plans that have the effect of encouraging early retirement.

The issue has particular importance in the context of current demographic trends. The average number of years spent in retirement has increased steadily, partly as a result of increasing life expectancy, and partly as a result of people retiring at younger ages. Between 1950 and 1997, labor force participation rates of older men dropped significantly—from 46 percent to 17 percent among men aged sixty-five and older, and from 87 percent to 67 percent among men between ages fifty-five and sixty-four. Among women, the large increase in labor force participation at younger ages is absent at older ages, suggesting the offsetting decision to retire earlier among women as well. The financial incentives in pension plans are an important factor affecting trends in retirement behavior and inducing earlier retirement decisions. To the extent that these early retirement decisions are made based on distorted (or unintended) economic incentives, they represent a loss in both labor productivity and social welfare—which will only grow larger as the population ages.

Woodbury's study is based on the experiences of twenty large U.S. corporations. The analysis draws in particular on a series of discussions about policy history and objectives with executives at each company, and on a review of internal business documents relating to the design of the policies.

1. The primary theoretical framework for this assumption derives from the literature on implicit contracts. According to the theory, workers are paid less than their productive value at younger ages, and more than their productive value at older ages, creating an incentive for workers not to change jobs, and to work harder in anticipation of the future reward. Pensions then serve as a means of inducing retirement (or at least reducing the effective compensation) among those older workers who would otherwise be paid more than their productive value (see Lazear 1981).

For some of the companies, several days were spent visiting the corporate headquarters, meeting with corporate personnel (including human resource executives, financial affairs executives, and employee benefits planners and administrators), and reading through business documents.

Woodbury emphasizes that the analysis identified a number of objectives and motivations for the design of business retirement policies, including, in some cases, the desire for older workers to retire. In most cases, however, retirement incentives were either unintentional or secondary to the policy's central motivation. In general, companies were much more concerned with providing competitive retirement policies (policies similar in structure and in value to those of their competitors in the labor market) and policies that adequately provided for the well-being of their retirees. The design and ongoing evaluation of the policies were targeted primarily toward monitoring the retirement policies offered by their competitors, as well as assessing the adequacy of their policies in satisfying (but not exceeding) the income replacement needs of their retirees.

Woodbury finds that at fourteen of the twenty companies participating in this study, all employees participate in a retirement policy with incentives to retire at particular ages. At another three of the companies, some categories of employees participate in a retirement policy with incentives to retire at particular ages. Only three companies have retirement policies that do not encourage the retirement of older workers. Despite the widespread use of policies that encourage retirement, the main finding of this study is that retirement incentives are typically not a central motivation for the policy design.

Two motivations have dominated the design of current business retirement policies: concern about retiree welfare, and concern about competitiveness in the labor market. A great deal of the current structure of business retirement policies is based on paternalistic company values. Many executives indicate that their companies have a responsibility to insure the well-being of retired employees, and because of this responsibility, many executives view their retirement policies more as entitlements or welfare for retired employees than as compensation for working employees. This view of retirement policies is reflected in pension plans and postretirement medical plans that are designed to support the needs of retired employees.

The effect of these company values on the economic structure of retirement policies is to encourage retirement. The benefits of those retiring early cannot be reduced too dramatically, or early retirees will be unable to maintain their preretirement standard of living. Similarly, the benefits of those retiring late need not be increased, since their preretirement standard of living can be maintained with normal benefit levels. Thus, the retirement policies have an economic structure that encourages retirement, even though retirement incentives are not a central motivation in the policy design.

Business concerns about competitiveness in the labor market have the effect of spreading these traditional policies more widely through the business community. In order to be competitive, companies choose policies with a similar structure and a similar value to those offered by competing employers. Thus, companies without strong paternalistic values are driven by competitive pressures to implement policies with the same economic structure. Whether the policies at a company are motivated more by a concern for retiree welfare or by a concern for competitiveness in the labor market, the same policies with the same economic structure and the same retirement incentives are chosen. In either case, it is not the retirement incentives that motivate the policy design.

Given the loss in productive activity caused by retirement in the United States, it is potentially worrisome, says Woodbury, that businesses do not consider the effect of their policies on retirement behavior more carefully. At the same time, however, most businesses are not unsatisfied with the retirement behavior taking place under their policies. While influencing retirement behavior is not the motivation for retirement policies, the policies seem to be affecting retirement behavior in a way that is roughly consistent with company preferences. Executives at many of the companies in this study are quite satisfied that older workers retire, and they claim that many older workers are paid more than their productive value. Thus, one need not conclude from this study that the retirement induced by pension plans represents an economic distortion.

There is even some indication that companies unsatisfied with the retirement behavior of their workers look to their retirement policies as potential instruments for changing retirement behavior. Most obviously, the increasing use of early retirement window plans has focused a great deal of attention on the potential for retirement policies to influence retirement behavior. Most executives also broadly recognize the behavioral incentives in their regular retirement policies.

In short, the assumption that pensions are deliberately designed to encourage retirement is not supported by this study. However, Woodbury concludes, as the population continues to age, and as retirement policies consume an even larger percentage of corporate payrolls, businesses are likely to focus much more attention on the retirement behavior of their workers and, consequently, on the relationships between retirement policies and retirement behavior. Indeed, if this same study were conducted in 2020, when the baby boom generation would be retiring in record numbers, it would likely reach some very different conclusions about the key motivations for retirement policy decisions.

In Japan

Returning to incentives in Japan, in their paper titled "Promotion, Incentives, and Wages," Toshiaki Tachibanaki and Tetsuya Maruyama consider labor market incentive effects not at retirement age but rather over the working life in Japan. There is a growing interest in the relationship between incentive pay and careers in organizations, and in particular between incentive pay and promotion up the hierarchical ladder. This study considers evidence on this issue in Japan. The authors suggest that population aging in Japan and slower firm growth rates have increased motivation to develop internal labor policies that enhance the work incentives of employees. In their paper, the authors focus on the relationship between worker effort and incentive effects, based on data from several large Japanese firms. The central conclusion of the paper is that the effect of incentives differs according to an employee's level in the firm hierarchy: The wage rate provides work incentive at early career stages; at mid-level stages promotion is the important incentive; and at the top level neither matters.

The authors emphasize that there has been growing awareness in Japan that average labor productivity of blue-collar workers is quite high, but productivity of white-collar workers is low, compared with other industrialized nations. The authors cite several reasons that they believe support this view. First, team production is common among manual workers in the manufacturing industries, and the authors believe that such a production system can increase labor productivity without necessarily requiring strong individual leadership. Second, the authors observe that nonmanufacturing industries in which the majority of workers are white-collar show lower labor productivity than do firms populated primarily by production workers. Third, the authors say, leadership and the capability of able and motivated persons are crucial to the productivity of white-collar employees, if they are engaged in complicated jobs. Fourth, the authors propose that a compressed wage structure and a seniority-based promotion system—which are typical features of internal labor markets in Japan—are perhaps appropriate for manual workers but not for white-collar workers. The focus of the paper is whether the latter proposition is supported by the evidence.

The study investigates the relationship between work effort on the one hand and wages and promotion on the other hand. Evidence from white-collar workers in several large Japanese firms was used to investigate this issue. The authors present several conclusions. For example, the position an employee holds in the hierarchical ladder is crucial in understanding the relationships among promotion, effort, and wages. The effect of wages on effort is important for employees early in their careers: the higher the wage payment, the higher the effort for these employees. However, promotion is the key reward that increases the efforts of mid-career employees. For employees at the top, the authors conclude that neither incentive works to promote productivity. Unobservable factors, including "pull" or "luck," seem to be important determinants of the advancement of these employees. The authors say that one reason incentive mechanisms work only for employees in early careers is that employees who have been promoted rapidly to higher positions have already shown that they are highly motivated in any case.

What are the implications for human resource management, in view of recent population aging and slower firm growth rates in Japan? The authors point to the importance of increasing worker productivity incentives. The authors conclude that competition among employees, in particular among younger employees, will work to increase productivity. Such competition, they say, is likely to distinguish between capable employees and less-capable employees early in their careers. Quicker promotions for capable employees and a wider wage dispersion among employees, the authors conclude, are unavoidable.

Population Projections in Japan

Poor population projections have been one important reason why forecasts of the financial status of the Social Security trust fund have been so inaccurate in the United States. Indeed, many prominent demographers have been critical of the way in which Social Security Administration forecasts are obtained. As it turns out, forecasts are incorrect elsewhere as well. In "What Went Wrong with the 1991–92 Official Population Projection of Japan?" Seiritsu Ogura explores the reasons for the error in 1992 projections in Japan.

On two grounds one can say that the track record of the last two Japanese official population projections is very poor. One is the absence of accuracy in the projections, even in the medium run. The other is making the wrong assumptions in the long-run trend. Every five years, the National Institute of Population Research makes three projections based on high-, middle-, and low-fertility assumptions, and it is the projection based on the middle-fertility assumption that is regarded as the official population projection. The projection is automatically linked to many long-term plans that the government agencies make, from public pensions projections to energy projections. The 1986 projection, which predicted a recovery of Total Fertility Rate (TFR) to 2.0, overestimated 1991 births by almost 300,000, or 20 percent. In fact, during this period, TFR dropped from 1.764 in 1985 to 1.51 in 1991. Despite this experience, demographers at the Institute predicted a recovery in TFR starting in 1995. At this time, however, there seems to be no sign of the predicted recovery, and the TFR has continued to slip during the last five-year period.

Despite this rather poor performance from the purely technical point of view, Ogura says that the 1992 projection was a very innovative one. Most significant, he says, was the way it tried to estimate age-specific fertility rates of the cohorts that had recently entered into the reproduction stage by fitting the data to a class of statistical distributions. Thus armed, it declared that Japanese women have been temporarily delaying marriage and childbearing, which would come to an end by the mid-1990s to raise the TFR to where it was in the mid-1980s. According to Ogura, however, their attempt to introduce science into the population projection was not very successful in terms of its outcome, and it seems to have been abandoned in the latest projection.

In fact, the 1997 projections, which were made public in January 1997, used fertility rates based on marriage rates and the marital fertility rates of recent cohorts. These methods were used in the last two Japan Center for Economic Research (JCER) population projections, which were made by Ogura himself. As marriage precedes births by many years, it seems natural to assume that using marriage data would be far more powerful in predicting the number of future births than the sole use of women's age, in a given cohort, Ogura concludes. The JCER population projection has been constructed on this simple idea, and so far it has been quite accurate, says Ogura.

References

Kotlikoff, Laurence J., and David A. Wise. 1989. *The wage carrot and the pension stick.* Kalamazoo, Mich.: Upjohn Institute for Employment Research.
Lazear, Edward. 1981. Agency, earnings profiles, productivity, and hours restrictions. *American Economic Review* 71 (4): 606–20.
Lumsdaine, Robin, and David Wise. 1994. Aging and labor force participation: A review of trends and explanations. In *Aging in the United States and Japan,* ed. Y. Noguchi and D. Wise, 7–41. Chicago: University of Chicago Press.
Shoven, John, and David Wise. 1997. Keeping savers from saving. In *Facing the aging wave,* ed. D. Wise, 57–87. Stanford, Calif.: Hoover Institution Press.
———. 1998. The taxation of pensions: A shelter can become a trap. In *Frontiers in the economics of aging,* ed. D. Wise, 173–211. Chicago: University of Chicago Press.

1

Choice, Chance, and Wealth Dispersion at Retirement

Steven F. Venti and David A. Wise

Why do some households have substantial wealth at retirement while others have very little? Indeed, why do some households with given lifetime earnings have substantial wealth at retirement, while other households with the same lifetime earnings accumulate very little wealth? In an earlier paper (Venti and Wise 1999), we evaluated the extent to which the different wealth accumulation of households with similar lifetime earnings could be accounted for by random shocks, such as health status and inheritances, that could reduce or increase the available resources out of which saving could be drawn. We concluded that only a small fraction of the dispersion in wealth accumulation within lifetime earnings deciles could be accounted for by random shocks and thus that most of the dispersion could be attributed to choice; some people save while young, others do not. We continue that analysis in this paper but with two additions: First, we attempt to evaluate the effect of investment choice on the accumulation of assets—in particular, how much of the dispersion in wealth can be accounted for by the choice between investment in the stock market and investment in presumably less risky assets such as bonds or bank saving accounts. Second, we attempt to understand the relationship between asset accumulation and individuals' assessment, just prior to retirement, of the adequacy of their saving and their saving behavior. This very exploratory

Steven F. Venti is professor of economics at Dartmouth College and a research associate of the National Bureau of Economic Research. David A. Wise is the John F. Stambaugh Professor of Political Economy at the John F. Kennedy School of Government, Harvard University, and the director for health and retirement programs at the National Bureau of Economic Research.

This research was supported by the National Institute on Aging. We are also grateful to the Unicon Research Corporation for providing a copy of their *CPS Utilities* data and software.

analysis is an attempt to evaluate the usefulness of an experimental saving module administered to a subsample of Health and Retirement Study (HRS) respondents.

People, of course, accumulate different amounts of wealth in part because they have different earnings. We essentially set that dispersion aside by considering persons with similar lifetime earnings. Thus the discussion here is about the dispersion of asset accumulation among persons with the same lifetime earnings. Given lifetime earnings, we consider the importance of "chance" events versus the choice to save in determining asset accumulation. Over the course of a lifetime many events not directly under the control of the household may affect the accumulation of wealth. We refer to these as *chance events*. They may include both unfavorable shocks, such as health care costs, and positive shocks, such as inheritances.

We distinguish between such *chance* events, which affect the resources from which saving could be drawn, and the *choice* of how much to save of the resources that are available. In fact, we consider two components of saving choice: One is the choice to save or not to save; the other is saving mode or investment choice. Households with similar lifetime resources may invest in different assets that earn different rates of return. We might think of three groups: nonsavers, savers who invest conservatively and have low rates of return, and savers who invest in more risky assets and have higher rates of return. Persons who invest in bonds or bank savings accounts will have lower rates of return on average than those who invest in stocks.

Whether accumulated wealth is attributable to the choice to save rather than to chance can have significant implications for government policy. Many policies impose ex post taxes on accumulated assets. For example, elderly Americans who saved when young and thus have higher capital incomes when old pay higher taxes on Social Security benefits. Shoven and Wise (1997, 1998) show that those who save too much in pension plans in particular face very large "success" tax penalties when pension benefits are withdrawn. In addition, pension assets left as a bequest can be virtually confiscated through the tax system. The spend-down Medicaid provision is another example. The belief—perhaps unstated—that chance events determine the dispersion in wealth may weigh in favor of such taxes in the legislative voting that imposes them.

If, on the other hand, the dispersion of wealth among the elderly reflects conscious lifetime spending-versus-saving decisions—rather than differences in lifetime resources—these higher taxes may be harder to justify and appear to penalize savers who spend less when they are young. From an economic perspective, if wealth accumulation is random, taxing saving has no incentive effects. On the other hand, if wealth accumulation results from conscious decisions to save versus spend, penalizing savers may have substantial incentive effects, discouraging individuals from saving for their own retirement and limiting aggregate economic growth. It is important to understand that this paper is about the dispersion in the accumulation of assets of persons with similar lifetime earnings. The issue raised here is not about progressive taxation, but rather about differences in taxes imposed on persons who spend tomorrow versus today, given the same after-tax lifetime earnings.

The same issue arises with respect to return on investments. In this case, higher expected returns come at the expense of more risk when young, just as higher saving rates come at the expense of lower consumption when young. And, just as it may be harder to justify imposing higher taxes on older households who choose to consume less and save more while young, it may also be harder to justify imposing higher taxes on older households for assuming greater risk while young. In addition, of course, the higher taxes may discourage saving and limit economic growth. Again, the question raised here is not about progressive taxation; it is about the different taxing of persons who assume risk while young versus those who do not, given the same lifetime earnings.

We begin this paper by controlling for lifetime earnings as reported in individual Social Security records. Given lifetime earnings, we examine the distribution of wealth, finding a very wide dispersion in the distribution of accumulated saving, even among families with the lowest lifetime earnings. We then show that only a small fraction of the dispersion can be explained by individual circumstances that may have limited the ability to save out of earnings. For persons in the *same lifetime earnings decile,* we do this by comparing the unconditional dispersion in wealth at retirement with the dispersion after controlling for chance events that may have affected lifetime resources out of which saving could have been drawn. Then we attempt to determine how much of the dispersion might be attributed to investment choices. Here we are limited by available data, having to rely on the allocation of assets at the time of the HRS.

We conclude that the bulk of the dispersion in wealth at retirement results from the choice of some families to save while other similarly situated families choose to spend. For the most part, controlling for lifetime earnings, persons with little saving on the eve of retirement have simply chosen to save less and spend more over their lifetimes. It is particularly striking that some households with very low lifetime resources accumulate a great deal of wealth, and some households with very high lifetime resources accumulate little wealth. We find these saving disparities cannot be accounted for by adverse financial events, such as poor health, or by inheritances. While better control for individual circumstances that may limit resources could change somewhat the magnitudes that we obtain, we believe that the general thrust of the conclusions would not change.[1]

1. It may be useful to view our estimates in the context of the broader literature on saving and consumption. Our focus is on the dispersion in saving among households with similar lifetime resources. The idea is to isolate empirically the portion of the saving variance attributable to individual choice (or "tastes") once differences in lifetime earnings are accounted

We then consider the wealth that would have been accumulated if families in our sample had followed specific saving plans throughout their working lives. This exercise shows that even families with modest lifetime earnings would have accumulated substantial wealth had they saved consistently and invested prudently over the course of their working lives.

Finally, we consider how asset accumulation, again controlling for lifetime earnings, is related to individual attitudes about saving and saving adequacy.

1.1   The Data

The analysis is based on household data collected in the baseline interview of the Health and Retirement Study (HRS).[2] The household heads were aged fifty-one to sixty-one in 1992 when the baseline survey was conducted. The analysis relies on the wealth of households at the time of the survey and on lifetime earnings, which is measured by historical earnings reported to the Social Security Administration.[3] The Social Security earnings data are available for 8,257 of the 12,652 HRS respondents. Comparison of respondents for whom we do and do not have Social Security records suggests that they are very similar. Selected characteristics of the two groups are shown in table 1.1. The groups have almost the same household income, the same average age, and the same years of education; the same proportion are married; and almost the same proportion are female. A slightly larger proportion of those for whom we have Social Security records are HRS primary respondents (64 percent versus 60 percent).

Our analysis is based on household rather than individual respondent data, however. Historical earnings for a single-person household required only that Social Security earnings records be available for that person. But for a two-person household, it was necessary to have historical earnings for both persons in the household if both had been in the labor force for a significant length of time. The HRS obtained such data for 1,625 single-

---

for. In most standard consumption models, dispersion in saving arises primarily from differences in household incomes. Such models do not aim to explain the variation in wealth among families with the same lifetime incomes. Some authors, such as Attanasio et al. (1995) and Venti and Wise (1990) allow saving choices to depend on household characteristics, like education and marital status. Another way to account for taste variation is to estimate a distribution of rates of time preference that fits the variation in saving, given income. This approach has been adopted by Samwick (1996). This approach equates taste and time preference but does not aim to distinguish choice (taste) from chance. Still another—and quite different—explanation for saving variation among households with similar resources is provided by behavioral models in which households differ in the level of discipline or self-control required to commit to a saving plan, as proposed by Shefrin and Thaler (1988). The aim is to explain why households make different choices, but, again, not to isolate the effects of choice versus chance events.

2. This section and the data appendix are largely reproduced from our earlier paper (Venti and Wise 1999). Some components of later sections also rely heavily on that paper.

3. See Juster and Suzman (1995) for a discussion of the structure and content of the HRS. Mitchell, Olson, and Steinmeier (2000) describe the attached Social Security earnings file.

Table 1.1   **Comparison of Social Security Data for Health and Retirement Study (HRS) Respondents**

Characteristic	Persons without Social Security Records	Persons with Social Security Records
Mean household income	$54,252.64	$53,434.20
Percent female	53.00	54.00
Mean age	55.57	55.40
Percent nonwhite	15.00	13.00
Mean years of education	12.37	12.40
Percent married	76.00	76.00
Percent primary respondent	60.00	64.00

Source: Weighted estimates from the HRS Wave I.

person households and for 2,751 two-person households, together comprising 4,376 of the 7,607 HRS households. Two additional sample adjustments were made. First, we retained households in which one or both members reported never having worked, even if the household member was missing a Social Security earnings record. We assumed zero earnings for such persons. Second, we excluded from the sample all households that included any member who had zero social security earnings *and* who reported working for any level of government for five (not necessarily consecutive) years. This latter restriction is intended to exclude households that have zero Social Security earnings due to gaps in coverage. The final sample includes 3,992 households.[4]

The other important data component is wealth at the time of the survey. We need a complete accounting of assets, including personal retirement assets such as IRAs and 401(k) balances, other personal financial assets, employer-provided pension assets, home equity, and assets such as real estate and business equity. In most instances the value of each asset is reported directly. For non-pension assets, the HRS survey reduces nonresponse considerably by adopting bracketing techniques for important wealth questions.[5]

In other cases asset values are not easily determined. The most important asset that is not directly reported is the value of benefits promised under employer-provided defined benefit pension plans. For persons who are retired and receiving benefits, this value can be approximated by using life tables to determine the expected value of the future stream of benefits. But for nonretired persons covered by a defined benefit plan—and for whom the benefit is not known—the value of future benefits can be only imprecisely imputed. The imputation process relies on the respondent de-

4. The present value of Social Security benefits is unavailable for an additional 167 households, and these have been excluded in preparing tables 1.3 and 1.4, leaving a sample of 3,825. Thus the sample is slightly smaller than was used in similar tables in Venti and Wise (1999).

5. Juster and Smith (1999) and Smith (1995) provide details.

scription of pension provisions and is described in detail in the appendix. The HRS also surveyed employers about the features of respondent pensions, but those data are not used in this analysis.

1.2 Lifetime Earnings and the Wealth of Households

Social Security earnings form a good measure of lifetime labor earnings for persons whose earnings are consistently below the Social Security earnings maximum and who have been in jobs covered by the Social Security system. Historically, the Social Security earnings maximum has been adjusted on an ad hoc basis. The percentage of HRS respondents exceeding the maximum was at its highest in the early 1970s, peaking at 26.9 percent in 1971. The percentage has been below 10 percent since 1981 and was 4.8 percent in 1991.

For persons with incomes above the limit, reported Social Security earnings can significantly underestimate actual earnings. (In addition, as explained above, some persons may report zero Social Security covered earnings because they were employed in sectors not covered by the Social Security system, and we have excluded certain government employees from the sample.) Thus we do not rely directly on Social Security earnings to establish the level of lifetime earnings, but use reported Social Security earnings to *rank* families by lifetime earnings. Then we group families into Social Security earnings deciles, to which we refer hereafter as *lifetime earnings deciles*. We believe that the ranking by Social Security earnings represents a good approximation to a ranking based on actual total earnings, and that thus the deciles are a good approximation to actual lifetime earnings deciles. However, the problems caused by the earnings maximum and by zeros may make results based on the lowest and highest deciles less reliable than results based on the other deciles.

The mean present value of lifetime Social Security earnings within each decile is shown in table 1.2. To obtain lifetime Social Security income, the Consumer Price Index (CPI) was used to convert past earnings to 1992 dollars. The means range from about $36,000 in the lowest decile to just over $1,600,000 in the highest decile. Within the deciles the medians are essentially the same as the means.

The medians of assets, including Social Security wealth, are shown in table 1.3. For single persons Social Security wealth is the mortality-adjusted present value of benefits. For two-person families it is the sum of the mortality-adjusted present value of benefits calculated separately for each person. We have made no additional adjustments for joint mortality or survivorship benefits. Excluding Social Security, the median of total wealth ranges from $5,000 for families in the lowest lifetime earnings decile to almost $388,000 for families in the top lifetime earnings decile. Including Social Security wealth, the median ranges from $33,006 in the lowest decile to $577,107 in the top decile. Many assets are held by fewer

Table 1.2   **Present Value of Social Security Earnings by Lifetime Earnings Decile**

Lifetime Income Decile	Present Value ($)
1st	35,848
2nd	193,664
3rd	372,534
4th	567,931
5th	741,587
6th	905,506
7th	1,055,782
8th	1,186,931
9th	1,333,162
10th	1,637,428

Source: Weighted estimates based on sample of 3,992 households as described in section 1.1 of the text.

than half of the households—indicated by zero medians. The 5th and 6th income deciles span the median of lifetime earnings, and the medians of total wealth in these earnings deciles are $105,166 and $144,188, respectively, excluding Social Security. Fewer than half of the families in these deciles have IRA or 401(k) accounts. Fewer than half have business equity or real estate. And the value of other assets is low. The median of employer-provided pension assets (excluding 401[k] accounts) is $4,000 for the 5th and $14,035 for the 6th lifetime income decile, not much higher than the median values of vehicles—$6,000 and $8,000 respectively. The median levels of financial assets are only $3,000 and $7,000 respectively. The largest component of the wealth of these families is home equity; the medians are $29,000 and $39,000, respectively.

The means of assets by lifetime earnings decile are shown in table 1.4. Comparison of the means and medians foretells the wide dispersion in assets, even among families with similar lifetime earnings. The means are typically much higher than the medians, and in some lifetime earnings deciles the mean of financial assets is more than ten times as large as the median.

1.3   The Distribution of Wealth for Given Lifetime Earnings

We discuss first the distribution of wealth within lifetime earnings deciles. We then consider how much of the dispersion can be accounted for investment choice and by chance shocks to resources. Personal chance events—like health status or children—that might be expected to limit the resources out of which saving might be drawn. Investment choice—e.g., between stocks and bonds—that may be expected to affect the accumulation of assets given saving out of available resources. To the extent that chance events and investment choices are correlated, however, there is of

Table 1.3   Median Level of Assets by Lifetime Earnings Decile and Asset Category, Health and Retirement Study (HRS)

Asset Category	Income Decile									
	1st	2nd	3rd	4th	5th	6th	7th	8th	9th	10th
Financial assets	0	70	80	2,000	3,000	7,000	9,500	17,000	25,000	36,500
Personal retirement assets	0	0	0	0	0	1,500	5,000	12,000	25,000	40,000
IRA	0	0	0	0	0	0	1,700	5,000	12,000	21,000
401(k)	0	0	0	0	0	0	0	0	0	0
Traditional pension	0	0	0	0	4,000	14,035	33,793	40,808	58,000	83,259
Defined contribution	0	0	0	0	0	0	0	0	0	0
Defined benefit	0	0	0	0	0	0	0	1,497	3,083	22,690
PV pension income	0	0	0	0	0	0	0	0	0	0
Vehicles	300	1,700	3,000	5,000	6,000	8,000	10,000	10,000	12,000	15,000
Business equity	0	0	0	0	0	0	0	0	0	0
Other real estate	0	0	0	0	0	0	0	0	0	3,000
Home equity	0	8,000	19,000	23,000	29,000	39,000	50,000	60,000	70,000	77,000
Home value	0	17,000	35,000	35,000	45,000	67,000	75,000	85,000	100,000	120,000
Mortgage debt	0	0	0	0	0	9,000	5,600	11,000	15,000	20,000
Social Security wealth	0	54,754	75,335	88,692	101,234	108,619	117,764	119,950	137,673	175,542
Total wealth, excluding Social Security	5,000	34,429	52,803	82,620	105,166	144,188	189,832	221,692	305,536	387,609
Total wealth, including Social Security	33,006	85,448	125,759	168,878	203,084	261,072	312,037	349,549	453,265	577,107

Source: Weighted estimates based on the HRS sample described in section 1.1 of the text.
Note: Zero medians indicate that asset is held by less than 50 percent of households.

Table 1.4   Mean Level of Assets by Lifetime Earnings Decile and Asset Category, Health and Retirement Study (HRS)

	Income Decile									
Asset Category	1st	2nd	3rd	4th	5th	6th	7th	8th	9th	10th
Financial assets	20,566	16,369	18,635	31,871	34,245	36,988	50,339	56,837	112,356	88,420
Personal retirement assets	5,628	4,337	6,266	10,185	10,340	16,000	28,291	40,531	65,461	76,454
IRA	3,730	3,683	4,325	6,843	8,035	11,219	18,904	24,528	39,391	52,706
401(k)	1,898	654	1,941	3,341	2,305	4,781	9,386	16,003	26,070	23,748
Traditional pension	12,382	19,285	22,301	32,603	38,107	55,383	79,646	91,843	132,369	145,626
Defined contribution	20	2,008	2,498	4,431	3,461	5,137	8,886	14,193	22,498	18,185
Defined benefit	8,224	8,563	11,436	17,089	18,821	28,614	37,574	50,684	73,454	93,074
PV pension income	4,138	8,713	8,368	11,083	15,825	21,633	33,206	26,966	36,416	34,367
Vehicles	3,353	4,291	7,022	8,519	11,155	12,691	18,694	15,700	16,142	19,698
Business equity	85	2,884	5,107	23,140	42,628	28,716	45,793	27,982	78,164	55,817
Other real estate	19,213	12,884	20,548	39,257	38,350	54,481	45,940	55,894	57,611	80,771
Home equity	17,842	32,488	33,129	38,941	44,342	53,143	65,596	73,628	91,297	98,326
Home value	23,997	43,997	46,674	57,834	62,417	76,721	96,452	104,887	126,176	139,148
Mortgage debt	6,155	11,508	13,544	18,893	18,076	23,578	30,857	31,259	34,879	40,821
Social Security wealth	16,494	49,665	67,962	82,951	95,980	108,749	116,674	119,172	135,626	172,476
Total wealth, excluding Social Security	79,069	92,538	113,009	184,515	219,166	257,402	334,298	362,413	553,400	565,112
Total wealth, including Social Security	95,563	142,203	180,971	267,466	315,146	366,151	450,972	481,586	689,026	737,588

Source: See table 1.3.

course no way to parcel out a separate effect for each of these factors. Thus we proceed in a way that indicates the maximum portion of dispersion that could be attributed to each.

1.3.1   Dispersion in Asset Accumulation Given the Same Lifetime Earnings

The dispersion in total accumulated wealth by lifetime earnings decile is shown in figure 1.1. For each earnings decile, the figure shows five quantiles: the 10th, 30th, 50th, 70th, and 90th. The median is the 50th quantile. Ten percent of families have wealth below the 10th quantile, 30 percent have wealth below the 30th quantile, and so forth. Several features of the data stand out. Perhaps not surprising, a noticeable proportion of households in the lowest lifetime earnings deciles have accumulated almost no wealth by the time they have attained ages fifty-one to sixty-one. Half of those in the lowest earnings decile have less the $5,000 in wealth, as do 30 percent of those in the 2nd decile, 20 percent of those in the 3rd, and 10 percent of households in the 4th earnings decile. But even among households with the highest lifetime earnings, some households have very limited wealth. For example, 10 percent of households in the 6th earnings decile have less than $30,000 in assets, and 10 percent of those in the 9th earnings decile have less than $100,000.

To address the principle question of this paper, it is the dispersion of wealth that is the most critical, and here the data are striking. Even controlling for lifetime earnings, the range of wealth is enormous. In the 5th lifetime earnings decile, the 90th quantile is thirty-five times the size of the 10th quantile. The range is less extreme in higher earnings deciles but still very wide: the 90th quantile is 16, 19, 12, 10, and 9 times as large as the 10th quantile in the 6th through the 10th lifetime income deciles, respectively.

While many families with low lifetime earnings have very limited wealth—as do some who earned the most—the wide dispersion in accumulated wealth is evident among those with low and high lifetime earnings alike. Thus some families with the lowest lifetime earnings have accumulated noticeable wealth. For example, the 90th quantile is approximately $150,000 for the lowest decile and is well above $200,000 for the 2nd and 3rd deciles.

The dispersion at the highest levels of wealth accumulation is itself substantial and is presented separately in figure 1.2, which shows the 90th, 95th, and 98th quantiles by lifetime earnings decile. The 98th quantile is typically two and a half to three times the size of the 90th quantile. Overall there is enormous variation in wealth accumulation among households whose members had similar earnings over their lifetimes. The wide variation in wealth will not be new to many readers; not so widely appreciated is the vast variation in wealth among households with similar lifetime earnings.

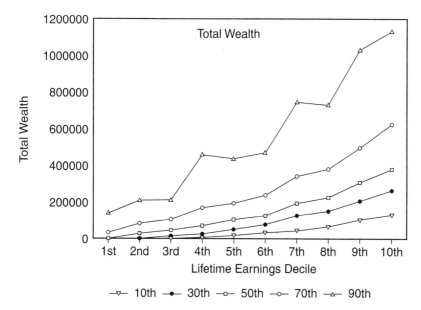

Fig. 1.1   Wealth quantiles: total wealth

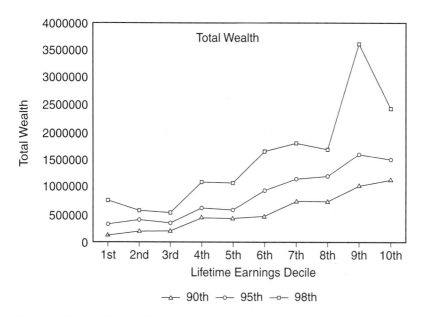

Fig. 1.2   Top wealth quantiles: total wealth

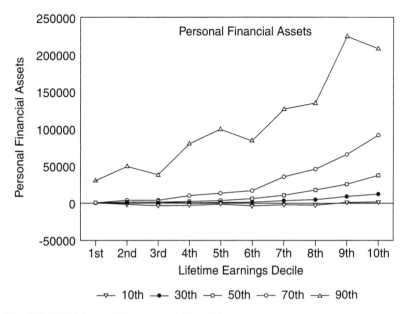

Fig. 1.3   Wealth quantiles: personal financial assets

Figure 1.3 shows the dispersion of personal financial assets (excluding personal retirement assets such as IRA and 401[k] accounts). That most people don't save much is not new. That many of those with high earnings save so little is, however, striking. The 10th quantile is negative or close to zero for every lifetime earnings decile! The same is true for the 20th quantile, with the exception of the highest earnings decile, for which the 20th quantile is a paltry $6,400. The medians range from zero for the lowest three deciles, to $3,000 and $5,800 for the 5th and 6th quantiles, to $10,000 for the 70th, to $36,500 for the highest income decile. Like the dispersion in total wealth, the range of personal financial assets from the 10th to the 90th quantiles is extremely broad and the dispersion is even greater when the top quantiles are considered, as in figure 1.4.

Almost all of the HRS respondents have had the opportunity to contribute to either an IRA or a 401(k) plan. It is not surprising, then, that personal retirement saving has become an important component of the wealth of some HRS households. Quantiles of personal retirement saving assets by lifetime earnings decile are shown in figure 1.5. Although personal retirement accounts are now an important form of personal saving, only about half of HRS households have such accounts. Most households in the highest lifetime earnings deciles have such accounts but households in the lowest deciles do not. Like the dispersions in personal financial saving and in total wealth, even for households with similar lifetime earnings the

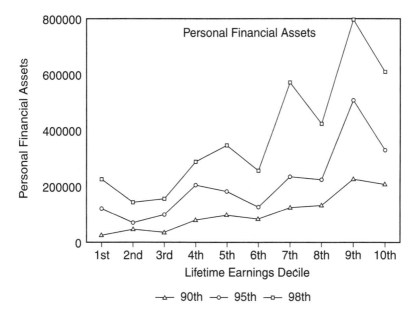

Fig. 1.4   Top wealth quantiles: personal financial assets

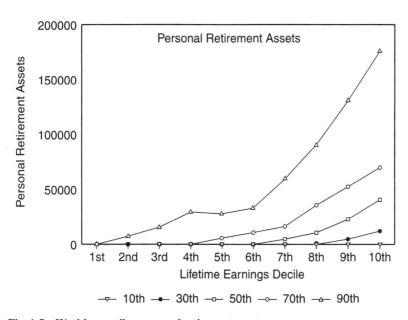

Fig. 1.5   Wealth quantiles: personal retirement assets

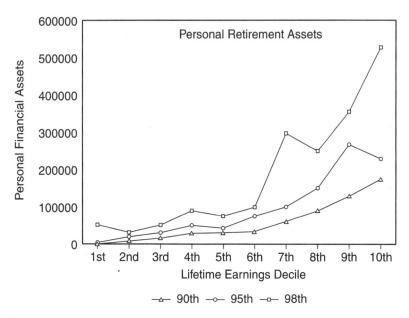

Fig. 1.6   **Top wealth quantiles: personal retirement assets**

variation in personal retirement assets is very large. Again, substantial variation is observed in the top quantiles as shown in figure 1.6. Although we have no way of knowing how much the IRA and 401(k)—as well as Keogh—limits constrained the personal retirement saving of HRS households, it is likely that many households at the top quantiles were constrained by the limits.

1.3.2   Chance Events versus Saving Choice and Investment Choice

We want to obtain an indication of how much of the dispersion in saving can be attributed to chance and how much to choice: *Chance* is intended to represent circumstances that may affect the resources available for saving, given lifetime resources. We attribute to *saving choice* the dispersion that remains after accounting for chance circumstances that limit or enhance resources. We also consider how much of the dispersion in wealth can be attributed to the *investment choice* of savers. We proceed in two steps: First, we consider how much of the dispersion in wealth can be attributed to chance events; what is not accounted for by chance events, we attribute to saving choice. Then we consider separately the effect of investment choice on the dispersion of wealth. We emphasize the effect of adjustment for chance events and investment choices on the distribution of wealth within lifetime earnings deciles. Thus the exposition is necessarily graphical, for the most part. We do present, however, some more-standard measures of reduction in dispersion when chance events and investment choices are accounted for.

In considering chance events that affect resources we do not want to control for education, ethnic group, and other attributes that may be correlates of the taste for saving. Rather, we want to consider individual circumstances that may enhance or limit funds out of which saving could be drawn. We consider inheritances and gifts, health status, age, number of children, and marital status. Age, of course, is not a chance event, but the range of ages of HRS household heads is likely to be systematically related to asset accumulation. Children and marital status are also not truly chance events. They might more properly be thought of as choices made early in one's lifetime that may later limit resources out of which saving can be drawn. Thus we include these with chance events. In effect, including these household attributes tends to exaggerate the dispersion that might be attributed to truly chance events.

That inheritances and gifts might ease the burden of saving seems clear. Poor health and associated health expenditures may increase the burden of saving. Health status may also affect lifetime earnings and thus the earnings deciles of households. However, the question here is whether, given earnings, health status may affect the resources out of which households might plausibly save. Unfortunately, we have only limited indicators of health status and know little about health over a person's lifetime. Thus we use health status at the time of the survey as an imperfect control for medical circumstances. It is likely that expenses associated with children also reduce the pool of resources that could be saved. Indeed, under some circumstances children could be a substitute for saving for retirement. Finally, marital status, if only because of economies of scale, may be a determinant of resources out of which saving could plausibly be drawn.

Within each lifetime earnings decile, we first predict wealth with a simple specification of the form

(1)   Wealth = Constant + β_1(Married) + β_2(Never Married)

+ β_3(Widowed, Divorced, or Separated) + β_4(No Children)

+ β_5(Number of Children if > 0) + β_6(Age)

+ β_7(Poor Health Single Person) + β_8(Poor Health 1 of 2 in Family)

+ β_9(Poor Health 2 of 2 in Family) + β_{10}(No Inheritances)

+ β_{11}(Amount of Inheritances Received < 1980)

+ β_{12}(Amount of Inheritances Received 1980 to 1988)

+ β_{13}(Amount of Inheritances Received > 1988),

with appropriate normalizing restrictions for the indicator variables. From this equation, we obtain predicted wealth. Then, within each earnings decile, adjusted wealth is determined by

(2) Adjusted Wealth = (Unadjusted Wealth) − (Predicted Wealth)

+ (Mean of Wealth),

which gives distributions of adjusted and unadjusted (observed) wealth with the same means.

We follow a similar procedure to determine the effect of investment choice on wealth dispersion. Even among households that save the same proportion of earnings, accumulated wealth may differ because some households have invested savings in the stock market (for example), while others have saved through bank saving account or money market funds. The average rate of return on stock investments is much higher than the rate of return in money market funds, but the risk associated with stock investments is also higher—or at least is perceived to be higher. Other households invested primarily in housing, and so forth. We don't know the investment choices that households made over their lifetimes. The HRS did, however, obtain information on the percent allocation of financial asset saving (excluding IRA and 401[k] accounts) for five components of financial assets. We use this information, together with information on the proportion of wealth in housing and five other asset categories, as an indicator of the lifetime investment choices of a household. Within each lifetime earnings decile, we again predict wealth, but based on investment choices, with a specification of the form

(3) Wealth = Constant + β_1(% Wealth in Personal Financial Assets)

+ β_2(% Financial Assets in Stocks) + β_3(% Financial Assets in Bonds)

+ β_4(% Financial Assets in Money Market Accounts)

+ β_5(% Wealth in IRA, 401(k), and Keogh Accounts)

+ β_6(% Wealth in Employer Pensions)

+ β_7(% Wealth in Business Equity) + β_8(% Wealth in Vehicles)

+ β_9(% Wealth in Housing) + β_{10}(% Wealth in Other Real Estate).

To evaluate the dispersion in total financial assets—including IRA, 401(k), and Keogh accounts—that might be accounted for by investment choice, we use

(4)   Total Financial Assets = Constant

$\quad$ + β_1(% Financial Assets in Stocks) + β_2(% Financial Assets in Bonds)

$\quad$ + β_3(% Financial Assets in Money Market Accounts)

$\quad$ + β_4(% Financial Assets in Certificates of Deposit)

$\quad$ + β_5(% Financial Assets in Other Interest-Bearing Accounts).[6]

Again, we determine adjusted total financial assets as in equation (2), above.[7]

We could, of course, adjust for both chance events and investment choice at the same time. Making separate adjustments to the same base, however, allows us to compare the effect of chance events on wealth dispersion with the effect of investment choices on dispersion. The two sets of variables may be correlated, however. To the extent that they are positively correlated, some of what is attributed to chance in the first adjustment should be attributed to investment choice instead, and some of what is attributed to investment choice in the second adjustment should be attributed to chance events. Thus, this procedure maximizes the adjustment attributed to each. (Standard measures of reduction in dispersion presented below suggest that the correlation between the two sets of variables is rather small, however.)

In referring to investment decisions as choice, it is important to distinguish this choice from risk—or the chance outcomes that the choice may yield. It seems clear that part of the wealth accumulation of savers is due to choice—conservative versus risky assets—and that part is due to chance. Chance may play a particularly prominent role in housing investments. For example, a person who purchased a home in Boston twenty years ago likely benefitted from large capital gain. On the other hand, a person who purchased in Houston may well have lost money. We will find, however, that the wide dispersion in accumulated wealth pertains to all forms of assets; dispersion is not peculiar to housing equity. There is, of course, a chance aspect to financial asset accumulation as well. Given the level of

---

6. Stocks include shares of stock in publicly held corporations, mutual funds, and investment trusts. Bonds include corporate, municipal, government, or foreign bonds, and bond funds. Money market accounts include checking or saving accounts and money market funds. Certificates of deposit include certificates of deposit, government saving bonds, and treasury bills. Other interest-bearing accounts include other saving or assets, such as money owed to the individual by others; a valuable collection made for investment purposes; an annuity; and rights in a trust or estate.

7. Because the shares of total wealth, or total financial assets, can be calculated only if wealth is positive, only observations with positive wealth values are included in the estimation samples. This reduces the sample from 3,992 to 3,584 households.

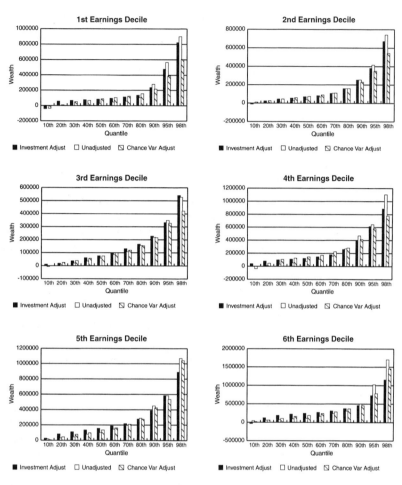

Fig. 1.7   1st–10th earnings deciles, adjusted v. unadjusted wealth quantiles

risk, some savers will be winners and have large returns while others will have lower returns. However, unlike a random shock to financial resources due, for example, to illness, this risk and associated distribution of shocks to accumulation is chosen.

Figure 1.7 shows graphs of the adjusted compared to the unadjusted quantiles for each lifetime earnings decile. The middle bar of each panel shows unadjusted wealth quantiles. The bars behind show the quantiles adjusted for investment choice. The bars in front show quantiles adjusted for chance events, or individual circumstances. Overall, the adjustment for individual circumstances does not have much effect on the dispersion of wealth. Thus we conclude that, for the most part, within-decile differences in saving can be attributed to differences in the amount of earnings that

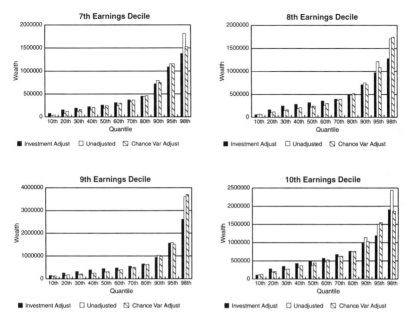

Fig. 1.7   (cont.)

households choose to save; some choose to save a good deal, many choose to save very little. Some of the dispersion can be attributed to investment choices. But investment choice, too, accounts for only a small part of the dispersion in wealth within earnings deciles. Overall, the small reduction in dispersion that can be attributed to chance events is about the same as the reduction that can be attributed to investment choices. Or, put another way: The increase in dispersion that results from differing household investment choices is approximately the same as the increase that can be attributed to chance events; both are small.

The comparison of adjusted and unadjusted distributions, however, does reveal some systematic patterns. With respect to the adjustment for chance events: First, the adjustment reduces the 95th and 98th quantiles in almost every decile, and the reduction in the 98th quantile is especially noticeable. Second, for the 5th to the 10th deciles, the adjustment for chance events has very little effect on all but the extreme quantiles. Modest leveling occurs within the 3rd and 4th deciles, with the 90th quantile reduced a bit and the lower quantiles raised a bit. Third, the greatest leveling occurs in the 1st and 2nd lifetime earnings deciles, in which the highest quantiles are reduced and the lowest quantiles raised. Still, in all deciles an enormous dispersion in assets remains after adjusting for the individual circumstances.

The adjustment for investment choices also reveals some systematic patterns. This adjustment has little effect on wealth dispersion in the bottom three lifetime earnings deciles. The greatest effects are in the upper deciles. The 98th quantile is reduced in almost every decile, especially in the upper ones. The 95th quantile is reduced in most deciles as well, but only marginally in all but the 6th, 8th, and 10th deciles. The lower quantiles tend to be raised in each earnings decile.

Finally, controlling for education and ethnic group (which are typically found to be related to saving and presumably influence the taste for saving) has only a very modest effect on the distributions. By way of illustration, figure 1.8 shows the quantiles for the 7th earnings decile when these variables are added to the list of individual circumstances. The principle effect of the addition of these "taste" variables is to increase a bit the lower quantiles. Nonetheless, the major dispersion remains: Some people choose to save, and others don't.

For comparison, more traditional measures of unconditional versus conditional variance (controlling for individual circumstances) are shown in table 1.5. Starting with the unconditional variance in wealth, controlling for lifetime earnings decile reduces the residual standard deviation by 5.05 percent. When lifetime earnings decile plus the individual chance events are controlled for (with complete interaction of earnings decile and attributes), the reduction is 9.08 percent. Thus 4.03 percent (9.08 percent − 5.05 percent) might be attributed to the chance events. When lifetime earnings decile plus investment choices are controlled for (again with complete interaction of earnings decile and investment choice), the reduction is

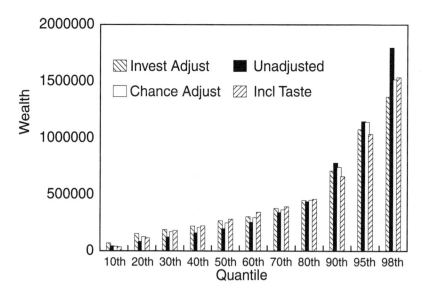

Fig. 1.8   7th earnings decile: adjusted v. unadjusted wealth quantiles

Table 1.5   Percent Reduction in Residual Variance of Total Wealth, by Control Variables

Total Sample

Control Variables	Percent Reduction vs. Unconditional Standard Deviation
(A). Lifetime earnings decile	5.05
(B). (A) + chance variables	9.08
(C). (A) + investment choice variables	12.98
(D). (A) + (B) + (C)	15.32
(E). (D) + "taste variables" (education and race)	16.00

By Lifetime Earnings Decile

Control Variables

Decile	Chance Variables (B)	Investment Choice Variables (C)	(B) + (C) (D)	(D) + "Taste Variables" (education and race) (E)
1st	6.84	7.18	10.29	10.12
2nd	23.15	8.29	26.41	27.90
3rd	1.47	9.39	10.33	10.54
4th	26.55	15.01	32.67	32.83
5th	3.35	16.30	16.91	17.82
6th	5.22	12.17	14.29	25.58
7th	9.88	13.78	19.52	20.70
8th	2.32	13.53	13.67	15.45
9th	1.88	19.67	19.76	19.98
10th	4.00	17.52	19.49	21.02

Source: See table 1.3.

Notes: Because shares could not be computed if total wealth is less than or equal to zero, only families with positive levels of total wealth are used. The following investment shares were used: financial assets, personal retirement saving, traditional pension assets, business equity, vehicles, home equity, and other real estate.

12.98 percent, and 7.93 percent (12.98 percent − 5.05 percent) might be attributed to investment choice. Thus, by this conventional measure, only a small proportion of the dispersion in wealth can be attributed to chance events. Little of the dispersion can be attributed to the investment choices of savers. By these measures, the effect of investment choice is somewhat greater than the effect of chance.

Controlling for earnings decile, chance events, and investment choice reduces the residual standard deviation by 15.32 percent. Or, 10.27 percent (15.32 percent − 5.05 percent) can be attributed to both chance events and investment choices together. The maximum that can be attributed to chance events, plus the maximum that can be attributed to investment choice, which is 11.96 percent (4.03 percent + 7.93 percent), is not much greater than the reduction of 10.27 percent that can be attributed to both jointly. Thus there is little correlation between the two sets of factors; if there were no correlation, the sum of the individual reductions would equal the joint reduction.

The effect of controlling for chance events and for investment choice within earnings decile is shown in the second panel of table 1.5. Controlling for chance events typically reduces the residual standard deviation by only a few percentage points (although as high as 23 percent in the 2nd and 27 percent in the 4th decile). Thus, within earnings deciles, little of the dispersion can be ascribed to these individual attributes. Controlling for investment choice typically yields a larger reduction in residual variance than controlling for the chance events. In this case the reduction ranges from about 3 percent to 16 percent. In the higher deciles, in particular, the reduction due to investment choice is around 13 percent on average, whereas the reduction due to chance events is around 4 percent on average. Although these measures are not inconsistent with the graphical information, they provide no detail on how the distribution of wealth may be affected by the individual attributes, and that is what we wish to emphasize; thus the figures highlighted above.

We have focused on the dispersion of total wealth. Within lifetime earnings deciles, wide dispersion characterizes all asset categories. Little of the dispersion can be attributed to individual household circumstances. For example, figure 1.9 shows adjusted and unadjusted quantiles for personal financial assets (including personal retirement assets) for households in

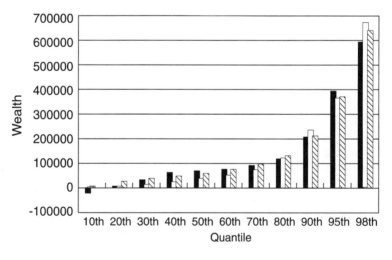

Fig. 1.9   7th earnings decile: adjusted v. unadjusted financial wealth

the 7th lifetime earnings decile. Although the top adjusted quantiles are lower than the unadjusted quantiles, overall, the adjustment has only a modest effect on the dispersion.

1.4   The Wealth That Consistent Saving Would Have Produced

We see that a large fraction of households on the eve of retirement have meager financial asset saving and, indeed, limited total wealth. We now ask what the wealth of HRS respondents might have been had they saved consistently for retirement throughout their working lives. The answer to this question can be illustrative only, because it requires a choice of saving rate out of income and a choice of rate of return. We make calculations based on several different saving rates and rate of return values. Basically, we ask, What if a proportion s of earnings had been saved each year, and each year this saving had been invested in assets earning a rate of return r?[8] Using a given s and a given r, we calculate the resulting asset accumulation of our sample. There is one important limitation to this method: Historical earnings are reported only up to the Social Security earnings limit, as emphasized above. Actual earnings in these deciles may be substantially higher than Social Security reported earnings.

Because of this limitation of the Social Security data, we also make calculations based on the annual March Current Population Survey (CPS), which reports earnings well above the Social Security maximum.[9] We follow this procedure: (a) We identify lifetime earnings deciles, as described above, using the Social Security earnings histories of each family in the HRS. (b) Using the annual March CPS, we calculate earned income deciles by age for the years 1964–91. Using published data on median earnings prior to 1964, we extrapolate this series back to 1955. Thus we obtain CPS earnings histories by decile for the years 1955 to 1991. (c) To compare the Social Security with the analogous CPS data, we assign each HRS household to a CPS decile according to the household Social Security earnings decile. The CPS earnings histories begin at age twenty-five, and a given household is assumed to have been in the same decile since age twenty-five. (d) Using this earnings profile and these saving and rate of return values, we calculate accumulated wealth up to the age of the respondent at the time of the survey in 1992.

Results for several saving rates (s) and nominal investment returns (r) are shown in table 1.6. For each combination of s and r, the first column presents results using only the Social Security earnings data. The second column shows the results of the alternative calculation based on the CPS

8. These calculations assume a constant rate of saving as a person ages.
9. The ratio of the CPS maximum to the Social Security maximum has ranged from a low of just under 2 in 1981 to a high of over 20 in 1964. In 1991 the CPS reported earnings up to a maximum of $200,000; the Social Security maximum was $53,400 in that year.

Table 1.6   Assets at the Time of the Health and Retirement Study (respondents having saved throughout their working lives)

Earnings Decile	Saving Rate (s) and Rate of Return (r)											
	s = .05, r = 6%		s = .05, r = 12.5%		s = .10, r = 6%		s = .10, r = 12.5%		s = .15, r = 6%		s = .15, r = 12.5%	
	SS	CPS	SS	CPS	SS	CPS	SS	CPS	SS	CPS	SS	CPS
1st	1,608	34	4,329	137	3,216	69	8,658	275	4,824	103	12,987	412
2nd	9,178	11,402	24,887	38,066	18,356	22,804	49,773	76,133	27,534	34,207	74,660	144,199
3rd	18,321	23,738	50,004	73,290	36,642	47,475	100,008	146,580	54,962	71,213	150,012	219,870
4th	28,236	33,627	78,897	100,608	56,472	67,253	157,794	201,216	84,708	100,880	236,690	301,825
5th	37,083	42,606	105,962	124,198	74,166	85,212	211,925	248,395	111,249	127,819	317,887	372,593
6th	45,490	51,079	125,965	144,557	90,981	102,158	251,930	289,113	136,471	153,237	377,896	433,670
7th	53,617	61,056	150,462	173,856	107,234	122,112	300,923	347,712	160,851	183,168	451,385	521,567
8th	60,073	71,689	163,745	199,094	120,147	143,378	327,490	398,189	180,220	215,068	491,236	597,283
9th	67,457	88,701	183,935	251,229	134,914	177,401	367,869	502,459	202,370	266,102	551,804	753,688
10th	83,810	125,418	226,230	354,536	167,620	250,835	452,460	709,072	251,430	376,153	678,690	1,063,609
All	40,487	50,935	111,442	145,957	80,975	101,870	222,883	291,914	121,462	152,805	334,325	437,872

Source: See table 1.3.

earnings data. Calculations are made for three values of s (5, 10, and 15 percent) and two values of r (6 and 12.5 percent). The assumed values of s reflect what we believe to be "reasonable" rates of saving for households. Indeed, if saving is broadly defined to include investments in housing, businesses, pensions, and vehicles, then a rate of even 15 percent may be conservative. The rates of return of 6 percent and 12.5 percent are the mean annual returns for long-term corporate bonds and the Standard and Poor's (S&P) index, respectively, between 1926 and 1995.

For the most part, the Social Security earnings histories and the CPS constructed histories yield rather similar results, although the CPS histories are associated with greater wealth accumulation. The greatest differences occur at the top earnings deciles and are typically larger for large saving rates and rates of return. The actual assets with which these accumulations should be compared is unclear. We are inclined to compare these values to all financial assets that might be used for support in retirement— that is, personal retirement assets, firm pension assets, and other personal financial assets. For convenience, the medians of these assets are shown by lifetime earnings decile in the first column of table 1.7. Since housing equity typically is not used to finance retirement spending, at least not until advanced ages, it is convenient to make comparisons excluding housing equity, which is the largest asset of the majority of households. In any case, total wealth is also shown in the second column of table 1.7. (The comparison should be with the actual median, and not the mean, because the same saving and rates of return are assigned to all households. In addition, within a decile, the same CPS earnings are assigned to all households.)

Saving rates of 10 percent would typically yield much larger assets than the median of actual total financial assets. Consider the 6th lifetime in-

Table 1.7	Actual Median Total Financial Assets and Total Wealth, by Lifetime Earnings Decile	
Lifetime Earnings Decile	Total Financial Assets ($)	Total Wealth ($)
1st	0	3,000
2nd	431	28,800
3rd	6,770	47,025
4th	22,000	72,504
5th	35,668	105,166
6th	46,882	126,082
7th	86,000	195,000
8th	111,465	224,000
9th	162,825	305,536
10th	213,855	380,115

Source: See table 1.3.

Note: Total financial assets include personal retirement, firm pension, and other financial assets.

come decile, for example. The figure for actual median total financial assets in this decile is $46,882. With a rate of return of 6 percent, a saving rate of 10 percent would have produced median assets of about $100,000 at the time of the survey. At the average rate of return for the S&P 500, the accumulation would have been between $250,000 and $300,000. The actual median of total (financial and nonfinancial) wealth in the 6th decile is $126,082. In all income deciles, the "as if" accumulation of financial assets is much larger than the actual accumulation of financial assets. Indeed, for saving rates of 10 percent and the S&P 500 rate of return, the "as if" potential accumulation is much larger than total actual wealth. The average age of the HRS respondents is only fifty-six, however, so assets projected to age sixty-five could easily be more than double those reported in table 1.6. Nonetheless, these potential saving accumulations are in stark contrast with the actual saving of these families. With the illustrative lifetime saving rates and investment returns, families in all but the lowest decile would have accumulated sizable wealth by the time of the HRS survey.[10]

Saving rates like those used in these illustrative calculations are likely to be increasingly common with the continuing spread of 401(k) plans. For example, if current trends continue, it would not be unusual for a person to contribute 10 percent of earnings to a 401(k) and to invest in an S&P 500 index mutual fund. It is easy to see that consistent lifetime saving, perhaps through a 401(k) plan, could yield large asset accumulations for a very substantial fraction of households. This prospect is considered in some detail by Poterba, Venti, and Wise (1998).

1.5 Self-assessed Saving Adequacy, Attitudes toward Saving, and Asset Accumulation

Two experimental saving modules were administered to subsamples of respondents in the third wave of the HRS. Each of the two modules was given to 10 percent of respondents, although not the same respondents. The goal of these experimental modules was to explore possibilities for discovering more about the attributes of persons who save compared to those who don't, with the ultimate goal of understanding more about what determines saving behavior. In addition, the modules asked respondents about the adequacy of their retirement saving. We explore here the relationship between responses to the saving module questions and realized saving as described in section 1.3.

The experimental module sample sizes are small. There are 460 observa-

---

10. In the CPS data, families in the lowest Social Security earnings decile are assumed to have been in the lowest earnings decile in all years. Thus in most years these families are assumed to be zero earners.

Table 1.8   Adequacy of Saving versus Q

Question	Response	Percent	Total Wealth Q	Total Financial Assets Q
Over the past twenty or thirty years, do you think now what you saved was (M9-4):	About right	24	61	64
	Too little	76	46	43
	Too much[a]			
If you could do it again, do you think you would save (M9-4c):	About the same	31	57	55
	More	69	45	46
	Less[b]			
Including Social Security and pensions, will you have enough saving to maintain your living standard after retirement? (M10-10)	Yes	67	58	57
	No	33	46	46
If yes: How do you expect your standard of living in retirement to compare to your present standard of living? (M10-11f)	Higher	8	44	50
	Same	75	60	58
	Lower	17	60	54

Source: Tabulations from experimental savings modules of the 1996 HRS.
[a]Less than 2 percent of the respondents answered "Too much," and these responses have been excluded.
[b]Less than 1 percent of the respondents answered "Less," and these responses have been excluded.

tions in one of the two that we use, and 390 in the other. About half of these observations are not used here, primarily because of missing Social Security records.[11] Thus, we need a convenient way to measure the realized saving of each household in such a way that we can avoid separate analyses by lifetime earnings decile. The 10 percent samples do not yield large enough sample sizes to do this reliably. Thus we calculate a variable Q, which in this paper is the within-decile wealth quantile of each household. For example, if a household has wealth just at the median of other households within an earnings decile, the Q assigned to this household is 50. This measure is independent of earnings decile. It tells us how the wealth of each household compares to the wealth of other households with similar lifetime earnings. Thus two households in different lifetime earnings deciles but with the same Q can be thought of as having a similar taste for saving. Households with different Q values have different tastes for saving.

We first consider the relationship between self-assessed adequacy of saving and Q. Table 1.8 shows respondent answers to several questions, together with their Q values. The first question asked whether the respondent's saving over the past twenty or thirty years was "About right," "Too little," or "Too much." Almost 75 percent of the respondents said "Too little." About 25 percent said "About right." Virtually no one said

11. There is no reason to believe that these exclusions are not random, as shown in table 1.1.

"Too much." Those who said "About right" had an average Q with respect to total wealth of 61—meaning that, on average, they were at the 61st percentile of the total wealth distribution within their lifetime earnings decile. Those who responded "Too little" had an average Q of 46. Thus a large fraction of respondents say they saved too little, and they have Q values substantially lower than those who say they saved enough. (To judge the difference in wealth of these two groups, the 61st quantile is typically about one and one-half to two times the size of the 46th quantile.) The last column of the table reports Q values based on total financial assets, including IRAs and 401(k) balances. Comparisons based on financial assets typically parallel those based on total wealth, as they do in this case. Apparently consistent with responses to the first question, the next question reveals that about two-thirds of respondents said they would save more if they could do it again, and about a third said they would save about the same.

The third question asked whether, including Social Security and pensions, the respondent would have enough saving to maintain his or her standard of living after retirement, 67 percent said yes and only 33 percent said no. Thus, many households who say they did not save enough also say they will be able to maintain their standard of living in retirement. However, of those who said yes, the average Q was 58; it was only 46 for those who said no. Apparently a substantial portion of respondents with relatively low Q say they will be able to maintain their standards of living (e.g., if those who said yes have Q values between 16 and 100, the average would be 58), even though many of these also say they have saved too little. Of those who answered yes, about 75 percent said they could maintain the *same* standard.

From the experimental modules, can we learn anything about the relationship between individual attributes and realized asset accumulation? Apparently we can. Table 1.9 shows responses to a series of questions about individual behavior or attitudes together with average Q values. It is clear that there is a strong relationship between the age at which respondents started saving for retirement and Q: Those who started saving before age twenty-five have an average Q of 63. Q declines consistently with postponement of retirement saving; respondents who never started to save for retirement have an average Q of 37.

It also appears that having a target or planned level of saving makes a difference. Those who said they had such a target have an average Q of 56, while those who had no target have an average Q of 48. Most of those who had a target also said they had a plan for achieving that target, and most also said the plan included trying to save something out of each paycheck. If the plan included saving out of each paycheck, the average Q was 59; if not, the average Q was 36. A question on a different module asked simply: "Over the past years, did you have a plan for retirement

Question	Response	Percent	Total Wealth Q	Total Financial Assets Q
At what age did you start saving for retirement? (M9-3)	≤25	13	63	58
	26–35	17	57	56
	36–45	21	54	53
	46–55	20	48	49
	≥56	3	47	45
	Never	26	37	34
Thinking over the past twenty or thirty years, did you have some target or planned level of saving? (M9-5)	Yes	23	56	54
	No	77	48	46
If yes: Did you have a plan for achieving that goal? (M9-5a)	Yes	81	59	56
	No	19	55	47
If yes: Did the plan include trying to save something out of each paycheck? (M9-5b)	Yes	92	59	56
	No	8	36	41
Over the past years, did you have a plan for retirement saving? (M10-4)	Yes	47	60	63
	No	53	48	44
How well do these statements describe you? (0 means doesn't, 10 means closely) (M10-20)				
I never seemed to get caught up on my bills so I could save for the future.	0–3	43	53	54
	4–6	28	57	58
	7–10	28	51	47
I could never stick to a saving plan.	0–3	44	57	61
	4–6	26	50	45
	7–10	30	53	51
I thought Social Security or employer pensions would take care of my retirement income.	0–3	44	58	59
	4–6	28	52	52
	7–10	28	50	46
If you put $10,000 in a saving account when age twenty-five, how much would you have now, at a 5 percent interest rate?	<$35,000	16	54	52
	$35,000–75,000	33	46	45
	$75,000–105,000	29	48	46
	>$105,000	22	58	58
Thinking of your planning for retirement over the past twenty or thirty years, how important did you think the following sources would be in providing your retirement income? (0 means unimportant, 10 means very important) (M9-2)				
Social Security	0–3	8	68	55
	4–6	24	54	49
	7–10	68	47	48
Employer-provided pension	0–3	23	44	41
	4–6	16	41	39
	7–10	62	55	54

(continued)

Table 1.9   (continued)

Question	Response	Percent	Total Wealth Q	Total Financial Assets Q
IRAs, 401(k) or Keogh	0–3	36	45	39
	4–6	22	49	47
	7–10	41	54	56
Other personal saving or investment	0–3	21	36	33
	4–6	27	45	42
	7–10	52	58	57
Other sources	0–3	47	44	44
	4–6	31	51	50
	7–10	23	61	54

Source: See table 1.8.

saving?" In response to this question, 47 percent said yes, and they had an average Q of 60; 53 percent said no and had an average Q of 48. The implications are that having a plan to save for retirement contributes to asset accumulation, and that trying to save something out of each paycheck may be the key to greater asset accumulation.

The questions asking how respondents would characterize themselves seem only weakly related to asset accumulation. Those who said they could never "get caught up on [their] bills" or that they could "never stick to a saving plan" accumulated about the same as those who said these attributes did not describe them. Given the promise of Social Security benefits, it may be that many households rationally choose to save little, in particular those with low lifetime earnings, for whom the Social Security replacement rate is relatively high. But only about a quarter of respondents said they "thought Social Security or employer pensions would take care of [their] retirement income." The average Q of this group was 50, not much lower than the average of 58 for those who said this view did not characterize them. The difference in Q values for total financial assets is greater—46 versus 59. Thus the responses suggest some relationship between expected Social Security and employer pension benefits and other saving, but certainly not enough to explain the very low asset accumulation of a large fraction of respondents. Even for respondents in the lower lifetime earnings deciles there appears to be little relationship between the anticipated importance of Social Security and Q values for total wealth, as shown in the tabulation that follows. The responses do suggest, however, that respondents in the lower earnings deciles who anticipated that Social Security and pensions would be important have lower total financial asset Q values than those who thought Social Security and pensions would be less important.

	Earnings Decile		
Response	1st–3rd	4th–7th	8th–10th
Total Wealth Q			
0 to 3	59	63	56
4 to 6	61	56	42
7 to 10	60	45	52
Total Financial Asset Q			
0 to 3	56	65	57
4 to 6	59	54	45
7 to 10	36	42	51

This sort of finding might be contrasted with results based on theoretical models of economic behavior. Hubbard, Skinner, and Zeldes (1995), for example, use a life-cycle model of saving, which accounts for precautionary motives for saving, to simulate the dispersion in wealth of low-income households in particular. They show how under their model social insurance programs with asset-based means testing can discourage saving by households with low expected lifetime incomes.

Could limited financial literacy be one reason some people don't save? To explore this possibility, the survey posed a question intended to test respondents' understanding of compound interest. Respondents were asked what they thought would be the current value of $10,000 saved at age twenty-five if the interest rate had been 5 percent. Depending on the age of the respondent in 1992, the appropriate answer is between $40,000 and $70,000. Although a small proportion of respondents give answers below this range, more than half give answers well above this range; about a third are within the range. However, there seems to be no clear relationship to asset accumulation.

Finally, the saving modules include a series of questions about anticipated sources of retirement income. Respondents who thought Social Security benefits would be important have an average Q of 47; those who thought Social Security benefits would be unimportant have an average Q of 65. The question discussed above, which asked whether the statement that "Social Security or employer pensions would take care of [the respondent's] retirement income" described the respondent's saving behavior, seemed related only to the saving of persons with low lifetime earnings. The response to this question suggests a more general correspondence between reliance on Social Security and saving. Greater anticipated importance of IRAs and 401(k) plans would almost surely be associated with greater wealth because they are included in total wealth and in total financial assets. Employer-provided pensions, however, are not included in total financial assets. Keeping in mind that Q controls for earnings decile, it is rather striking to find that respondents who anticipate that pensions will be important in retirement have an average Q of 55, while those who say pensions will be unimportant have an average Q of only 44. Such evidence may perhaps support the view that saving has a multiplier effect: Saving in one way induces saving in other forms, as well. Having an employer pension, for example, may be accompanied by information about financial needs in retirement.

In addition to the questions discussed above, the experimental modules asked respondents whether, in thinking about their financial futures, they were concerned about several events: job loss, financial market collapse, and health care costs. The results are presented in table 1.10. Few were very concerned about job loss or financial market collapse, but a large number of respondents were concerned about potential health care costs. The concern with health care costs is weakly related to Q. Job loss, on the other hand, is a much greater concern for those with low Q than for those with higher Q: Those who say they aren't concerned with job loss have an average Q of 55, while those who are very concerned have an average Q of only 39. Concern with financial market collapse is not strongly related to Q, although those who are more concerned about this event have some-

Table 1.10   Financial Concerns versus Q

Question	Response	Percent	Total Wealth Q	Total Financial Assets Q
In thinking about your financial future, how concerned are you with (M9-7):				
health care costs?	Hardly	19	54	50
	Some	29	52	53
	A lot	52	47	44
job loss?	Hardly	67	55	52
	Some	15	44	50
	A lot	18	39	36
financial market collapse?	Hardly	43	45	43
	Some	31	55	55
	A lot	26	53	51
costs of supporting parents?	Hardly	78	51	51
	Some	13	47	38
	A lot	8	45	42
costs of supporting children?	Hardly	64	51	51
	Some	23	54	49
	A lot	13	39	38

Source: See table 1.8

what higher Q values than those who are unconcerned, perhaps as should be expected.

1.6   Conclusions and Discussion

In 1953, Milton Friedman wrote a paper he titled "Choice, Chance, and the Personal Distribution of Income." In this paper he states:

> Differences among individuals or families in the amount of income received are generally regarded as reflecting . . . circumstances largely outside the control of the individuals concerned, such as unavoidable chance occurrences and differences in natural endowment and inherited wealth. . . . The way that individual choice can affect the distribution of income has been less frequently noticed. The alternatives open to an individual differ, among other respects, in the probability distribution of income they promise. Hence his choice among them depends in part on his taste for risk. . . . The foregoing analysis is exceedingly tentative. . . . Yet I think it goes far enough to demonstrate that one cannot rule out the possibility that a large part of the existing inequality of wealth can be regarded as produced by men to satisfy their tastes and preferences. (277–78, 289–90)

Now, more than forty years later, "People earn just enough to get by" is a phrase often used to explain the low personal saving rate in the United States. The implicit presumption is that households simply do not earn enough both to pay for current needs and to save. Yet in other developed countries the saving rate at all income levels is much higher than in the United States. Even in Canada—in many respects similar to the United States—the personal saving rate is almost twice as high as in the United States. Such international comparisons alone suggest that saving depends on much more than lifetime earnings.

We show in this paper that at all levels of lifetime earnings there is an enormous dispersion in the accumulated wealth of families approaching retirement. In the United States it is not only households with low incomes that save little. A significant proportion of high-income households also save very little. Furthermore, not all low-income households are non-savers. Indeed, a substantial proportion of low-income households saves a great deal. We then consider the extent to which differences in household lifetime financial resources explain the wide dispersion in wealth, given lifetime earnings. We find that very little of this dispersion can be explained by chance differences in individual circumstances—"largely outside the control of the individuals"—that might limit the resources from which saving might plausibly be made. Thus we conclude that the bulk of the dispersion must be attributed to differences in the amount that households choose to save. Choices vary enormously across households. Some choose to save more and spend less over their working lives while others choose to save little and spend more while working. Wide dispersion in saving is evident at all levels of lifetime earnings, from the lowest to the highest. The differences in saving choices among households with similar lifetime earnings lead to vastly different levels of asset accumulation by the time retirement age approaches.

Perhaps more closely related to the choice of risk that Friedman emphasized, we also consider how much of the dispersion in wealth might be accounted for by different investment choices of savers—some more risky, some less risky—again, given lifetime earnings. We find that investment choice matters but that it is not a major determinant of the dispersion in asset accumulation. It matters about as much as chance events that limit the available resources of households with the same lifetime earnings. Thus, although investment choices make a difference, the overwhelming determinant of the accumulation of wealth at retirement is simply the choice to save.

As a benchmark, we also considered the assets that the HRS respondents would have accumulated had they saved given amounts over their working lives and had earned given returns on their saving. Saving 10 percent of earnings and earning the average annual S&P 500 return (which has been 12.2 percent since 1926) would have led to accumulated assets much much greater than the typical financial assets of HRS households at the time of the survey.

Perhaps based on the presumption—contrary to Friedman's conjecture—that differences in wealth can be attributed more to differences across households in adverse circumstances that limit saving, rather than to explicit individual choices, government policy often penalizes persons who have saved over their lifetimes. For example, persons with the same lifetime earnings will face very different tax rates on Social Security benefits: Those who saved will pay higher taxes while those who didn't will pay lower taxes. Shoven and Wise (1997, 1998) show that persons who save too much through personal or employer-provided pensions face enormous tax penalties when they use these accumulated assets for retirement support. The evidence that differences in retirement wealth are due largely to saving choice while younger brings into question this tendency in tax policy. Although the distribution of the tax burden will inevitably be based on many factors, most observers believe that the extent to which older persons with more assets are taxed more should depend in part on how they acquired the assets. Chance accumulation may weigh on the side of heavier taxes on those who have accumulated. On the other hand, accumulation by choosing to consume less when young, while others choose to consume more when young, weighs against heavier taxes on those who accumulate assets for retirement. As emphasized at the outset, this paper is about the dispersion in the accumulation of assets of persons with *similar lifetime earnings.* The issue raised here is not about progressive income taxation, but rather, given the same after-tax earnings, about differences in the tax imposed on persons who save today in order to spend more tomorrow, versus those who spend all today. Our analysis suggests that a very large proportion of the variation in the wealth of older households can be attributed to household saving choices while younger rather than to chance events that may have limited the resources available for saving. To the extent that most asset accumulation is due to choice rather than chance, our results also suggest that ex ante taxing of saving may have more serious consequences for saving than may previously have been thought.

Finally, we explored the relationship between household saving and information about household saving that was obtained through two experimental saving modules administered in the third wave of the HRS. In general, the experimental module responses were consistent with household realized asset accumulation. About three fourths of respondents said they had saved too little over the past twenty or thirty years, and we found a strong relationship between our Q value—a household's percentile level of assets, given lifetime earnings—and whether respondents thought they had saved enough. The accumulation of retirement assets is very strongly related to the age at which persons began to save for retirement. In addition, persons who accumulated more retirement assets tended to have a saving target or plan, and the plan typically included saving a portion of each paycheck. Those who accumulated little were more likely to say that they just couldn't get caught up on their bills or that they had a hard time sticking to a saving plan. Low saving rates seem to be related only weakly to an expectation that Social Security or employer pension plans would take care of retirement income, even among households with low lifetime earnings. The potential cost of health care is an important concern of a large fraction of households, and this concern appears to be unrelated to asset accumulation. On the other hand, there appears to be relatively little concern about job loss, supporting children or parents, or financial market collapse. The results from the HRS experimental saving modules suggests to us that this type of information collection might fruitfully be pursued in more depth.

Appendix

The Sample

The analysis is based on the first wave of the Health and Retirement Study (HRS), which sampled families with heads aged age fifty-one to sixty-one in 1992. This wave of the HRS includes 12,652 respondents in 7,702 households. For two reasons our analysis was based on only 3,992 households.

First, in 379 married or partnered households, one of the respondents did not respond to the survey. Because the pension wealth of both members is a critical component of the analysis, we have deleted these households from the sample.

Second, the analysis relies heavily on lifetime income as measured by Social Security earnings records. These records are available for only 8,257 of the 12,652 HRS respondents. The analysis is based on household rather than individual respondent data. Historical earnings for a single-person household required only that Social Security earnings records be available for that person. For a two-person household, it was necessary to have historical earnings for both persons in the household if both had been in the labor force for a significant length of time. The HRS obtained such data for 1,625 single-person households and for 2,751 two-person households, together comprising 4,376 of the 7,607 HRS households.

Two related sample adjustments were made. First, we retained households in which one or both members reported never having worked, even if the household member was missing a Social Security earnings record. We assumed zero earnings for such persons. Second, we excluded from the sample all households that included any member who had zero Social Security earnings *and* who reported working for any level of government for five (not necessarily consecutive) years. This latter restriction is intended to exclude households that have zero Social Security earnings due to gaps in Social Security coverage. The final sample includes 3,992 households.

Wealth

Total wealth is comprised of the following broad categories:

Financial Assets: Stocks, mutual funds, investment trusts, checking or saving account balances, money market funds, CDs, government saving bonds, treasury bills, bonds, bond funds, and other savings or assets, less unsecured debt.

Personal Retirement Assets: IRA, Keogh, and 401(k) balances.

Firm Pension Assets: Defined-contribution plan balances (other than 401[k]) and the present value of promised defined-benefit plan benefits. (See the section "Pension Wealth," following.)

Net Vehicle Equity

Net Business Equity

Real Estate: Real estate other than main home, net of debt

Home Equity: Value of primary residence less outstanding balances on all mortgages, home equity loans, and lines of credit used.

Pension Wealth

Imputation of Key Missing Data

It is particularly difficult to produce a measure of pension wealth for this sample.[12] Many respondents were missing key pieces of data needed to construct pension wealth. For some types of pensions, less than half of the respondents provided data complete enough to calculate pension wealth directly. A brief overview of the procedures used to impute these missing data follows.

In the HRS, the information required to construct pension wealth comes from three sources: the pension on the current job for persons still working, the pension on the last job for persons no longer working, and pension income by source for persons receiving benefits.[13]

All currently employed workers were asked if they were "included in" a pension plan "through your work" (if self-employed), or if they were "included" in a pension plan "sponsored by your employer or union" (if not self-employed). Each respondent could list up to three plans. About 76 percent of the respondents listed a single plan, 21 percent listed two plans, and the remaining 3 percent of the respondents listed three plans. Respondents were most likely to cite a defined benefit (DB) plan as their first plan. Of the first plans reported, 61 percent were DB and 34 percent were defined contribution (DC) plans. Of the second plans reported, only 16 percent were DB; 81 percent were DC. Most of the third plans reported were DC.

For each of the three plans, if the reported plan type was DB, "both," or "don't know," then the respondent was first asked the expected age of retirement, then asked to give an estimate of the pension benefit at retirement. The benefit could be expressed as a percentage of final salary, as an amount ($) per unit of time (month, quarter, year, etc.), or as a lump sum at retirement. Most respondents (44 percent) gave an amount per unit of time, and we have converted these to annual pension benefits. For those providing a percent of final salary (15 percent) we have also computed an annual pension benefit using an assumed (see below) annual rate of growth of earnings until the expected date of retirement. Still, data are missing;

---

12. Our estimates of pension wealth are based on the respondent's report of the provisions of employer-sponsored pension plans. The HRS also conducted a survey of employers. Information from this latter survey is not used in this analysis.

13. There is also some information on pensions associated with previous jobs (other than the last job), but we judged these data to be too incomplete to use at this time.

the remaining 41 percent of the plans require imputation. To impute pension benefits we first divide the sample by the number of plans (three could be listed), type of response (DB, DC, or both), and ten wage-and-salary income deciles. We then used a hotdeck imputation procedure using these ninety cells.[14]

If the reported plan type is "DC" or "both," then the survey asks for the balance accumulated in the plan. Missing data, although still a problem, are not as severe as for DB plans: For 71 percent of DC plans an account balance is reported. If the plan type is DC, then further details on the type of plan are requested. Responses to these detailed questions are used to categorize DC contributions as contributions to either "401(k) plans" or to "traditional DC plans." Our definition of "401(k) plans" broadly includes the HRS response categories "401(k)/403(b)/SRA," "thrift of saving plan," "tax shelter," "IRA/SEP," "SEPP," or any response combination that includes these (e.g., some respondents indicate their plans to be a combination of a 401[k] and a thrift plan). The category "traditional DC plans" covers the remaining types of DC plans, including ESOPs and money purchase plans. If a respondent indicated plan type "both," then no detailed questions about plan type were asked. For these plans the entire balance is assumed to be in a "traditional DC plan," thus perhaps underestimating 401(k) balances. For plans known to be DC, but for which the balance is unknown, the hotdeck imputation method is again used, based on plan number, plan type (traditional DC and 401[k]), and ten wage-and-salary income deciles.

Persons not currently employed are asked about their most recent job. As above, they can specify four pension types: DB, DC, both, and don't know (DK). However, each respondent could provide information on only one plan. In general, the follow-up questions parallel the questions asked for the current job discussed above. We will note only the differences here. First, persons covered by DB plans are asked about expected future benefits, benefits currently being received, and benefits already distributed as a lump sum. We disregard all but the former because benefits currently received are picked up elsewhere in the survey (the income section, see below), and benefits already paid out will show up as IRA balances if rolled over (and do not represent pension wealth if not). If covered by a DC plan, the balance is included only if "left to accumulate" with the former employer. DC balances rolled over into an IRA, converted to an annuity, or withdrawn are not included. Finally, respondents who indicated coverage by "both" plan types were asked, "How much money was in your account when you left that employer?" The survey does not ask how much remains in the account as of the survey date. Based on the proportion of

14. About 9 percent of the DB plans were also missing the expected age of retirement. We use the modal response of age sixty-two in these cases.

DC balances remaining with the employer to accumulate, we randomly include the balances of 33 percent of these respondents. Again, missing DB benefits and DC data are imputed by the hotdeck method described above. Unfortunately, there is no way to distinguish between 401(k) balances and traditional DC plan balances acquired on prior jobs. Thus, all DC balances are assumed to be from traditional DC plans.

The final source of information on pension wealth is from income currently being received. We use income streams from pensions, annuities, and veterans' benefits. There is no way to distinguish between DC and DB sources, so we report these data as a separate category (PV pension income) in tables 1.3 and 1.4.

Constructing Pension Wealth

For DC-type pensions the reported balance is our measure of pension wealth. For persons expecting DB pension benefits and persons currently receiving pension income, we compute the present value of the benefit stream using the following assumptions: Mortality data are based on population averages by gender, age, and birth cohort provided by the Social Security Administration; see Mitchell, Olson, and Steinmeier (2000) for a discussion of these data. For discounting and earnings growth we use the "intermediate" interest rate assumptions used by the Social Security Administration; see Board of Trustees (1995). Public pensions are assumed to be fully indexed, again using the "intermediate" projections of the Social Security Administration; see Board of Trustees (1995). Private-sector pension benefits are not indexed.

Respondents were asked to provide the expected pension benefits at their expected dates of retirement. If benefits are not currently being received, they are assumed to commence at the expected age of retirement (the mean is sixty-two). The average age of HRS respondents is fifty-five. Thus, for the typical HRS respondent, retirement benefits do not begin for another seven years. We have assumed that their responses to the expected pension-benefits question are denominated in future (date of retirement) dollars. Moreover, we have assumed that the benefit amount is a single-survivor benefit. Accordingly, we use individual survival probabilities in the computation of the present value. If we assumed instead that the responses represented joint-survivor benefits, calculated pension wealth would be somewhat higher.

We further assume that when respondents report expected pension benefits, they do not anticipate separating from their employers prior to retirement. This assumption allows us to calculate the present value of retirement wealth conditional on continued years of service until retirement. The component of this wealth "earned" as of the survey date is this present value multiplied by the ratio of years of service at the survey date to years of service at the expected date of retirement. This adjustment is necessary to make the present value of DB benefits comparable to the accumulated balance in a DC plan at the date of the survey.

References

Attanasio, Orazio, James Banks, Costas Meghir, and Guglielmo Weber. 1995. Humps and bumps in lifetime consumption. NBER Working Paper no. 5350. Cambridge, Mass.: National Bureau of Economic Research, November.

Board of Trustees, Federal Old-Age and Survivors Insurance and Disability Insurance Trust Funds. 1995. *The 1995 annual report.* Washington, D.C.: GPO.

Friedman, Milton. 1953. Choice, chance, and the personal distribution of income. *Journal of Political Economy* 41:277–90.

Hubbard, R. Glenn, Jonathan Skinner, and Stephen P. Zeldes. 1995. Precautionary saving and social insurance. *Journal of Political Economy* 103 (2): 360–99.

Juster, F. Thomas, James P. Smith, and Frank Stafford. 1999. The measurement and structure of household wealth. *Labour Economics* 6 (2): 253–75.

Juster, F. Thomas, and Richard Suzman. 1995. An overview of the Health and Retirement Study. *Journal of Human Resources* 30:S7–S56.

Mitchell, Olivia, Jan Olson, and Thomas Steinmeier. 2000. Social Security earnings and projected benefits. In *Forecasting retirement needs and retirement wealth,* ed. Olivia Mitchell, Brett Hammond, and Anna Rappaport, 327–59. Philadelphia: University of Pennsylvania Press.

Poterba, James M., Steven F. Venti, and David A. Wise. 1998. Implications of rising personal retirement saving. In *Frontiers in the economics of aging,* ed. David A. Wise, 125–67. Chicago: University of Chicago Press.

Samwick, Andrew A. 1996. Discount rate heterogeneity and social security reform. Paper presented at the ninth annual Inter-American Seminar on Economics. November, Buenos Aires.

Shoven, John B., and David A. Wise. 1997. Keeping savers from saving. In *Facing the aging wave,* ed. David A. Wise, 57–87. Stanford, Calif.: Hoover Institution Press.

———. 1998. The taxation of pensions: A shelter can become a trap. In *Frontiers in the economics of aging,* ed. David A. Wise, 173–211. Chicago: University of Chicago Press.

Smith, James P. 1995. Racial and ethnic differences in wealth in the Health and Retirement Study. *Journal of Human Resources* 30:S158–S183.

Venti, Steven F., and David A. Wise. 1990. Have IRAs increased U.S. saving? Evidence from consumer expenditure surveys. *Quarterly Journal of Economics* 55 (3): 661–98.

———. 1999. Lifetime earnings, saving choices, and wealth at retirement. In *Wealth, work, and health: Innovations in measurement in the social sciences,* ed. James P. Smith and Robert J. Willis, 87–120. Ann Arbor: University of Michigan Press.

2

Household Portfolio Allocation over the Life Cycle

James M. Poterba and Andrew A. Samwick

The recent and prospective aging of the populations in developed countries has attracted attention in many nations, as the prominent discussion in a World Bank (1994) report attests. The potential effects of population aging on social security systems and on the levels of private and national saving have drawn the most interest from academics and policy analysts. In the United States, particular attention has focused on the adequacy of the baby-boom generation's level of retirement saving; for conflicting reports on this question, see the Congressional Budget Office (1993) and Bernheim (1995). The way households allocate their accumulated saving across different assets, such as stocks, bonds, and real estate, has attracted less discussion, even though future economic security can depend as much on the way assets are invested as on the level of those assets. Understanding asset allocation is also essential for understanding the behavior of individuals in the increasingly popular defined contribution pension plans that allow participants some discretion in their investment choices, and for analyzing recent proposals for Social Security reform that call for mandatory saving accounts, with investment responsibility delegated to individuals.[1]

James M. Poterba is the Mitsui Professor of Economics at the Massachusetts Institute of Technology and director of the Public Economic Research Program at the National Bureau of Economic Research. Andrew A. Samwick is professor of economics at Dartmouth and a research associate of the National Bureau of Economic Research.

The authors thank Makoto Saito, Steve Venti, and conference participants for helpful comments and Arthur Kennickell for assistance with the Surveys of Consumer Finances. Financial support from the National Institute of Aging and the National Science Foundation is gratefully acknowledged.

1. Samwick and Skinner (1998) examine the adequacy of defined contribution plans relative to the defined benefit plans that were popular before the transition began. Advisory Council on Social Security (1996) reports on various reform proposals for the United States system.

Although there is little empirical work on asset allocation, there is a theoretical literature on the optimal portfolio behavior of individuals at different ages. This work is characterized by some controversy, in part between academics and practical financial advisers. In the standard portfolio-choice paradigm that underlies most of financial economics, the only factor that should explain age-related differences in portfolio structure is differential risk aversion. In this setting, if a household is endowed with a time-invariant risk tolerance, then there should be no age-related patterns of portfolio allocation. Conditional on a household's risk aversion, there are strong predictions regarding the mix of risky and riskless assets that a household should hold. Moreover, regardless of their risk aversion, all households should hold risky assets in the same proportions within their risky asset portfolios.

A number of studies have tried to relate this theoretical result to the common practical recommendation, documented by Canner, Mankiw, and Weil (1997), that households should change the relative proportions of risky assets in their portfolios as they age. Samuelson (1989, 1990) has considered the conditions on utility functions and asset returns that will lead to age-related differences in risky asset holdings; in essence, his analysis allows for time-varying risk tolerance. Other studies expand the traditional model of portfolio choice to study related aspects of life-cycle asset allocation. For example, if individuals can vary their labor supply to offset fluctuations in asset returns, as in Bodie, Merton, and Samuelson (1992), or if they accumulate assets in part for precautionary reasons, as in Kimball (1993), and nonfinancial risks increase with age, then rational behavior may lead to a reduction in risky asset exposure as households age.[2]

This paper complements the substantial theoretical discussion of age-related patterns in asset allocation. It presents systematic empirical evidence on the basic patterns of household asset allocation over the life cycle. This information can help to evaluate competing models of household portfolio behavior, and more generally to assess proposals for greater reliance on household choices in retirement preparation. Using multiple waves of the Surveys of Consumer Finances, we are able to control for systematic differences across birth cohorts in the age-specific pattern of asset ownership. We find that it is not possible to aggregate households born at different ages for the purpose of portfolio modeling: There are statistically and economically significant "cohort effects" for most types of financial and nonfinancial assets.

The paper is organized as follows. Section 2.1 describes the Surveys of Consumer Finances and presents summary statistics for each wave of data. Section 2.2 presents our econometric methodology for distinguishing age and cohort effects and analyzes the patterns of ownership and allocation

---

2. See Gakidis (1997), Hochguertel (1998), and Campbell et al. (1999) for recent life cycle analyses of portfolio choice in the presence of income uncertainty.

of financial assets. Section 2.3 places the analysis of financial assets within the context of households' comprehensive balance sheets. The final section discusses several implications of our results, as well as directions for further research.

2.1   Data Description

The Surveys of Consumer Finances (SCFs) conducted by the Federal Reserve Board are designed to be the most comprehensive sources of wealth data in the United States. They are collected every three years, with the first one done in 1983 and the latest one in 1998. Although there are limited panel dimensions between the 1983 and 1986 and 1989 surveys, our analysis uses the SCFs from 1983, 1989, and 1992 as repeated cross-sections. We omit the 1986 survey because it was a limited reinterview survey of the households from the 1983 survey, which does not permit us to distinguish among all of the asset and debt categories that are found in the other surveys.[3] Avery and Elliehausen (1988), Avery and Kennickell (1988), and Kennickell (1999a,b) provide documentation of the SCFs from 1983, 1986, 1989, and 1992, respectively. An important feature of the SCFs is that they combine an area probability sample of U.S. households with a sample of high-income households drawn from tax records. The oversampling of high-income households allows the SCFs to provide an accurate assessment of the upper tail of the distribution of wealth in the United States.[4] In total, there are 4,103, 3,143, and 3,906 observations in the three SCFs. In this section, we present summary statistics on financial and total assets.[5]

Table 2.1 provides descriptive statistics for holdings of financial assets in each of the survey years; we consider the allocation of net worth in a later table. The six main categories of financial assets are taxable equity; tax-exempt bonds; taxable bonds; tax-deferred accounts such as Individual Retirement Accounts (IRAs), Keoghs, and defined contribution pension plans (including 401(k) plans); bank accounts (including certificates of deposit and money market accounts); and other financial assets such as whole life insurance and trusts. In each case, we assign mutual fund assets to the asset category corresponding to the assets held by the mutual fund. In addition, we distinguish between taxable equity held directly in brokerage accounts and that held indirectly through mutual funds.

---

3. The final public releases of the 1995 and 1998 SCFs were not available as of the initial draft of this paper. Subsequent analyses including more recent data did not change the results qualitatively from those we report below.
4. Curtin, Juster, and Morgan (1989) compare the SCF 1983 to the wealth information in the 1984 Panel Study of Income Dynamics and the 1984 Survey of Income and Program Participation.
5. See Pence and Sabelhaus (1998) for a more comprehensive, cohort-based analysis of the rate of the overall rate of saving using the SCFs.

Table 2.1   **Ownership and Allocation of Financial Assets for All Households, by Year**

Financial Asset	1983	1989	1992
Probability of Ownership			
Taxable equity held either directly or through			
mutual funds	20.15	19.04	20.98
Taxable equity held directly in brokerage accounts	19.07	15.91	16.90
Tax-exempt bonds	3.31	6.23	6.77
Taxable bonds	23.99	27.95	27.23
Tax-deferred accounts	32.86	37.85	39.33
Bank accounts	87.63	85.65	87.21
Other financial assets	36.52	36.62	36.60
Average Share of Household Portfolio			
Taxable equity held either directly or through			
mutual funds	5.78	5.53	6.15
Taxable equity held directly in brokerage accounts	5.50	4.58	4.43
Tax-exempt bonds	0.76	1.84	1.96
Taxable bonds	3.61	4.63	4.57
Tax-deferred accounts	15.14	19.59	21.67
Bank accounts	58.53	54.41	52.15
Other financial assets	16.19	14.01	13.49
Share of Aggregate Household Portfolio			
Taxable equity held either directly or through			
mutual funds	27.32	17.08	19.84
Taxable equity held directly in brokerage accounts	26.43	14.82	16.18
Tax-exempt bonds	7.15	9.69	9.37
Taxable bonds	6.26	7.68	6.42
Tax-deferred accounts	14.67	21.39	26.61
Bank accounts	27.73	30.61	25.44
Other financial assets	16.87	13.54	12.32

Source: Authors' tabulations of 1983, 1989, and 1992 SCFs. Taxable equity held directly through brokerage accounts is a subset of taxable equity held either directly or through mutual funds.

Table 2.1 is divided into three sections. The three sections show the probability that a household owns a given asset, the average share of the household's portfolio in a given asset, and the share of total financial assets accounted for by each asset. More formally, for each financial asset j in each survey year, we define y_{ij} as household i's holdings of asset j; Y_i is household i's total financial assets; w_i is the sample weight of household i; and N is the number of households in the given year's sample.[6] We then tabulate

6. Wolff (1987, 1994, 1997) has argued that the SCFs need to be reweighted in order to match the aggregate totals in the Flow of Funds accounts of household net worth. Because it is not clear that the Flow of Funds are a more appropriate benchmark, we use the recommended weights provided with the SCFs without any adjustment.

(1)   Probability of Ownership $= \dfrac{\displaystyle\sum_{i=1}^{N} w_i(y_{ij} > 0)}{\displaystyle\sum_{i=1}^{N} w_i}$

Average Portfolio Share $= \dfrac{\displaystyle\sum_{i=1}^{N} w_i(y_{ij}/Y_i)}{\displaystyle\sum_{i=1}^{N} w_i}$

Aggregate Portfolio Share $= \dfrac{\displaystyle\sum_{i=1}^{N} w_i y_{ij}}{\displaystyle\sum_{i=1}^{N} w_i Y_i}.$

The average portfolio share measures the allocation of the typical household, while the aggregate portfolio share measures the allocation of all households taken together. These portfolio shares will diverge to the extent that households with higher wealth levels have different allocations of financial assets than those with lower wealth.

The results on ownership probabilities under the first heading of table 2.1 suggest several broad patterns. First, the probability of owning taxable equity, excluding ownership through retirement accounts, was relatively constant over the 1983–92 period. This constancy occurs even though the probability of direct equity ownership declined over this time period. A rising probability of equity ownership through mutual funds accounts for the difference. The rising ownership of tax-deferred accounts during this period, however, and the attendant equity ownership through these accounts, results in a substantial increase in the total number of households who own corporate stock.

Second, the fraction of households owning tax-exempt bonds increased by about three percentage points between 1983 and 1992. This reflects the declining ownership of tax-exempt securities by commercial banks and insurance companies over this period. There is also a roughly equal increase in the probability of owning taxable bonds.

Third, there is a sharp increase in tax-deferred asset ownership. The probability of ownership rises by roughly 5.5 percentage points between 1983 and 1992. This reflects the expansion of IRAs in the early 1980s and the rapid growth of 401(k) plans and related retirement saving plans in the late 1980s and early 1990s. Poterba, Venti, and Wise (1996) summarize these developments.

Fourth, the probabilities of owning bank accounts and other financial assets were roughly unchanged over the period. This reflects in part the high initial market penetration for these accounts and the continued household reliance on these accounts for a variety of financial functions.

The second and third headings of table 2.1 underscore the important difference between the average portfolio and the aggregate portfolio. For example, while assets in bank accounts represented 52.2 percent of the total financial assets in the average portfolio in 1992, they accounted for only 25.4 percent of total financial assets in household portfolios of the same year. The portfolios of higher net worth households are less heavily invested in bank accounts and similar assets than are those of lower net worth households. There are corresponding differentials between the average portfolio and aggregate portfolio share in taxable equity (also in 1992), 6.15 percent versus 19.8 percent, and in tax-exempt bonds, 2.0 versus 9.4 percent.

The data on aggregate portfolio shares shown under the last heading of table 2.1 track the substantial growth of assets held in tax-deferred accounts between 1983 and 1992. Assets in these accounts represented 14.7 percent of total financial assets in 1983, compared with 26.7 percent in 1992. The importance of these assets in the average portfolio also rose sharply during this period. Table 2.1 presents summary information on portfolio allocation for all households, pooling those of different age categories. One group of households that attracts particular attention in studies of saving behavior and portfolio choice is the elderly. Because wealth accumulation typically takes place over a household's entire working life, elderly households have higher assets, on average, than younger households. Their behavior is therefore weighted more than the behavior of younger households in determining the composition of the aggregate household portfolio. In addition, for the elderly who have accumulated limited assets, the portfolio choices made early in retirement can determine the resources available for the later years of retirement.

Because the elderly are of special interest, table 2.2 presents information analogous to that in table 2.1, but only for those households headed by someone over the age of sixty-five. Many of the broad patterns resemble those in the earlier table. The bank account share of the average household's portfolio, 65.5 percent in 1992, is almost twice the share in the aggregate portfolio for elderly households (36.9 percent). Tax-deferred assets grew less quickly between 1983 and 1992 for elderly households than for the entire population, reflecting the link between employment and access to these accounts. The aggregate portfolio held by elderly households differs from that for all households in that it includes more equity (23 percent versus 20 percent of total financial assets), more assets in bank accounts (37 percent versus 25 percent), and more holdings of taxable and tax-exempt bonds (20 percent versus 16 percent). The greater portfolio shares in each of these categories are counterbalanced by significantly lower holdings in tax-deferred accounts, 11 percent versus 27 percent, for elderly as opposed to all households.

Table 2.3 presents more detailed information on the total holdings of financial assets by households of different ages in each of our sample years.

Table 2.2   **Ownership and Allocation of Financial Assets for Households over Age Sixty-Five, by Year**

Financial Asset	1983	1989	1992
Probability of Ownership			
Taxable equity held either directly or through			
mutual funds	22.77	20.63	21.73
Taxable equity held directly in brokerage accounts	21.41	18.04	17.44
Tax-exempt bonds	5.80	9.05	11.01
Taxable bonds	20.44	23.49	23.84
Tax-deferred accounts	7.92	17.78	20.74
Bank accounts	86.75	91.11	90.37
Other financial assets	37.28	36.52	40.97
Average Share of Household Portfolio			
Taxable equity held either directly or through			
mutual funds	7.89	6.53	6.76
Taxable equity held directly in brokerage accounts	7.45	5.55	4.74
Tax-exempt bonds	1.36	2.81	3.55
Taxable bonds	4.35	5.71	4.84
Tax-deferred accounts	2.50	6.56	7.63
Bank accounts	72.37	68.60	65.50
Other financial assets	11.54	9.79	11.73
Share of Aggregate Household Portfolio			
Taxable equity held either directly or through			
mutual funds	32.75	18.87	23.00
Taxable equity held directly in brokerage accounts	31.49	16.75	19.21
Tax-exempt bonds	10.56	13.28	11.84
Taxable bonds	8.92	11.31	7.87
Tax-deferred accounts	4.71	9.31	10.52
Bank accounts	32.54	37.96	36.90
Other financial assets	10.53	9.27	9.88

Source: See table 2.1.

The table is designed to highlight cohort-related differences in both the level of financial assets and the accumulation of financial assets over the nine years spanned by the data. Table 2.3 presents the mean and median financial asset holdings in each survey year by various birth cohorts, which we define as including households headed by individuals who were born within three years of each other. We identify each cohort by the age that the households born in that cohort's middle year had attained in 1983. The age twenty-eight cohort, for example, includes all households in which the head of household was born in 1954, 1955, or 1956.[7] This cohort was be-

7. We define the head of household for a married couple to be the spouse that earned more labor income or, if neither worked, the older spouse. It is therefore possible that a given household would be part of different cohorts in different years if the head of the household stops being the primary earner or leaves the household. This may account for some of the anomalies in the tabulations of assets at older ages.

Table 2.3 Financial Asset Holdings by Cohort and Year

Age in 1983	Mean 1983	Mean 1989	Mean 1992	Median 1983	Median 1989	Median 1992
19	3,850	6,861	14,172	419	1,019	2,76
	(1,641)	(2,297)	(4,026)	(285)	(334)	(76
22	4,362	21,351	20,380	1,029	3,450	5,05
	(930)	(9,763)	(5,632)	(256)	(1,602)	(1,05
25	7,687	20,914	25,777	1,759	3,730	3,57
	(1,014)	(9,579)	(6,989)	(354)	(1,545)	(1,31
28	9,818	30,583	27,315	1,970	5,329	4,50
	(1,235)	(21,500)	(9,668)	(431)	(1,048)	(1,22
31	13,923	43,207	40,793	2,890	12,899	9,10
	(7,872)	(11,043)	(10,198)	(576)	(3,067)	(1,90
34	33,182	36,765	54,339	10,880	11,989	12,10
	(8,545)	(40,992)	(16,492)	(2,064)	(1,840)	(2,848
37	31,195	61,509	74,160	8,750	9,649	8,77
	(44,949)	(31,017)	(20,004)	(1,380)	(2,797)	(2,73
40	35,983	63,865	78,316	8,750	8,369	16,47
	(6,603)	(39,118)	(27,374)	(1,793)	(2,948)	(2,61
43	37,911	84,058	124,963	9,170	11,390	22,20
	(9,625)	(28,683)	(31,557)	(2,609)	(3,847)	(10,43
46	81,064	81,352	104,504	11,520	20,370	19,80
	(111,616)	(18,713)	(27,794)	(3,534)	(4,751)	(5,91
49	67,821	89,496	144,769	10,170	20,479	32,27
	(33,285)	(39,970)	(56,449)	(2,731)	(8,974)	(16,94
52	49,144	96,129	124,017	12,479	10,520	30,60
	(13,479)	(44,938)	(29,567)	(3,678)	(6,884)	(8,643
55	87,258	109,603	94,693	13,409	12,449	15,26
	(38,070)	(28,301)	(50,803)	(2,104)	(4,551)	(4,793
58	94,010	102,525	80,019	21,040	20,250	10,00
	(28,594)	(38,764)	(39,221)	(5,096)	(5,687)	(4,452
61	91,179	107,870	112,358	19,930	11,989	23,60
	(37,106)	(45,402)	(47,727)	(3,738)	(3,756)	(7,759
64	162,507	105,022	96,608	14,140	31,450	17,89
	(68,483)	(30,246)	(45,657)	(4,147)	(9,395)	(7,558
67	126,708	91,994	96,321	14,090	21,500	28,899
	(44,063)	(43,808)	(31,806)	(5,613)	(10,848)	(10,550
70	123,968	106,879	97,555	20,559	42,259	14,550
	(36,374)	(37,031)	(58,157)	(5,111)	(13,891)	(7,487
73	117,941	74,874	94,085	15,890	5,539	6,000
	(59,195)	(43,876)	(34,098)	(5,392)	(4,806)	(13,079
76	85,727	107,124	125,394	8,430	20,819	8,000
	(74,049)	(98,454)	(98,233)	(3,216)	(10,832)	(6,596
79	75,315	52,666	134,576	12,710	11,310	48,029
	(56,431)	(46,839)	(147,614)	(5,887)	(8,539)	(28,254
Over 62	117,782	94,749	101,407	13,779	23,760	15,680
	(23,292)	(18,331)	(23,209)	(1,696)	(4,579)	(3,961
Over 65	107,915	91,998	102,917	13,590	20,370	14,550
	(23,875)	(21,947)	(27,022)	(2,112)	(4,655)	(4,314

Table 2.3   (continued)

Age	Mean			Median		
in 1983	1983	1989	1992	1983	1989	1992
All cohorts	57,816	63,350	70,028	7,599	9,279	9,779
	(8,793)	(7,333)	(6,515)	(410)	(731)	(604)

Source: Authors' tabulations of the 1983, 1989, and 1992 SCFs.
Notes: All dollar amounts are in constant 1992 dollars. Standard errors are listed in parentheses. "Age in 1983" refers to all households in which the head is within one year (above or below) of the specified age.

tween twenty-seven and twenty-nine years old in 1983, between thirty-three and thirty-five in 1989, and between thirty-six and thirty-eight in 1992. All of the entries in table 2.3 are reported in constant 1992 dollars, and standard errors are reported in parentheses below the means or medians.

Table 2.3 shows a number of interesting patterns in asset accumulation. For example, the information in the table can be used to compare asset accumulation across households in different cohorts. To illustrate these comparisons, consider the cohort that was aged twenty-eight in 1983. The mean financial assets for this cohort, $30,583 in 1989 and $27,315 in 1992, were somewhat lower than those of the cohorts that were aged thirty-four ($33,182) and thirty-seven ($31,195) in 1983, respectively. This could lead to a conclusion that households in the younger cohort were saving less than were those in older cohorts. Bernheim and Scholz (1995) focus on comparisons of this type in their study of retirement saving by the baby boom generation.

The data in table 2.3 show that households enter a period of fairly rapid accumulation of financial assets when they are about thirty-four years old, and that their holdings of financial assets peak at about age fifty-eight. Movements in mean asset holdings are more pronounced than movements in the median, reflecting the well-documented fact that many households never accumulate particularly large stocks of financial wealth.[8]

The last three rows of table 2.3 present summary information on total financial assets for three groups of households in each sample year: all households, all households with a head over the age of sixty-two, and all households with a head over the age of sixty-five. The comparisons of these groups illustrate the greater financial assets of the elderly than of households in general. In 1992, the average household headed by someone

8. Poterba, Venti, and Wise (1994) show that the wealth distribution for households at retirement age is highly skewed, and that many households reach retirement with virtually no resources other than the annuity value of Social Security and the equity in their home.

over the age of sixty-five held $102,917 in financial assets, compared with $70,028 for all households. Median financial assets for both the elderly ($14,550) and all households ($9,779) are much lower than mean assets, but they show the same pattern as the means.

Comparisons of mean and median financial assets for the elderly households in the three SCFs raise some questions. The mean financial assets of households over the age of sixty-five in 1989 was nearly 20 percent lower than the comparable mean assets for households over age sixty-five in 1983, and 10 percent lower than the value for comparable households in 1992. Yet median assets were higher for the cohort aged sixty-five and up in 1989 than in either 1983 or 1992. The patterns of mean and median asset holdings for all households do not exhibit such reversals of trend; both mean and median financial assets for the whole population were higher in 1992 than in 1989, and higher in 1989 than in 1983.

Table 2.3 focuses on total financial assets, the sum of all of the asset categories we considered in table 2.1. We also construct a measure of household net worth. One component of net worth is total assets, which includes total financial assets as well as holdings of owner-occupied real estate, other real estate assets, net equity in personally owned businesses, and miscellaneous assets. The other component is total debt, which equals the sum of financial debt, owner-occupied real estate debt, other real estate debt, and miscellaneous debt. We do not include the actuarial present value of Social Security benefits (net of taxes), or of benefits paid by defined benefit pension plans, in our measure of net worth.

Table 2.4 presents summary statistics on the ownership and allocation of the various components of net worth. The table is structured in the same way as table 2.1, which described financial assets. Several findings on the ownership patterns for nonfinancial assets bear comment. Between 1983 and 1992, the probability of holding owner-occupied real estate assets stayed roughly constant, while the probability of owing debt on owner-occupied real estate increased. There were decreases in the probabilities of holding other real estate assets, business assets, and miscellaneous debt, and little change in the probabilities of owning financial assets, financial debt, and other real estate debt.

Table 2.4 shows an increase in the share of household debt between 1983 and 1992, and it suggests that this increase is particularly important for lower net worth households.[9] Table 2.4 also shows that in 1989, for the average household, as a share of total assets, financial debt rose by 1.2 percentage points, owner-occupied real estate debt rose by 2.8 percentage

---

9. To scale the value of net worth components relative to the average and aggregate portfolio, we divide each component by total assets, rather than net worth, since approximately 10 percent of the households report negative net worth in each year, and for these households, dividing by net worth would yield unreliable data values.

Table 2.4   **Ownership and Allocation of Net Worth for All Households, by Year**

Wealth Component	1983	1989	1992
Probability of Ownership			
Financial assets	89.79	87.56	88.95
Financial debt	41.12	40.90	41.33
Owner-occupied assets	63.41	64.72	63.93
Owner-occupied debt	36.94	39.55	39.03
Other real estate assets	21.00	20.40	19.35
Other real estate debt	8.19	6.97	7.72
Business net worth	14.22	10.89	11.31
Miscellaneous assets	85.34	85.53	87.51
Miscellaneous debt	48.17	51.72	45.41
Average Share of Household Total Assets			
Financial assets	28.84	26.98	27.88
Financial debt	9.25	4.54	10.44
Owner-occupied assets	40.24	41.22	40.51
Owner-occupied debt	10.31	11.70	13.13
Other real estate assets	6.80	6.31	5.46
Other real estate debt	1.29	0.97	1.08
Business net worth	4.72	3.52	3.79
Miscellaneous assets	19.39	21.97	22.35
Miscellaneous debt	18.83	36.16	22.63
Share of Aggregate Household Total Assets			
Financial assets	29.65	26.70	30.02
Financial debt	0.60	0.53	0.56
Owner-occupied assets	31.45	33.59	32.96
Owner-occupied debt	7.31	8.92	10.66
Other real estate assets	15.18	15.72	14.62
Other real estate debt	2.73	3.90	3.25
Business net worth	19.22	16.58	16.20
Miscellaneous assets	4.50	7.41	6.20
Miscellaneous debt	2.19	2.55	1.69

Source: Authors' tabulations of 1983, 1989, and 1992 SCFs.

points, and other debt rose by 3.6 percentage points. The aggregate household balance sheet shows an increase in owner-occupied real estate debt of 3.3 percentage points over the same period, but little increase in other debt components.

Table 2.4 shows that between 1983 and 1989 a shift in the composition of total assets away from personally owned businesses and toward miscellaneous assets occurred, with little or no change in the proportion of financial and real estate assets. Table 2.4 also shows in 1992 that total assets are on average composed of 30 percent financial assets, 33 percent owner-occupied assets, 15 percent other real estate, 16 percent business net worth, and 6 percent miscellaneous assets.

Table 2.5 presents information similar to that in table 2.4, but the

Table 2.5   Ownership and Allocation of Net Worth for Households over Age
                 Sixty-Five, by Year

Wealth Component	1983	1989	1992
Probability of Ownership			
Financial assets	88.73	91.96	91.19
Financial debt	13.20	17.54	23.65
Owner-occupied assets	74.56	77.18	77.68
Owner-occupied debt	10.24	14.05	11.60
Other real estate assets	23.17	20.58	20.49
Other real estate debt	2.93	2.03	2.47
Business net worth	9.45	5.35	6.03
Miscellaneous assets	71.46	77.03	80.84
Miscellaneous debt	13.05	16.91	17.52
Average Share of Household Total Assets			
Financial assets	37.22	36.20	34.76
Financial debt	15.73	1.38	1.73
Owner-occupied assets	44.90	46.23	47.62
Owner-occupied debt	1.86	2.05	2.07
Other real estate assets	6.94	4.90	5.15
Other real estate debt	0.18	0.15	0.25
Business net worth	3.34	1.41	1.92
Miscellaneous assets	7.60	11.26	10.55
Miscellaneous debt	1.71	4.85	2.20
Share of Aggregate Household Total Assets			
Financial assets	41.56	38.29	37.99
Financial debt	0.12	0.20	0.30
Owner-occupied assets	24.26	30.12	28.78
Owner-occupied debt	0.99	1.02	1.36
Other real estate assets	17.21	14.45	16.59
Other real estate debt	0.86	1.44	1.49
Business net worth	14.88	11.76	12.18
Miscellaneous assets	2.10	5.38	4.46
Miscellaneous debt	0.96	0.62	0.73

Source: Authors' tabulations of 1983, 1989, and 1992 SCFs.

sample is restricted to households with heads over the age of sixty-five in
each year. There are some differences between the elderly and the population at large in the evolution of net worth. Owner-occupied housing, for
example, became a more important component of net worth between 1983
and 1992 for elderly households, but not for households in general. The
probability that an elderly household would own a home rose from 74.6
percent to 77.7 percent over this nine-year period, and the aggregate share
of owner-occupied housing as a fraction of total assets held by elderly
households rose from 24.3 percent to 28.8 percent. This increase is not
substantially offset by an expansion of mortgage debt. Over the 1983–92
time period, financial assets became less important as a fraction of total
assets for elderly households, with a decline from 41.6 percent to 38 per-

cent. This coincided with an increase in the importance of financial assets, relative to total assets, for the entire population.

Comparisons between the elderly population and the population in general also reveal differences in the composition of net worth. Owner-occupied real estate constitutes a smaller share of total assets, 28.8 percent, for the elderly than for households of all ages (33 percent). Financial assets are substantially more important for the elderly, and business net worth, an asset that is likely to be correlated with active participation in a business, is less important. Total debt, and especially owner-occupied debt, as a fraction of total assets are lower for the elderly than for the general population.

Table 2.6 shows the age-specific pattern of mean and median net worth for each of the sample years. Once again, households are categorized by the age of the household head in 1983; this is the same classification scheme used in table 2.3 above. The data in this table provide the most direct evidence on the extent of household wealth accumulation at different ages. Several findings deserve commentary. First, net worth tends to peak when households are in their early sixties. Median net worth at this peak, in 1992, was roughly $130,000; mean net worth was roughly three times greater. Second, both mean and median net worth rose between 1983 and 1992 for households that were less than fifty-two years old in 1983, but beyond this age, net worth did not increase and in many cases declined. Finally, the large standard errors on the net worth entries make it difficult to draw strong conclusions at some ages. This is particularly important to remember when evaluating the findings for older households, where there is some evidence that net worth moves in one direction between 1983 and 1989, and then in another direction between 1989 and 1992.

Table 2.7 is similar to table 2.6, except that it shows the age-specific pattern of total asset holdings rather than net worth. These summary statistics are of interest for two reasons. First, they provide important background for interpreting the graphs shown below on the share of total assets that are allocated to various asset categories at different ages. Second, they present some information on gross asset accumulation profiles. As an illustration of this use of the data, the results suggest that young households, those between the ages of roughly twenty and thirty-five, accumulated assets over the 1983–92 period. For older households, the large standard errors on the cohort-specific asset values in each year make it more difficult to draw strong conclusions about the slope of the age-assets profile.

2.2   Financial Asset Allocations

The summary statistics presented in the last section provide important evidence on the nature of household portfolios in a cross-section of house-

Table 2.6 Net Worth Holdings by Cohort and Year

Age in 1983	Mean			Median		
	1983	1989	1992	1983	1989	1992
19	12,692	34,429	43,027	3,559	3,640	10,600
	(5,649)	(11,141)	(19,119)	(1,098)	(2,388)	(2,828)
22	15,591	68,203	64,151	3,000	15,050	21,549
	(3,131)	(32,811)	(15,314)	(766)	(3,854)	(4,782)
25	27,048	67,639	83,892	7,059	10,979	28,409
	(6,452)	(15,942)	(18,289)	(1,489)	(5,051)	(5,047)
28	34,061	89,351	113,924	10,659	22,309	29,276
	(4,402)	(38,760)	(69,959)	(2,017)	(4,235)	(4,662)
31	59,174	146,219	121,372	16,319	59,759	50,799
	(40,199)	(39,610)	(35,501)	(3,721)	(10,252)	(6,366)
34	102,608	149,136	174,983	46,520	70,769	66,400
	(22,971)	(83,200)	(47,394)	(5,652)	(10,452)	(12,066)
37	122,283	229,282	201,460	49,299	79,199	54,049
	(52,928)	(94,758)	(51,784)	(5,246)	(8,980)	(9,941)
40	125,330	261,377	252,401	56,450	86,330	81,300
	(15,902)	(91,228)	(88,956)	(5,006)	(16,034)	(10,276)
43	139,495	275,855	300,262	66,849	104,989	98,500
	(21,681)	(87,207)	(78,445)	(11,430)	(19,541)	(20,739)
46	262,211	337,379	316,458	90,389	106,129	127,230
	(125,622)	(156,663)	(74,703)	(15,178)	(26,894)	(16,171)
49	270,937	279,117	357,069	75,779	101,809	133,300
	(79,596)	(103,127)	(121,208)	(8,888)	(15,255)	(18,553)
52	203,575	293,317	358,761	91,790	111,500	130,679
	(43,348)	(125,381)	(128,429)	(9,962)	(15,658)	(21,685)
55	269,377	335,652	256,498	88,760	95,610	82,099
	(118,305)	(101,528)	(104,563)	(16,018)	(20,020)	(17,159)
58	292,612	344,166	277,621	107,059	111,050	87,419
	(62,470)	(205,060)	(131,290)	(15,831)	(28,337)	(18,390)
61	299,167	299,373	296,988	127,029	70,150	103,440
	(109,138)	(143,490)	(157,152)	(14,171)	(12,058)	(19,882)
64	348,270	298,177	257,417	86,269	105,230	97,529
	(108,733)	(134,406)	(147,107)	(11,060)	(15,693)	(15,454)
67	364,771	236,069	217,193	98,059	99,569	117,949
	(132,656)	(116,156)	(64,389)	(15,804)	(18,400)	(24,983)
70	300,125	243,804	259,474	90,400	111,260	88,500
	(94,164)	(60,066)	(181,154)	(10,955)	(28,769)	(11,196)
73	240,507	176,476	168,679	73,470	49,779	42,700
	(74,403)	(181,932)	(53,405)	(11,117)	(15,495)	(26,263)
76	167,327	209,846	213,156	62,520	100,699	70,699
	(82,805)	(117,350)	(134,761)	(19,669)	(16,965)	(11,343)
79	203,574	126,895	230,709	73,150	49,439	86,099
	(89,658)	(101,769)	(198,478)	(7,946)	(10,348)	(41,080)
Over 62	269,486	232,101	229,822	77,480	95,949	86,900
	(39,448)	(53,797)	(57,221)	(4,059)	(8,308)	(6,450)
Over 65	252,104	214,407	221,141	74,559	87,120	86,599
	(41,520)	(57,636)	(57,954)	(4,493)	(10,296)	(6,978)

Table 2.6   (continued)

Age in 1983	Mean			Median		
	1983	1989	1992	1983	1989	1992
All cohorts	173,635	200,471	195,375	51,919	62,229	58,400
	(15,521)	(22,721)	(18,602)	(1,802)	(4,040)	(2,278)

Source: Authors' tabulations of 1983, 1989, and 1992 SCFs.
Notes: All dollar amounts are in constant 1992 dollars. Standard errors are listed in parentheses. "Age in 1983" refers to all households in which the head is within one year (above or below) of the specified age.

Table 2.7   **Total Asset Holdings by Cohort and Year**

Age in 1983	Mean			Median		
	1983	1989	1992	1983	1989	1992
19	15,636	53,596	70,036	3,659	9,850	18,739
	(6,325)	(13,109)	(20,843)	(1,459)	(2,513)	(4,677)
22	21,769	98,828	109,249	5,849	23,079	39,979
	(3,786)	(33,690)	(17,147)	(880)	(5,635)	(9,607)
25	42,212	107,443	124,134	11,669	26,290	52,130
	(6,748)	(18,116)	(23,368)	(2,231)	(13,226)	(11,154)
28	53,550	137,356	159,089	20,579	57,700	61,349
	(5,178)	(40,134)	(70,784)	(4,426)	(10,819)	(14,089)
31	82,974	202,935	170,710	29,810	102,169	104,000
	(40,298)	(43,300)	(36,822)	(7,611)	(14,377)	(11,752)
34	142,963	199,395	226,656	80,889	113,470	104,569
	(23,705)	(86,787)	(50,520)	(8,279)	(16,955)	(12,681)
37	166,289	309,543	254,761	94,939	132,600	103,750
	(53,537)	(134,137)	(58,159)	(7,184)	(15,396)	(15,476)
40	165,970	329,990	315,472	96,529	125,729	115,099
	(19,237)	(106,255)	(92,122)	(10,598)	(25,017)	(17,200)
43	179,442	323,463	349,924	101,419	132,139	127,449
	(179,442)	(95,543)	(83,774)	(11,625)	(22,972)	(23,158)
46	299,935	379,894	355,593	129,039	139,679	139,500
	(126,825)	(163,085)	(80,892)	(14,325)	(27,332)	(15,927)
49	321,129	333,108	109,372	100,950	141,679	167,649
	(95,517)	(118,559)	(127,382)	(12,296)	(21,246)	(27,387)
52	228,999	335,278	390,753	115,659	130,350	154,300
	(45,437)	(150,167)	(132,970)	(11,052)	(8,948)	(19,170)
55	295,926	358,332	285,804	109,519	116,180	98,099
	(121,699)	(108,612)	(116,594)	(16,088)	(21,234)	(20,028)
58	325,506	370,565	300,889	137,130	114,269	87,419
	(67,749)	(252,822)	(157,531)	(16,816)	(25,345)	(18,237)
61	320,726	310,893	303,674	135,990	76,569	104,309
	(112,048)	(144,862)	(159,057)	(13,551)	(11,751)	(19,695)
64	365,917	309,283	265,967	94,500	109,750	97,529
	(113,134)	(167,223)	(163,438)	(16,377)	(13,908)	(15,454)

(continued)

Table 2.7 (continued)

Age in 1983	Mean 1983	Mean 1989	Mean 1992	Median 1983	Median 1989	Median 1992
67	377,039	252,422	227,279	98,889	99,559	125,000
	(133,288)	(158,361)	(71,180)	(16,141)	(17,574)	(22,511)
70	313,354	247,760	270,004	99,269	114,260	94,349
	(96,412)	(60,332)	(184,700)	(15,671)	(24,123)	(18,062
73	244,194	180,738	169,808	74,860	50,919	42,700
	(74,801)	(182,536)	(53,484)	(11,125)	(13,914)	(26,263
76	176,245	213,574	215,686	62,510	100,699	70,699
	(85,189)	(118,623)	(142,087)	(19,666)	(14,994)	(11,343
79	(206,733)	127,208	234,424	73,150	49,439	86,099
	(94,511)	(101,860)	(198,466)	(7,977)	(10,342)	(45,202
Over 62	278,894	239,619	236,992	81,000	99,559	89,579
	(40,439)	(61,850)	(61,098)	(4,339)	(9,381)	(7,846
Over 65	259,694	220,964	227,876	77,489	87,120	88,400
	(42,317)	(63,727)	(59,865)	(5,122)	(11,123)	(7,821
All cohorts	200,016	238,725	232,573	73,000	91,319	88,430
	(16,102)	(26,070)	(19,935)	(2,213)	(4,728)	(3,467

Source: Authors' tabulations of 1983, 1989, and 1992 SCFs.

Notes: All dollar amounts are in constant 1992 dollars. Standard errors are listed in parentheses. "Age in 1983" refers to all households in which the head is within one year (above or below) of the specified age.

holds, and on the evolution of household portfolios over time. In this section, we impose additional structure on the net worth and asset ownership data, and we decompose changes in financial asset allocation into age and cohort effects. Our methodology is based on a specification of the form

$$(2) \qquad f(y_{ij}) = \alpha + \sum_{n=2}^{24} \beta_n \text{age}_{i,n} + \sum_{m=2}^{21} \gamma_m \text{cohort}_{i,m} + \varepsilon_{i,j},$$

where y_{ij} is the holdings of asset j by household i, $\text{age}_{i,n}$ is a dummy variable for whether the current age of the household head is in the three-year interval centered on age $= 3 \times n + 16$, and $\text{cohort}_{i,m}$ is a dummy variable for whether age of the household head in 1983 fell in the three-year interval centered on age $= 3 \times m + 16$. Because of the oversampling of high-income households in the Surveys of Consumer Finances, we estimate equation (2) using the year-specific sample weights, normalized so that the sum of the weights for the whole population in each year is the same.

We estimate equation (2) for each financial asset category with two forms of the dependent variable. The first is a probit for whether the household has positive amounts of the asset category ($y_{ij} > 0$ in equation [1]). The second is a Tobit for the share of the household's total financial assets held in each category (y_{ij}/Y_i in equation [1]). These dependent variables correspond to summary information presented in the earlier tables.

For each specification, we focus on three issues in interpreting the results. The first is whether the cohort effects are significantly different from zero, or alternatively, whether there appear to be year-of-birth related differences in the asset allocation patterns of households. Consider the null hypothesis

(3) $H_0 : \gamma_m = 0, \forall\ m.$

Estimates of equation (2) with this constraint imposed are "no cohort effects" specifications; estimates without this constraint allow for cohort effects. We use a likelihood ratio test to determine whether the cohort effects are jointly significant. If they are, then different birth cohorts have significantly different probabilities of holding or portfolio shares of given financial assets. Finding that there are cohort effects in asset demands implies that data from different birth cohorts that comprise a single cross-section may be difficult to aggregate. Much of this section is devoted to describing the pattern of cohort effects for different asset categories.

The second issue that we consider is whether patterns are present in or absent from the estimated age coefficients, β_n. These estimates reveal whether households follow the precepts of the simplest models of portfolio choice with time-invariant risk aversion, which imply that $\beta_n = 0$ for all n, or the precepts of financial planners, who often suggest $\beta_{n+1} < \beta_n$ for risky assets.

Finally, we are interested in the methodological question of how the estimated age coefficients (β_n) change when cohort effects are introduced into the specifications. Any changes will illustrate the importance of utilizing repeated cross-sections, as opposed to single cross-sections, to analyze portfolio allocations.

Figure 2.1 illustrates our graphical methodology for presenting the results of this estimation. The first graph displays two age-ownership profiles for equity held in taxable brokerage accounts. The profile depicted with triangles represents the predicted values from a regression of equation (2) without cohort effects. This profile is therefore the age-ownership profile that one would expect to find in any population cross-section. The profile is increasing with age until age forty-three, when it peaks at around 22 percent of households owning corporate stock directly. The profile levels off after age forty-three, with a slight decline at much older ages.

The profile depicted with circles in figure 2.1 represents the predicted values from equation (2) allowing for cohort effects. The predicted values at each age are based on the cohort effect for those households who were aged twenty-eight in 1983. This particular cohort is roughly the middle cohort in the U.S. baby boom generation. The slope of the age-ownership profile for this cohort is very close to the cross-sectional profile until roughly age forty-three, but after that age, the cohort-specific profile is much lower. This difference implies that a given cohort of households can

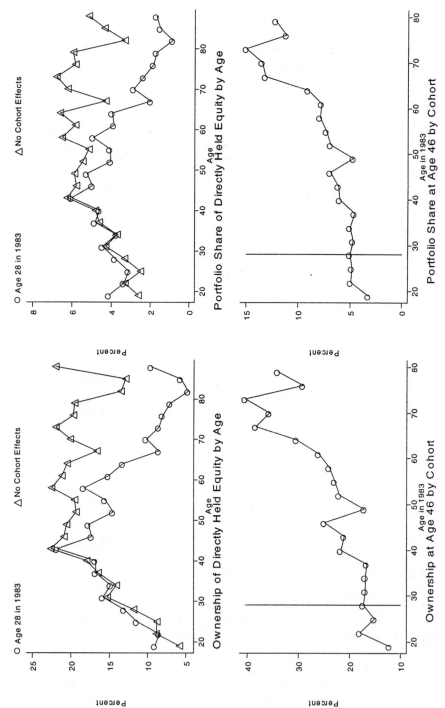

Fig. 2.1 Directly held equity

Table 2.8   **Tests for Joint Significance of Cohort Effects in Ownership
                        and Allocation**

Financial Asset	Ownership Probits	Portfolio Share Tobits
Taxable equity held directly	0.0072	0.0134
Taxable equity held either directly or indirectly through mutual funds	0.1508	0.1555
Tax-exempt bonds	0.0000	0.0000
Taxable bonds	0.0010	0.0001
Tax-deferred accounts	0.0000	0.0000
Bank accounts	0.0006	0.0000
Other financial assets	0.0750	0.0017

Source: Authors' estimates from 1983, 1989, and 1992 SCFs.
Notes: Joint significance tests for probits are based on a chi-square distribution with 20 degrees of freedom. Joint significance tests for tobits are based on an *F*-distribution with 20 (numerator) and 9,759 (denominator) degrees of freedom.

be expected to divest their direct equity holdings as they age faster than the cross-section evidence suggests (i.e., the cohort-specific probabilities of directly owning corporate stock have been declining over time).

The cohort effects are identified by the differences in the ownership probabilities of different cohorts at the same age, which naturally occurs in different years of the survey. The second graph, located in the lower left-hand corner of figure 2.1, shows the predicted probability that households born in each cohort will own taxable equity when they reach age forty-six. The use of age forty-six is only a normalization; the shape of this curve would be the same for any age, since it depends only on the pattern of cohort effects. The vertical line in this figure indicates the cohort that was aged twenty-eight in 1983; this point corresponds to the same point on the first graph (line with circles).

Table 2.8 reports statistical tests for the importance of cohort effects for various asset categories. The entries in the first row are the *p*-values for the joint significance of the cohort effects in the two specifications we consider. The results show that there are statistically significant differences in ownership probabilities across different cohorts. Figure 2.1 helps the interpretation of this finding, since it shows that older cohorts were more likely to hold equity directly than were younger cohorts over this time period.[10]

The two graphs in the right panel of figure 2.1 present the predicted values, by age and cohort, for estimates of equation (2) in which the depen-

---

10. It is not possible to estimate age, cohort, and year effects simultaneously without imposing functional form restrictions, such as a quadratic specification in age or a linear time trend. As a result, our identifying assumption may in fact be the result of secular trends toward lower directly held equity ownership.

dent variable is the household's share of financial assets allocated to directly held stock.[11] The divergence between the age-allocation profiles with and without cohort effects mirrors the divergence in the age-ownership profiles. Average asset allocations to directly held equity peak at about 5 percent at age forty-three and decline thereafter. Compared to the ownership profile, the allocation profile rises to this peak less rapidly and declines more rapidly.

Table 2.8 shows the p-value for the joint significance of the cohort effects. The null hypothesis of no cohort effects is rejected at standard significance levels. As in the estimates of ownership probabilities, the cohort effects are increasing with the household's age. This suggests that currently older cohorts of households tend to devote a higher fraction of their assets to directly held stock.

We now employ the graphical analysis of figure 2.1 for other asset categories. Figure 2.2 shows analogous graphs for all taxable equity, including brokerage accounts as well as equity mutual funds. These graphs demonstrate that the patterns in figure 2.1 reflect changes in the institutional arrangements for holding the equity, rather than changes in age-specific patterns of equity ownership per se. The graphs in the upper panel of figure 2.2 reveal virtually no differences in the age profiles of ownership and allocation when cohort effects are included in the model. The relatively flat age profiles suggest that households do not necessarily follow the popular financial advice to switch from stocks to bonds as they approach retirement.[12] The cohort differences in ownership and allocation in the bottom graphs do not display a strong pattern with the household's age in 1983. Additionally, the p-values shown in table 2.8 for the joint significance of the cohort effects show that the null hypothesis of no cohort effects is not rejected at standard significance levels.

Figure 2.3 shows the age profiles for tax-exempt bonds. Both direct and indirect holdings of tax-exempt bonds (through mutual funds) are included in the statistics that underlie both of these figures. The age profiles for tax-exempt bonds are sharply increasing when cohort effects are included, in contrast to the flat profile found in the cross-section. The difference is due primarily to the statistically significant and downward-sloping pattern of cohort effects shown in the bottom graphs. Although the current generation of older cohorts does not hold tax-exempts, the youngest generations do hold them, and this is reflected in the estimated cohort effects.

11. The estimates of equation (2) with asset shares as the dependent variable do not impose the adding-up constraint on the asset shares for taxable equity, tax-exempt bonds, taxable bonds, tax-deferred accounts, bank accounts, and other financial assets, that they must sum to unity.

12. Since tax-deferred accounts may also be invested in equities, households could be reducing their overall equity positions if they were lowering the equity shares of their tax-deferred accounts.

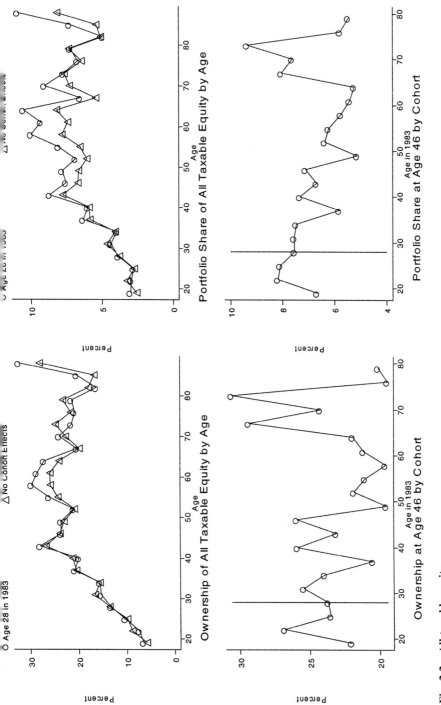

Fig. 2.2   All taxable equity

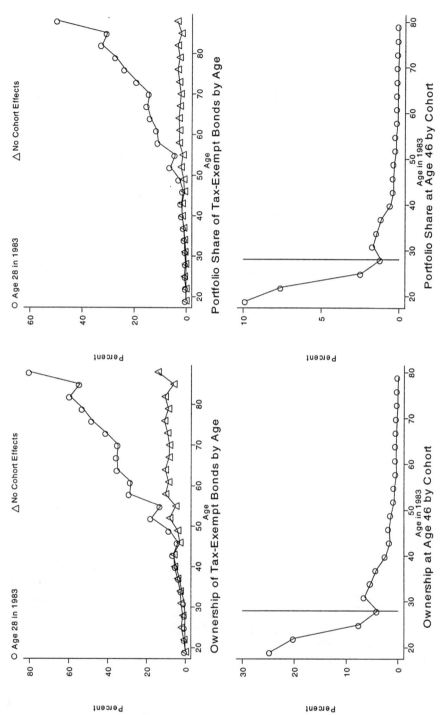

Fig. 3.3   Tax-exempt bonds

These findings are consistent with the growing importance of municipal bonds as a retail financial asset, and with the greater experience with this asset on the part of younger households.

The age profiles for taxable bonds in figure 2.4 resemble those for taxable equity, in that the profiles increase rapidly until about age forty and remain steady thereafter. The profiles for taxable bonds that exclude cohort effects turn sharply lower after the peak, indicating that a cross-sectional analysis would overstate the reduction in taxable bond holdings over the life cycle. The bottom graphs show a sharply declining pattern of cohort effects in both ownership and allocation.

Figure 2.5 presents the graphs for assets held in tax-deferred accounts, including IRAs, Keoghs, defined contribution (DC) pension plans, and other employer-sponsored retirement accounts, such as 401(k) plans.[13] In all cases, the investment earnings on these accounts are not taxed as they compound, and, in most cases, the initial contributions to the accounts are tax-deductible. Income tax typically is due only when the proceeds of the account are received as income in retirement.[14] As in the case of taxable bonds, the profiles with cohort effects do not slope downward later in life to the extent that the profiles without cohort effects do. The estimates predict that the cohort that was aged twenty-eight in 1983 will hold approximately 33 percent of its financial assets in tax-deferred accounts when it reaches age sixty, and more generally, that younger cohorts will rely much more heavily on tax-deferred accounts than did earlier generations.

There is some decline with age in the reliance on traditional bank accounts, including certificates of deposit and money market accounts, and in the holdings of other financial assets, which are primarily the cash value of whole life insurance and trust accounts. Figure 2.6 presents the four graphs for bank accounts.[15] The cohort effects in the portfolio-share equation are statistically significant and increasing for older ages, suggesting that younger cohorts rely less on these fixed income assets for holding wealth. Additionally, the age-ownership profiles increase slowly with age while the age-allocation profiles decline over most of the life cycle. The

13. The SCFs from 1989 and 1992 also report information on the assets that are actually owned in the tax-deferred accounts (e.g., stocks or bonds). Because the SCF from 1983 does not provide this information, we do not disaggregate this category further. Poterba, Venti, and Wise (1998) project the current rates of age-specific 401(k) contributions for individuals born in 1960 and 1970. They find that assuming that 401(k) assets are invested in bonds, the mean 401(k) assets at retirement will be $50,111 (in constant 1992 dollars) for the 1960 cohort and $66,765 for the 1970 cohort. If these assets are invested in the S&P 500, however, and if the average return on stocks in coming decades is similar to that in the last seven decades, then the balances in 401(k)'s will be $181,567 and $256,056, respectively. These asset balances would represent very large shares of household wealth at retirement, and could be compared with an actuarial value of Social Security wealth of $103,392 on average.

14. See Shoven and Wise (1998) for a careful analysis of the effective tax rates on tax-deferred accounts.

15. The graphs for other financial assets are similar and therefore not presented.

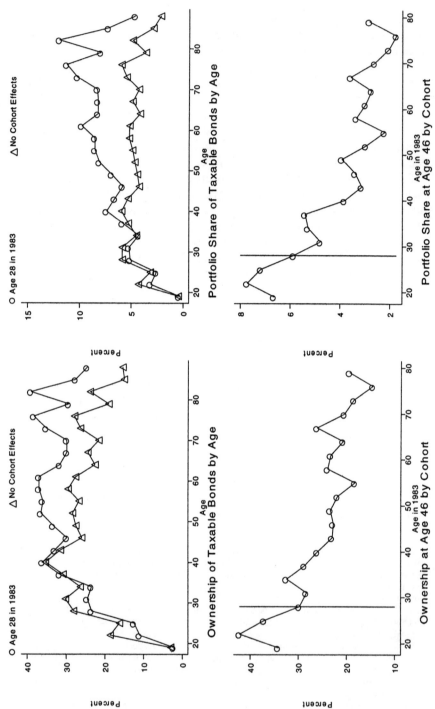

Fig. 2.4   Taxable bonds

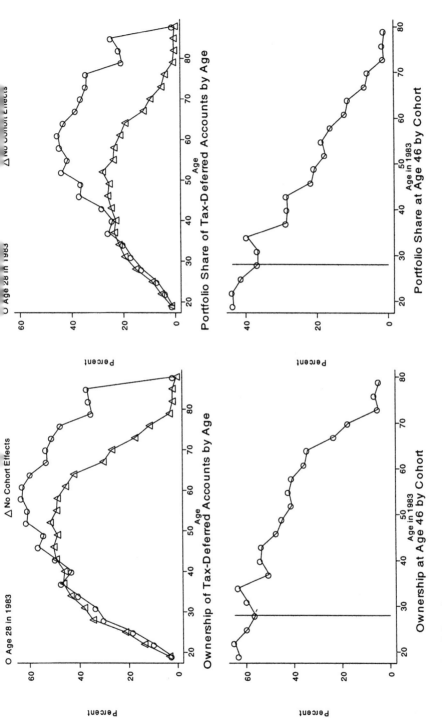

Fig. 2.5   Tax-deferred accounts

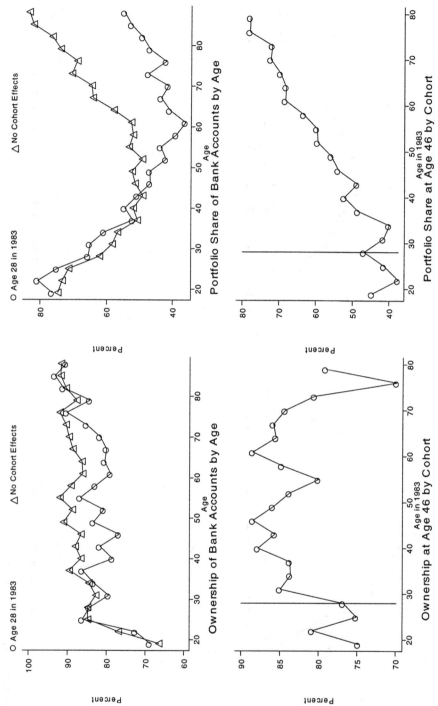

Fig. 2.6 Bank accounts (including CDs and MMAs)

Table 2.9   **Tests for Joint Significance of Cohort Effects in Ownership and Allocation of Total Assets**

Wealth Component	Ownership Probits	Total Asset Share Tobits
Financial assets	0.0018	0.0454
Financial debt	0.0000	0.0000
Owner occupied assets	0.0005	0.0418
Owner occupied debt	0.0003	0.0000
Other real estate assets	0.0484	0.0108
Other real estate debt	0.3106	0.2804
Business net worth	0.0001	0.0003
Miscellaneous assets	0.0001	0.0000
Miscellaneous debt	0.0071	0.0678

Source: Authors' estimates from the Surveys of Consumer Finances, 1983, 1989, and 1992.
Notes: Joint significance tests for probits are based on a chi-square distribution with 20 degrees of freedom. Joint significance tests for tobits are based on an *F*-distribution with 20 (numerator) and 10,292 (denominator) degrees of freedom.

cohort effects in the ownership specifications do not follow an obvious pattern over the life cycle, and in the case of other financial assets, they are statistically indistinguishable from zero.

2.3   Financial Assets in Total Net Worth

This section extends our analysis of the asset ownership and allocation profiles to broader components of net worth. We consider aggregate financial assets, owner-occupied real estate, and holdings of business assets. The discussion and presentation parallel those for distinct classes of financial assets in the previous section.

Figure 2.7 graphs the ownership and allocation of financial assets as a share of total assets. The estimated age profiles for both ownership and allocation show an increase when households are young, followed by a decline until the household reaches age forty. Thereafter, financial assets comprise a steadily increasing share of total assets. The cohort effects for ownership increase and then decrease over the life cycle. The cohort effects for the share of financial assets in total assets show a slightly increasing pattern with age in 1983.

Table 2.9 presents the results of tests for the joint significance of the cohort effects in the ownership and asset allocation equations based on total assets. For the asset share equations for total financial assets, the null hypothesis of equal cohort effects is rejected at standard significance levels. The table also shows results for other asset categories, and with the exception of other real estate debt, finds statistically significant cohort effects for all asset categories.

Figure 2.8 presents the graphs showing ownership and share profiles for

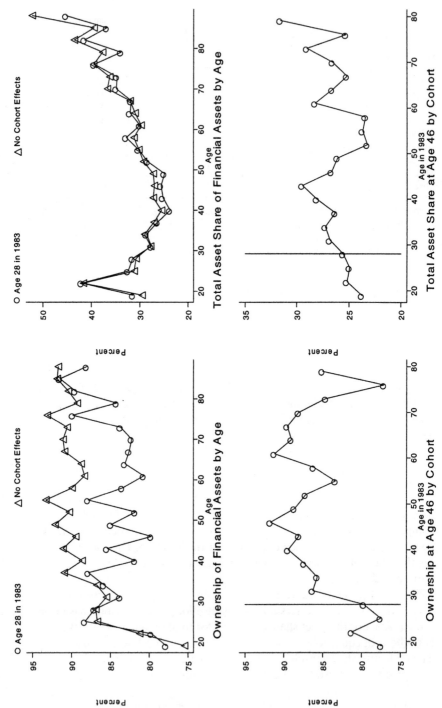

Fig. 2.7 Financial assets

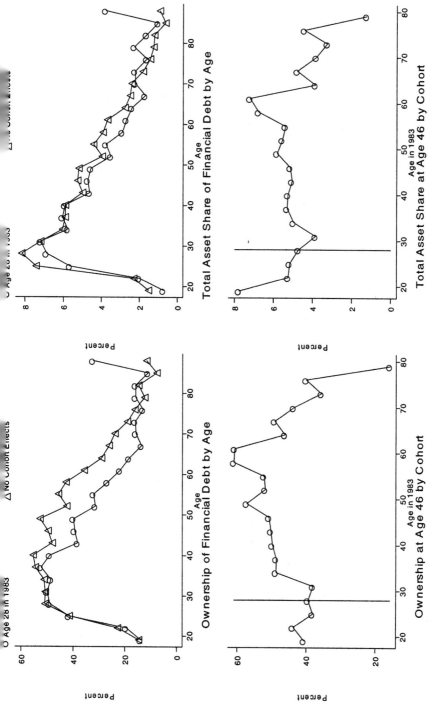

Fig. 2.8   Financial debt

financial debt, which is the sum of outstanding balances on credit cards and lines of credit that are not directly secured by the value of real estate. The age-ownership profile shows increasing ownership with age at young ages, peaking at about 50 percent by age forty-three and then falling steadily to below 20 percent at the oldest ages. Controlling for cohort effects leads to a somewhat sharper decline with age. Controlling for cohort effects has little effect on the age profile of financial debt as a share of total assets, which shows a similar pattern of a more rapid increase to a peak of about 7 percent at age thirty-one, declining to below 2 percent at the oldest ages. In both the ownership and allocation specifications, the cohort effects are statistically significant and the point estimates of these effects rise, slightly, between ages thirty and sixty (these ages correspond to the age of the household head in 1983).

Figures 2.9 and 2.10 show the graphs for owner-occupied real estate assets and associated debt. Owner-occupied real estate assets are simply the value of the household's primary residence. Owner-occupied real estate debt includes the amounts remaining on mortgages and home equity loans on that property plus the outstanding balances on any lines of credit secured by the home. The age-ownership profile of owner-occupied assets rises from about 10 percent for the youngest ages and then remains fairly steady above 70 percent for ages above forty-five. More surprisingly, the fraction of total assets comprised by the value of owner-occupied assets remains steady at about 40 percent for all ages above the mid-thirties. Though we reject the null hypothesis of no cohort effects in both cases, in neither case do cohort effects show a systematic pattern across different ages in 1983 or affect the shape of the age profiles.

The age-ownership profile of owner-occupied debt more closely resembles that of financial debt than of owner-occupied assets. It rises to a peak of about 60 percent at age fifty and then declines to about 10 percent at the oldest ages. As a percentage of total assets, the amount of owner-occupied debt peaks at about 25 percent between ages forty-three and fifty-two and then declines to below 10 percent at the oldest ages. The cohort effects show a declining pattern with age in 1983, with the cohort aged twenty-eight in 1983 predicted to have almost twice the share of debt in total assets when it reaches age forty-six than the cohort aged sixty-one in 1983 had when it was forty-six. Younger generations clearly borrow against the value of their homes to a greater extent than did earlier generations. Controlling for cohort effects shifts the peak of the age-allocation profile by about twenty years, from thirty-five to fifty-five.[16]

---

16. Figure 2.11 is the most obvious example of a sharp increase in the age profile for one of the later age groups. Another example is figure 2.9, which also pertains to a debt measure. Such upturns were present to a lesser extent in taxable equity and tax-exempt bonds in the previous section. One reason such irregularities are possible is that we have fewer observations at the higher ages than in the middle of the age distribution.

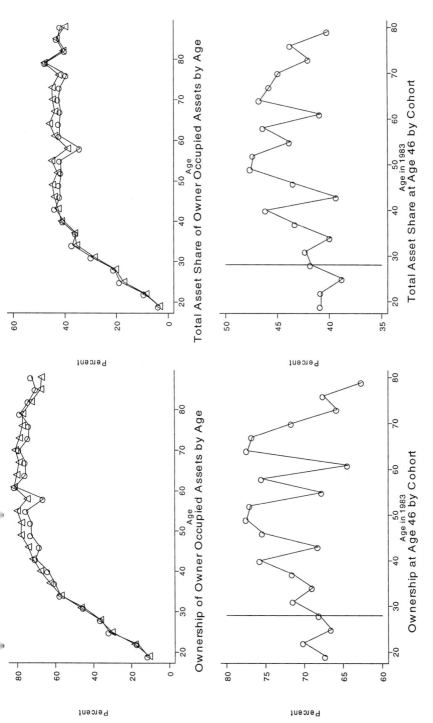

Fig. 2.9 Owner occupied real estate assets

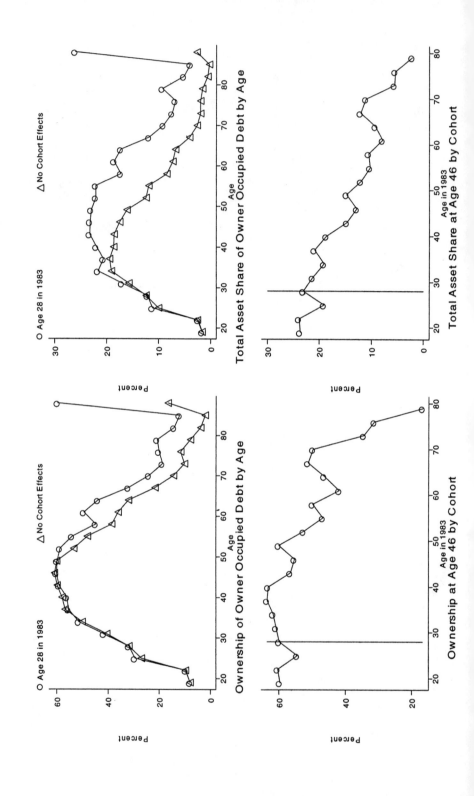

Ownership of Owner Occupied Debt by Age

Total Asset Share of Owner Occupied Debt by Age

Ownership at Age 46 by Cohort

Total Asset Share at Age 46 by Cohort

O Age 28 in 1983   △ No Cohort Effects

Figure 2.11 plots the results for other real estate equity, which includes all real estate other than the primary residence, such as second homes and properties held for investment purposes. We have combined both assets and debt into the same category in the graphs. The age profiles reach their peaks of 27 percent ownership and 7 percent allocation at about age sixty, and the inclusion of cohort effects tends to flatten the profile. The cohort effects are statistically significant and show both an increasing pattern with age and substantial variation around this trend.

Figure 2.12 presents the results for net equity in personally owned businesses. These enterprises could be sole proprietorships, partnerships, or Subchapter S Corporations. In most instances, at least one member of the household actively manages the business. In other cases, the household holds a passive interest in the enterprise, such as a limited partnership. The age profile for ownership of net equity in a personally held business increases rapidly until about age thirty-seven and then declines as the household ages. In the late thirties, about 15 percent of households own businesses and the average share of total assets comprised by business net worth is 5 percent. The declines are much more pronounced in the profile that includes cohort effects than in the profile that does not. The cohort effects are statistically significant and increasing with age in 1983.[17]

The results presented in this section and the previous one suggest two broad conclusions. First, there are important differences across asset classes in the age-specific probability of asset ownership and in the fraction of household assets allocated to different assets at different ages. The notion that all assets can be treated as identical from the standpoint of analyzing household wealth accumulation is clearly not supported by the data. Households tend to accumulate liquid financial assets early in the life cycle, followed by accumulation of real estate and retirement saving assets. Second, there are evident differences in the asset-ownership probabilities of different birth cohorts. Older households were more likely to hold corporate stock and less likely to hold tax-exempt bonds than younger households, at any given age. These differences across cohorts are important to recognize when analyzing asset accumulation profiles.

2.4 Discussion and Conclusions

The results presented in the previous two sections describe the evolution of household portfolios over the life cycle. Empirical evidence on the structure of household portfolios bears on a variety of questions in financial economics and public finance.

One question that our results address is the degree to which the standard

17. In order to conserve space, the figures for miscellaneous assets and debts (consisting primarily of vehicles, collectibles, and other loans owed to or by the household) are omitted.

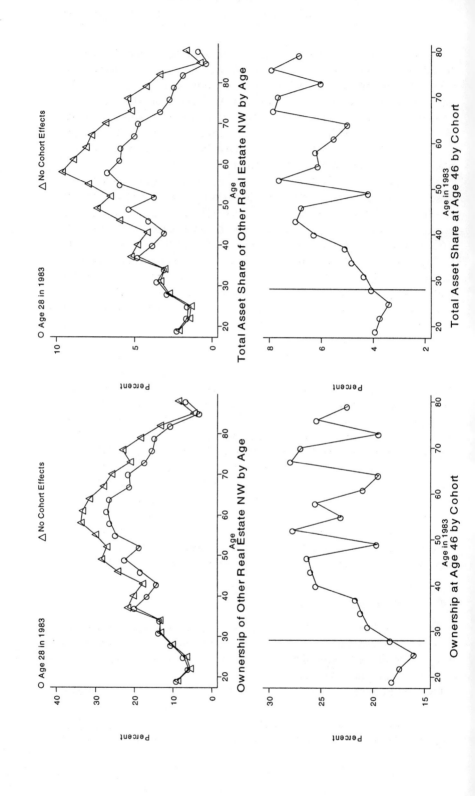

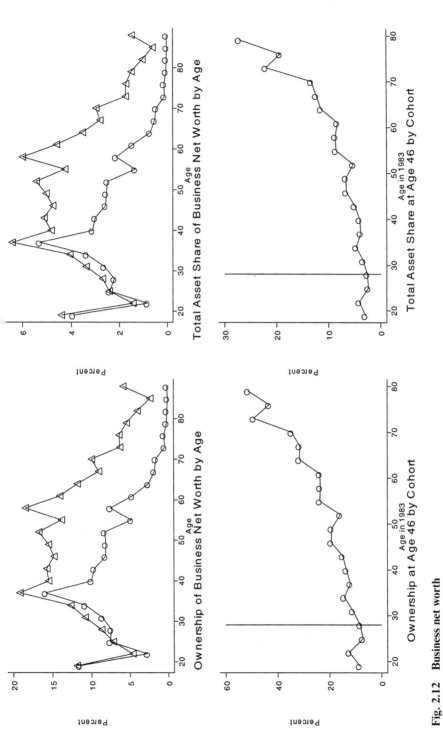

Fig. 2.12   Business net worth

life-cycle framework of asset accumulation can be applied to different components of wealth. The life-cycle model posits a "hump-shaped" pattern of asset accumulation as households age: They accumulate assets during their working years and spend down those assets during their retirement years. Our results suggest that the hump-shaped pattern is not uniform across all assets. For example, as a percentage of total assets, financial assets show just the opposite pattern. They decline as households age, then begin to increase at advanced ages. Investment real estate and equity in privately held businesses do display a hump-shaped pattern, as in the life-cycle model, but owner-occupied housing does not, since there is no evident decline in its ownership at older ages.[18] The standard life-cycle model does not distinguish among various types of assets. Yet when assets exhibit different degrees of liquidity, with (for example) financial assets more liquid than business net worth or other real estate assets, the age pattern of asset holdings may contain important clues for evaluating competing theories of saving behavior. Precautionary saving models suggest that households should seek assets that can be liquidated in the event of financial need. The different age profiles that we identify should therefore provide grist for future research on motives for saving.

A second issue that our findings address is the importance of cohort-specific factors, such as experience with historical returns on different assets, or exposure to financial advertisements, in shaping portfolio patterns. One result that our findings suggest is the important heterogeneity in the composition of portfolios across different cohorts. Our statistical tests show that cohort effects are significant for most components of financial assets and net worth. Among financial assets, the only category in which there was no trend in the cohort effects by age in 1983 was taxable equity. Baby boomers show roughly the average propensity to hold taxable equity and the average portfolio share of taxable equity. Younger cohorts show greater investments in taxable bonds, tax-exempt bonds, and tax-deferred accounts than do older cohorts. They show lower investments in bank accounts and other financial assets. Compared to previous cohorts, the baby boom generation appears to be more willing to take advantage of the more sophisticated financial instruments that have become available over the past twenty years. Younger cohorts have also leveraged their assets to a greater extent than older cohorts. The greater use of debt may also be the result of liberalization of financial markets over the last two decades. Nonetheless, the burden of servicing this debt will reduce the extent to which the baby boomers can use their assets to support consumption in retirement. Our results suggest that borrowing behavior should re-

18. Venti and Wise (1990) discuss the absence of substantial dissaving out of housing assets among the elderly.

ceive attention, along with asset accumulation, in studies of financial preparation for retirement.

We explored some simple explanations for the estimated cohort effects by estimating asset holding and asset-share specifications, including other explanatory variables (e.g., the level of family income, the marginal tax rate on interest income, household size, and marital status), as well as the set of variables in equation (2).[19] While these additional covariates generally improved the fit of the model, for most of the asset and debt categories we analyzed, the estimated age and cohort coefficients changed very little as a result of these specification changes.

Detailed analysis of particular asset categories may be needed to explain some of the cohort effects. For example, Samwick (1996) analyzes the market for tax-shelter investments in real estate, oil and gas, and other areas, before and after the Tax Reform Act of 1986 reduced the incentives for investing in tax shelters. Older cohorts may hold assets that were originally purchased as part of these tax shelter investments, while younger households may not hold these assets, because of the historical investment environment in which they made portfolio decisions. Further work modeling and explaining the nature of the cohort effects clearly is needed. The important cohort patterns we identify suggest that it is essential to distinguish between the saving and asset accumulation of various cohorts as they approach retirement. The experience of one cohort as it approaches retirement may not translate to other, younger, cohorts. These results provide a warrant for the type of research now being undertaken, in many contexts, on the retirement planning and preparation of the baby boom cohort in the United States.

One significant issue that we have not addressed is the role of financial market frictions in explaining age-specific patterns of asset holding and portfolio structure. Down-payment requirements for purchasing owner-occupied homes are an example of such a friction. In most cases, households must accumulate a down payment of between 10 and 20 percent of house value before they can obtain a mortgage for the balance of their home. This could explain a pattern of financial asset accumulation for young households before they purchase a home, as well as the high level of real estate assets (and low level of financial assets) for households in the years immediately after home purchase.

Another example of institutional constraints that might affect accumulation profiles arises from tax-deferred retirement saving accounts. The rapid growth of these accounts has led to a substantial increase in the share of assets that many households hold through these accounts. Be-

---

19. Poterba and Samwick (2000) report more detailed results on some of these specifications, with a particular focus on how taxation affects asset demand.

cause these accounts make it easier for households to purchase some types of assets than others (traded equity or bonds are easy to hold in these accounts; net worth in private businesses would be much harder), the diffusion of these accounts may in part explain the shifting asset-ownership patterns of different cohorts.

Further work is needed to explore the implications of life-cycle models with realistic financial market frictions, and alternative models of saving behavior based on precautionary or other factors, for the structure and development of household portfolios. The rich variation in portfolio structure provides a substantial body of information on motives for saving that has yet to be fully exploited.

References

Advisory Council on Social Security. 1996. *Quadrennial report.* Washington, D.C.: Social Security Administration.

Avery, Robert B., and Gregory E. Elliehausen. 1988. *1983 Survey of Consumer Finances: Technical manual and codebook.* Washington, D.C.: Board of Governors of the Federal Reserve System.

Avery, Robert B., and Arthur B. Kennickell. 1988. *1986 Survey of Consumer Finances: Technical manual and codebook.* Washington, D.C.: Board of Governors of the Federal Reserve System.

Bernheim, B. Douglas. 1995. Do households appreciate their financial vulnerabilities? An analysis of actions, perceptions, and public policy. *Tax policy and economic growth,* 1–30. Washington, D.C.: American Council for Capital Formation.

Bernheim, B. Douglas, and J. Karl Scholz. 1995. U.S. household saving in the 1980s: Evidence from the Surveys of Consumer Finances. Stanford University, Department of Economics, Manuscript.

Bodie, Zvi, Robert C. Merton, and William F. Samuelson. 1992. Labor supply flexibility and portfolio choice in a lifecycle model. *Journal of Economic Dynamics and Control* 16 (July-Oct.): 427–49.

Campbell, John Y., Joao F. Cocco, Francisco J. Gomes, and Pascal J. Maenhout. 2001. Investing retirement wealth: A life-cycle model. In *Risk aspects of investment-based Social Security reform,* ed. John Y. Campbell and Martin S. Feldstein, 439–73. Chicago: University of Chicago Press.

Canner, Niko, N. Gregory Mankiw, and David N. Weil. 1997. An asset allocation puzzle. *American Economic Review* 87 (March): 181–91.

Congressional Budget Office. 1993. *Baby boomers in retirement: An early perspective.* Washington, D.C.: GPO.

Curtin, Richard T., F. Thomas Juster, and James N. Morgan. 1989. Survey estimates of wealth: An assessment of quality. In *The measurement of saving, investment, and wealth,* ed. Robert E. Lipsey and Helen Stone Tice, 473–552. Chicago: University of Chicago Press.

Gakidis, Harry. 1997. Stocks for the old? Earnings uncertainty and life-cycle portfolio choice. Massachusetts Institute of Technology. Manuscript, November.

Hochguertel, Stefan. 1998. A buffer stock model with portfolio choice: Implications of income risk and liquidity constraints. Uppsala University. Manuscript, February.

Kennickell, Arthur B. 1999a. Codebook for 1989 SCF cross-section. Washington, D.C.: Board of Governors of the Federal Reserve System. Manuscript. Available at http://www.federalreserve.gov/pubs/oss/oss2/89/codebk89.txt.

———. 1999b. Codebook for 1992 SCF. Washington, D.C.: Board of Governors of the Federal Reserve System. Manuscript. Available at http://www.federalreserve.gov/pubs/oss/oss2/92/codebk92.txt.

Kimball, Miles S. 1993. Standard risk aversion. *Econometrica* 61 (May): 589–611.

Pence, Karen M., and John Sabelhaus. 1999. Household saving in the '90s: Evidence from cross-section wealth surveys. *Review of Income and Wealth* 45 (4): 435–53.

Poterba, James M., and Andrew A. Samwick. 2000. Taxation and household portfolio composition: Evidence from tax reforms in the 1980s and 1990s. Massachusetts Institute of Technology, Department of Economics. Mimeograph.

Poterba, James M., Steven F. Venti, and David A. Wise. 1994. Targeted retirement saving and the net worth of elderly Americans. *American Economic Review* 84 (May): 180–85.

———. 1996. How retirement saving programs increase saving. *Journal of Economic Perspectives* 10:91–112.

———. 1998. Implications of rising personal retirement saving. In *Frontiers in the economics of aging,* ed. David A. Wise, 125–67. Chicago: University of Chicago Press.

Samuelson, Paul A. 1989. A case at last for age-phased reduction in equity. *Proceedings of the National Academy of Sciences* 86 (November): 9048–51.

———. 1991. Long-run risk tolerance when equity returns are mean regressing: Pseudoparadoxes and vindication of "businessman's risk." In *Money, macroeconomics, and economic policy: Essays in honor of James Tobin,* ed. William C. Brainard, William D. Nordhaus, and Harold W. Watts, 180–200. Cambridge: MIT Press.

Samwick, Andrew A. 1996. Tax shelters and passive losses after the Tax Reform Act of 1986. In *Empirical foundations of household taxation,* ed. Martin S. Feldstein and James M. Poterba, 193–226. Chicago: University of Chicago Press.

Samwick, Andrew A., and Jonathan S. Skinner. 1998. How will defined contribution plans affect retirement income? NBER Working Paper no. 6645. Cambridge, Mass.: National Bureau of Economic Research, July.

Shoven, John B., and David A. Wise. 1998. The taxation of pensions: A shelter can become a trap. In *Frontiers in the economics of aging,* ed. David A. Wise, 173–211. Chicago: University of Chicago Press.

Venti, Steven F., and David A. Wise. 1990. But they don't want to reduce housing equity. In *Issues in the economics of aging,* ed. David A. Wise, 13–29. Chicago: University of Chicago Press.

Wolff, Edward N. 1987. Estimates of household wealth inequality in the United States, 1962–1983. *Review of Income and Wealth* 33 (September): 231–56.

———. 1994. Trends in household wealth in the United States, 1962–1983 and 1983–1989. *Review of Income and Wealth* 40 (June): 143–74.

———. 2000. Who are the rich? A demographic profile of high-income and high-wealth Americans. In *Does Atlas shrug? The economic consequences of taxing the rich.* ed. Joel Slemrod, 74–113. New York: Russell Sage Foundation.

World Bank. 1994. *Averting the old age crisis: Policies to protest the old and promote growth.* Policy Research Report Series. Oxford: Oxford University Press.

The Social Security System and the Demand for Personal Annuity and Life Insurance
An Analysis of Japanese Microdata, 1990 and 1994

Seki Asano

3.1 Introduction

The two most important objectives of the social security system are to support workers in their retirement and, in the case of unexpected death (or disability) of the breadwinner, to provide a stable financial base for the surviving family members. The current social security system offers partial insurance for these risks, but by no means provides customized protection for individual households. Individual workers must prepare for the risk of living beyond retirement, and for the risk of unexpected death. They prepare for these risks by allocating their wealth to various assets.

For example, households can adjust their future asset positions by purchasing two types of insurance. Those who want more protection against living for many years in retirement than the public pension system offers would purchase a private annuity. Those who want protection for family members in the event of the breadwinner's death soon after retirement would purchase life insurance. The resulting asset allocation would reveal the relative strengths of these two motives.

This study examines the effects of public pension benefits on Japanese households' choice of life insurance versus private annuity. Two waves of microdata, constituting the Nikkei Radar Survey (RADAR) and obtained in 1990 and 1994, provide a unique opportunity to observe the effects of changes in social security benefits, total asset values, and expectations on households' asset allocations.

In 1994, at the time of the second-wave survey, the Japanese Diet passed the Social Security Reform Bill. Its main change from the previous 1985

Seki Asano is professor of economics at Tokyo Metropolitan University.

system was to shift the starting age of basic pension provision from sixty to sixty-five. This reform affected males under age fifty-two (in 1994), whose benefits were delayed by one to five years. One focus of this study is to ask how households reacted to this reform.

Also important to this study are the sharp decline in stock prices and the falling real estate values that began in early 1990. The average market value of households' total assets fell about 40 percent by 1994, according to the sample shown later in table 3.1. In addition, the Japanese economy was then in a deep recession; thus the public's prospects for the future became less optimistic. I look at three age groups—people in their thirties, forties, and fifties—to see how households react to these changing economic conditions in various stages of their life cycles.

In the past, empirical studies of the effect of public pensions on life insurance and private annuity purchase yielded varied results. Bernheim (1991) examined the life insurance and personal annuity holdings of retirees and concluded that pension benefits had a significant positive effect on life insurance holdings but depressed personal annuities. Hence, a substantial portion of saving is motivated by bequests. In his analysis, however, life insurance was measured at total face value, not net of saving. Using the same data set, Hurd (1989) examined the wealth and consumption trajectory of retirees and concluded that the bequest motive is weak. Iwamoto and Furuie (1995, 1996) examined the 1990 RADAR data and found a weak effect of bequestable assets on the demand for life insurance. In a somewhat different approach, Chuma (1994) estimated the effect of the intended bequest motive on the demand for life insurance from the same 1990 RADAR data. He found that there was a significant effect for the younger age group, but not for the older group.

This study differs from previous studies in the following aspects: it looks at a sample of household heads of working age (thirty to fifty-nine); it isolates savings in life insurance and personal annuities from gross savings; and it analyzes two data sets from periods when drastic changes in the social security system and the Japanese economy were taking place.

In this analysis, I consider market assets (the sum of monetary and real assets), annuities, and life insurance. Life after retirement is supported by accumulated market assets and annuities. On the other hand, in the case of the breadwinner's death, market assets and life insurance payments will be bequeathed to the surviving family members.

Annuities consist of both public pensions and personal annuities, and life insurance consists of both public and private life insurance. In the case of the insured's death, the social security system becomes a form of life insurance. Although it is compulsory to join social security, the level of benefits provided by the system may not be the same as the individual's desired amount: Desired levels of annuities and life insurance vary from person to person depending on values, education, life stage, family composition, social status, and other factors. Hence, the observed pattern of holding (private) life insurance and personal annuities can be interpreted as the result of adjusting the gap between the desired level and the compulsory provided benefits of the social security system. Also, because negative holdings of life insurance and private annuities are practically impossible, public pensions provide a lower limit for individual annuities and life insurance.

If a person has a strong bequest motive, any increase in pension benefits will be countered by an increase in life insurance. The other side of this adjustment is a reduction in personal annuities or market assets. If the person has no bequest motive, increased pension benefits result in a reduction of personal annuities, leaving the level of life insurance constant.

However, identifying the relative importance of these various motives is a difficult task. Since social security pension benefits are closely tied to public life insurance coverage, an increase in the former also brings about an increase in the latter. Private life insurance both provides bequests to the surviving family (pure bequest), and saving for the insured person. Most life insurance contracts in Japan serve these two functions, and thus a substantial portion of them should be regarded as saving (market assets).

My data sets contain unique information enabling the calculation of the amount of pure life insurance, annuity, and saving (market assets) for both public and personal insurance/annuity, under plausible assumptions. Using data on these assets, I estimate a model in which individuals choose personal annuity and life insurance in order to maximize utility.

The next section presents a theoretical model and an econometric specification of binding nonnegative choice. Section 3.3 describes the data sets, and explains some of the variables. Section 3.4 discusses estimation results. Section 3.5 concludes the paper. The appendix gives a brief description of the Japanese social security system and of other variables in the paper.

3.2   The Model and Econometric Specification

3.2.1   The Model

This model may lead to four types of private annuity and life insurance holding patterns, based on rational choice of a household:

(private annuity, life insurance) = $(+,+)$, $(+,0)$, $(0,+)$, and $(0,0)$.

I assume that the utility of the household depends on marketable wealth (M), which is the sum of marketable monetary and real wealth including demand deposits, stocks, bonds, real estate, etc., annuity (A), which is the annuity and pension received after retirement; and life insurance (L), which is life insurance to be received by the surviving family if the holder dies. A natural formulation of the choice of these three assets may be the following expected utility function:

$$U(M,A,L) = PU_L(M + A) + (1 - P)U_B(M + L),$$

where P is the individual's probability of survival to retirement age. U_L is individual utility when one lives to retirement age and holds market assets, M, and annuities, A. U_B is the utility from bequests when the individual dies before retirement, with the surviving family receiving M and L. This is the model adopted by Bernheim (1991). However, this formulation leads to the prediction that nobody holds a personal annuity and life insurance at the same time. Obviously, that prediction is violated by the data.

In order to avoid such a deficiency, I assume that the functional form is of the linear expenditure system type, written as

(1) $U = \alpha_M \ln(M - M_0) + \alpha_A \ln(A - A_0) + \alpha_L \ln(L - L_0).$

Marketable wealth (monetary and real assets), M, includes all the financial and real assets that can be bought and sold in the markets. The parameters, M_0, A_0, and L_0, may be interpreted as the minimum level of the three assets, but such strict interpretation is not necessary. We can assume that $\alpha_M + \alpha_A + \alpha_L = 1$.

Annuity consists of two components, the first provided by the government in the form of social security pension benefits, and the second a personal annuity purchased by the householder. Thus A is written as

(2) $A = A_P + A_G,$

where A_P indicates private annuity and A_G indicates public pension.

Life insurance is the conditional payment to the surviving family members when the head of household dies. In this sense, the social security system plays the role of public life insurance. If the recipient of a social security pension dies, the surviving family members will receive some part of pension payments for a certain period. Hence, total life insurance is the sum of private and public life insurance.

(3) $L = L_P + L_G,$

where L_P indicates private life insurance and L_G indicates public life insurance.

The householder will allocate total private wealth to three assets, M, A_P, and L_P, under the wealth constraint.

(4) $W = M + aA_P + lL_P,$

where a and l are prices of A_p and L_p, respectively.

Since it is not possible to hold a negative personal annuity (A_p) and life insurance (L_p), the first-order conditions are the Kuhn-Tucker conditions shown in equations (5), (6), and (7).

$$(5) \qquad M: \frac{\alpha_M}{M - M_0} - \lambda \leq 0 \leq M,$$

$$(6) \qquad A_p: \frac{\alpha_A}{A_p + A_G - A_0} - a\lambda \leq 0 \leq A_p, \text{ and}$$

$$(7) \qquad L_p: \frac{\alpha_L}{L_p + L_G - L_0} - l\lambda \leq 0 \leq L_p,$$

where double inequalities ($\leq 0 \leq$) imply that if the inequality holds on the left, equality holds on the right, and vice versa. Although it is possible to have negative M, I assume that all households have positive M, i.e., that equation (5) holds with equality on the left. Thus,

$$(8) \qquad \lambda = \frac{\alpha_M}{M - M_0}.$$

Substituting equation (8) into equations (6) and (7) yields

$$(9) \qquad A_p: \frac{\alpha_A}{A_p + L_G - L_0} - \frac{a\alpha_M}{M - M_0} \leq 0 \leq A_p, \text{ and}$$

$$(10) \qquad L_p: \frac{\alpha_L}{L_p + L_G - L_0} - \frac{l\alpha_M}{M - M_0} \leq 0 \leq L_p.$$

An alternative representation of equations (9) and (10) is obtained by replacing (M by $M = W - aA_p - lL_p$), where W is the total wealth.

$$(11) \quad A_p: \frac{\alpha_A}{A_p + A_G - A_0} - \frac{a\alpha_M}{W - aA_p - lL_p - M_0} \leq 0 \leq A_p$$

$$(12) \quad L_p: \frac{\alpha_L}{L_p + L_G - L_0} - \frac{l\alpha_M}{W - aA_p - lL_p - M_0} \leq 0 \leq L_p$$

3.2.2 Econometric Specification

Solving equations (11) and (12) for A_p and L_p, respectively, and adding disturbance terms u_A and u_L, the structural form of the personal annuity and private life insurance demand functions is

$$(13) \qquad A_P = \left(\frac{1}{a}\right)\left(\frac{\alpha_A}{\alpha_M + \alpha_A}\right)L_P + \left(\frac{\alpha_M}{\alpha_M + \alpha_A}\right)(A_0 - A_G)$$

$$+ \left(\frac{\alpha_A}{\alpha_M + \alpha_A}\right)\frac{W - M_0}{a + u_A}, \text{ and}$$

$$(14) \qquad L_P = \left(\frac{a}{1}\right)\left(\frac{\alpha_L}{\alpha_M + \alpha_L}\right)A_P + \left(\frac{\alpha_M}{\alpha_M + \alpha_L}\right)(L_0 - L_G)$$

$$+ \left(\frac{\alpha_L}{\alpha_M + \alpha_L}\right)\frac{W - M_0}{1 + u_L}.$$

The right-hand side of equations (13) and (14) are the latent demand for A_P and L_P, but the observed demands for A_P and L_P are nonnegative. When the RHS of equation (13) is negative, $A_P = 0$, the same relationship holds for equation (14) and L_P.

I assume that the joint distribution of (u_A, u_L) is independently and identically distributed (i.i.d.) bivariate normal.

$$(15) \qquad \begin{bmatrix} u_A \\ u_L \end{bmatrix} \sim N\left\{\begin{bmatrix} 0 \\ 0 \end{bmatrix}, \begin{bmatrix} \sigma_{AA} & \sigma_{AL} \\ \sigma_{LA} & \sigma_{LL} \end{bmatrix}\right\} = N(0, \Sigma_u)$$

The system in equations (13), (14), and (15) is a bivariate simultaneous Tobit model for which both A_P and L_P take nonnegative values ($A_P \geq 0$, $L_P \geq 0$).

In estimating the model, I have reliable data on L_P, L_G, A_P, and A_G, but W is not observable and A_0, L_0, and M_0 are unknown parameters. Assuming that W, A_0, L_0, and M_0 are linear functions of the observables, the estimable form of the structural equation is

$$(16) \qquad A_P = \gamma_L L_P + x'\beta_A + u_A, \text{ and}$$

$$(17) \qquad L_P = \gamma_A A_P + x'\beta_L + u_L,$$

where, x' is the vector that consists of observed exogenous variables.

I divide the observations into four groups, denoted by I, II, III, and IV.

$$\text{I.: } A_P > 0, \quad L_P > 0$$

$$\text{II.: } A_P > 0, \quad L_P = 0$$

$$\text{III.: } A_P = 0, \quad L_P > 0$$

$$\text{IV.: } A_P = 0, \quad L_P = 0$$

Then, the likelihood function is given by the following:

$$(18) \quad L = \Pi_{i\in I}(1 - \gamma_L\gamma_A)f(A_{Pi} - \gamma_L L_{Pi} - \mathbf{x}_i'\beta_A, L_{Pi} - \gamma_A A_{Pi} - \mathbf{x}_i'\beta_L)$$

$$\Pi_{i\in II}\int_{-\infty}^{-\gamma_A A_{Pi} - \mathbf{x}_i'\beta_L} f(A_{Pi} - \mathbf{x}_i'\beta_A, u_L')du_L,$$

$$\Pi_{i\in III}\int_{-\infty}^{-\gamma_L L_{Pi} - \mathbf{x}_i'\beta_A} f(u_A, L_{Pi} - \mathbf{x}_i'\beta_A)du, \text{ and}$$

$$\Pi_{i\in IV}\int_{-\infty}^{-\mathbf{x}_i'\beta_A}\int_{-\infty}^{-\mathbf{x}_i'\beta_L} f(u_L, u_A)du_L du_A,$$

where $f(\cdot)$ is a bivariate normal density function with zero means and the variance matrix Σ_u. The maximum likelihood estimates of (γ_A, γ_L, β_A, β_L, Σ_u) can be obtained by maximizing equation (18).

3.3 Data

3.3.1 Nikkei Radar Survey

As mentioned earlier, the data sets used in this study are taken from the two waves (1990 and 1994) of an annual survey conducted by the Data Bank Bureau of Nihon Keizai Shimbun, called the Nikkei Radar Survey (RADAR). In RADAR, about 5,000 individuals aged twenty-five to sixty-nine were interviewed each year. The observations were collected from the Tokyo area (metropolitan Tokyo, Saitama, Chiba, and Kanagawa prefectures, excluding offshore islands). The response rates were 56.4 percent (2,818) in 1990 and 54.4 percent (2,721) in 1994. The survey asked detailed questions about household income: financial asset holding patterns, including life insurance and private annuities, and various monetary and real assets. The survey also collected information on each household's family background, ages, education, family composition, life stage, and work status of husband and wife.

For the econometric analysis, I limited observations to the families of married couples whose husbands are between the ages of thirty and fifty-nine and work full time as wage earners. After observations with missing values or improbable figures were removed, the sample size was 789 in 1990 and 610 in 1994.

3.3.2 Definition of Variables

The following variables were used in the model.

Variable Name	Description	Unit
H_AGE	Age of husband	year
ERN_P	Annual permanent earnings of household	million yen
RASST	Real asset	million yen
D_OWN_H	Owns home	dummy (0,1)
TFASST	Total financial asset	million yen
A_p	Private annuity	million yen

Variable Name	Description	Unit
L_P	Private life insurance	million yen
A_G	Public pension	million yen
L_G	Public life insurance	million yen
NDEPKID	Number of dependent children	person
H_CLLG	Husband graduated college	dummy (0,1)
H_LARG	Husband works in large firm (500+ employees)	dummy (0,1)
H_PUBS	Husband works in public sector	dummy (0,1)
W_EMPF	Wife works full time	dummy (0,1)

Public pension (A_G) is the sum of public pension benefits beginning at age sixty discounted by mortality risk. Mortality risk comes from the 1990 Japanese Population Census, and the discount rate is set at 5 percent. I also assume that the individual will retire at age sixty.

The life insurance component of public pension (L_G) is defined as the expected receipt of a survivor's pension benefit conditional on the head of household's being alive at the time of the survey. I then consider death at age H_AGE+1, H_AGE+2, . . . up to age eighty (see appendix).

Of course, the value of L_G is related closely to the public pension benefit (A_G), because the Employees' Pension Insurance Survivors' Benefit (EPISB) is three fourths of the public pension benefit. The total value of L_G is the sum of EPISB and additional benefits that depend on family composition and wife's age and work status.

(Private) life insurance (L_P) is the expected sum of life insurance coverage from private sources.

Net life insurance is the discounted sum of expected life insurance receipts from life insurance and personal annuities, conditional on the person's being alive at age H_AGE, minus any cancellation value of insurance contracts (see appendix).

The value of private annuity (A_P) is defined as the expected value of a discounted sum of private annuity flow beginning at age sixty. As in the case of public pension, A_P is discounted by mortality risk.

Total financial assets (TFASST) is defined as the sum of the usual financial assets (such as demand deposits, time deposits, bonds, stocks, money in trust, and other monetary assets) and the cancellation value of life insurance and private annuities, minus the present value of home loan payments. I classify single-payment old age life insurance (*ichiji harai yoro hoken*) as a financial asset instead of life insurance, because it usually has a short maturity period (five years) and mostly is purchased as a short-term saving asset. For this reason I do not include it in the calculation of life insurance payments to survivors. Its financial value is set as the amount of reimbursement at maturity. Also, variable life insurance (*hengaku hoken*) is usually purchased as a financial asset. Half of its guaranteed minimum life insurance coverage is included in TFASST.

RASST is the sum of the market value of land, condominiums, and other assets including gold, coins, membership in golf clubs, and the like.

In RADAR, the response to the questions relating to real assets may contain serious errors. The questionnaire first asks the value of "own land" where the owner resides, then asks the value of "other" land and real estate, including condominiums. With this setup, some owners of owner-occupied condominiums may answer "zero" to both questions, in which case the value of the RASST is zero even though the respondent owns real estate. In fact, about 200 homeowners responded in this manner in both waves. Though I excluded these observations from the sample, other errors may be contained in this variable. For example, homeowners may report the value of the land excluding the value of the house. For this reason I display RASST and TFASST separately in the list of explanatory variables.

3.3.3   Descriptive Statistics

Table 3.1 shows the mean values of the variables by age group for 1990 and 1994. As shown, the decline in the real estate market and the stock market lowered the value of land to about 50 percent of its 1990 level, and lowered the value of high-risk financial assets. Total market assets declined to about 50 percent of their 1990 level for those in their thirties, 66 percent of their 1990 level for those in their forties, and about 60 percent of the 1990 level for those in their fifties.

The effect of changes in the social security system for household portfolios is apparent in the shift in personal annuities. The proportion of A_P holders increased across all age groups: from 19 percent to 33 percent for those in their thirties, 23 percent to 34 percent for those in their forties, and 29 percent to 40 percent for those in their fifties. The mean value of A_P, however, appears to have stayed about the same.

On the other hand, the proportion of life insurance holders declined by anywhere from 6 percent to 10 percent across all age groups. Gross life insurance coverage stayed about the same, but saving from life insurance fell by 2 million yen (for those in their fifties) and by 0.4 million yen (for those in their forties). Also, although it is not indicated in the table, all the annuity holders held life insurance in both waves.

Public pension benefits (A_G) declined a little for those in their thirties and forties but stayed the same for those in their fifties. Public life insurance (L_G) increased about 10 percent. Thus, in my sample social security reform, life insurance increased slightly and pension benefit declined.

3.4   Results

3.4.1   Structural Form Estimates

I estimate the structural form of the model using the maximum likelihood method for individuals in their thirties, forties, and fifties. I use L_G as an instrument for L_P in the A_P equation, and A_G for A_P in the L_P equation. The results are shown in table 3.2.

Table 3.1   Descriptive Statistics by Age

		Ages 30–39		Ages 40–49		Ages 50–59		All	
		1990	1994	1990	1994	1990	1994	1990	1994
Permanent earnings (million yen)	ERN_P	6.02	6.76	7.95	8.97	9.18	9.44	7.61	8.41
Total monetary asset[a] (million yen)		6.36	5.14	10.04	9.75	16.28	12.61	10.42	9.18
Real asset, land (million yen)		21.55	6.06	40.82	21.61	65.21	37.78	40.61	21.73
Total real asset (million yen)	RASST	26.08	10.23	48.97	30.06	79.64	45.68	49.16	28.64
Proportion of home owners (%)	D_OWN_H	44	33	78	63	84	80	68	59
Total net financial asset[b] (million yen)	TFASST	5.22	4.16	9.79	6.83	20.06	14.57	10.93	8.41
Total market asset[c] (million yen)		31.3	14.38	58.75	36.88	99.71	60.25	60.09	37.04
Personal annuity	A_P	1.21	1.55	1.06	1.39	1.25	1.97	11.16	1.62
Saving from personal annuity (million yen)		0.04	0.03	0.31	0.31	1.23	1.71	0.46	0.66
Proportion of personal annuity holders (%)		19	33	23	34	29	40	23	36

Life insurance, gross (million yen)		29.21	29.39	30.67	29.73	23.58	22.87	28.27	27.48
Life insurance, net (million yen)	L_P	26.03	27.13	24.96	24.42	15.93	17.16	22.93	23.01
Saving from life insurance (million yen)		3.18	2.26	5.71	5.31	7.65	5.72	5.35	4.47
Proportion of life insurance holders (%)		82	73	87	80	84	79	85	77
Public pension (million yen)	A_G	19.71	19.19	19.86	18.79	21.54	22.56	20.26	20.11
Public life insurance (million yen)	L_G	7.63	8.59	9.94	10.76	11.09	11.93	9.44	10.44
Dependent children	NDEPKID	1.52	1.53	1.96	1.78	1.02	0.98	1.56	1.45
College degree (%)	H_CLLG	59	57	45	49	42	41	49	49
Public sector (%)	H_PUBS	15	12	10	16	13	15	12	15
Large firm (%)	H_LARG	44	41	40	45	43	41	42	42
Wife employed full time (%)	W_EMPF	13	14	18	20	20	12	17	16
Sample size		275	194	304	225	210	191	789	610

[a]Sum of demand deposit, time deposit, stocks, bonds, bank debenture, foreign currency saving, and other monetary assets.

[b]Sum of total monetary asset, and cancellation value of personal annuity and life insurance, minus present value of home loan.

[c]RASST + TFASST.

Table 3.2 **Structural Form Estimate**

	1990			1994		
Variable	Estimate	Structural Estimate	*t*-ratio	Estimate	Structural Estimate	*t*-rati
		Dependent A_P (ages 30–39)				
L_P	0.10	0.10	0.97	0.13	0.04	3.1
CONST	−3.17	22.24	−0.14	−25.35	16.56	−1.5
A_G	−2.03	0.98	−2.08	0.44	0.63	0.6
TFASST	−0.05	0.14	−0.37	0.09	0.11	0.8
RASST	0.01	0.02	0.41	−0.05	0.04	−1.2
D_OWN_H	3.49	3.06	1.14	−0.63	2.12	−0.3
ERN_P	3.67	1.83	2.01	−0.66	1.31	−0.5
NDEPKID	−1.07	1.22	−0.88	−1.43	0.83	−1.7
H_AGE	0.33	0.50	0.66	0.52	0.38	1.3
H_CLLG	−2.53	2.40	−1.05	0.46	1.51	0.3
H_PUBS	−6.60	5.69	−1.16	7.04	4.34	1.6
H_LARG	−0.85	2.46	−0.35	−1.03	1.69	−0.6
W_EMPF	−2.74	4.09	−0.67	1.71	3.07	0.5
Structural Estimate	10.93			5.53		
		Dependent L_P				
A_P	−0.27	0.75	−0.36	2.47	1.10	2.24
CONST	3.07	19.87	0.15	46.97	31.13	1.51
L_G	−3.09	1.95	−1.58	1.60	3.62	0.44
TFASST	0.27	0.12	2.37	0.38	0.23	1.66
RASST	0.02	0.03	0.67	0.06	0.13	0.50
D_OWN_H	2.76	3.97	0.69	−0.25	5.91	−0.04
ERN_P	5.45	1.94	2.82	2.09	4.09	0.51
NDEPKID	0.45	1.79	0.25	2.07	2.95	0.70
H_AGE	0.35	0.64	0.55	−1.76	0.96	−1.83
H_CLLG	−3.26	3.24	−1.01	0.48	5.09	0.09
H_PUBS	2.43	5.69	0.43	5.03	10.45	0.48
H_LARG	1.38	3.26	0.43	3.27	5.05	0.65
W_EMPF	−15.65	6.09	−2.57	−3.06	11.86	−0.26
Structural Estimate	23.27			26.61		
rho		0.04			−0.43	
N		275 (+,+ = 51; 0,+ = 182; 0,0 = 42[a])			194 (+,+ = 60; 0,+ = 95; 0,0 = 39)	
Log likelihood		−1,373.75			−1,043.98	
		Dependent (ages 40–49)				
L_P	0.11	0.08	1.37	0.10	0.05	1.96
CONST	−39.78	12.77	−3.12	−1.49	11.23	−0.13
A_G	0.83	0.45	1.82	−0.18	0.33	−0.56
TFASST	0.06	0.05	1.20	0.04	0.03	1.05
RASST	0.01	0.01	0.74	−0.02	0.02	−1.07
D_OWN_H	5.02	2.02	2.49	2.43	1.67	1.46
ERN_P	−1.39	0.65	−2.14	0.40	0.42	0.94
NDEPKID	−1.11	1.07	−1.03	−0.47	0.75	−0.63
H_AGE	0.47	0.28	1.65	−0.05	0.24	−0.20
H_CLLG	−0.35	1.51	−0.23	0.39	1.30	0.30
H_PUBS	0.56	2.43	0.23	0.87	2.13	0.41

	1990			1994		
ariable	Estimate	Structural Estimate	t-ratio	Estimate	Structural Estimate	t-ratio
_LARG	4.85	1.38	3.52	−0.96	1.47	−0.65
_EMPF	5.89	1.84	3.20	−1.25	1.53	−0.82
tructural Estimate	7.07			5.40		
		Dependent L_P				
$_P$	−0.01	0.77	−0.01	2.18	1.34	1.62
ONST	50.32	20.34	2.47	60.88	27.73	2.20
$_G$	−0.83	0.90	−0.93	−0.72	0.89	−0.80
FASST	0.27	0.06	4.31	0.14	0.09	1.54
ASST	0.04	0.02	2.32	0.06	0.06	0.95
_OWN_H	2.14	3.37	0.64	−0.29	4.70	−0.06
RN_P	1.38	0.77	1.80	2.54	0.97	2.63
NDEPKID	3.62	1.54	2.35	0.24	2.14	0.11
_AGE	−0.94	0.49	−1.94	−1.28	0.65	−1.98
_CLLG	−3.27	2.79	−1.17	0.56	3.67	0.15
_PUBS	−5.81	4.65	−1.25	−6.33	4.96	−1.28
_LARG	3.44	2.85	1.21	2.04	3.80	0.54
W_EMPF	3.51	3.46	1.01	−3.79	4.79	−0.79
tructural Estimate	19.49			23.08		
ho		−0.15			−0.33	
V	304 (+,+ = 69; 0,+ = 201; 0,0 = 34[a])			225 (+,+ = 77; 0,+ = 115; 0,0 = 33)		
Log likelihood		−1,543.97			−1,249.60	
		Dependent (ages 50–59)				
L_P	0.12	0.09	1.26	0.20	0.06	3.24
ONST	5.22	14.09	0.37	−36.37	20.71	−1.76
$_G$	−0.19	0.26	−0.74	−0.08	0.31	−0.26
FASST	0.01	0.04	0.14	0.04	0.05	0.86
RASST	0.00	0.01	−0.10	−0.01	0.02	−0.57
D_OWN_H	0.20	1.86	0.11	1.74	2.46	0.71
ERN_P	0.68	0.37	1.84	0.44	0.44	0.99
NDEPKID	−0.84	0.83	−1.01	1.49	1.01	1.48
H_AGE	−0.21	0.25	−0.84	0.48	0.39	1.22
H_CLLG	−0.19	1.80	−0.10	0.53	1.76	0.30
H_PUBS	1.22	2.33	0.52	2.03	2.37	0.86
H_LARG	0.68	1.41	0.48	−1.71	1.81	−0.95
W_EMPF	−0.49	1.97	−0.25	−0.87	2.67	−0.33
Strutural Estimate	5.71			6.59		
		Dependent L_P				
A_P	0.70	0.98	0.71	1.31	0.61	2.13
CONST	48.84	29.31	1.67	37.34	42.91	0.87
L_G	−0.16	0.60	−0.27	0.81	0.66	1.22
TFASST	0.31	0.06	5.12	0.42	0.08	4.95
RASST	0.00	0.01	0.21	0.01	0.03	0.17
D_OWN_H	2.85	4.87	0.58	11.88	5.38	2.21
ERN_P	0.45	0.66	0.68	−0.03	0.84	−0.04
NDEPKID	0.24	1.75	0.14	−2.53	2.42	−1.05

(*continued*)

Table 3.2   (continued)

	1990			1994		
Variable	Estimate	Structural Estimate	t-ratio	Estimate	Structural Estimate	t-ratio
H_AGE	−0.86	0.52	−1.64	−0.90	0.77	−1.16
H_CLLG	−4.02	2.79	−1.44	1.28	4.20	0.30
H_PUBS	1.97	4.31	0.46	−3.63	6.02	−0.60
H_LARG	6.59	2.79	2.37	3.52	3.85	0.91
W_EMPF	1.08	3.66	0.29	0.98	5.87	0.17
Structural Estimate	16.25			19.93		
rho	−0.13			−0.33		
N	210 (+,+ = 60; 0,+ = 124; 0,0 = 26[a])			191 (+,+ = 76; 0,+ = 82; 0,0 = 33)		
Log likelihood	−1,067.76			−1,054.73		

Note: N = Number of observations. See text for explanation of variables.

[a] +,+ 0,+, and 0,0 indicate (AP > 0, LP > 0), (AP = 0, LP > 0), and (AP = 0, LP = 0), respectively.

The theoretical model predicts that the coefficient on L_p in the A_p equation and the one on A_p in the L_p equation are both negative. Contrary to this prediction, neither coefficient comes out significantly negative, and both are positive and significant in five out of twelve instances (three age groups, two waves, and two dependents). Although the coefficients on A_G in the A_p equations and on L_G in the L_p equations tend to have negative signs as I expected, they are not significant, except in one case (ages thirty to thirty-nine in 1990). Based on these results, I cannot say that this model specification and estimation are correct descriptions of household asset choice.

There are several possible explanations for this result. First, measurement error in A_p and L_p are unavoidable in this data set, and can cause bias in estimates. However, this cannot explain consistent positive signs of endogenous variable coefficients.

A more plausible explanation of the positive signs may be that they are caused by a positive association between A_p and L_p. The main reason for this association may be heterogeneity in time preference. That is, those who have higher time (future) preference tend to have higher A_p and L_p, and vice versa. When we can successfully control for time preference by including variables representing it, we can expect to observe a trade-off between life insurance and personal annuity. My results indicate that the control variables included in the model are not rich enough to explain heterogeneity in time preference.

3.4.2   Reduced-Form Estimates

Although tight parameterization in theoretical models is not enough to explain the observed pattern of asset holding, it is interesting to see how holding private annuities and life insurance is affected by exogenous variables.

To examine how households reacted to a decline in asset values and reduced pension benefits between the two waves, I estimate tobit regressions of A_P and L_P for a set of exogenous variables: L_G, A_G, TFASST, NDEPKID, and other control variables. As in the structural form, the observations are divided into six groups: three age groups and two waves (1990 and 1994).

3.4.3 Marginal Effects

Table 3.3 and figure 3.1 summarize the marginal effects on A_P and L_P of public pension (A_G), public life insurance (L_G), total financial asset (TFASST), number of dependent children (NDEPKID), and intercept (CONST).

In table 3.3, tests of significance of individual coefficients are indicated in column t, and tests of equality of coefficients in 1990 and in 1994 ($\beta_{j90} = \beta_{j94}$) are indicated in column s. Except for a few cases, the marginal effects of these variables change by age group within the same wave. I do not present results of formal statistical tests, but it is obvious that the marginal effects change with one's life stage.

The coefficients of A_G in the A_P equation are significantly negative for people in their thirties in both 1990 and 1994: -1.247 in 1990 and -0.649 in 1994. This implies that, holding other variables constant, reduction in public pension benefits is countered by roughly the same amount of increase in private annuities for this age group. In other age groups, the marginal effects are insignificant or positive (as for those in their forties in 1990).

The effects of public life insurance (L_G) on private life insurance (L_P) are all negative in 1990 and are significant for those in their thirties and fifties. This strongly supports the life-cycle hypothesis. The effects are insignificant in 1994, however. Also, the coefficient for A_P in 1994 is significantly positive, which again supports the life cycle hypothesis.

The effects of total financial assets are mostly positive and significant as one would expect. However, the marginal effects on A_P increased significantly from 1990 to 1994 for those in their thirties and fifties. The number of dependent children (NDEPKID) has a negative effect on personal annuities (A_P) for two age groups, household heads in their thirties and their forties. The coefficient is significant for the latter group in 1990, and for the former group in 1994. It may be that when parents are younger (and presumably their children are young), they place a higher priority on investing in their children rather than preparing for retirement. Also, the effect of NDEPKID on L_P is significantly positive for those in their forties in 1990. These two observations support the bequest motive. In 1994, however, all the coefficients for L_P become insignificant. This pattern suggests that the bequest motive had become negligible by 1994.

A possible reconciliation of these conflicting observations is that, faced with less optimistic future prospects for their children and themselves,

Table 3.3   Marginal Effects Based on Reduced Form Estimates

Age	A_P						L_P					
	1990	t	s	1994	t	s	1990	t	s	1994	t	s
A_G												
30s	−1.25	**		−0.65	*		1.95			−4.21	*	*
40s	0.75	**		−0.34		**	−0.14			−0.02		
50s	−0.20			0.17			2.51	**		−1.29		**
L_G												
30s	0.13			1.64	**		−5.38	*		7.63	*	**
40s	−0.22			−0.01			−0.74			−0.90		
50s	0.17			−0.23			−2.01	**		0.89		**
TFASST												
30s	−0.02			0.12	**	**	0.27	*		0.59	**	
40s	0.08	**		0.06	**		0.28	**		0.17	*	
50s	0.03	*		0.11	**	**	0.32	**		0.41	**	
NDEPKID												
30s	−0.61			−1.87	**	*	2.11			0.23		
40s	−0.70	**		−0.29			3.60	**		0.34		
50s	−0.42			0.90	*	**	1.27			−0.26		
CONST												
30s	−8.64			−0.53			−39.02			132.07	**	**
40s	−39.34	**		3.22		**	52.13	*		63.76	*	
50s	2.96			−4.81			53.17	*		18.82		

Notes: t indicates test of significance. *s* indicates test of difference, $\beta_{1990} = \beta_{1994}$. See text for explanation of variables.

**Significant at the 5 percent level (two-tailed).

*Significant at the 10 percent level.

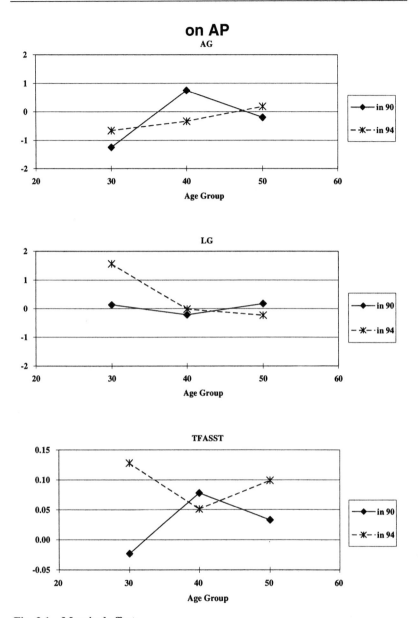

Fig. 3.1   **Marginal effect**

parents make a priority of leaving bequests to their heirs by investing in education, which yields a higher return than monetary assets in the long run. Their second priority is preparing for retirement. To that end, they purchase personal annuities and trade in their monetary assets. When they are younger, the purchase of A_p is more dependent on the level of total

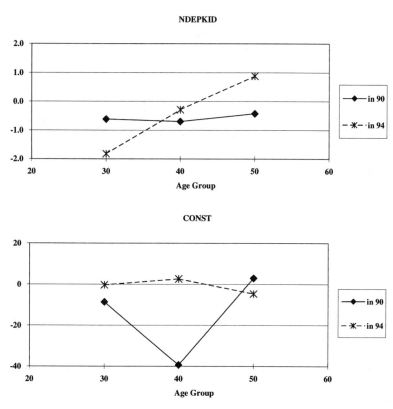

Fig. 3.1   (cont.)

financial assets and the number of dependent children; the marginal effects
of those two factors are large.

The level of the intercept coefficient itself is not of interest, but its shift
between the two waves reflects a uniform adjustment made by the people
within the same age group. The intercept showed a significant increase for
the group in their forties in the A_p equation, and for those in their thirties
in the L_p equation. The marginal effects of other variables on A_p are very
stable for people in their forties. This implies that, facing a reduction in
pension benefits, those in their forties raised their private annuity holdings,
regardless of the level of other factors. These adjustments presumably were
made by a compensating reduction in other financial assets.

It is difficult to explain all of these results in one simple framework.
However, it seems that household priorities regarding these two objectives,
their own retirement life and the later life of their surviving family members, change with both their life stage asset levels and their expectations
for the future. One common pattern suggested by these estimation results
is that a households' first priority is to achieve at least a minimum level of

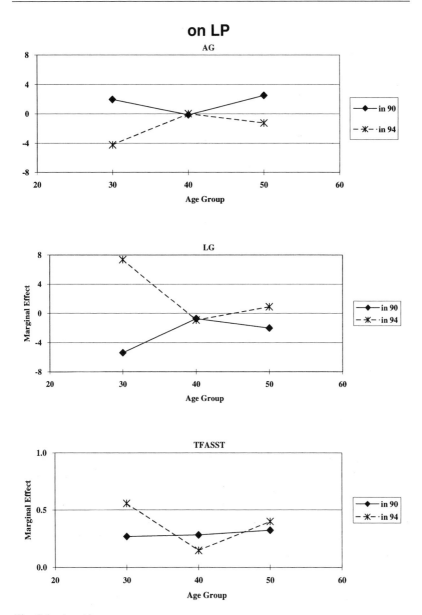

Fig. 3.1   (cont.)

preparation for retirement and a minimum level of bequests to their heirs. For that purpose, they are willing to sacrifice current consumption.

We also look at changes in total annuity and life insurance demand in the two waves. The sum of the predicted values of private annuities from the tobit coefficients and public pensions (A_G) may be interpreted as "de-

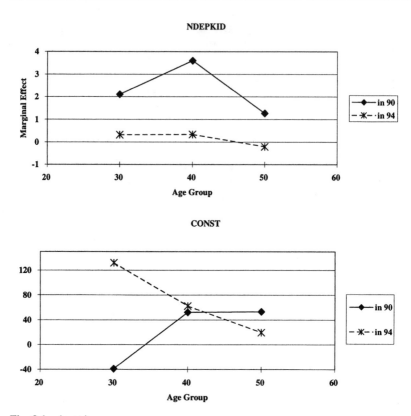

Fig. 3.1   (cont.)

sired total annuity." The same interpretation applies to life insurance. I look at the level and shift of these total annuity and life insurance variables. Table 3.4 and figure 3.2 present means and standard deviations of these two variables for six age groups: thirty to thirty-four, thirty-five to thirty-nine, and so on, up to fifty-five to fifty-nine.

As the upper half of figure 3.2 shows, the mean total annuity increased in all age groups by 2 million (for those aged fifty-five to fifty-nine) to 4.5 million yen (for those forty-five to forty-nine). Younger generations tend to start accumulating annuities earlier in the 1994 data. Within the 1994 wave, the means of total annuity are fairly stable across age groups, with a range of 2.9 million yen (15.6–18.5 million yen). Variations within and across age groups are stable, with the standard deviations between 5 and 6 million in both years.

A contrasting picture emerges for total life insurance. The lower half of figure 3.2 shows that the means of total life insurance stayed at about the same level in both years. The variation within each age group, on the other hand, increased in all age groups, with those aged thirty-five to thirty-nine

Table 3.4		Desired Life Insurance and Annuity, by Age Group		
		1990		1994
Age	Mean	Standard Deviation	Mean	Standard Deviation
		Total Annuity		
30–34	12.77	6.39	16.72	6.03
35–39	12.91	6.05	17.02	5.37
40–44	14.49	5.66	17.35	6.07
45–49	14.05	5.25	18.52	9.00
50–54	14.18	5.00	16.31	7.98
55–59	13.85	5.76	15.61	5.73
		Total Life Insurance		
30–34	28.78	8.58	32.35	12.56
35–39	35.31	8.99	33.90	18.36
40–44	35.24	8.82	35.29	11.78
45–49	34.10	9.40	33.86	11.84
50–54	27.72	9.39	29.91	13.79
55–59	26.20	12.91	27.19	15.30

Note: Total annuity is the sum of predicted private annuity and life insurance (million yen). Total life insurance is the sum of public pension and life insurance (million yen).

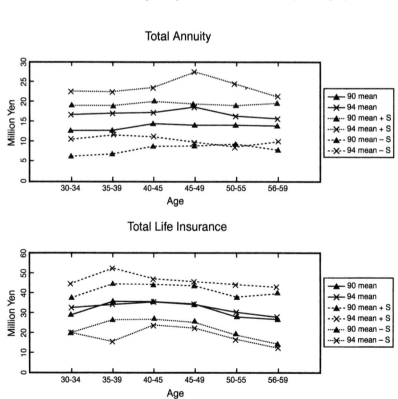

Fig. 3.2   Desired total annuity and life insurance

having the largest variation. As noted earlier, this age group is the first generation of both males and females to begin receiving full pension benefits beginning at age sixty-five. The response to the shift in the public pension system is more heterogeneous in this age group than in other groups.

3.5   Conclusion

This study examined the relationship between Japanese households' personal annuity and life insurance choices and the public pension system. From the two waves of microdata sets obtained in 1990 and 1994, I separate pure life insurance and pure annuity from their gross values, and thereby isolate the saving component of life insurance and personal annuity. The sample period is characterized by declining asset values, a reduction in public pension benefits, and less optimistic future prospects for the Japanese economy.

I find that the intended level of total annuities increased by about 4 million yen on average from 1990 to 1994, which more than compensated for a reduction in public pension benefits. Furthermore, the age profile for mean total annuities became flatter from 1990 to 1994 across all age groups because of the younger generation's early accumulation of personal annuities. In contrast to total annuities, the mean total of life insurance stayed quite flat and stable in both periods across age groups, while intragenerational variations widened to as much as twice their 1990 levels.

One hypothesis to explain this result is that households have a minimum target level of annuity and bequest. Facing declining benefits from public pensions and unfavorable future income prospects, individuals begin to accumulate personal annuities at earlier stages of their lives. To leave a bequest, it is a rational choice to invest in the asset that yields the highest return to heirs, namely, education. If parents decide to leave a bequest in the form of human capital via education, they are constrained during the period of high educational expenses. Since educational expense is lumpy in nature, households must reduce their consumption, saving, and life insurance purchases during this period, typically beginning in their midthirties and up to their early fifties. Once the minimum level is achieved, households choose their consumption/wealth accumulation path from a wider variety of menus.

These results are consistent with Horioka et al.'s (1996) finding that, in Japan, the purpose and priority of wealth accumulation (saving) changes with age and life stage. In particular, the primary purpose of saving among those in their thirties is education, while for those over forty-five it is preparation for retirement.

Appendix

Japanese Social Security System

This section gives an outline of Japan's social security system, which provides public pensions and public life insurance (see Social Insurance Agency 1995a,b; Shimada 1995 for details). Old-age public pensions provided by the Japanese system have two parts: the base (fixed) part, and the remuneration (proportional) part, which is also called the "second floor."

Base Part

The base of the system is the National Pension (NP, or Kokumin Nenkin). It is compulsory for all individuals aged twenty to sixty. Those who paid the premium for the NP will receive a fixed annual payment beginning at age sixty in the 1985 system, and beginning between age sixty and sixty-five (depending on year of birth) in the 1994 system (see fig. 3A.1).

Benefits from the NP include Old-Age Basic Pension, Survivors' Basic Pension, and Disability Basic Pension. The insured person who has paid the premium for more than twenty-five years is eligible for Old-Age Basic Pension benefits. Those who paid the premium for forty years will receive full benefits: 666,000 yen per year in 1990, and 780,000 yen in 1994. The

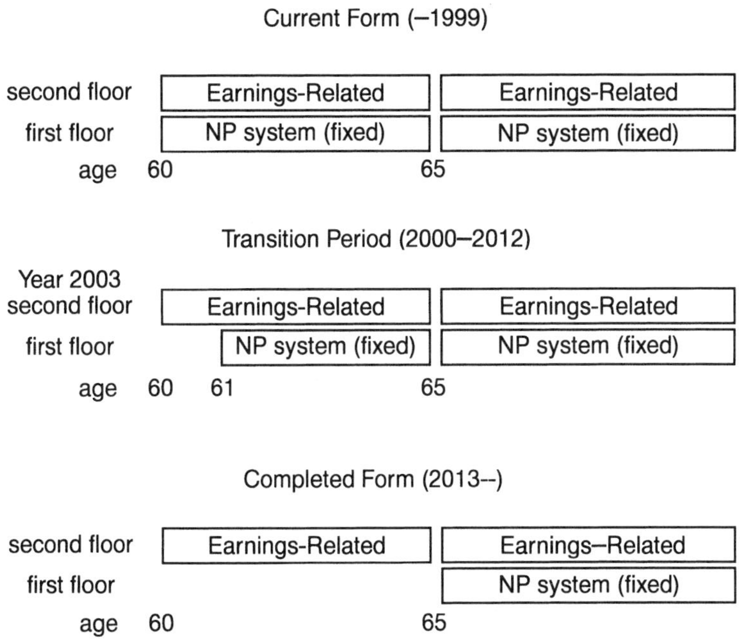

Fig. 3A.1   Transition of social security system (1985–94)

Survivors' Basic Pension benefit depends on family composition and the age of the widow.

Second Floor

The proportional remuneration consists of various employees' pension systems. Among those, the Employees' Pension Insurance system (EPI, or Kōsei Nenkin) is the most common one in Japan. It covers all employees in the private sector, excluding only public employees, teachers and employees of private schools, and seamen. Those insured by EPI pay the premium according to their remuneration level, and upon reaching their retirement age (sixty), they receive pension payments based on their premiums. Employees not covered by EPI are covered by mutual aid associations (MAA, *kyō-sai kumiai*), which offer similar premium/benefits schemes as the EPI, to the insured. The premiums for the EPI are determined on the basis of "standard remuneration," SR, which is basically equal to the regular monthly wage and allowance, excluding bonus payments. The premiums are determined by the SR multiplied by the prescribed ratio.

The benefit levels of the Old-Age Employees' Pension and the Survivor's Employees' Pension are determined as follows:

Old-Age Employees' Pension =

(Average Monthly SR)x(1% ~ 0.75%)* x(Insured Period in Months),

where x is the indication ratio and the asterisk indicates that the ration varies by the year of birth.

Survivor's Employees' Pension is paid to the surviving family members when the insured person dies. The pension is 75 percent of the Old-Age Employees' Pension, and an additional amount is paid if there are children under eighteen years old, or if the widow is of advanced age.

Calculation of Public Life Insurance (L_G)

The life insurance part of social security (L_G) is defined as the expected value of a discounted sum of social security payments:

$$\sum_{t=\text{H\_AGE}+1}^{80} \text{SSB}_t \times \Pr(\text{Die at age } t \,|\, \text{Alive at age H\_AGE}),$$

where SSB_t indicates the discounted sum of social security benefit flow when husband dies at age t ($>$H_AGE). SSB_t is obtained under the following assumptions:

1. The householder started working at the age indicated in the following table, and did or will pay social security premiums throughout the employment period.

Final School Attended	Age When Started Working
Junior high school	17
High school	20
Junior college	22
College	24

2. The wage profile of the husband before and after the survey, up to his death, is given by equations from Iwamoto and Furuie (1995), which were obtained from cross-sectional regressions of the 1990 RADAR data.

3. The SR when the husband dies at age t is the average wage of the husband before his death multiplied by the factor determined by the firm size.

4. The couple will not have additional children after the RADAR survey.

5. The discount rate is $1/1.05$.

6. The indexation factor is 1.01 (1 percent annual growth).

Family Composition

RADAR asked questions on the number of dependent children and the family's life stage, but did not ask the ages of the children. In order to obtain the social security benefits flow for the surviving family members, I assume that the ages of the children are given by the following table.

Life Stage	Description	Age of the Eldest Child
3	First child is born.	3
4	First child is in elementary school.	9
5	First child is in junior high school.	14
6	First child is in high school.	17
7	First child is in college.	21
8	First child becomes independent.	25

The age difference between children is assumed to be two years. If the age of the youngest child becomes negative by this convention, then the age of the youngest is set to be zero and all ages are spaced evenly between the eldest and the youngest.

Life Insurance (L_p)

The following variables on life insurance are used to calculate the expected life insurance payment to surviving family members. Note that survey questions regarding the types of insurance held by the household differ in 1990 and 1994.

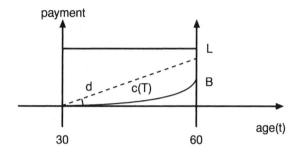

L   : death payment
B   : reimbursement at maturity
C(t)   : cancellation value
d   : premium payment

Fig. 3A.2   Life insurance

1990

1. Husband's death insurance payment (LI_H), and the amount of reimbursement at maturity (LI_B).
2. Types of insurance purchased by the household. Dummies for:
    a. term insurance (D_TI);
    b. insurance with maturity and reimbursement (D_MR);
    c. insurance with maturity (D_M);
    d. whole life–type insurance (D_WL).

1994

1. Husband's death insurance payment (LI_H), and the amount of reimbursement at maturity (LI_HB).
2. Types of insurance which cover husband. Dummies for:
    a. term insurance (D_TI);
    b. whole life–type insurance (D_H_WL);
    c. saving-type insurance (D_H_SV).

As mentioned earlier, life insurance has two functions: pure term and savings (see fig. 3A.2). To measure the amount of bequest from life insurance, I look at the expected discounted value of life insurance payment, net of saving. This approach makes it possible to compare benefits from public life insurance and private life insurance.

The expected life insurance payment to surviving family members is calculated by the following formula:

$$\sum_{t=\text{H\_AGE}+1}^{80-\text{H\_AGE}} \rho^{t-\text{H\_AGE}} \times \text{Death Insurance Payment}$$

$$\times \text{Pr}(\text{Die at age } t \,|\, \text{Alive at age H\_AGE}),$$

where ρ is the discount factor, which is set to be 1/1.05. The conditional probability of death at age t given that the husband is alive at age H_AGE is calculated from the seventeenth Japanese mortality table, based on the 1990 population census. The summation is taken up to age eighty, because the conditional death rate is not available for age eighty and over.

The saving component of life insurance at time t is defined as reimbursement for canceling the contract at time t. I obtain the figures under the following assumptions:

1. Household purchased the contract at age thirty.
2. Premium is paid by annual (or monthly) installment.

Calculation of Personal Annuity (A_p)

The following variables relating to private annuity are available in RADAR.

1. Dummies for subscriber as husband or wife (multiple answer is possible).
2. The expected total annual annuity payment upon retirement.
3. Duration of receiving annuity. Dummies for
   a. whole life (D_PA_WL);
   b. over eleven years (D_PA11);
   c. six to ten years (D_PA6_11);
   d. five years or less (D_PA_5) (multiple answer is possible).

The typical personal annuity arrangement is in the following form (see fig. 3A.3): The contract holder pays a fixed annual installment, d, until age $T^* - 1$ (typically age fifty-nine or sixty-four). At age T^*, he starts receiving an annuity of A for TA years. If he dies before age T^*, his surviving family receives roughly the amount of total installments paid before his death. In the case of death during the annuity period, the heir will receive the remaining balance of the annuity payments during the guarantee period, G years. For example, if the husband dies at age t, $T^* < t < T^* + G$, the payment is roughly $A(T^* + G - t)$. There is no payment to his heir if the holder dies after age $T^* + G$. Also, if he cancels the contract before age T^*, reimbursement is paid according to the pre-specified schedule (see fig. 3A.3). In the case of cancellation after age T^*, the payment is the same as in the case of death.

Thus the personal annuity contract has three functions: personal annuity, life insurance, and saving (cancellation value). The total figure of personal annuity receipt of the household is in the questionnaire, but other information about husband's annuity, such as amount of coverage for the husband, age of the person when the contract was signed, (T_0), age when the person starts receiving the annuity (T^*), period of receipt (TA), or the guaranteed period (G), are not available.

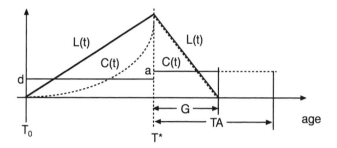

T_0	: Age at contract
T^*	: Age, start receiving annuity
G	: Guaranteed period
TA	: Annuity period
a	: annuity
d	:premium
L(t)	: Life insurance payment
C(t)	: cancellation value

Fig. 3A.3   Personal annuity life insurance

I construct the cancellation value, the discounted expected sum of annuity flow, and the life insurance under the following assumptions:

1. Personal annuity contract started when the husband was age thirty ($T_0 = 30$).
2. Premium is paid by annual (or monthly) installment.
3. Husband will start receiving annuity at age sixty ($T^* = 60$).
4. There are three types of personal annuity: ten-year guarantee/whole life ($G = 10$, $TA = \infty$); five-year fixed ($G = TA = 5$); and ten-year fixed ($G = TA = 10$).

References

Bernheim, B. D. 1991. How strong are bequest motives? Evidence based on estimates of the demand for life insurance and annuities. *Journal of Political Economy* 99:899–927.

Chuma, H. 1994. Intended bequest motives, savings and life insurance demand. In *Savings and bequests,* ed. T. Tachibanaki, 15–38. Ann Arbor: University of Michigan Press.

Horioka, C., N. Yokota, T. Miyaji, and N. Kasuga. 1996. Purposes of Japanese household saving. In *Saving and bequest: Inheritance in an aging society* (in Japanese), ed. N. Takayama, C. Horioka, and K. Ohta, 9–53. Tokyo: Nihon Hyōron Sha.

Hurd, M. D. 1989. Mortality risk and bequests. *Econometrica* 57:779–813.

Iwamoto, Y., and Y. Furvie. 1995. Demand for life insurance and bequest motive (in Japanese). *Yūsei Kenkyū Review* 6:59–60.

———. 1996. Role of survivor's annuity as a public life insurance (in Japanese). *Yūsei Kenkyū Review* 7:97–124.

Shimada, T. 1995. *Introduction to public pension* (in Japanese). Tokyo: Iwanami.

Social Insurance Agency. 1995a. *Guidebook of social insurance in Japan 1995.* Tokyo: Japan International Social Security Association.

———. 1995b. *Outline of social insurance in Japan.* Tokyo: Yoshida Finance and Social Security Law Institute.

4

An Empirical Investigation of Intergenerational Consumption Distribution
A Comparison among Japan, the United States, and the United Kingdom

Makoto Saito

4.1 Introduction

When evaluating economic growth, it is fundamentally important to recognize not only what constitutes rapid growth, but also how the results of that growth are distributed between generations. When an economy grows rapidly, public transfers from the young or middle-aged to the elderly often are justified on the grounds that the elderly devoted their youth to the growing economy and thus should be rewarded financially in their twilight years. For this reason, intergenerational transfer schemes have been implemented in most developed countries.

However, the implications of recent population aging and slow economic growth are causing concern in regard to the consequences of these intergenerational transfers. That is, there are serious questions about the validity of existing social welfare programs that tend to favor the elderly excessively. These social welfare programs will have their costs passed on to the younger generation, and this trend may continue for future generations. Such concerns are especially important in Japan, where the population is aging the most quickly among all industrial countries.

This paper empirically analyzes how the results of successful economic growth have been distributed among generations during the past thirty years in Japan, the United States, and the United Kingdom. These three countries provide a controlled experiment for evaluating the consequences of intergenerational transfers on the wealth distribution. In comparison with both Japan and the United States, the United Kingdom is relatively free from any negative effects of intergenerational transfer schemes, for the

Makoto Saito is professor of economics at Hitotsubashi University.

following reasons: First, no large-scale public pension system was implemented in the United Kingdom. The existing public pension system is therefore not as generous as those found in the other two countries, and is more a flat-rate scheme. Although an earnings-related element (the State Earnings-Related Pension Scheme) was introduced to the United Kingdom by the 1975 Social Security Pension Act, this was scaled down in the 1986 Social Security Act.[1]

Second, although there was a population increase immediately after World War II in the United Kingdom, it was not as great as the baby boom phenomenon experienced in Japan and the United States. A more even distribution of population alleviates some potential problems associated with intergenerational transfers. Finally, the United Kingdom has not experienced a major slowdown in economic growth for the past thirty years mainly because of its poor economic performance in the 1960s. Levels of social security benefits, which might have been determined initially under optimistic growth expectations, would be politically difficult to modify later. Therefore, serious economic slowdown indeed may cause financial problems under a pay-as-you-go pension system. Without a major slowdown in the economy, the United Kingdom has been free of such problems.

For these three reasons, the United Kingdom is less subject to the negative effects of intergenerational transfers than is either Japan or the United States. Hence, if there were any difference in the intergenerational wealth distribution between Japan and the United Kingdom or between the United States and the United Kingdom, it would be because of cross-country differences in the size and impact of public intergenerational transfer schemes.

The first half of this paper examines how the cross-sectional distribution of consumption goods between elderly and young consumers has evolved over time. Using age-classified consumption data, I find that in both Japan and the United States, the percentage of youth consumption has declined substantially on a per capita basis while elderly consumption has increased dramatically. By contrast, young consumers in the United Kingdom are receiving an increasingly greater percentage of consumption goods. As discussed above, the observed pattern of consumption distribution in both Japan and the United States suggests that resources are transferred publicly on a large scale from the young or middle-aged to elderly consumers.

In the second half of the paper, I present an analytical framework for evaluating quantitatively the evolution of the cross-age distribution of consumption goods (Saito 1997). The framework treats this evolution as if the observed cross-age distribution were along a general equilibrium path with spot markets as well as future markets. This method can be used to analyze

---

1. See Atkinson (1995) for a detailed discussion of the development of state pensions in the United Kingdom.

the change in the distribution of cross-age consumption patterns into two distinct effects: (a) the *age effect,* or the effect of the difference in the age consumption pattern (e.g., the middle-aged consume more than the elderly); and (b) the *cohort effect,* or the effect arising from differences in lifetime income among cohorts (e.g., the elderly currently receive higher lifetime income as a result of the implementation of welfare programs).

This framework allows for a theoretical interpretation of the observed evolution of the cross-age distribution of consumption goods and allows us to evaluate a lifetime income relative to resource availability on a cohort-by-cohort basis. Applying this method to the age-classified data, I find that the value of the lifetime income peaked for the cohort born between 1932 and 1936 in Japan and for the American cohort born between 1947 and 1951. In both countries, lifetime income has declined among younger cohorts. This deterioration in lifetime income is more serious in the United States than in Japan, however. By contrast, the value of lifetime income is higher for younger cohorts in the United Kingdom.

Since the real price per unit of consumption goods has decreased because of economic growth, a resulting decrease in the value of lifetime income does not necessarily imply a decline in the living standard. My calculation suggests, however, that without sound economic growth, the living standard of future generations may be unsustainable under existing welfare programs in the United States.

This paper is organized as follows: Section 4.2 describes how the cross-age distribution of consumption goods has evolved in Japan, the United States, and the United Kingdom. Section 4.3 presents an analytical framework for quantitatively evaluating the age-classified consumption data, and derives a set of empirical predictions. Section 4.4 applies this framework to the age-classified consumption data of Japan, the United States, and the United Kingdom. Section 4.5 concludes.

4.2   The Evolution of the Cross-Age Consumption Distribution

4.2.1   Data

In this section, I examine how the consumption goods generated by economic growth have been allocated among the different age groups, and then compare the evolution of the cross-age consumption distribution in the three countries. Research on consumption distribution is important, in that the level of consumption better indicates the level of economic welfare of a household than do such other variables as disposable income. In the next section, I give a rigorous theoretical interpretation to this evolution of the cross-age consumption distribution.

The data used in this research include household surveys summarized according to the age of the household head. This type of household data is considerably easier to obtain than household microdata; government agencies from many countries, including the three studied here, regularly publish summarized data sets. Using the successive years of the cross-age household survey data, I construct a consumption and expenditure cohort data set, with data indexed by both date of birth and age of household head.

The Japanese data come from the National Survey on Family Income and Expenditure (NSFIE). This survey has been conducted every five years since 1959, has collected data on more than 40,000 households, and is the most representative among Japanese government household surveys. I use the age-classified consumption and expenditure data taken from 1959 to 1994.[2] There are two categories of household in this survey: one headed by a worker (hereafter, workers' households); and another, including household heads who are self employed (hereafter, all households). Expenditure items are reported for both categories while income items are reported for the former only.

I use U.S. data from the Consumer Expenditure Survey (CES), which has been conducted annually since 1980, collecting between 5,700 and 8,300 observations. Other similar surveys were carried out in 1972–73 and 1960–61. I use the 1980–94 surveys as well as the 1972–73 versions of the CES.

The British data come from the Family Expenditure Survey (FES). This annual survey has been conducted since 1954 and collects information from approximately 7,000 households annually. I use the official British 1971–91 summarized versions of the FES for this research.

One conceptual problem with the above-mentioned summarized data sets is that consumption and income data are both measured at the household level. In other words, the data indexed by the age of the household head include the consumption of other household members of different ages. To overcome this problem, household expenditures must be allocated to individual household members (Gokhale, Kotlikoff, and Sabelhaus 1996). Another solution would be to control for the effect of household consumption attributable to multiple members of the household by using an adult equivalence scale (Deaton and Paxson 1994). Both research methods require detailed information about the household composition, which is available only from microdata. The data sets I use do not provide such detailed information. This is particularly the case with the NSFIE summarized tables, where only the size of the household is recorded. For this reason, I use per-member consumption indexed by the age of the household head as a first approximation.

Another concern is that total consumption may include medical and

2. The 1969 survey report does not include the age-classified consumption and expenditure data.

educational expenditures, the age consumption patterns of which have changed dramatically over the past three decades. Therefore, I report the results based not only on total consumption, but also on food/clothes consumption patterns, which have not changed substantially.

4.2.2   The Cross-Age Consumption Distribution

Tables 4.1–4.4 show annual relative consumption patterns. In all these tables, the consumption of the young and the elderly is compared with that of the middle-aged (which includes those aged forty). These tables illustrate the evolution of the cross-age consumption distribution, thus indicating whether consumption has increased or decreased within an age group.

Table 4.1 shows that elderly consumption among Japanese workers' households has increased considerably compared to middle-aged consumption. For example, the ratio of total consumption for those aged fifty to fifty-four increased from 1.18 in 1959 to 1.51 in 1994. This pattern is also observed in food and clothes consumption. Further, relative food consumption by youth has decreased more than the relative food consumption by the middle-aged; the ratio for those aged twenty-five to twenty-nine declined from 1.03 in 1959 to 0.88 in 1994. Even if the self-employed are included in the household category, these cross-age patterns do not change substantially (table 4.2).

Table 4.3 illustrates the cross-age consumption distribution in the United States. Youth consumption here has increased more slowly for both the total and the food/clothes categories. For example, the ratio of total consumption for those aged twenty-five to thirty-four decreased from 1.16 in 1972–73 to 0.93 in 1994. Consumption by the elderly, especially for those in their late sixties and seventies, has increased considerably since 1980. This observation from household data is similar to the findings of Gokhale, Kotlikoff, and Sabelhaus (1996) drawn from individual consumption data.

Table 4.4 illustrates the evolution of the consumption distribution in the United Kingdom. The relative ratio of youth total consumption has been stable since the early 1970s. For those aged fifty to sixty-four, on the other hand, consumption grew at a slower rate in total and for food/clothes; for total consumption, the ratio declined from 1.38 in 1971 to 1.26 in 1991.

These tables illustrate a striking contrast between Japan and the United Kingdom and between the United States and the United Kingdom. In both Japan and the United States, the results of economic growth have been distributed more to the elderly and less to the youth on a per capita consumption basis. In the United Kingdom, the fruits of economic growth have been distributed more to the young or middle-aged populations.

As discussed in the introduction, the cause of this striking difference may lie in the extent to which implementation of social security schemes has affected intergenerational wealth distribution. That is, economic

Table 4.1 Relative Per-Member Consumption in Workers' Households in Japan

	-24	25-29	30-34	35-39	40-44	45-49	50-54	55-59	60-64	65-; 65-69	70-; 70-74	75-
A. Total Consumption												
1959	0.95	1.09	0.99	0.99	1.00	1.07	1.18	1.15	1.18	1.04		
1964	1.05	1.08	0.98	0.98	1.00	1.11	1.23	1.22	1.11	1.21		
1974	1.13	1.06	0.95	0.93	1.00	1.17	1.28	1.28	1.20	1.08		
1979	1.13	1.06	0.94	0.93	1.00	1.22	1.45	1.42	1.34	1.30		
1984	1.11	1.09	0.93	0.93	1.00	1.20	1.46	1.53	1.48	1.42	1.38	1.57
1989	1.12	1.07	0.97	0.91	1.00	1.25	1.48	1.56	1.49	1.44	1.51	1.23
1994	1.02	1.11	1.01	0.94	1.00	1.27	1.51	1.60	1.56	1.58	1.49	
B. Food Consumption												
1959	1.01	1.03	0.98	0.99	1.00	1.01	1.07	1.07	1.13	1.04		
1964	0.98	1.03	0.98	0.99	1.00	1.03	1.07	1.07	1.06	1.14		
1974	1.05	0.99	0.93	0.95	1.00	1.05	1.07	1.08	1.06	1.09		
1979	0.95	0.95	0.89	0.94	1.00	1.07	1.11	1.10	1.15	1.13		
1984	0.92	0.91	0.86	0.91	1.00	1.05	1.09	1.12	1.13	1.18	1.21	1.15
1989	0.85	0.86	0.86	0.90	1.00	1.07	1.12	1.18	1.22	1.24	1.34	1.25
1994	0.81	0.88	0.87	0.91	1.00	1.09	1.17	1.23	1.30	1.39	1.37	
C. Clothes Consumption												
1959	0.91	1.13	1.02	1.02	1.00	1.09	1.42	1.17	1.22	1.14		
1964	1.07	1.06	1.01	0.99	1.00	1.18	1.33	1.29	1.02	1.07		
1974	1.09	1.01	0.87	0.89	1.00	1.24	1.36	1.27	1.15	0.90		
1979	1.26	1.01	0.90	0.89	1.00	1.31	1.56	1.58	1.50	1.24		
1984	1.22	1.10	0.90	0.89	1.00	1.22	1.57	1.73	1.53	1.66	1.65	1.40
1989	1.09	1.04	0.98	0.89	1.00	1.20	1.42	1.67	1.47	1.42	1.36	1.19
1994	0.92	1.09	1.01	0.97	1.00	1.21	1.49	1.62	1.61	1.59	1.42	

Source: National Survey on Family Income and Expenditure (1959–94).

Table 4.2   Relative Per-Member Consumption in All Households in Japan

	−24	25–29	30–34	35–39	40–44	45–49	50–54	55–59	60–64	65–; 65–69	70–; 70–74	75–
					A. Total Consumption							
1964	1.01	1.04	0.96	0.96	1.00	1.08	1.13	1.11	1.03	1.01		
1974	1.15	1.05	0.94	0.92	1.00	1.16	1.20	1.18	1.07	0.93		
1979	1.13	1.05	0.93	0.92	1.00	1.20	1.40	1.33	1.21	1.10		
1984	1.14	1.09	0.94	0.92	1.00	1.18	1.35	1.34	1.24	1.13	1.08	1.03
1989	1.13	1.08	0.97	0.91	1.00	1.24	1.43	1.44	1.32	1.24	1.18	1.13
1994	1.01	1.11	1.00	0.93	1.00	1.25	1.46	1.51	1.42	1.36	1.32	1.21
					B. Food Consumption							
1964	0.96	1.01	0.97	0.98	1.00	1.02	1.03	1.02	1.03	1.00		
1974	1.04	0.98	0.93	0.94	1.00	1.04	1.04	1.06	1.02	0.98		
1979	0.94	0.92	0.88	0.93	1.00	1.06	1.09	1.09	1.07	1.03		
1984	0.93	0.91	0.87	0.91	1.00	1.04	1.05	1.01	1.00	1.00	0.50	0.96
1989	0.86	0.87	0.86	0.90	1.00	1.07	1.10	1.14	1.13	1.10	1.09	1.05
1994	0.80	0.87	0.87	0.90	1.00	1.09	1.16	1.20	1.23	1.25	1.24	1.19
					C. Clothes Consumption							
1964	1.01	0.97	0.94	0.95	1.00	1.09	1.15	1.13	0.99	0.88		
1974	1.09	0.97	0.86	0.87	1.00	1.20	1.24	1.20	1.02	0.82		
1979	1.16	0.95	0.87	0.89	1.00	1.30	1.51	1.51	1.29	1.02		
1984	1.23	1.07	0.88	0.88	1.00	1.20	1.46	1.43	1.27	1.16	0.98	0.89
1989	1.08	1.02	0.98	0.89	1.00	1.22	1.45	1.55	1.24	1.15	1.06	1.05
1994	0.90	1.08	0.99	0.97	1.00	1.23	1.47	1.55	1.51	1.32	1.16	0.92

Source: National Survey on Family Income and Expenditure (1959–94).

Table 4.3 **Relative Per-Member Consumption in U.S. Households**

	−24	25–34	35–44	45–54	55–64	65–	65–74	75
			A. Total Consumption					
1972–73	1.45	1.16	1.00	1.23	1.40	1.17		
1980–81	1.06	1.10	1.00	1.16	1.25	1.09		
1982–83	0.93	1.03	1.00	1.11	1.17	1.05		
1984	0.90	0.96	1.00	1.12	1.13	0.95	1.00	0.8
1985	0.88	0.99	1.00	1.15	1.19	1.00	1.03	0.9
1986	0.86	0.93	1.00	1.21	1.13	0.93	1.00	0.8
1987	0.86	0.93	1.00	1.18	1.21	1.00	1.07	0.8
1988	0.91	0.92	1.00	1.14	1.17	0.96	1.00	0.8
1989	0.85	0.92	1.00	1.11	1.15	0.98	1.03	0.9
1990	0.85	0.93	1.00	1.18	1.18	1.01	1.02	0.9
1991	0.84	0.95	1.00	1.15	1.26	1.05	1.08	0.9
1992	0.78	0.91	1.00	1.15	1.14	1.04	1.09	0.9
1993	0.81	0.90	1.00	1.29	1.26	1.11	1.10	1.0
1994	0.78	0.93	1.00	1.26	1.30	1.13	1.19	1.1
			B. Food Consumption					
1972–73	1.13	1.02	1.00	1.16	1.28	1.22		
1980–81	1.00	1.00	1.00	1.16	1.26	1.17		
1982–83	0.88	0.94	1.00	1.13	1.20	1.16		
1984	0.92	0.88	1.00	1.11	1.10	1.00	1.07	0.8
1985	0.92	0.96	1.00	1.15	1.18	1.04	1.07	0.9
1986	0.90	0.90	1.00	1.21	1.10	0.98	1.03	0.9
1987	0.90	0.93	1.00	1.17	1.24	1.10	1.15	1.0
1988	0.97	0.93	1.00	1.18	1.28	1.02	1.07	0.9
1989	0.88	0.91	1.00	1.13	1.21	1.02	1.06	0.9
1990	0.94	0.90	1.00	1.16	1.18	1.06	1.07	0.9
1991	0.86	0.93	1.00	1.06	1.12	1.11	1.11	1.0
1992	0.85	0.92	1.00	1.15	1.11	1.15	1.24	1.0
1993	0.85	0.92	1.00	1.21	1.24	1.18	1.18	1.1
1994	0.83	0.89	1.00	1.20	1.23	1.14	1.17	1.1
			C. Clothes Consumption					
1972–73	1.13	1.02	1.00	1.17	1.16	0.75		
1980–81	1.05	0.99	1.00	1.05	1.03	0.69		
1982–83	1.06	0.97	1.00	1.05	1.01	0.74		
1984	0.94	0.88	1.00	0.94	0.96	0.71	0.84	0.48
1985	0.89	0.87	1.00	1.07	1.13	0.79	0.93	0.54
1986	0.83	0.91	1.00	1.16	1.00	0.63	0.71	0.51
1987	0.84	0.87	1.00	1.14	1.03	0.81	0.92	0.62
1988	0.95	0.88	1.00	1.19	1.01	0.69	0.80	0.49
1989	0.97	0.88	1.00	1.03	1.06	0.77	0.92	0.55
1990	0.82	0.80	1.00	1.07	0.97	0.64	0.73	0.44
1991	0.94	0.86	1.00	1.05	0.99	0.83	0.94	0.60
1992	0.97	0.95	1.00	1.16	0.98	0.75	0.82	0.64
1993	1.00	1.00	1.00	1.25	1.17	0.88	0.98	0.68
1994	0.86	0.97	1.00	1.26	1.12	0.80	0.91	0.66

Source: Consumer Expenditure Survey (1972–73, 1980–94).

Table 4.4 Relative Per-Member Consumption in U.K. Households

	−29	30–49	50–64	65–	65–74	75–
			A. Total Consumption			
1971	1.03	1.00	1.38	1.05		
1972	1.06	1.00	1.36	1.04		
1973	1.09	1.00	1.35	1.00		
1974	1.07	1.00	1.35	1.03		
1975	1.05	1.00	1.33	1.02		
1976	1.04	1.00	1.35	1.04		
1977	1.06	1.00	1.25	1.02		
1978	1.08	1.00	1.28	1.02		
1979	1.08	1.00	1.28	0.95		
1980	1.04	1.00	1.34	1.01		
1981	1.03	1.00	1.30	1.01		
1982	1.00	1.00	1.30	0.96		
1983	0.97	1.00	1.30	1.04		
1984	1.01	1.00	1.34		1.06	0.94
1985	0.97	1.00	1.29		1.05	0.90
1986	0.99	1.00	1.22		1.05	0.89
1987	0.97	1.00	1.23		1.05	0.88
1988	1.06	1.00	1.26		1.05	0.90
1989	0.97	1.00	1.27		1.08	0.86
1990	1.06	1.00	1.26		1.06	0.86
1991	0.99	1.00	1.26		1.06	0.90
			B. Food Consumption			
1971	0.93	1.00	1.31	1.10		
1972	0.98	1.00	1.30	1.12		
1973	0.97	1.00	1.29	1.11		
1974	0.98	1.00	1.30	1.12		
1975	0.97	1.00	1.27	1.11		
1976	1.00	1.00	1.31	1.15		
1977	0.98	1.00	1.26	1.15		
1978	1.00	1.00	1.28	1.12		
1979	0.98	1.00	1.26	1.11		
1980	0.98	1.00	1.26	1.08		
1981	0.98	1.00	1.25	1.11		
1982	.96	1.00	1.26	1.13		
1983	0.92	1.00	1.23	1.11		
1984	0.94	1.00	1.25		1.14	1.06
1985	0.95	1.00	1.24		1.13	1.06
1986	0.94	1.00	1.22		1.14	1.00
1987	0.96	1.00	1.21		1.11	1.00
1988	0.99	1.00	1.20		1.12	0.97
1989	0.92	1.00	1.21		1.08	0.97
1990	0.94	1.00	1.21		1.09	0.96
1991	0.94	1.00	1.23		1.08	0.97
			C. Clothes Consumption			
1971	0.93	1.00	1.31	0.82		
1972	0.99	1.00	1.31	0.80		

(continued)

Table 4.4   (continued)

	−29	30–49	50–64	65–	65–74	75
1973	0.97	1.00	1.19	0.71		
1974	1.02	1.00	1.27	0.81		
1975	0.98	1.00	1.28	0.80		
1976	0.93	1.00	1.27	0.70		
1977	0.96	1.00	1.14	0.72		
1978	0.98	1.00	1.25	0.73		
1979	1.00	1.00	1.21	0.68		
1980	0.98	1.00	1.26	0.71		
1981	0.99	1.00	1.25	0.72		
1982	0.91	1.00	1.11	0.73		
1983	0.96	1.00	1.17	0.70		
1984	1.10	1.00	1.12		0.76	0.6
1985	0.96	1.00	1.08		0.72	0.5
1986	1.05	1.00	1.14		0.79	0.5
1987	0.97	1.00	1.05		0.74	0.4
1988	1.02	1.00	1.07		0.72	0.4
1989	0.95	1.00	1.11		0.72	0.5
1990	1.01	1.00	1.02		0.75	0.4
1991	0.97	1.00	1.09		0.76	0.4

Source: Family Expenditure Survey (1971–91).

resources are transferred from the young or middle-aged to the elderly in countries such as Japan and the United States, where large-scale public pension schemes have been established. The next section provides an analytical framework for interpreting the described evolution of the cross-age consumption distribution and for quantifying the differences in lifetime income among cohorts.

4.2.3   The Cross-Age Distribution of Labor Income

The simplest interpretation of the above evolution of consumption distribution is that relative consumption simply reflects relative labor income among age groups when consumers are myopic or liquidity-constrained. Any parallel movement between the consumption and income distributions is a necessary condition for this view. Before concluding this section, I explore the validity of this assertion by examining the cross-age distribution of labor income.

Tables 4.5–4.7 illustrate the movement of relative labor income per household member in Japan, the United States, and the United Kingdom. For Japan, I can report only on workers' households, as in table 4.5, because there is no income item that is common to all households. The pattern of labor-income distribution broadly follows the consumption distribution; the relative ratio of those in their fifties has increased in terms of both labor income and consumption.

Table 4.5   Relative Per-Member Labor Income in Workers' Households in Japan

	-24	25-29	30-34	35-39	40-44	45-49	50-54	55-59	60-64	65-; 65-69	70-; 70-74	75-
1959	0.80	1.07	0.99	0.99	1.00	1.08	1.25	1.15	1.15	1.09		
1964	0.87	1.03	0.96	0.98	1.00	1.11	1.26	1.22	1.04	1.22		
1974	1.04	1.00	0.92	0.91	1.00	1.18	1.32	1.27	1.10	0.99		
1979	1.00	1.00	0.90	0.92	1.00	1.19	1.45	1.46	1.19	1.10		
1984	1.00	1.00	0.89	0.91	1.00	1.17	1.43	1.48	1.16	1.06	1.02	1.08
1989	0.94	0.98	0.92	0.91	1.00	1.19	1.47	1.60	1.20	0.98	1.23	0.95
1994	0.92	1.07	0.98	0.94	1.00	1.20	1.54	1.69	1.27	1.02	1.01	

Source: National Survey on Family Income and Expenditure (1959–94).

Table 4.6   Relative Per-Member Labor Income in U.S. Households

	−24	25–34	35–44	45–54	55–64	65–	65–74	75
1972–73	1.18	1.14	1.00	1.27	1.36	0.32		
1980–81	0.92	1.13	1.00	1.17	1.14	0.23		
1982–83	0.74	1.06	1.00	1.10	0.95	0.20		
1984	0.75	0.97	1.00	1.01	0.86	0.20	0.27	0.
1985	0.68	1.01	1.00	1.10	0.95	0.22	0.29	0.
1986	0.69	0.96	1.00	1.16	0.98	0.20	0.27	0.
1987	0.66	0.99	1.00	1.18	1.05	0.20	0.26	0.
1988	0.72	0.06	1.00	1.21	1.01	0.22	0.30	0.
1989	0.68	0.95	1.00	1.08	0.98	0.19	0.28	0.
1990	0.63	0.96	1.00	1.18	0.98	0.19	0.27	0.
1991	0.61	0.99	1.00	1.21	1.09	0.21	0.29	0.
1992	0.59	0.91	1.00	1.17	0.94	0.21	0.29	0.
1993	0.62	0.88	1.00	1.25	0.97	0.21	0.28	0.
1994	0.54	0.87	1.00	1.19	1.08	0.19	0.25	0.

Source: Consumer Expenditure Survey (1972–73, 1980–94).

However, the income and consumption distributions have evolved differently in the United States (table 4.6) and the United Kingdom (table 4.7). In the United States, the ratio for those in their twenties has declined much faster for labor income than for consumption; the opposite is true for those in their fifties, with a faster increase in their consumption than in their labor income. In the United Kingdom, the ratio for those in their twenties has been stable for consumption but has shown a substantial increase for labor income.

Given these observations, one might say that households are subject to liquidity constraints or behave myopically in Japan. However, the parallel movement is a necessary condition, and therefore is not sufficient evidence for any liquidity constraints. When both labor income and consumption include common permanent shocks or are influenced by common fixed effects, both move together even in the absence of liquidity constraints. One cannot reach any definite conclusion without applying theoretical models to these data sets. In the next section, after presenting theoretical framework, I will reexamine this issue.

4.3   Analytical Framework

4.3.1   Simple Model with Cohort Structure

Extending my earlier work (Saito 1997), this section presents an analytical framework for assessing the evolution of the consumption distribution among different age groups. Let us assume that there are both spot and future markets in which the future delivery of goods on a certain date is

Table 4.7   **Relative Per-Member Labor Income in U.K. Households**

	-29	30–49	50–64	65–	65–74	75–
1971	1.04	1.00	1.35	0.34		
1972	1.11	1.00	1.30	0.32		
1973	1.08	1.00	1.37	0.29		
1974	1.12	1.00	1.38	0.32		
1975	1.12	1.00	1.29	0.28		
1976	1.11	1.00	1.33	0.24		
1977	1.14	1.00	1.32	0.25		
1978	1.15	1.00	1.28	0.23		
1979	1.09	1.00	1.29	0.22		
1980	1.38	1.00	1.43	0.56		
1981	1.49	1.00	1.40	0.48		
1982	1.45	1.00	1.40	0.45		
1983	1.34	1.00	1.32	0.44		
1984	1.42	1.00	1.34		0.44	0.32
1985	1.35	1.00	1.25		0.38	0.37
1986	1.46	1.00	1.27		0.37	0.36
1987	1.42	1.00	1.22		0.39	0.23
1988	1.46	1.00	1.20		0.39	0.29
1989	1.37	1.00	1.25		0.35	0.25
1990	1.41	1.00	1.19		0.40	0.27
1991	1.45	1.00	1.13		0.36	0.23

Source: Family Expenditure Survey (1971–91).

contracted. A claim for a unit of time t goods is traded at the price $p(t)$. The price of time 0 goods is the numeraire. It is assumed that a set of prices is determined by a certain resource allocation mechanism.[3]

Given the above market structure, a cohort born at time i solves the following maximization problem:

$$(1) \qquad \max \sum_{j=1}^{J} \mu_j \frac{c_i(i + j)^{1-1/\varepsilon}}{1 - \dfrac{1}{\varepsilon}}$$

subject to

$$\sum_{j=1}^{J} p(i + j)[e_i(i + j) + d_i(i + j) - c_i(i + j)] = 0,$$

3. When all agents participate in markets at the specified time 0, competitive markets where all agents take prices as given can determine a set of prices of contingent claims. Since new cohorts enter markets later in this economy, competitive markets may not be an appropriate device for determining prices of contingent claims. In order for prices to be determined at time 0, this economy may require some institutions, such as banks and insurance companies, to form rational expectations and to exploit arbitrage opportunities.

where ε is the elasticity of intertemporal substitution, and μ_j is a weight on period utility of age j ($j = 1,2, \ldots J$).[4] These parameters are common among cohorts. $c_i(t)$, $e_i(t)$, and $d_i(t)$ are the cohort i's consumption, exogenous income, and transfer from different cohorts at time t. λ_i denotes the Lagrange multiplier on the cohort i's lifetime budget constraint. The first-order condition with respect to the consumption goods at age j by cohort i is

(2) $$\mu_j c_i(i + j)^{-1/\varepsilon} = \lambda_i p(i + j).$$

Taking the logarithm from both sides, we obtain

(3) $$\ln c_i(i + j) = \varepsilon[\ln\mu_j - \ln\lambda_i - \ln p(i + j)].$$

Equation (3) implies that consumption at age j by cohort i can be divided into three factors: age-specific, cohort-specific, and time-specific. Each factor on the right-hand side of equation (3) is intuitively understandable. First, the higher the age-specific weight μ_j, the more consumption increases. Second, the lifetime income of cohort i is a decreasing function in the Lagrange multiplier λ_i (the marginal utility with respect to lifetime income), and the consumption of cohort i consequently decreases in λ_i due to lower lifetime income. Third, the price of a unit of time $i + j$ goods $p(i + j)$ represents the degree of resource scarcity. As fewer goods are provided at time $i + k$, $p(i + j)$ increases, and consumption decreases. In other words, the third effect represents an aggregate supply factor or a macroeconomic effect.

4.3.2   Empirical Implication

By using equation (3), I give a theoretical interpretation to the cross-sectional consumption distribution among the age groups, which was examined in the previous section. Let us now examine the difference in log-consumption at time $i + j$ between the two cohorts, such that $i + j = i' + j'$.

(4) $$\ln\frac{c_i(i + j)}{c_{i'}(i' + j')} = \varepsilon\left(\ln\frac{\mu_j}{\mu_{j'}} - \ln\frac{\lambda_i}{\lambda_{i'}}\right)$$

Equation (4) implies that relative consumption is the result of two effects: the difference in the age weight, and the difference in the Lagrange multiplier. Hereafter, the former is termed the *age effect* and the latter the *cohort effect*. Equation (4) can also be written as

4. In this model, we treat each cohort as a representative agent, and abstract the issue of the within-cohort consumption distribution. Deaton and Paxson (1994) address this issue using U.S. and U.K. microdata while Ohtake and Saito (1998) replicate the issue using Japanese microdata.

$$(5) \quad \ln \frac{c_i(i + j)}{c_{i'}(i' + j')} = \sum_{m=1}^{J} \alpha_m \text{age dummy}_m + \sum_{n=1}^{I} \beta_n \text{cohort dummy}_n,$$

where age dummy$_j$ is $+1$, age dummy$_{j'}$ is -1, and the other age dummies are zero. In contrast, cohort dummy$_i$ is -1, cohort dummy$_{i'}$ is $+1$, and the other cohort dummies are zero. α_j corresponds to $\varepsilon \ln \mu_j$ while β_i corresponds to $\varepsilon \ln \lambda_i$. One major advantage of equation (5) as an empirical specification is that the right-hand side includes only fixed effects—that is, the year of birth and age, both of which are outside the control of each cohort.

4.3.3   The Altruistic Motive versus the Life Cycle Hypothesis

Equation (5) provides a hypothesis that tests the altruistic motive against the life-cycle hypothesis. If cohorts are linked through the altruistic motive, á la Barro (1974), and the lifetime utility of all cohorts is weighted equally within a dynasty, then all cohorts are subject to the same budget constraint. Thus, the Lagrange multiplier has an identical value across all cohorts. That is,

$$\lambda_i = \lambda_{i'} \quad \forall \ i, \ i'$$

must hold when cohorts are linked altruistically.

The cross-cohort difference in the Lagrange multiplier λ_i, on the other hand, implies that lifetime income differs among cohorts. At the optimal level of consumption, we obtain

$$\lambda_i^{\varepsilon} = \frac{1}{w_i} \sum_{j=1}^{J} [\mu_j^{\varepsilon} p(i + j)^{1-\varepsilon}],$$

where w_i is the value of the cohort i's lifetime income evaluated at the real price of goods, or where

$$w_i = \sum_{j=1}^{J} p(i + j)[e_i(i + j) + d_i(i + j)].$$

When the elasticity of intertemporal substitution is close to one, the effect of market prices on λ_i is represented solely by w_i. The difference in $\varepsilon \ln \lambda_i$ between two cohorts can be, accordingly, approximated by the difference in the logarithmic lifetime income. In other words,

$$(6) \quad \varepsilon \ln \frac{\lambda_i}{\lambda_{i'}} \approx -\ln \frac{w_i}{w_{i'}},$$

when ε is close to one. Thus, the relative differences in lifetime incomes are inferable from the estimated coefficient on the cohort effect of equation (5) under the assumption of a unit elasticity of intertemporal substitution.[5]

4.3.4   The Sustainability of the Living Standard

This subsection emphasizes that the value of cohort i's lifetime income can be inferred from λ_i and can be evaluated in terms of the real price of goods. In other words, an evaluation of lifetime income of any cohort group takes into consideration resource scarcity and then measures this lifetime income level relative to the resource availability. In most cases, this feature embodied in λ_i itself is economically relevant when comparing welfare levels among cohorts. Without considering resource abundance (scarcity), it is obvious that younger cohorts enjoy more consumption goods in a growing economy.

Comparing the absolute level of consumption, or the living standard, among cohorts may also be important in the current context. In particular, whether the living standard of the youth and their future generations will be sustained is becoming increasingly important. To compare, the Lagrange multiplier λ_i, or the value of lifetime income w_i, must be converted into the absolute level of consumption, or the living-standard term.

It should be observed that higher λ_i or lower w_i does not necessarily imply that the living standard of cohort i deteriorates, because the real price of goods declines as a result of economic growth. Thus, consumption levels may be even greater when λ_i is higher or w_i is lower. Suppose that the real price of goods is determined according to the marginal period utility of a representative agent, or

$$(7) \qquad\qquad p(t) = C(t)^{-1/\varepsilon},$$

where $C(t)$ is an aggregate level of consumption at time t.[6] Substituting equation (7) to equation (3), we obtain the following result:

$$\ln c_i(t) = \varepsilon \ln \mu_j - \varepsilon \ln \lambda_i + \ln C(t).$$

---

5. My approach is related to Mace (1991), Cochrane (1991), Altug and Miller (1990), and Hayashi, Altonji, and Kotlikoff (1996) in the sense that all of them have empirically tested theoretical restrictions imposed on the marginal utility in a complete market setup. These empirical models differ, however, from my empirical specification because they cancel the Lagrange multiplier by taking a first difference of individual consumption instead of estimating the multiplier. My main goal in this paper is to estimate the Lagrange multiplier cohort by cohort.

6. More precisely, when the same technique used in the aggregation theorem (Rubinstein 1974) is applied, the real price at time t is determined by $p(t) = C(t)^{-1/\varepsilon} \{\Sigma_{j=1}^{J}[s_j(t)\lambda_{t-j}^{-\varepsilon}\mu_j^{\varepsilon}]\}^{1/\varepsilon}$, where $s_j(t)$ is the population share of cohort j at time t. On the right-hand side, the first term $C(t)^{-1/\varepsilon}$ represents the aggregate supply effect while the terms in the brackets correspond to the aggregate demand effect. I abstract the latter in characterizing the real price $p(t)$ by equation (7).

By abstracting the age effect, and denoting the cohort i's average consumption (living standard) by c_i and the average aggregate consumption level realized when cohort i is alive by C_i, we can derive any difference in the living standard between the two cohorts

(8) $\ln c_i - \ln c_{i'} = -\varepsilon(\ln\lambda_i - \ln\lambda_{i'}) + (\ln C_i - \ln C_{i'})$.

According to equation (8), $\lambda_i > \lambda_{i'}$ or $w_i < w_{i'}$ does not necessarily imply $c_i < c_{i'}$ when an economy grows fast or $C_i >> C_{i'}$.

4.3.5   Examples

This subsection presents several examples to explain the implication of equation (4) intuitively. Throughout this subsection, I assume that each cohort lives for three periods—young, middle-aged, and old—and that one household enters the economy at each period.

As discussed above, the difference in logarithmic consumption between any two cohorts at a given point in time is free of any macroeconomic effect. To illustrate this independence, I must compare figure 4.1 and figure 4.2. The former shows that in a time of economic boom the level of consumption for all generations increases simultaneously at time 3. The latter shows that a recession decreases the level of consumption. The relative logarithmic consumption among three generations at time 3 does not differ between the two cases, however.

I then examine the case where the altruistic motive is compared with the life cycle hypothesis. For the sake of simplicity, it is assumed that neither the age effect nor the business cycle effect is present. When lifetime income is distributed equally over the generations as a result of the altruistic motive, the consumption profile is identical among all generations (see fig. 4.3). In this case, the ratio of log-consumption for each age group

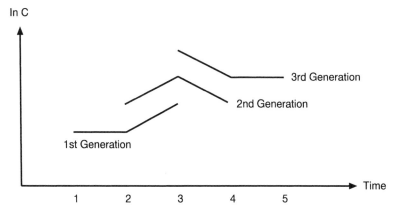

Fig. 4.1   Effects of business cycles in the case of a boom

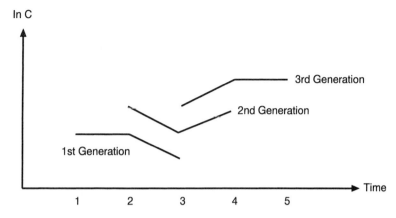

Fig. 4.2   Effects of business cycles in the case of a recession

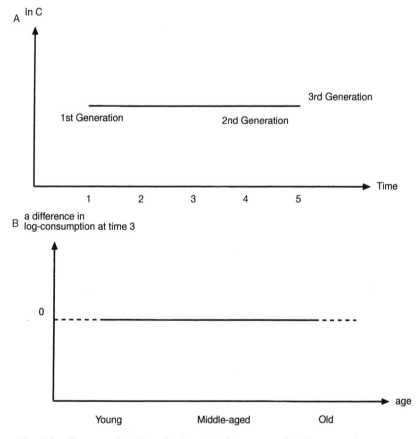

Fig. 4.3   The case of perfect altruism; (*A*), intergenerational consumption pattern, and (*B*), relative logarithmic consumption profile

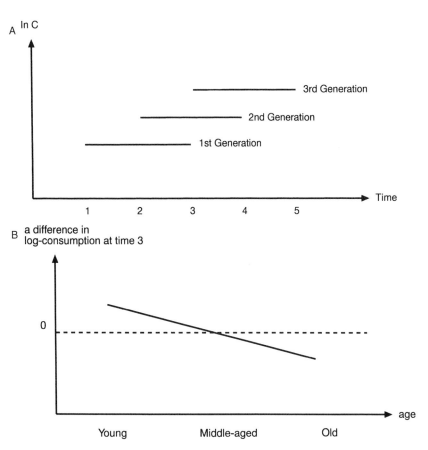

Fig. 4.4   The case of increasing welfare; (*A*), intergenerational consumption pattern, and (*B*), relative logarithmic consumption profile

relative to that of the middle-aged group is completely flat. On the other hand, when lifetime income increases for youth, the ratio is downward sloping (see fig. 4.4). Similarly, when lifetime income decreases for youth, the same ratio shows an upward trend (see fig. 4.5).

This suggests that cohort effects are identifiable from the evolution of the cross-age distribution of log-consumption. By using the consumption data—for example, as represented by figure 4.6—the above-defined ratio is downward sloping at the beginning of the sample period; it is almost flat in the middle; and finally, it tends to slope upward as time runs out. Thus, the difference in lifetime income among generations is inferable from the evolution of the cross-age consumption distribution.

Contrarily, if we find time-invariant patterns in the cross-age consumption distribution, we can infer that the cohort effect is absent and that only

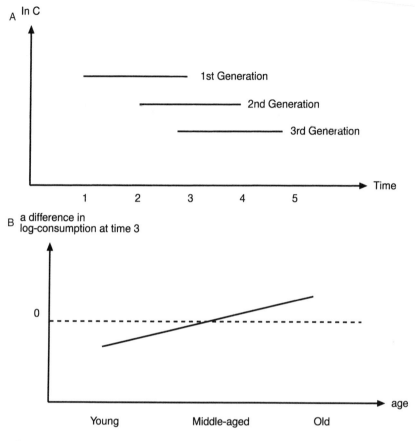

Fig. 4.5 The case of declining welfare; (*A*), intergenerational consumption pattern, and (*B*), relative logarithmic consumption profile

the age effect is significant. In summary, the cohort effect can be identified by the time-varying nature of the cross-age consumption distribution, while the age effect can be identified by the time-invariant nature.

4.3.5   Effects of Liquidity Constraints

So far I have maintained that each cohort can trade at both spot and future markets without any constraints. This subsection explores the possibility that cohorts may be subject to liquidity constraints. That is, agents may fail to smooth consumption because of liquidity constraints.

When liquidity constraints are binding on some cohorts, unlike those in equation (5), then the relative log-consumption between two cohorts depends not only on fixed effects (both the age and cohort effects) but also on current liquidity positions. One way to examine the extent of liquidity

log-consumption

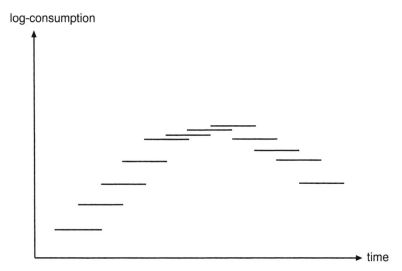

Fig. 4.6   The evolution of cross-age consumption profiles

constraints is to add the relative logarithmic labor income (endowment), or the equation

$$\ln \frac{e_i(i + j)}{e_{i'}(i' + j')}$$

to the right-hand side of equation (5). The explanatory power of this additional term may suggest that liquidity restraints are binding on some cohorts.

4.4   Estimation Results

4.4.1   The Comparison of Cohort Effects

In this section, I apply the empirical specification (equation [5]) to the cross-age consumption distributions of Japan, the United States, and the United Kingdom. These were all examined in depth in section 4.2. The goal of this section is to quantify the cross-cohort differences in lifetime income for these countries. In particular, I am interested in whether the lifetime incomes of the current youth have declined in comparison with the lifetime incomes received by the current elderly generation.

As in section 4.2, age bands were chosen as points of reference for each age group in formulating the relative log-consumption ratio. To avoid any linear dependence of age dummies, I excluded the age dummy group that included individuals aged forty. The cohort dummy is formulated according to the following year bands: those born before 1907, those born during the years 1907–11, 1912–16, 1917–21, 1922–26, 1927–31, 1932–36, 1937–41, 1942–46, 1947–51, 1952–56, 1957–61, 1962–66, and finally, those born after 1966. Similarly, I exclude cohorts born between 1942 and 1946 in order to remove any linear dependence on cohort dummies.

Accordingly, the estimated α_j of equation (5) implies the ratio of the age-specific weight on period utility relative to that of the age band including the age forty, while the estimated β_i is the ratio of the logarithmic Lagrange multiplier relative to that of the cohort 1942–46. As equation (6) implies, the latter coefficient approximates an inverse of the ratio of the lifetime income of each cohort to that of the cohort 1942–46.

Tables 4.8–4.10 report the estimation results for Japan, the United States, and the United Kingdom, respectively. In all these countries, the estimated cohort effect (the estimated relative logarithmic Lagrange multiplier, β_i's) differs substantially among cohorts; the equality of all β_i's is rejected strongly for total consumption as well as for food/clothes consumption. These findings suggest that the altruistic motive is either absent or weak in these countries. This is consistent with the existing empirical results based on the microdata sets; for example, Hayashi (1995) for Japan and Altonji, Hayashi, and Kotlikoff (1992) for the United States.

A closer look at the estimated cohort effect gives us more detailed information concerning the cross-cohort difference in the Lagrange multiplier or lifetime income for each country. In Japan (see table 4.8), the estimation result from total consumption indicates that lifetime income peaked at the cohort 1932–36 while it decreased for younger cohorts. Figure 4.7, which plots the estimated β's with the 95 percent confidence interval, illustrates this cross-cohort pattern. This same pattern is observed in results from food consumption. However, there is no statistical decrease for younger cohorts in lifetime income in the results from clothes consumption.

In the United States, the results from total consumption indicate that lifetime income peaked at the cohort 1947–51 and deteriorated substantially for younger cohorts (see table 4.9 and fig. 4.8). A less serious decline in the younger cohorts' lifetime income is shown in the results from food consumption, while there is no evidence for such a deterioration from clothes consumption. United Kingdom estimates based on total consumption as well as on food and clothes consumption show, by contrast, that lifetime incomes are higher for younger cohorts (see table 4.10 and fig. 4.9).

4.4.2 The Sustainability of the Living Standard

Using the estimation results for total consumption, figure 4.10 contrasts this cross-cohort pattern for Japan, the United States, and the United Kingdom. In both Japan and the United States, lifetime income has deteriorated for younger cohorts while it has improved among younger cohorts in the United Kingdom. Deterioration in the lifetime income of young

Table 4.8   **Estimation Results of Age and Cohort Effects in Workers' Households
in Japan**

	Total Consumption		Food		Clothes	
	Estimate	Standard Error	Estimate	Standard Error	Estimate	Standard Error
Age dummy						
−24	0.166	(0.035)	0.045	(0.033)	0.161	(0.081)
25–29	0.109	(0.026)	−0.017	(0.025)	0.059	(0.060)
30–34	−0.019	(0.020)	−0.088	(0.019)	−0.066	(0.046)
35–39	−0.062	(0.016)	−0.068	(0.015)	−0.087	(0.037)
45–49	0.196	(0.017)	0.065	(0.016)	0.200	(0.038)
50–54	0.361	(0.023)	0.111	(0.022)	0.385	(0.053)
55–60	0.403	(0.032)	0.152	(0.030)	0.446	(0.072)
60–64	0.395	(0.041)	0.207	(0.039)	0.406	(0.093)
65–	0.418	(0.054)	0.277	(0.051)	0.428	(0.123)
Cohort dummy						
1902–06	0.302	(0.078)	0.204	(0.074)	0.451	(0.178)
1907–11	0.136	(0.069)	0.153	(0.065)	0.199	(0.156)
1912–16	0.170	(0.066)	0.158	(0.062)	0.183	(0.149)
1917–21	0.078	(0.049)	0.069	(0.046)	0.025	(0.112)
1922–26	0.039	(0.043)	0.066	(0.041)	0.005	(0.098)
1927–31	−0.012	(0.033)	0.020	(0.031)	−0.062	(0.076)
1932–36	−0.037	(0.022)	0.020	(0.020)	−0.080	(0.049)
1937–41	−0.014	(0.013)	0.009	(0.012)	−0.012	(0.029)
1947–51	0.015	(0.013)	0.026	(0.012)	−0.016	(0.029)
1952–56	0.043	(0.020)	0.078	(0.019)	−0.018	(0.046)
1957–61	0.038	(0.034)	0.125	(0.032)	−0.040	(0.077)
1962–66	0.051	(0.044)	0.201	(0.041)	0.006	(0.100)
1967–71	0.014	(0.031)	0.281	(0.029)	0.071	(0.070)
Adjusted R^2	0.985		0.973		0.943	

Source: National Survey on Family Income and Expenditure (1959–94).

cohorts has been much more rapid in the United States than in Japan. The value of lifetime income has declined by 26 percent in a twenty-year period, or between the 1947–51 cohort and the 1967–71 cohort in the United States. By contrast, it decreased 9 percent in a thirty-year period in Japan, or between the 1932–36 cohort and the 1962–66 cohort.

As discussed in the previous section (section 4.3), when an economy is growing and the real price of goods is decreasing, a corresponding decline in the value of lifetime income does not necessarily imply a decline in the living standard. Therefore, an important policy question is whether high economic growth can compensate for a decline in the value of lifetime income for the younger cohorts, thus allowing their living standard to be sustained.

Equation (8) allows us to calculate the minimum growth rate required to sustain the living standard of the current young generation. For instance,

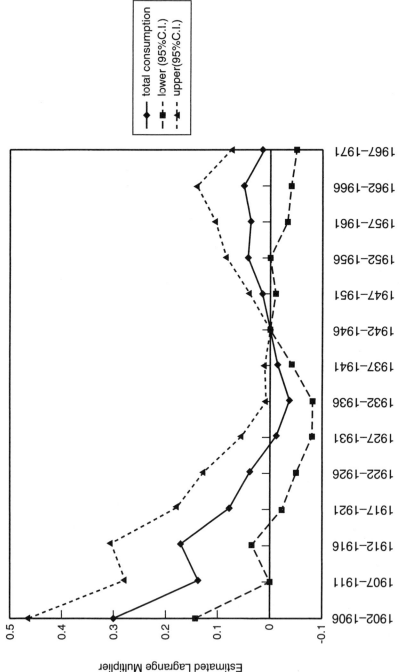

Fig. 4.7 Estimated Lagrange multipliers in workers' households in Japan (cohort: 1942 → 1946 = 0)

Table 4.9   **Estimation Results of Age and Cohort Effects in U.S. Households**

	Total Consumption		Food		Clothes	
	Estimate	Standard Error	Estimate	Standard Error	Estimate	Standard Error
Age dummy						
−24	−0.017	(0.045)	−0.103	(0.044)	−0.270	(0.095)
25–34	−0.003	(0.033)	−0.095	(0.032)	−0.223	(0.069)
45–54	0.274	(0.031)	0.238	(0.030)	0.328	(0.065)
55–64	0.412	(0.055)	0.356	(0.054)	0.506	(0.116)
65–	0.307	(0.073)	0.323	(0.071)	0.337	(0.153)
Cohort dummy						
1907–11	0.424	(0.081)	0.376	(0.079)	0.986	(0.171)
1912–16	0.329	(0.071)	0.290	(0.069)	0.730	(0.148)
1917–21	0.271	(0.064)	0.234	(0.063)	0.539	(0.135)
1922–26	0.251	(0.057)	0.208	(0.056)	0.453	(0.120)
1927–31	0.207	(0.049)	0.152	(0.048)	0.395	(0.104)
1932–36	0.199	(0.029)	0.146	(0.028)	0.294	(0.061)
1937–41	0.087	(0.024)	0.086	(0.024)	0.108	(0.051)
1947–51	−0.039	(0.018)	−0.027	(0.017)	−0.119	(0.037)
1952–56	0.003	(0.026)	−0.016	(0.025)	−0.124	(0.054)
1957–61	0.062	(0.044)	−0.024	(0.043)	−0.192	(0.092)
1962–66	0.092	(0.055)	−0.027	(0.054)	−0.298	(0.116)
1967–71	0.219	(0.071)	0.051	(0.070)	−0.334	(0.150)
Adjusted R^2	0.844		0.807		0.763	

Source: Consumer Expenditure Survey (1972–73, 1980–94).

consider the U.S. cohort 1947–51 (the current middle-aged) compared to the cohort 1967–71 (the current youth). As mentioned earlier, the value of lifetime income has declined by 26 percent from the former cohort to the latter. Thus, the U.S. economy would have to grow at no less than 1.3 percent per year for the next twenty years in order for the living standard of the current young generation to catch up with that of the current middle-aged one. This required growth rate is less demanding from the viewpoint of past growth experience of the United States (where per capita consumption grew at 1.9 percent annually from 1974 to 1994). If the U.S. economy were to grow as steadily as it did in the past, then the living standard of the current young generation would still improve. Without sound economic growth, however, their living standard may be unsustainable under the existing U.S. welfare program.

4.4.3   Effects of Liquidity Positions

In this subsection, I examine the effects of the liquidity position on the cross-age distribution of consumption or the presence of liquidity constraints. To achieve this, I regress the estimated residuals of equation (5) on the relative logarithmic labor income per household member. In addi-

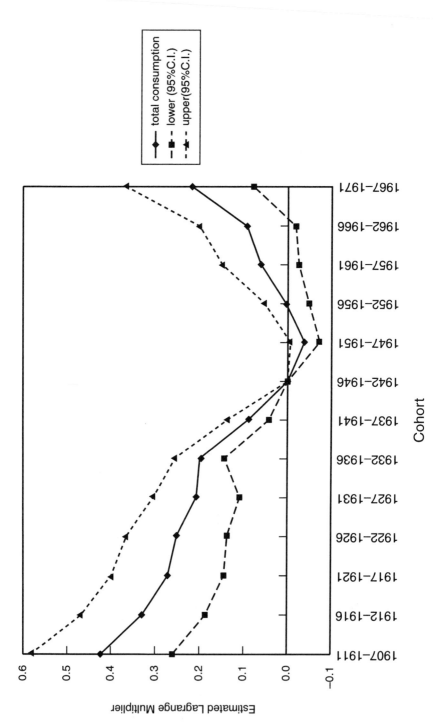

Fig. 4.8 Estimated Lagrange multipliers in the United States (cohort: 1942 − 1946 = 0)

Table 4.10   **Estimation Results of Age and Cohort Effects in U.K. Households**

	Total Consumption		Food		Clothes	
	Estimate	Standard Error	Estimate	Standard Error	Estimate	Standard Error
Age dummy						
−29	−0.044	(0.019)	−0.104	(0.013)	−0.291	(0.040)
50–64	0.402	(0.028)	0.324	(0.019)	0.511	(0.057)
65–	0.246	(0.045)	0.249	(0.030)	0.219	(0.093)
Cohort dummy						
1907–11	0.333	(0.055)	0.214	(0.037)	0.755	(0.114)
1912–16	0.255	(0.044)	0.166	(0.030)	0.645	(0.091)
1917–21	0.176	(0.040)	0.114	(0.027)	0.437	(0.082)
1922–26	0.152	(0.034)	0.114	(0.023)	0.389	(0.069)
1927–31	0.137	(0.024)	0.087	(0.016)	0.352	(0.050)
1932–36	0.106	(0.018)	0.075	(0.012)	0.258	(0.036)
1937–41	0.023	(0.015)	0.023	(0.010)	0.095	(0.030)
1947–51	−0.065	(0.014)	−0.068	(0.009)	−0.181	(0.029)
1952–56	−0.030	(0.024)	−0.045	(0.016)	−0.284	(0.049)
1957–61	−0.117	(0.030)	−0.120	(0.020)	−0.455	(0.062)
Adjusted R^2	0.914		0.948		0.913	

Source: Family Expenditure Survey (1971–91).

tion, to learn which age groups are more subject to liquidity constraints, the estimated residuals are regressed on a set of

$$\text{age dummy}_j \times \ln \frac{e_i(i + j)}{e_{i'}(i' + j')},$$

where j denotes age groups. In both cases, the reference age group is assumed to be the age band that includes a head of household aged forty.

Table 4.11 reports the estimation results for all three countries. The overall result suggests that liquidity positions do not help to explain the evolution of the cross-age consumption distribution. The only exceptions are the liquidity positions of the Japanese in their twenties (food/clothes) and Americans in their sixties (both total and food/clothes consumption). As far as these estimation results are concerned, there is no conclusive evidence in support of liquidity constraints, and the evolution of the cross-age consumption distribution has not been influenced directly by the cross-age distribution of liquidity positions in either Japan, the United States, or the United Kingdom.[7]

7. Using a different data set of the Japanese expenditure survey (the Family Income and Expenditure Survey), Saito (1997) finds that the consumption distribution depends on the labor income distribution not only in young groups, but also in old groups.

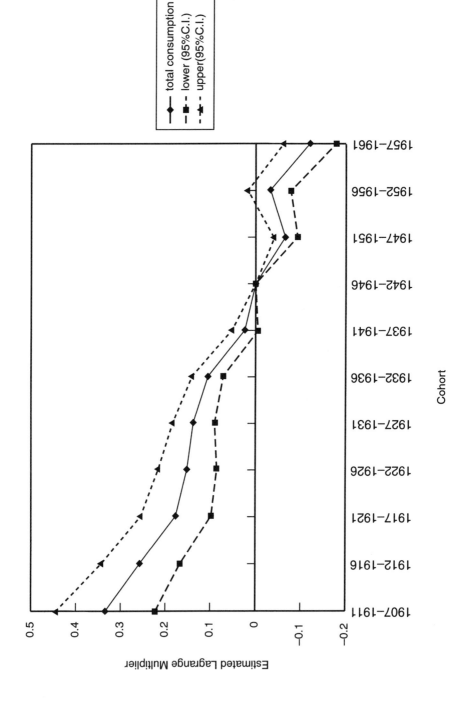

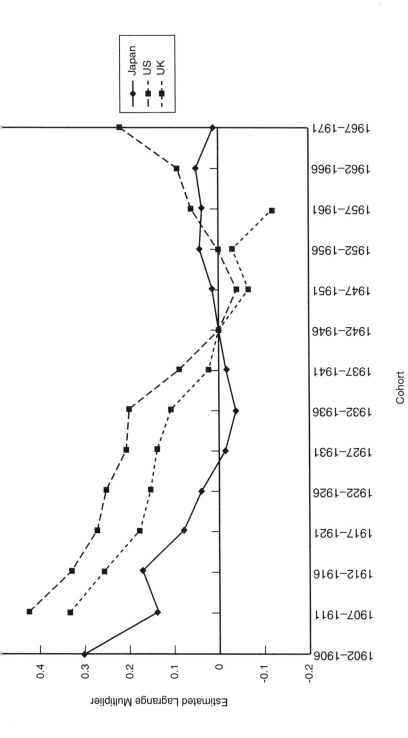

Fig. 4.10 A comparison of estimated Lagrange multipliers among Japan, the United States, and the United Kingdom (cohort: 1942 – 1946 = 0)

Table 4.11 Estimation Results of Labor Income on Estimated Residuals

	Total Consumption		Food		Clothes	
	Estimate	Standard Error	Estimate	Standard Error	Estimate	Standard Error
	A. Workers' Households in Japan					
Relative labor income	0.013	(0.013)	0.006	(0.012)	0.031	(0.029)
Relative labor income × age dummy						
−24	0.261	(0.244)	0.402	(0.221)	0.555	(0.534)
25–29	0.187	(0.247)	0.313	(0.225)	0.901	(0.542)
30–34	0.086	(0.097)	0.063	(0.088)	0.125	(0.213)
35–39	0.042	(0.043)	0.041	(0.039)	0.049	(0.095)
45–49	−0.002	(0.052)	−0.013	(0.047)	0.014	(0.113)
50–54	0.003	(0.024)	−0.009	(0.021)	0.007	(0.052)
55–60	0.005	(0.021)	−0.002	(0.019)	0.030	(0.046)
60–64	−0.024	(0.049)	−0.006	(0.045)	0.011	(0.108)
65–	0.089	(0.153)	−0.120	(0.139)	0.522	(0.336)

B. United States						
Relative labor income	0.006	(0.005)	0.005	(0.005)	0.019	0.010
Relative labor income × age dummy						
–24	0.057	(0.033)	0.029	(0.033)	0.052	(0.071)
25–34	–0.069	(0.154)	0.029	(0.154)	–0.110	(0.330)
45–54	–0.085	(0.084)	–0.072	(0.084)	–0.037	(0.180)
55–64	0.230	(0.112)	0.139	(0.112)	0.216	(0.241)
65–	0.008	(0.005)	0.007	(0.005)	0.020	(0.011)
C. United Kingdom						
Relative labor income	0.003	(0.005)	0.001	(0.004)	0.008	0.011
Relative labor income × age dummy						
–29	–0.007	(0.033)	–0.004	(0.022)	–0.022	(0.068)
50–64	–0.008	(0.035)	–0.009	(0.024)	–0.038	(0.073)
65–	0.005	(0.008)	0.003	(0.005)	0.015	(0.016)

Sources: National Survey on Family Income and Expenditure (1959–94); Consumer Expenditure Survey (1972–73, 1980–94); Family Expenditure Survey (1971–91).

Before concluding this subsection, I would like to point out that the above empirical result does not necessarily contradict the fact that other papers often find the presence of liquidity constraints from microdata (Zeldes 1989). While most existing studies examine whether idiosyncratic (person-specific) shocks on labor income affect the current consumption level, my research was concerned with the effect of age-specific shocks only. This investigation, therefore, could not have examined any effect of idiosyncratic shocks because those shocks would have been cancelled by the age-classified income data.

4.5 Conclusion

This paper analyzes the distribution of economic growth among different generations and compares this intergenerational distribution in Japan, the United States, and the United Kingdom. First, I examined the evolution of the consumption distribution between young and elderly consumers. In both Japan and the United States, the youth are receiving an increasingly smaller percentage, while the British youth are receiving a larger percentage.

The paper then presents an analytical framework, which gives a theoretical interpretation to the evolution of the cross-age consumption distribution. One major advantage of this model is that it can evaluate the level of cohorts' lifetime income relative to resource availability. Using this framework, I find that the value of lifetime income has declined significantly for younger cohorts in both Japan and the United States. Such a decrease in lifetime income in younger cohorts is, however, more substantial in the United States than in Japan. By contrast, younger cohorts have received higher lifetime income in the United Kingdom.

As I suggested in the introduction, the sharp contrast between Japan and the United Kingdom or between the United States and the United Kingdom may be caused by the impact of public transfer schemes on the intergenerational wealth distribution. That is, large-scale intergenerational transfer schemes in both Japan and the United States, which may have been politically justified during the high-growth periods of the 1960s, favor the current older generation. The youth are forced to bear the costs of these welfare programs. As a consequence, the economic resources that younger cohorts are allowed to consume have increased much more slowly than aggregate resources.

The deterioration in lifetime income of the youth in Japan and the United States does not automatically imply a decline in their living standard. Moreover, the current young generation is still improving its purchasing power in terms of consumed resources. However, my calculation indicates that without sound economic growth, the living standard of future generations may be unsustainable under the existing welfare programs. Japan and the United States will be forced not only to maintain economic growth but also to reform their welfare programs, thereby changing the consumption distribution between the young and the elderly.

References

Altonji, J. G., F. Hayashi, and L. J. Kotlikoff. 1992. Is the extended family altruistically linked? Direct tests using micro data. *American Economic Review* 82: 1177–98.

Altug, S., and R. Miller. 1990. Household choices in equilibrium. *Econometrica* 58:543–70.

Atkinson, A. B. 1995. *Incomes and the welfare state: Essays on Britain and Europe.* Cambridge: Cambridge University Press.

Barro, R. J. 1974. Are government bonds net wealth? *Journal of Political Economy* 82:1095–117.

Cochrane, J. H. 1991. A simple test of consumption insurance. *Journal of Political Economy* 99:957–76.

Consumer Expenditure Survey (CES). 1972–73 and 1980–94. U.S. Department of Labor, Bureau of Labor Statistics.

Deaton, A., and C. Paxson. 1994. Intertemporal choice and inequality. *Journal of Political Economy* 102:437–67.

Family Expenditure Survey (FES). 1971–91. Office for National Statistics, U.K.

Gokhale, J., L. Kotlikoff, and J. Sabelhaus. 1996. Understanding the postwar decline in U.S. saving: A cohort analysis. *Brookings Papers on Economic Activity,* issue no. 1:315–90. Washington, D.C.: Brookings Institution.

Hayashi, F. 1995. Is the Japanese extended family altruistically linked? A test based on Engel Curves. *Journal of Political Economy* 103:661–74.

Hayashi, F., J. G. Altonji, and L. J. Kotlikoff. 1996. Risk-sharing between and within families. *Econometrica* 64:261–94.

Mace, B. J. 1991. Full insurance in the presence of aggregate uncertainty. *Journal of Political Economy* 99:928–56.

National Survey on Family Income and Expenditure (NSFIS). 1959–94. Statistics Bureau, Management and Coordination Agency, Japan.

Ohtake, F., and M. Saito. 1998. Population aging and consumption inequality in Japan. *Review of Income and Wealth* 44:361–81.

Rubinstein, M. 1974. An aggregation theorem for securities markets. *Journal of Financial Economics* 1 (1): 225–44.

Saito, M. 1997. An empirical investigation of intergenerational consumption distribution. Kyoto University. Mimeograph.

Zeldes, S. P. 1989. Consumption and liquidity constraints: An empirical investigation. *Journal of Political Economy* 97:305–46.

5

The Third Wave in
Health Care Reform

David M. Cutler

The title of this paper refers to a forecast of coming trends in health care reform. I believe a "third wave" of health care reform, focusing on improving the efficiency of medical care provision, will become common in the countries of Organization for Economic Cooperation and Development (OECD) in the next five to ten years.

I date the first wave of health care reform from the late 1940s through the early 1980s. In this era, most OECD countries built up their health insurance systems. Universal coverage was guaranteed, and benefits were expanded. There were few restrictions on the provision of services. As a result, medical spending consumed an increasing part of the economy of every OECD country.

The growing cost of medical care led to the second wave of reform—a focus on cost containment. The most obvious way to limit medical spending is to limit the total amount of resources the medical sector can consume. Since governments in the OECD typically paid for most, if not all, of, medical care spending, the government could easily limit its overall cost. Spending limits did not conflict with the goal of universal insurance coverage with low cost sharing. Thus, the 1980s saw the advent of wide-scale restrictions on medical spending in the aggregate: global budgets for hospitals, payments inversely related to volume increases for physicians, and caps on pharmaceutical payments.

However, limiting spending without altering the underlying demand or supply for medical care does not necessarily lead to efficient service provi-

David M. Cutler is professor of economics at Harvard University and a research associate of the National Bureau of Economic Research.

The author is grateful to Monica Singhal for research assistance and to the National Institute on Aging for research support.

sion. In many countries, tight budget constraints have led to inefficient resource allocations and to a growing role for the private sector in supplying care. Some countries have concluded—and I believe more will follow—that additional reforms strengthening the market in medical care are needed. I refer to this incipient trend as the *third wave of health care reform*.

In this paper, I document the trends in OECD medical systems over the past fifty years and the reasons for major changes in these systems.

5.1   The Organization of Medical Systems

The medical sector is characterized by three economic agents, shown in figure 5.1: patients, insurers, and providers. The dollars generally flow from left to right. Patients give money to insurers, who in turn pay providers. There is some cost sharing that patients pay directly to providers, but this is typically small. In the United States, for example, the typical private insurance policy covers nearly 80 percent of medical spending; only 20 percent is paid out-of-pocket by the patient. In most other countries, the insurers' share of the bill is even greater.

Figure 5.1 depicts a fundamental representation of the medical sector. This figure encompasses a broad range of insurance arrangements. For example, the "patient" may be all taxpayers and the "insurer" may be the government, in which case figure 5.1 depicts a national health insurance scheme. Alternatively, the "insurer" and "provider" could be the same, as in a health maintenance organization (HMO) in the United States or a publicly run hospital in European countries. In both cases, one can distinguish among the three separate actors, even if more than one function physically occurs in the same place.

In developed countries, the insurer is almost always the government, or, in cases where insurance is private, it is heavily regulated by government. This is not surprising; government involvement is required in any universal benefit system. Because of this, I conduct the rest of the discussion in terms of the decisions that governments have historically made about the medical sector.

5.2   The First Wave of Health Care Reform

Prior to World War II, few countries had universal health insurance coverage. Social insurance as a whole dates back to Bismark in the 1880s, but health insurance coverage was always limited. Bismark's Germany, for example, covered the working age population, leaving the poor uncovered. In only a few countries (Austria, Germany, the United Kingdom, the Netherlands, France, and Norway) was any serious effort at medical care insurance adopted prior to World War II. The countries that did have some coverage typically covered only certain groups in the population, such as

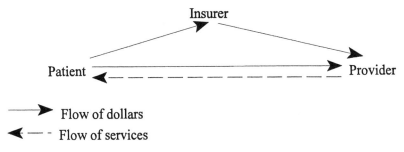

Fig. 5.1   The organization of the medical sector

workers or urban residents. Coverage was much more extensive for old-age insurance than for medical care insurance (Cutler and Johnson 1999).

After World War II, medical insurance expanded. A wave of countries—generally the rich Northern European countries such as the United Kingdom, Sweden, Belgium, and France—enacted universal insurance coverage in the 1940s. The advent of modern medicine, most strikingly illustrated by the penicillin antibiotic, drove demand for medical care to some extent. These countries are also notable for a strong egalitarian ethic: Health care is generally viewed as a basic right of all people, not as a good to be allocated through markets. The legacy of the Great Depression and World War II also fueled expanded coverage. Populations that had suffered for more than twenty years wanted some reward for their suffering, and medical insurance was an appropriate reward.

The late 1940s, 1950s, and 1960s saw the expansion of universal coverage. The United Kingdom, for example, implemented universal coverage in 1948. France achieved universal coverage a few years later. Canada, Denmark, Iceland, Luxembourg, Japan, and Sweden all guaranteed universal insurance coverage during the 1960s. The United States enacted Medicare and Medicaid in the middle of the 1960s.

For a few countries—Australia, Greece, Italy, and Portugal—the process of ensuring universal coverage extended into the 1970s. The "laggard" countries were typically poorer or had particular political situations (such as authoritarian regimes) that set back the expansion of social insurance for several decades.

By the 1980s insurance coverage had become universal in most developed countries. Twenty-two of the twenty-four OECD countries have universal insurance coverage.[1] Only in the United States and Turkey is medical insurance voluntary.

---

1. This statement applies to most of the population; in some countries, certain groups (such as guest workers) are not covered by health insurance. Switzerland only recently enacted universal insurance coverage, but it has had very generous subsidies to insurance, and thus very high rates of insurance coverage, for several decades.

In the United States, insurance coverage is spotty. For the elderly and very poor, insurance is free or heavily subsidized. Thus, insurance is nearly universal for the elderly and is high among the very poor. For the non-elderly, non-poor population, insurance is subsidized, but to a lesser extent. The principal subsidy is that employer payments to health insurance are not taxed as income to individuals in the way that wage payments are. As a result, the subsidy to medical insurance varies with the employee's marginal tax rate—generally 15 to 40 percent once federal and state income taxes and social security taxes are accounted for. This subsidy is large enough that virtually everyone with private health insurance obtains that insurance through an employer, but small enough that not everyone chooses to be insured; about 15 percent of the U.S. population is without health insurance.

Because countries began at different points, the method of guaranteeing universal coverage differs internationally. There are two fundamental ways of providing universal insurance. The first is a *tax* model. Countries with this system levy a payroll, income, or consumption tax, the proceeds of which are used to finance universal insurance. In such a system, the "insurance company" is the government. The second system is the *insurance* model.[2] Insurance is provided through regional associations, occupational groups, or religious or political associations. Often, "employers" are required to pay for health insurance in such a system (although the incidence of this is almost certainly on employees). Table 5.1 shows the division of countries by system of insurance provision. The tax system is typified in Canada, where the federal government raises a uniform tax that it distributes to the provinces to pay for medical costs. The insurance model is seen most clearly in Germany, which has over 1,000 sickness funds varying by region, industry, and occupation.

In practice, the distinction between tax and insurance systems is less important than it could be. Countries that use the insurance model generally do not let people choose among alternative insurance companies. As a result, people are effectively assigned to one insurance arrangement, as in the tax-financed model. The insurance companies are generally not-for-profit and are heavily regulated by the government, so that benefits and cost sharing do not vary across individuals.

As countries expanded their insurance coverage, they also expanded the benefits that people receive and reduced the cost sharing that people pay. Table 5.2 shows the characteristics of the guaranteed insurance policy in OECD countries.[3] It is easier to show the services that are not covered than those that are covered. Generally, almost all medical services are cov-

---

2. Frequently, these insurance companies are termed *sickness funds.*
3. For the United States, I show the coverage under the federal Medicare program.

Table 5.1   **The Provision of Health Insurance**

	Mandatory		Voluntary
	Tax Model	Insurance Model	
	Australia	Austria	Turkey
	Canada	Belgium	United States
	Denmark	France	
	Finland	Germany	
	Greece	Japan	
	Iceland	Luxembourg	
	Ireland	The Netherlands	
	Italy	Switzerland	
	New Zealand		
	Norway		
	Portugal		
	Spain		
	Sweden		
	United Kingdom		

Source: Information on insurance systems is from the Organization for Economic Cooperation and Development (OECD; 1995).

ered. The few exceptions tend to be eyeglasses, some dental care, or certain
pharmaceuticals (generally less expensive ones, including some that are
available over the counter in the United States). Frequently, even these services are covered for the very poor. Indeed, the services covered go far
beyond what most economists think of as insurance services; a classic example is spa benefits, which are covered under health insurance in some
countries (such as Germany).

Cost sharing is similarly low. Table 5.2 shows the cost sharing for visiting
a general practitioner. In about half the countries, there is no cost sharing
for visiting a primary care physician. In most other countries, cost sharing
is nominal—perhaps $5 to $15 per visit—and these amounts are frequently waived for the very poor. Specialist services (not shown) generally
are provided at the same levels of cost sharing. The out-of-pocket cost of
using medical care is, in most countries, trivial. Indeed, the United States,
which economists frequently criticize for having a low amount of cost sharing in its public programs, actually has very high cost sharing when compared with other OECD countries.[4]

The last column of table 5.2 shows whether each country imposes a
"gatekeeper" for access to specialty care. Typically, the gatekeeper is the
primary care physician, who must refer a patient to a specialist. Gatekeep-

---

4. Of course, this does not count the fact that most Medicare enrollees in the United States
have supplemental insurance that eliminates the cost sharing required under Medicare.

Table 5.2   Generosity of Insurance Coverage

Country	Noncovered Services	Cost Sharing for General Practitioner	Gatekeeper for Specialist
Australia	Dental; pharmaceuticals	$5	No
Austria	Some dental; eyeglasses	10–20%	Yes
Belgium	—	25%	No
Canada	Dental; pharmaceuticals; eyeglasses	—	Yes
Denmark	—	—	Yes
Finland	—	$17	No
France	Dental; eyeglasses	25%	No
Germany	—	—	No
Greece	—	—	No
Iceland	—	$9	Yes
Ireland	—	—	Yes
Italy	—	—	Yes
Japan	Innoculations; eyeglasses	10–30%	No
Luxembourg	—	5%	No
The Netherlands	Eyeglasses	—	Yes
New Zealand	Dental; eyeglasses	—	Yes
Norway	—	$11	Yes
Portugal	Some pharmaceuticals	—	Yes
Spain	—	—	Yes
Sweden	Some pharmaceuticals	$6–$19	No
Switzerland	Dental; eyeglasses	10%	No
United Kingdom	Dental; eyeglasses	—	Yes
United States	Pharmaceuticals; long-term care; dental; eyeglasses	20% above $100 deductible	No

Source: OECD (1995).
Note: Long dash indicates "none."

ers are relatively common in OECD countries; however, it is important to note that there is generally little financial penalty for their primary care physicians who make referrals to a specialists (unlike for HMO physicians in the United States). Primary care physicians paid on a salary basis, for example, bear no cost of authorizing a person to see a specialist. As a result, the gatekeeper provisions are generally much less onerous than they are in the United States.

On the supply side of the market, governments must specify a payment system for medical providers. There are many potential systems, shown in figure 5.2: the most generous is fee-for-service payment. In this system, a price is set for each service that providers can offer, and providers receive payment for the amount billed. Providers paid on a fee-for-service basis are insulated from the cost of the services they provide (assuming the fee-for-service payment is above marginal cost). As a result, providers have incentives to perform more services than are warranted.

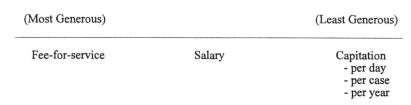

Fig. 5.2   Payment systems for medical care

A somewhat tighter system is a salary payment.[5] Salaried physicians receive an annual payment, with their practice expenses covered by the insurer. While physicians are not paid for performing additional medical care, they also have no financial incentive to limit the care they provide.[6]

Systems that place the provider at risk for medical care utilization are on the right-hand side of the figure. These are grouped under the term *capitation,* although there are many variants of such a system. One type of payment is a per diem in which a hospital receives a fixed amount for each day the patient is in the hospital. Hospitals bear the cost for patients who are more expensive than the per diem amount, but, conversely, make money on patients who are less expensive than the per diem amount. Not surprisingly, hospital stays are long in countries with per diem payments, since marginal days of care are less resource intensive than the average day of care. A related system is a per-case payment. In this system, the hospital is paid a fixed amount for the patient as a whole. Thus, the marginal costs of all services provided is borne by the hospital. Hospital stays generally fall as payment moves from a per diem or fee-for-service basis to a per-case basis (Cutler and Zeckhauser 1999). A final alternative is a per-year payment—a "global budget" for all hospital services provided during the year, or an annual fee to physicians that covers their salary and practice expenses. In these systems, providers are at even greater risk for the costs of the services that they provide. Money spent for one patient reduces money available for other patients or reduces physician take-home earnings. The exact level of risk varies with the nature of the capitation payment.[7]

Historically, medical providers in virtually every country were paid on a fee-for-service or salary basis. In part, this has been a response to the complexity of the medical care system. Medical care is an extremely difficult commodity to price. There are about 10,000 services that physicians can provide, and thousands more for hospitals. Since governments are rarely specialists in the provision of medical care, they must figure out

5. This system is relevant only for physicians (not for hospitals).
6. They also have few incentives to work hard where it is difficult to monitor their work hours or their effort.
7. This includes any additional payment for "outlier" patients.

how to pay for these varied services. Paying piece rates or salaries is more natural than capitated payment where knowledge of medical care delivery is important. Thus, many countries started off with piece rates or salaried reimbursement.

The use of fee-for-service and salaried payments has also been, in part, a response to concerns about the underprovision of services if marginal costs were not covered. In the United States, for example, the Medicare system was set up with a fee-for-service payment structure for exactly that reason; it was the only way to blunt the fears of doctors that their incomes would be reduced if they were to use an alternate pricing system. In other countries, a similar dynamic was at work.

The result was that there were few incentives to limit utilization. In essentially no country were supply-side constraints important in limiting medical care provision. This circumstance was coupled with the already weak incentives on the demand side to limit utilization.

By the beginning of the 1980s, therefore, most countries had a medical care system characterized by three features, each of which strongly encouraged the growth of medical costs:

- Universal insurance coverage;
- A generous set of benefits, with low cost sharing; and
- Fee-for-service or salaried providers who faced no financial incentives to limit care provision.

In effect, the systems were unconstrained on both the demand and the supply sides of the market. In such a system, one might naturally expect costs to grow rapidly; this was indeed the case. Table 5.3 shows the growth of medical costs in the Group of Seven (G7) nations and in the remainder of the OECD nations between 1960 and 1980. Between 1960 and 1980, medical spending for the average OECD country increased from 4.1 percent of GDP to 7.4 percent. In the G7 countries, growth was particularly rapid; in the United States, for example, medical care increased from 5.3 percent of GDP to 9.2 percent of GDP.

Some of the growth of medical spending as a share of GDP may be due to the growth of the economy as a whole. If the income elasticity of medical care is greater than 1, or if increases in income increase the opportunity cost of resources in the medical sector and thus increase overall medical spending (Baumol 1988), one would naturally expect medical care to expand as a share of GDP as the economy grows. To adjust for this, I estimate a regression for the growth of real per capita medical spending between 1960 and 1980 as a function of real per capita income growth. For the twenty-one OECD countries with data in both years, the coefficient on income growth is 1.26 (standard error = 0.22). Thus, at least some of the growth of medical spending as a share of GDP is to be expected.

Still, the third column of table 5.3 shows the growth of residual medical

Table 5.3   **Medical Spending between 1960 and 1980**

	Medical Care/ GDP (%)		Growth of Residual Medical Spending (%)	
Country	1960	1980	1960–80	1980–90
Canada	5.5	7.4	0.7	1.9
France	4.2	7.6	2.0	1.2
Germany	4.8	8.4	2.0	−0.7
Italy	3.6	6.9	2.2	0.8
Japan	2.9	6.4	2.5	−0.7
United Kingdom	3.9	5.8	1.5	0.2
United States	5.3	9.2	2.2	2.3
OECD Average	4.1	7.4	2.3	0.4

Source: OECD (1998).
Notes: Residual medical spending for 1960–80 is the growth of medical spending beyond the rate predicted by the increase in income. Residual medical spending for 1980–90 uses the income elasticity estimated for the 1960–80 period.

spending—medical spending growth beyond what can be explained by the growth of income alone. As the table shows, residual spending growth was generally 2.0 to 2.5 percent annually in the G7, and averaged 2.3 percent in the OECD countries. The only countries with residual growth rates below 2 percent annually are Canada and the United Kingdom, both of which had a longer history of cost containment, as noted below.

5.3   The Second Wave

At the beginning of the 1980s, countries throughout the OECD became concerned about spending on medical care. Public-sector concern was fueled by the large drain that medical costs placed on the public fisc. Governments paid for over 70 percent of medical costs in most countries. Beginning in the mid-1970s, the growth of wages, and thus the tax base, slowed; as the 1980s progressed, it became clearer to governments that they had a long-term funding crisis in medical care. Employers also became concerned about health care costs, particularly when employers wrote the checks for health insurance. In the United States, for example, employer concern about rising health costs was instrumental in driving reform. The general public also grew weary of rising costs, which led to ever-increasing tax burdens and less rapidly increasing wages.

As a result, the 1980s saw a concerted effort to control medical spending in most developed countries. Table 5.4 shows the particular measures taken in the G7 (Canada, France, Germany, Italy, Japan, the United Kingdom, and the United States). The most common reform was to place limits

Table 5.4   The Medical Care Experience in the 1980s and 1990s

Country	Reforms (1980s)	Current Issues
Canada	Global budgets for hospitals established with universal coverage	Cost containment; efficiency
France	Global budgets for hospitals Creation of "Sector 2" (allowing balance billing) for physicians Tighter fee schedules for physicians	Costs; efficiency; difference between public and private sectors
Germany	Global budgets for hospitals Aggregate fee limits on physicians (enforced by reducing fee-for-service payments)	Costs; efficiency; competition among sickness funds
Italy	Reduce hospital funding Move to diagnosis related group payment system for hospitals Limit federal subsidies	Waiting lists (rich opt out); low quality; costs
Japan	Reduce fee schedules Increase copayments	Costs; efficiency; aging
United Kingdom	Capitation of some general practitioners (fundholders) Competition among hospitals (trusts)	Waiting lists (rich opt out); quality
United States	Prospective payment for hospitals Fee schedule for physicians	Universal insurance coverage; public-sector costs

Source: See Cutler (1999) for more details.
Note: Reforms in the United States are for Medicare.

on overall medical spending. Since the government was paying for medical care, the simplest way the government could control overall spending was simply to limit aggregate spending for medical care.

This was most easily accomplished in the hospital sector. Rather than paying hospitals on a fee-for-service basis, countries moved toward a global payment for each hospital (termed a *global budget*) which was to cover all the care that was appropriate. Global budgets were implemented in France in 1984 (for public hospitals only) and in Germany in 1986. The United Kingdom, Canada, and Italy already had global budgets in place—they had been established with universal coverage—but both countries tightened their budgets in the 1980s, nonetheless. Among the universal insurance countries, only Japan did not move away from fee-for-service payment; instead, the fee schedule for hospitals in Japan was reduced.

Table 5.5 shows that this experience was not unusual. Most countries now pay hospitals on some type of capitated basis. Only a few countries have retained a fee-for-service payment system.

Limiting physician spending is more difficult, since full capitation for physicians makes much less sense than it does for hospitals—the risk to a physician in bearing the cost per year of a patient are simply too great.

Table 5.5   **Methods of Hospital Payment**

Fee-for-service	Per Diem	Per Case	Per Year
Japan	Austria	Belgium	Australia
Switzerland	Belgium	France (public)	Canada
	France (private)	Germany	Denmark
	Germany	Ireland	Finland
	Spain	Spain	Greece[a]
		United States	Iceland[a]
			Ireland
			Italy[a]
			New Zealand
			Norway[a]
			Portugal[a]
			Sweden
			United Kingdom

Source: Information on insurance systems is from OECD (1995).
Note: The United States is placed in the per-case column because that is how Medicare pays for hospital care.
[a] Hospitals run by the public sector.

Table 5.6   **Methods of Payment for Primary Care Physicians**

Fee-for-service	Salary	Capitation
Australia	Finland	Austria
Belgium	Greece	Denmark
Canada	Iceland	Italy
France	Norway	Ireland
Germany	Portugal	The Netherlands
Japan	Spain	United Kingdom
Luxembourg	Sweden	
New Zealand		
Switzerland		
United States		

Source: Information on insurance systems is from OECD (1995).

Table 5.6 shows how countries reduced payments for physician services, however. A few countries have capitated physicians, but this typically involves a salary payment that depends on the number of patients seen, not a system where primary care physicians bear the risks of individual patient costs.[8] More commonly, countries have implemented "global budgets" for the physician sector as a whole. In Canada and Germany, for example, aggregate payments for physicians are set in advance; payments for each individual physician are made on a fee-for-service basis, but the fees are

8. Although in the United States, capitation in the form of global budgets is used.

reduced if the aggregate volume of services provided exceeds the expected level. Other countries introduced fee schedules (as did the United States) or, as in the case of Japan, retained fee schedules but proceeded to lower the rates. In countries with salaried physicians (public-sector physicians in France and specialists in Italy and the United Kingdom), salaries grew less rapidly than they had in previous decades.

The result was a decade of relatively low medical-spending growth. The last column of Table 5.3 shows the growth of residual medical spending from 1980 to 1990, using the same income elasticity as in the 1960–80 period. That is, I report the growth of medical spending net of the amount predicted, given income growth that decade and the historical relation between growth in income and increases in medical spending.

In most countries, residual medical-spending growth was substantially lower in the 1980s than it had been in previous decades. In Germany and Japan, for example, residual spending growth was negative in the 1980s— medical spending increased less rapidly than income alone would dictate. In the United Kingdom and Italy, residual spending growth was positive but very small. Only in the United States and Canada was residual medical-spending growth close to what its value had been in the previous twenty years. In Canada this is understandable, since many cost containment initiatives had been implemented prior to the 1980s and the stringency with which limits were applied was generally reduced in the 1980s. The United States is the clear outlier. With no clear demand- or supply-side restraints, residual spending growth in the 1980s grew as rapidly as residual growth had during the 1960s and 1970s.

5.4   The Third Wave

Has the rest of the world (outside of the United States) discovered the answer? Are countries in long-run balance on their medical care systems, or are further reforms required? In this section, I speculate about future trends in health care reform.

It is clear that people in most countries are much happier with their medical care systems than are people in the United States. Blendon et al. (1990) reported on surveys of satisfaction with the health system in ten countries, including all of the G7 countries. The share of individuals who feel that only minor changes are needed in their health system[9] was 56 percent in Canada, 41 percent in France and Germany, 29 percent in Japan, 27 percent in the United Kingdom, and 12 percent in Italy. This compares to 10 percent in the United States.

Although people in most countries are more satisfied with their medical

---

9. The exact question was "On the whole, the health care system works pretty well, and only minor changes are necessary to make it work better."

care systems than are Americans, what is equally striking is the large number of people in every country who still want fundamental reform of the health system. Only in Canada did as many as 40 percent of the population think that the structure of the health system was sound; and in Canada, the share of people favoring fundamental reform of the medical care system has risen in recent years (Blendon et al. 1995).

The last column of table 5.4 shows the concerns that have arisen in G7 countries in the 1990s, particularly in the past few years. Despite lower overall spending growth, many countries are still concerned about medical costs. This is not surprising; even at its lower growth rate, medical care is consuming an increasing share of GDP—and public spending—in most countries. Moreover, the prices that have been paid for the less-rapid growth of medical costs have been high.

A second concern has risen to match the overall level of spending: the efficiency of the medical sector. Recall that medical care reforms in the 1980s did not reduce the underlying demand for medical care. Even after the 1980s, patients still faced little or no cost sharing for the use of covered services. The "rationing" of medical care was entirely on the supply side.

Supply-side rationing has predictable consequences, the most common of which are waiting lists. Waiting lists are common in Canada, Italy, and the United Kingdom. In Japan, although waiting lists are not common, excess demand for physicians is; the time involved in seeing a physician can be quite high.

Countries that spend more have shorter waiting lists than countries that spend less. Waiting lists are more common in the United Kingdom, for example, than in Canada, reflecting the greater level of medical care funding in the latter country than in the former.

Coupled with this excess demand is the difficulty of efficient planning in the public sector. Governments are rarely good at providing complex services, and this is particularly true in medical care, where the nature of optimal service provision changes very rapidly. Thus, medical care quality in supply-side rationing was uneven—good in some places and bad in others. Moreover, the incentives built into the systems became more noticeable. Salaried physicians did not work hard, and physicians who were paid little money for each visit did not spend much time with each patient.

The levels of funding and of the efficiency with which funds were allocated showed up directly in patient satisfaction with the medical care system. Cutler (1999) shows that the share of people expressing the need for fundamental health reform (based on the Blendon et al. survey) is strongly positively correlated with per capita medical spending. With the exception of the United States, countries that spend more on medical care have greater public satisfaction with the medical care system than countries that spend less on medical care. In the United States, in fact, the concern about the medical system probably refers more to the lack of universal coverage than to the rationing of medical services. Within countries that have universal coverage, the level of medical spending is strongly related to satisfaction with the medical system.

When waiting times are long and quality in the public sector is particularly low, the private sector is often the alternative source of medical care. The ability to go outside the national medical system varies across countries; some countries place restrictions on doing so, or offer inducements to stay in the national system. In Canada, for example, providers are not allowed to treat patients outside the national system for services the system covers, nor are they allowed to accept payments above the insured level.

In other countries, however, a robust private sector has developed to supplement the public system. This is the case in the United Kingdom, Italy, and France. In the United Kingdom, for example, a growing private insurance market allows people to "queue jump" to receive services more rapidly than they would be eligible for them under the national insurance system. In Italy, people also go outside the public system, paying out of pocket when they want services they cannot obtain rapidly enough through the public sector. In France, the issue of private provision has been particularly contentious. Some providers may see patients outside the public sector, which they do to increase their income. The result is that the rich get better (or at least faster) medical care than the poor.

The anecdotal information from the G7 suggests that supply-limited systems are not the ultimate resolution of the medical care struggle. Tight spending constraints reduce medical spending but also engender increasing dissatisfaction. It seems likely that further medical care reforms will be needed. As a result, a new round of reform efforts across countries may well begin. My suspicion is that reforms are likely to proceed on two tracks, which I discuss in the following subsections.

5.4.1   Measures to Increase Competition

One focus of reform efforts will be on increasing competition in the medical care system, in an effort to increase system efficiency. Almost certainly, this will involve more cost consciousness on the part of physicians. The United Kingdom is at the forefront here. In the late 1980s and early 1990s, the United Kingdom began capitation payments for physicians ("GP fundholders"). The capitation amount included primary care services as well as specialist and hospital services. At the same time, hospitals were encouraged to become, in effect, not-for-profit "trusts" that could compete for patients. The result is incentives for providers to monitor utilization more closely and to limit excessive medical care.

In other countries, there has been less emphasis on competition among providers than on competition among insurers. For example, Germany now allows people to choose among sickness plans, much as individuals may choose among insurance companies in the United States. The hope is that competition among funds will encourage the different funds to be more efficient.[10]

The issue of choice brings up a fundamental question about health insurance markets: Are the efficiency advantages of choice greater than the losses it brings about through adverse selection? While insurance choice is likely to lead to efficiency savings, it also creates adverse selection (Cutler and Reber 1998; Cutler and Zeckhauser 1999). As people sort themselves across insurance plans, the sickest people will choose the most generous insurance and the healthiest people will choose the least generous insurance. This will increase the premiums for the sick and reduce the premiums for the healthy, and may even lead to the abandonment of the most generous plans. Adverse selection is an inherent tendency of choice-based insurance systems (Cutler and Zeckhauser 1999). Thus, countries that move along this route will necessarily give up some of the redistribution that they currently maintain.

5.4.2   Increasing Patient Cost Sharing

The other avenue for change will be reducing benefits or increasing patient cost sharing. As supply-side constraints alone become less popular, demand-side controls will be an increasing option. In some countries (e.g., Japan), reforms in the 1980s increased cost sharing for covered services. Cost sharing has been increasing in the United States as well as for some services in other countries.

Countries that increase cost sharing face the question of whether people will be allowed to purchase supplemental insurance to buy down that cost sharing. In many countries (including the United States), supplemental insurance is allowed to cover the cost sharing required under the basic package. This creates significant problems, however; when individuals purchase supplemental insurance, they use more medical services than they otherwise would, driving up spending in the basic medical plan. Thus, allowing insurance to cover basic cost sharing is likely to limit the efficiency gains of increasing cost sharing.

In addition, increasing cost sharing raises concerns about the poor. The rich can afford greater cost sharing more readily than the poor can. Thus, countries that move toward increased cost sharing or fewer covered services inevitably face questions about their commitment to equity in medical care financing.

---

10. The model here is the recent reform in the Netherlands, which involved substantial competition among insurers.

5.5 Conclusions

The world's medical systems have been in flux for most of the past fifty years. At first, countries built up their medical care systems. Coverage was made universal, and benefits were generous. There was little demand- or supply-side cost sharing.

In the early 1980s, countries realized the unaffordability of generous demand incentives with no control over medical care supply. The typical response was to limit the supply side of the market by capping the total amount of services that could be provided. Given most countries' commitment to universal insurance and low cost sharing, supply-side restrictions were the logical response. This response saved money; the 1980s were characterized by much lower growth of medical costs than had taken place during the previous twenty years.

However, the strains in this approach ultimately became apparent. Excess demand led to waiting lists, non-pricing rationing, and the incentive to seek services outside the public sector. As a result, efficiency concerns rose in importance during the 1980s and 1990s.

A focus on efficiency is likely to involve two reforms, which I characterize as the "third wave" of health care reform: increased competition for services, either at the level of the provider or at the level of the insurer; and increased patient cost sharing. Neither of these is an easy reform to implement. Increased competition increases the incentives for adverse selection; increased cost sharing is more burdensome for the poor than for the rich. Nonetheless countries are finding, or are likely to find, they have no alternative but to try these reforms.

This debate between demand-side and supply-side limits is, in my estimation, the next great debate in the medical sector. Countries cannot have unlimited demand and unlimited supply, nor can they effectively rely on supply-side controls alone. What sort of demand-side controls they implement, and how they manage the inherent inequities in these systems, will determine the shape of medical care systems for the early part of the twenty-first century.

References

Baumol, William J. 1988. Containing medical costs: Why price controls won't work. *The Public Interest* 93:37–53.
Blendon, Robert J., John Benson, Karen Donelan, Robert Leitman, Humphrey Taylor, Christian Koeck, and Daniel Gitterman. 1995. Who has the best health care system? A second look. *Health Affairs* 14 (4): 220–30.
Blendon, Robert J., Robert Leitman, Ian Morrison, and Karen Donelan. 1990. Satisfaction with health care systems in ten nations. *Health Affairs* 9 (2): 186–92.

Cutler, David. 1999. Equality, efficiency, and market fundamentals: The dynamics of international medical care reform. Mimeograph.

Cutler, David, and Richard Johnson. 1999. The birth and growth of the social insurance state. Mimeograph.

Cutler, David, and Sarah Reber. 1998. Paying for health insurance: The tradeoff between competition and adverse selection. *Quarterly Journal of Economics* 113 (2): 433–66.

Cutler, David, and Richard J. Zeckhauser. 2000. The anatomy of health insurance. In *Handbook of health economics,* vol. 1, ed. Joseph Newhouse and Anthony Culyer, 563–643. Amsterdam: Elsevier.

Organization for Economic Cooperation and Development (OECD). 1995. *Health policy studies 7.* Paris: OECD.

———. 1998. *Health systems data 7* [CDRom]. Paris: OECD.

6

Concentration and Persistence of Health Care Costs for the Aged

Seiritsu Ogura and Reiko Suzuki

6.1 Introduction

There have been very few studies of the distribution of health care costs among individuals in Japan. The most likely explanation for this may be an absence of the appropriate longitudinal data sets that are indispensable to carrying out such analyses. Another reason, however, may be the implicit assumption that health care resources naturally are consumed by a small number of individuals who are in poor health or are in danger of dying. Moreover, even if we find that health care expenditures indeed are heavily concentrated among a few individuals, is there anything to be done about it? Are we ready to look at total health care resources and decide anew how they should be distributed?

It is interesting to note that it is common to discuss the regional variation in health care costs, even in Japan. Regional variations have been studied jointly with the physician-induced demand (PID) hypothesis; in PID studies, generally speaking, the main objective was not to judge whether given regions were spending too little or too much, but rather to test a particular hypothesis about how health care expenditures are determined.

This paper describes the distribution of health care expenditures among the elderly in Japan. We examine both regional and interpersonal variations in the hope of finding what determines each. Some have argued that it is not appropriate for us to discuss the interpersonal distribution of health care resources,[1] but we do not subscribe to such an "extreme" view.

Seiritsu Ogura is professor of economics at Hosei University. Reiko Suzuki is a senior economist at the Japan Center for Economic Research.

1. This is one of the reactions to a study on the costs of terminal care patients written by one of the coauthors of the present paper.

187

Even if we cannot find a way to improve the distribution of health care right away, we may obtain new insights into what health care is really about, why it costs so much, and why it grows so persistently.

The rest of this paper is constructed as follows: In section 6.2, we outline the distribution of health care costs among the elderly population, and single out the factors that characterize the high-cost elderly. In section 6.3, we focus on the high-cost elderly as represented by long-term inpatients and look into the effect that long-term hospitalization has on the regional variation in health care costs.

6.2   Distribution of Health Care Costs among the Japanese Elderly Population

As we stated at the beginning of this paper, there is virtually no information on the distribution of medical costs among elderly individuals (seventy years old or over) in Japan. It is the primary purpose of our exposition here to present a reasonably accurate picture of the distribution of medical expenditures among such individuals. We then focus on the characteristics of the "expensive" elderly and try to single out the factors that make them expensive.

6.2.1   Data Sources

We use a subset of the experimental Health and Medical Services System for the Elderly (HMSSE) data collected by a group of researchers at the National Institute of Public Health.[2] The original data were collected from participating municipalities of twelve prefectures during the period 1991–93. (Certain prefectures' data were ultimately excluded, as will be discussed later.) The original database consists of two different data sets: Part A provides a summary of the health insurance claims of individual elderly in each month of that year, and Part B provides a slightly more detailed accounting of health insurance claims in a given month of the year (cross-sectional data). As a basis of our analysis we have chosen samples that satisfy the following requirements:

Complete records for twenty-four months. We selected individuals with complete entries for each month in Part A for both 1992 and 1993, including months with zero claims.[3] Some prefectures, such as Hokkaido, Osaka, and Kochi, use different identification codes for different years; we eliminated their data.

---

2. The group was headed by professor Atsushi Gunji of Tokyo University; Mr. Tetsuji Fukawa almost single-handedly collected and prepared the data.
3. Again, we have excluded those who have become eligible for HMSSE benefits or those who have died sometime in the course of these two years.

Consistent identification coding for Part A and Part B. Unlike Part A, where the costs of all claims are aggregated for an individual, Part B contains the costs and primary diagnosis of each claim for one month in 1992 and 1993. Some municipalities (and all the municipalities in Okayama) used different identification codes for Part A and Part B, making it impossible to integrate them.

Matching 1993 for Part A and Part B. More municipalities provided Part B data in 1993 than in 1992. As a result, even in prefectures that used consistent identification codes for Part A and Part B and did so for both years, we have far more individuals matching in 1993 than in 1992. Instead of insisting that individual records match in 1992 and 1993, we require that they match only in 1993; we rely on 1993 diagnoses as our source of primary diagnosis.

Of the original data covering twelve prefectures, only data from Aomori, Fukushima, Toyama, Ishikawa, Fukui, Shizuoka, Shiga, and Wakayama met these criteria. So far, we have analyzed the data from Aomori, Fukushima, Toyama, Fukui, and Wakayama. Thus, our samples may not be nationally representative, because these five prefectures are concentrated heavily toward the rural north and are perhaps below average in terms of economic well-being. The number of individuals in our sample of five prefectures is 479,673 for Part A,[4] and 328,134 for Part B.

6.2.2   Individual Ranking of Health Care Expenditures

We added inpatient and outpatient health care costs for each individual during the twenty-four-month period, ranked each individual in order of total expenditures within each prefecture, then computed the percentile for each individual in the prefecture. No attempt has been made to generalize percentiles across prefectures or to the general population. In the five prefectures taken together, the health care costs during these two years totaled 952,602 yen per elderly patient,[5] of which 474,170 yen were for inpatient care and 478,432 yen were for outpatient care.

6.2.3   Concentration of Health Care Expenditures

In Japan as in the United States (Gornick, McMillan, and Lubitz 1993), at any point in time, health care expenditures are concentrated heavily on a relatively small number of individuals; this pattern tends to persist over

---

4. Of these, Aomori accounted for 110,323, Fukushima for 92,801, Toyama for 103,896, Fukui for 74,182, and Wakayama for 98,471.

5. The average total cost figure was 963,784 yen for Aomori, 855,449 yen for Fukushima, 1,101,504 yen for Toyama, 933,319 yen for Fukui, and 899,052 yen for Wakayama. The average total inpatient-care cost figure was 497,161 yen for Aomori, 407,956 yen for Fukushima, 606,050 yen for Toyama, 468,959 yen for Fukui, and 375,614 yen for Wakayama.

time. In our sample of almost half a million elderly in five prefectures observed over a two-year period, the median elderly spent slightly more than 500,000 yen in two years, while the mean elderly spent almost twice as much, slightly less than 1 million yen. The top 1 percent, on the other hand, spent about 9.5 million yen, or about twenty times the median amount, during the same period.

In terms of the proportion of the total expenditures on health care in a given prefecture, the results are even more dramatic. The bottom half of the elderly in terms of health care costs spent about 11 percent of the total, while the top 1 percent spent about 10 percent of the total. The top 3 percent spent about 22 percent of the total, the top 5 percent about 30 percent, and the top 10 percent about 45 percent. Now we know that, even among the elderly, health care expenditures are very heavily concentrated on a relatively small number of individuals. The degree of concentration is probably far beyond anything anyone has yet imagined.

6.2.4   Inpatient Care Costs, Outpatient Care Costs, and the Factors Leading to Concentration

In order to single out factors leading to this drastic concentration of health care expenditures, we decompose expenditures into inpatient and outpatient care costs. Figure 6.1 shows three cumulative distribution functions: for total costs, inpatient care costs, and outpatient care costs. The horizontal axis variable, the percentile ranking of health care costs, is common in three distributions. Clearly, compared with the distribution of total health care costs, outpatient costs are distributed far more equally among the elderly, and inpatient care costs are even more concentrated among the expensive few. In terms of the numbers, the bottom half of the elderly population consumed only about 1.2 percent of total inpatient care costs, but about 20 percent of total outpatient costs. The top 1 percent consumed about 3 percent of the total outpatient care costs, but almost 17 percent of the inpatient care costs. The top 10 percent consumed 18.4 percent of the outpatient care costs, but 73.5 percent of the inpatient care costs. Thus, it is the inpatient care costs that are producing the heavily concentrated health care expenditure patterns in the elderly population in Japan.

The two cumulative distributions in figure 6.2 look almost identical to those in figure 6.1, but are based on the number of days that health care services were received: the number of visits for outpatients and the number of days hospitalized for inpatients. Each distribution is shown separately in figures 6.3 and 6.4, respectively. Comparing these two, we may conclude that the primary determinant of the concentrated expenditure pattern is the extraordinarily large number of days that the highest percentile of elderly are hospitalized. For instance, not the proportion of individuals who stayed in the hospital for more than 730 days in each percentile of total health care costs. At the 95th percentile, only 2 percent of the elderly

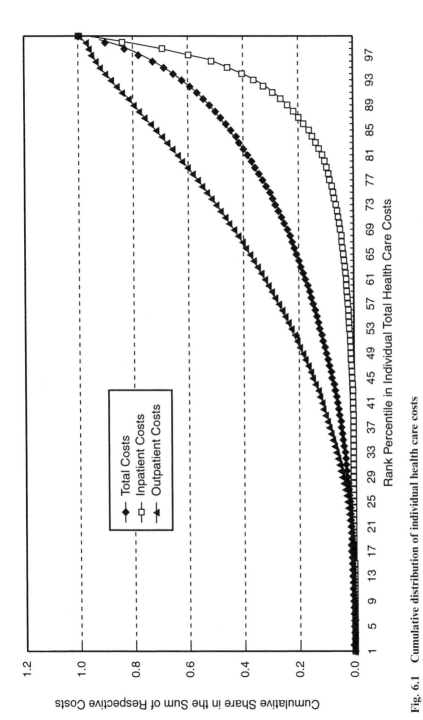

Fig. 6.1 Cumulative distribution of individual health care costs

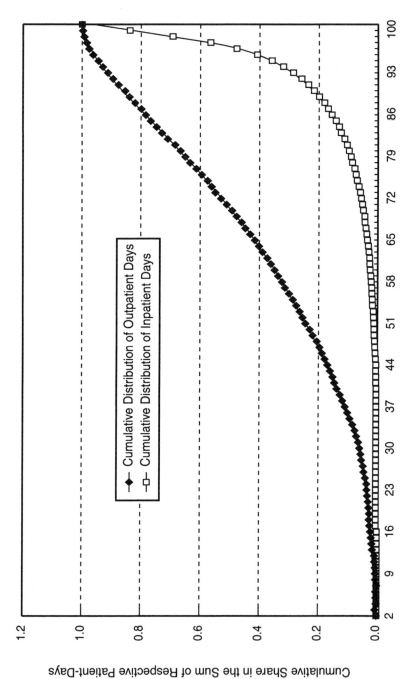

Fig. 6.2 Cumulative distribution of inpatient and outpatient days

Cumulative Share in the Sum of Respective Patient-Days

Rank Percentile in Individual Total Health Care Costs

- Cumulative Distribution of Outpatient Days
- Cumulative Distribution of Inpatient Days

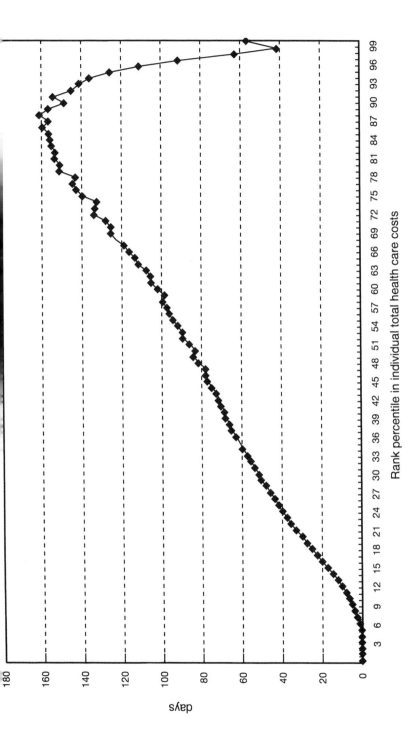

Fig. 6.3 Distribution of total outpatient days over a two-year period

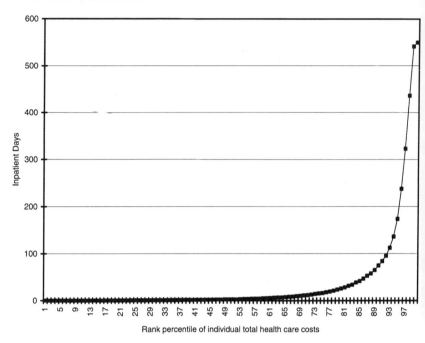

Fig. 6.4   Cumulative distribution of inpatient days

stayed in the hospital practically every day of the two-year period. At the 96th percentile, that proportion was 6 percent. But the proportion increases to 15 percent at the 97th percentile, 27 percent at the 98th percentile, 40 percent at the 99th percentile, and 45 percent at the top 1 percent.

6.2.5   Primary Diagnoses of the "Expensive Elderly"

In order to obtain information on diagnoses of the patients in Part B, we integrated Part B (cross-sectional data) with Part A (longitudinal data) for each patient. There were two problems associated with this process. First, since not everyone receives medical care in a given month, we lost some individuals who were in Part A. In fact, we lost about one-fourth of the individuals in Part A in this process, including those who never see a doctor during these twenty-four months. We were still left with almost 330,000 individuals in our combined sample. Second, in a given month, many patients see several doctors for an identical (or different) ailment(s); these several doctors may in turn give different diagnoses. For these patients, we had to choose a primary diagnosis. We simply chose the diagnosis for the most expensive claim of each patient in the month.

Table 6.1 gives the distribution of primary diagnoses of the patients whose Part A and Part B records are successfully integrated. In the same table, the distribution of primary diagnoses of the top 3 percent in health

Table 6.1 **Number of Individuals in Each Primary Diagnosis Group in a Given Month in 1993**

	Total Elderly Population						Top 3% of the Total Elderly Population					
	Total	Aomori	Fukushima	Toyama	Fukui	Wakayama	Total	Aomori	Fukushima	Toyama	Fukui	Wakayama
Contagious	4,458	1,086	477	921	779	1,195	199	58	26	34	37	44
Neoplastic	7,726	1,787	1,140	1,922	1,278	1,598	601	138	110	93	135	125
Endocrinal	14,395	3,584	1,735	4,123	2,060	2,893	607	168	64	182	77	116
Hematological	1,154	202	108	408	177	259	53	7	5	19	5	17
Mental	4,452	1,069	699	868	729	1,087	935	222	243	57	124	289
Ophthalmological/ Audiological	62,135	15,848	6,977	15,832	9,247	14,231	1,458	366	191	292	243	366
Respiratory	14,130	2,636	1,741	2,894	3,690	3,169	443	69	83	45	117	129
Digestive	27,855	6,794	4,075	5,534	4,249	7,203	674	164	98	110	102	200
Genitourinary	6,683	2,102	766	1,331	1,152	1,332	646	186	89	110	92	169
Dermatological	7,942	1,563	667	2,051	1,605	2,056	189	59	15	32	37	46
Skeletal	42,722	10,516	4,974	9,999	8,612	8,621	1,199	291	134	258	261	254
Unknown	2,517	424	319	450	319	1,005	56	4	8	2	5	37
Traumatic	5,757	1,298	567	1,334	1,116	1,442	328	92	30	58	44	104
Hypertensive	68,257	18,451	12,976	14,851	6,983	14,996	1,066	241	161	265	158	241
Coronary	23,638	5,846	3,874	5,040	4,151	4,727	1,005	248	152	238	152	215
Cerebrovascular	29,839	8,086	4,287	7,446	5,021	4,999	3,226	822	309	1,184	454	457
Other Circulatory	4,405	1,321	649	696	779	960	129	41	24	21	26	17
Total	328,134	82,625	46,047	75,707	51,964	71,791	12,816	3,176	1,743	3,001	2,069	2,827

Note: Total elderly population was taken from the five prefectures sampled: Aomori, Fukushima, Toyama, Fukui, and Wakayama.

care costs are given. In the general population of elderly, the most common diagnosis is hypertension (20.8 percent), followed by ailments of the nervous system (18.9 percent) and the musculoskeletal system. Among the group we describe as the "expensive" elderly, however, it is cerebrovascular disease (25.2 percent), followed by mental disease (11.4 percent). We have also computed the probabilities that a patient in each primary diagnosis group will join the expensive elderly.[6] Mental diseases rank the highest at 21.0 percent, or 7.0 times the average likelihood; cerebrovascular diseases rank second highest (10.8 percent); and diseases of the urinary system rank third highest (9.7 percent), or 3.0 times the average likelihood.

Tables 6.2 through 6.4 give the average total costs, average inpatient care costs, and average outpatient care costs, respectively. Table 6.5 computes how much more time the expensive elderly spend in inpatient and outpatient care than do the average elderly with the same primary diagnosis. On average, the expensive elderly consume about 10.8 times as much inpatient care as the average elderly, but only 1.3 times as much outpatient care. On the other hand, average patients with mental diseases, diseases of the urinary system, and cerebrovascular diseases are relatively expensive to begin with and consume relatively intensive inpatient care, which accounts for the relatively low numbers for these groups for inpatient care.

6.2.6   Relevance of the Type of Medical Institution

Part B provides some information on the type of medical institution where a patient has been treated. Unfortunately, the classification of medical institutions is very crude. It distinguishes a teaching hospital, an incorporated private hospital, a hospital that is neither teaching nor incorporated, a clinic, or an out-of-prefecture institution, but does not provide any information on the size or location of the institution.

Based on this limited information, we have computed distribution statistics for utilization and costs. Table 6.6 shows the distribution of elderly patients across different types of institutions in a given month of 1993 in each prefecture. Throughout the municipalities of these five prefectures, 57 percent of all patients chose clinics, 12 percent chose incorporated private hospitals, and 28 percent chose the other types of hospitals. Teaching hospitals and out-of-prefecture hospitals accounted for only 1 percent of patients each. As for the expensive elderly, the distributions are very different (table 6.7): Only 17 percent were in clinics, but 42 percent were in incorporated private hospitals, and 36 percent in the other types of hospitals. Thus, if one is computing the probability that a patient in a given type of institution belongs to the expensive elderly (table 6.8), incorporated pri-

---

6. As we have defined the "expensive" to be at the top 3 percent, if we sum over all the primary diagnosis groups, we should get 3 percent—but, in fact, we recovered 3.9 percent. This is due to the fact that top 3 percent are defined relative to all the elderly in Part A, from which we have lost about one-fourth in our attempt to combine Part A with Part B.

Table 6.2   Average Health Care Costs during Two Years in Each Primary Diagnosis Groups (in thousands of yen)

	Total Elderly Population						Top 3% of the Total Elderly Population					
	Total	Aomori	Fukushima	Toyama	Fukui	Wakayama	Total	Aomori	Fukushima	Toyama	Fukui	Wakayama
Contagious	1,251	1,303	1,143	1,380	1,276	1,131	6,899	6,705	6,435	8,463	6,628	6,447
Neoplastic	1,922	1,791	1,863	2,018	2,096	1,855	6,920	6,624	6,418	8,137	7,033	6,662
Endocrinal	1,314	1,357	1,143	1,456	1,215	1,230	7,613	6,865	6,389	8,646	7,616	7,747
Hematological	1,306	1,096	1,219	1,428	1,185	1,398	8,121	5,941	8,240	9,688	10,878	6,421
Mental	2,379	2,313	2,806	2,219	2,219	2,405	6,161	5,978	6,045	7,383	6,090	6,189
Ophthalmological/Audiological	1,123	1,112	1,016	1,190	1,149	1,096	7,020	6,708	6,080	8,661	6,726	6,708
Respiratory	1,114	1,125	1,158	1,076	1,086	1,147	6,651	6,875	6,069	8,026	6,361	6,691
Digestive	1,042	1,057	934	1,165	1,020	1,006	6,627	6,409	5,908	8,146	6,465	6,407
Genitourinary	2,092	2,005	2,163	2,259	1,831	2,245	10,474	10,375	10,524	11,104	9,959	10,426
Dermatological	1,032	1,141	898	1,122	991	935	7,496	7,110	5,966	9,756	6,507	7,712
Skeletal	1,107	1,098	973	1,254	1,087	1,045	6,775	6,270	5,945	8,039	6,728	6,549
Unknown	980	980	853	999	911	1,034	6,557	10,172	6,958	7,713	5,464	6,165
Traumatic	1,416	1,526	1,235	1,559	1,183	1,436	7,064	6,823	6,751	8,281	6,994	6,719
Hypertensive	852	857	733	993	877	799	6,853	6,461	5,773	8,247	6,653	6,565
Coronary	1,279	1,267	1,103	1,521	1,259	1,196	6,976	6,682	6,198	8,294	6,813	6,524
Cerebrovascular	1,827	1,665	1,343	2,613	1,603	1,558	7,245	6,632	6,468	8,065	6,996	6,992
Other Circulatory	1,092	1,092	939	1,255	1,176	1,007	7,086	6,489	6,340	8,464	7,815	6,759
Total	1,200	1,186	1,040	1,390	1,193	1,125	7,147	6,795	6,394	8,333	6,932	6,906

Note: See table 6.1.

Table 6.3   Average Inpatient Care Costs during Two Years According to Primary Diagnosis Groups (in thousands of yen)

	Total Elderly Population						Top 3% of the Total Elderly Population					
	Total	Aomori	Fukushima	Toyama	Fukui	Wakayama	Total	Aomori	Fukushima	Toyama	Fukui	Wakayama
Contagious	655	725	593	742	719	506	6,232	6,315	5,448	7,271	6,244	5,773
Neoplastic	1,142	1,097	1,119	1,221	1,316	973	5,995	5,868	5,446	7,515	6,028	5,453
Endocrinal	650	722	522	783	561	510	6,651	6,251	5,396	7,958	5,841	6,410
Hematological	719	632	806	740	643	769	6,309	5,483	8,005	6,116	10,703	5,073
Mental	1,893	1,894	2,405	1,638	1,736	1,873	6,059	5,888	6,004	7,054	5,981	6,073
Ophthalmological/ Audiological	441	460	406	496	469	358	5,842	5,877	4,939	7,368	5,439	5,329
Respiratory	533	540	620	506	521	518	5,896	5,860	5,484	7,314	5,525	6,029
Digestive	468	506	416	571	452	394	5,980	5,823	5,275	7,554	5,768	5,695
Genitourinary	998	1,057	1,077	1,070	812	950	5,944	7,054	6,077	5,354	5,289	5,394
Dermatological	422	526	380	470	421	307	5,731	5,791	5,052	6,674	5,388	5,497
Skeletal	492	504	400	609	499	390	6,121	5,721	5,123	7,396	6,134	5,792
Unknown	424	475	373	471	384	410	5,453	10,080	5,791	7,448	3,549	5,029
Traumatic	921	1,056	771	1,053	695	911	6,487	6,449	6,271	7,820	6,259	5,937
Hypertensive	322	334	253	420	379	241	6,309	6,045	5,193	7,602	6,299	5,903
Coronary	676	696	555	890	627	566	6,443	6,123	5,624	7,905	6,188	5,956
Cerebrovascular	1,251	1,139	769	2,067	996	887	7,062	6,448	6,153	7,979	6,761	6,705
Other Circulatory	491	521	409	649	547	347	6,349	5,872	5,701	8,080	6,717	5,715
Total	589	601	488	755	586	467	6,363	6,156	5,606	7,639	6,093	5,907

Note: See table 6.1.

Table 6.4   Average Outpatient Care Costs during Two Years According to Primary Diagnosis Groups (in thousands of yen)

	Total Elderly Population						Top 3% of the Total Elderly Population					
	Total	Aomori	Fukushima	Toyama	Fukui	Wakayama	Total	Aomori	Fukushima	Toyama	Fukui	Wakayama
Contagious	597	579	549	638	558	626	667	390	987	1,192	384	674
Neoplastic	780	694	744	796	780	883	925	756	972	621	1,004	1,210
Endocrinal	664	635	621	672	654	720	962	614	992	688	1,776	1,337
Hematological	587	463	413	688	542	629	1,812	459	235	3,572	175	1,347
Mental	485	419	401	580	482	531	102	90	41	328	109	116
Ophthalmological/ Audiological	682	652	610	694	679	737	1,178	832	1,141	1,294	1,287	1,379
Respiratory	581	585	538	570	565	629	753	1,015	584	712	835	662
Digestive	573	550	518	594	567	613	648	586	634	592	697	712
Genitourinary	1,093	948	1,086	1,189	1,019	1,295	4,529	3,321	4,447	5,750	4,670	5,032
Dermatological	610	614	518	652	570	628	1,764	1,319	914	3,082	1,118	2,215
Skeletal	615	594	573	646	588	655	654	550	822	643	594	757
Unknown	556	504	480	528	526	624	1,104	92	1,167	265	1,914	1,135
Traumatic	495	470	464	506	488	525	577	374	480	461	735	782
Hypertensive	531	523	481	573	498	557	544	415	580	645	354	662
Coronary	603	571	548	631	632	630	533	559	574	390	625	568
Cerebrovascular	576	527	574	546	607	671	183	184	315	86	235	288
Other Circulatory	600	571	530	606	628	660	736	617	639	384	1,098	1,044
Total	611	585	552	635	607	658	784	639	788	694	839	999

Note: See table 6.1.

Table 6.5   **Relative Sizes of Health Care Costs in Top 3 Percent Compared with the Averages of Primary Diagnosis Groups**

	Inpatient Care Costs						Outpatient Care Costs					
	Total in the Five Prefectures	Aomori	Fukushima	Toyama	Fukui	Wakayama	Total in the Five Prefectures	Aomori	Fukushima	Toyama	Fukui	Wakayama
Contagious	9.5	8.7	9.2	9.8	8.7	11.4	1.1	0.7	1.8	1.9	0.7	1.1
Neoplastic	5.3	5.3	4.9	6.2	4.6	5.6	1.2	1.1	1.3	0.8	1.3	1.4
Endocrinal	10.2	8.7	10.3	10.2	10.4	12.6	1.4	1.0	1.6	1.0	2.7	1.9
Hematological	8.8	8.7	9.9	8.3	16.6	6.6	3.1	1.0	0.6	5.2	0.3	2.1
Mental	3.2	3.1	2.5	4.3	3.4	3.2	0.2	0.2	0.1	0.6	0.2	0.2
Ophthalmological/ Audiological	13.2	12.8	12.2	14.9	11.6	14.9	1.7	1.3	1.9	1.9	1.9	1.9
Respiratory	11.1	10.9	8.8	14.5	10.6	11.6	1.3	1.7	1.1	1.2	1.5	1.1
Digestive	12.8	11.5	12.7	13.2	12.8	14.5	1.1	1.1	1.2	1.0	1.2	1.2
Genitourinary	6.0	6.7	5.6	5.0	6.5	5.7	4.1	3.5	4.1	4.8	4.6	3.9
Dermatological	13.6	11.0	13.3	14.2	12.8	17.9	2.9	2.1	1.8	4.7	2.0	3.5
Skeletal	12.4	11.4	12.8	12.1	12.3	14.9	1.1	0.9	1.4	1.0	1.0	1.2
Unknown	12.9	21.2	15.5	15.8	9.2	12.3	2.0	0.2	2.4	0.5	3.6	1.8
Traumatic	7.0	6.1	8.1	7.4	9.0	6.5	1.2	0.8	1.0	0.9	1.5	1.5
Hypertensive	19.6	18.1	20.5	18.1	16.6	24.5	1.0	0.8	1.2	1.1	0.7	1.2
Coronary	9.5	8.8	10.1	8.9	9.9	10.5	0.9	1.0	1.0	0.6	1.0	0.9
Cerebrovascular	5.6	5.7	8.0	3.9	6.8	7.6	0.3	0.4	0.5	0.2	0.4	0.4
Other Circulatory	12.9	11.3	13.9	12.5	12.3	16.5	1.2	1.1	1.2	0.6	1.7	1.6
Total	10.8	10.2	11.5	10.1	10.4	12.7	1.3	1.1	1.4	1.1	1.4	1.5

Table 6.6   Distribution of Elderly Patients across Institutions in a Given Month in 1993

	Types of Institutions						Percentage					
	Total	Other Types	Teaching	Incorporated	Clinics	Outside	Total	Other Types	Teaching	Incorporated	Clinics	Outside
Aomori	82,626	23,286	0	11,424	47,214	702	100	28.2	0.0	13.8	57.1	0.8
Fukushima	46,048	11,035	236	9,564	24,800	413	100	24.0	0.5	20.8	53.9	0.9
Toyama	75,708	27,736	811	5,623	40,977	561	100	36.6	1.1	7.4	54.1	0.7
Fukui	51,965	19,065	776	5,396	25,639	1,089	100	36.7	1.5	10.4	49.3	2.1
Wakayama	71,792	12,003	1,718	7,789	48,756	1,526	100	16.7	2.4	10.8	67.9	2.1
Total	328,139	93,125	3,541	39,796	187,386	4,291	100	28.4	1.1	12.1	57.1	1.3

Table 6.7   Distribution of the Expensive Elderly Patient Group (top 3 percent) across Institutions in a Given Month in 1993

	Types of Institutions						Percentage					
	Total	Other Types	Teaching	Incorporated	Clinics	Outside	Total	Other Types	Teaching	Incorporated	Clinics	Outside
Aomori	3,177	1,023	0	1,526	584	44	100	32.2	0.0	48.0	18.4	1.4
Fukushima	1,744	502	18	907	291	26	100	26.8	1.0	52.0	16.7	1.5
Toyama	3,002	1,469	40	1,153	301	39	100	48.9	1.3	38.4	10.0	1.3
Fukui	2,070	925	52	637	350	106	100	44.7	2.5	30.8	16.9	5.1
Wakayama	2,828	737	84	1,099	603	305	100	26.1	3.0	38.9	21.3	10.8
Total	12,821	4,656	194	5,322	2,129	520	100	36.3	1.5	41.5	16.6	4.1

Table 6.8   Probability of Belonging to the Expensive Elderly Patient Group (top 3 percent)
                   a Given Type of Institution

	Percentages					
	Total	Other Types	Teaching	Incorporated	Clinics	Outsi
Aomori	3.8	4.4		13.4	1.2	6.3
Fukushima	3.8	4.5	7.6	9.5	1.2	6.3
Toyama	4.0	5.3	4.9	20.5	0.7	7.0
Fukui	4.0	4.9	6.7	11.8	1.4	9.7
Wakayama	3.9	6.1	4.9	14.1	1.2	20.0
Total	3.9	5.0	5.5	13.4	1.1	12.1

vate hospitals rank at the top with about 13.4 percent, followed by out-of-prefecture hospitals (12.1 percent), teaching hospitals (5.5 percent), and the other types (5.0 percent). The patients at the clinics rank the lowest with only 1.1 percent probability, or one-fourth the average likelihood (3.9 percent).

The average health care costs of a patient treated for a certain primary diagnosis in a given type of institution during 1992–93 are given in table 6.9. In table 6.10, we have shown how many times more an expensive elderly patient costs than an average elderly patient for each type of institution in each prefecture. On the average, the ratio is 6.0, and except for clinics, the variation across different types of institutions is provided by the difference in the denominator (i.e., the cost of an average elderly), rather than the numerator (the cost of an expensive elderly). In the same table, the average health care cost of an expensive elderly patient in a given type of institution is given. Both of these cost measures can be subject to serious criticism, however, for two reasons. First, since we have nothing to impute the monthly expenditures to different institutions by Part A, we must rely on information supplied by Part B. In fact, we are imputing the costs incurred during a twenty-four-month period based on only one month of data. Second, in order to simplify the analysis, we impute all the health care costs of a patient incurred for all ailments and at all institutions to the institution where the patient is treated for the primary diagnosis. In spite of these shortcomings, we feel that the figures in table 6.9 are useful because, as we have seen, the major component of health care costs for the most expensive elderly is inpatient care, and many of these patients have been hospitalized for most of the twenty-four months studied.

Table 6.11 points to another source of concentration of health care expenditures among the elderly. Apparently, close to half (48.1 percent) of the revenues of the incorporated private hospitals come from the expensive elderly, or the top 3 percent of the elderly in the health care cost ranking, while other types of hospitals derive 25.4 percent of their revenue from

Table 6.9   Average Health Care Costs of a Patient, by Institution Type (primary diagnosis only) during 1992–93 (unit = 1,000 yen)

	All Elderly						Expensive Elderly (top 3%)					
	Total	Teaching	Incorporated	Clinics	Outside	Other	Total	Teaching	Incorporated	Clinics	Outside	Other
Aomori	1,186.5		1,945.6	932.0	1,450.8	1,322.1	6,794.6		6,885.2	6,450.1	8,176.9	6,796.4
Fukushima	1,040.3	1,503.1	1,514.9	764.4	1,407.7	1,225.4	6,393.8	5,687.9	6,459.9	6,037.3	7,008.1	6,474.5
Toyama	1,389.5	1,751.7	2,948.7	939.2	1,873.6	1,718.3	8,332.9	9,870.1	8,133.0	8,300.9	8,670.9	8,445.6
Fukui	1,192.6	1,696.4	1,861.7	920.8	1,733.4	1,317.4	6,932.1	7,967.8	7,021.4	6,739.0	6,910.0	6,888.0
Wakayama	1,125.1	1,418.0	1,960.2	868.0	2,378.4	1,426.5	6,905.7	6,998.1	6,894.3	6,669.0	7,505.4	6,857.4
Total	1,200.4	1,561.1	1,975.3	893.2	1,903.5	1,441.1	7,147.0	7,728.6	7,101.4	6,765.0	7,503.4	7,309.7

Table 6.10   Ratio of the Health Care Costs of the Expensive Elderly to Those of All Elderly, by Institution Type (primary diagnosis only)

	Total	Teaching	Incorporated	Clinics	Outside	Other
Aomori	5.7		3.5	6.9	5.6	5.1
Fukushima	6.1	3.8	4.3	7.9	5.0	5.3
Toyama	6.0	5.6	2.8	8.8	4.6	4.9
Fukui	5.8	4.7	3.8	7.3	4.0	5.2
Wakayama	6.1	4.9	3.5	7.7	3.2	4.8
Total	6.0	5.0	3.6	7.6	3.9	5.1

Table 6.11   Revenue Share (%) of the Expensive Elderly, by Institution Type (primary diagnosis only)

	Total	Teaching	Incorporated	Clinics	Outside	Other
Aomori	22.0		47.3	8.6	35.3	22.6
Fukushima	23.3	28.9	40.4	9.3	31.3	24.0
Toyama	23.8	27.8	56.6	6.5	32.2	26.0
Fukui	23.2	31.5	44.5	10.0	38.8	25.4
Wakayama	24.2	24.1	49.6	9.5	63.1	29.5
Total	23.3	27.1	48.1	8.6	47.8	25.4

these patients. For clinics, the proportion is only 8.6 percent. Table 6.12 computes the average inpatient days of an elderly patient treated at an institution for what is considered his or her primary diagnosis, versus those of an expensive elderly patient. Average inpatient days for patients treated for all primary diagnoses in incorporated private hospitals are 116.8 days, or more than twice those of hospitals other than teaching and incorporated (55.1 days), and more than three times those of teaching hospitals (38.6 days). This bias seems to cut across all diagnoses and can easily push up the costs for those treated at incorporated hospitals relative to other institutions. It is interesting to see that even among the most expensive elderly patients, such a bias can still be observed across all diagnoses.

6.3   Long-Term Inpatients and Regional Variations in the Distribution of Health Care Costs

In the analysis presented in the previous section, several facts concerning the concentration of health care expenditure were revealed. In particular, the following facts strongly indicate that the presence of large numbers of inpatients may explain the increasing cost of health care for the elderly in Japan.

1. There is a significant concentration of health care costs for the elderly in Japan: The top 1 percent of patients account for 10 percent of total

Table 6.12   **Average Inpatient Days of Patients Treated for Primary Diagnosis**

	All Elderly						Expensive Elderly					
	Total	Teaching	Incorporated	Clinics	Outside	Other	Total	Teaching	Incorporated	Clinics	Outside	Other
Contagious	51.0	41.4	113.9	25.1	55.1	73.5	511.4	323.4	540.9	461.6	547.0	518.5
Neoplastic	64.7	65.5	103.6	39.9	79.9	59.9	380.7	307.6	451.6	326.1	329.2	357.3
Endocrinal	46.2	32.7	113.4	23.1	57.1	50.9	504.2	214.5	595.2	381.1	571.2	458.4
Hematological	46.0	58.1	115.0	22.5	140.1	55.8	402.9	482.0	494.8	289.6	548.5	350.3
Mental	211.0	38.2	328.0	35.4	418.2	182.1	685.9	513.5	698.0	473.3	673.4	680.8
Ophthalmological/ Audiological	31.4	31.1	61.7	27.4	46.0	33.7	464.1	333.1	519.9	465.2	556.8	431.2
Respiratory	37.0	32.2	83.1	22.8	48.4	54.6	444.0	182.1	509.2	378.3	420.0	442.9
Digestive	33.6	33.8	69.9	20.4	66.5	43.5	459.7	251.6	533.8	355.5	543.6	439.8
Genitourinary	57.8	43.7	120.0	38.5	69.3	54.9	317.6	269.1	386.5	271.5	340.7	276.3
Dermatological	27.1	39.8	42.8	23.7	60.5	30.5	400.7	346.8	483.6	443.4	581.7	282.5
Skeletal	37.5	40.0	84.3	22.2	74.0	45.5	508.1	287.9	585.9	403.8	520.0	487.7
Unknown	26.5	34.3	33.9	18.0	59.6	34.4	330.4	158.0	358.8	349.3	450.3	303.1
Traumatic	69.6	64.8	125.8	37.7	117.9	74.2	501.8	417.0	532.3	453.2	546.7	480.7
Hypertensive	23.6	19.9	69.1	13.5	56.7	36.2	504.0	288.0	598.6	315.2	589.8	479.4
Coronary	47.1	37.5	96.7	24.5	99.6	51.6	475.6	250.7	540.6	361.6	463.5	448.0
Cerebrovascular	107.3	44.3	223.4	32.4	266.8	118.3	620.1	323.6	641.5	489.0	626.2	607.4
Other Circulatory	33.7	46.3	84.2	18.9	69.0	45.2	439.8	312.8	511.8	391.7	507.0	412.7
Total	44.3	38.6	116.8	22.5	95.3	55.1	517.2	296.6	588.6	408.1	565.4	489.3

health care costs, and the top 10 percent account for a staggering 45 percent of these costs.

2. This concentration derives from inpatient care rather than outpatient care.

3. The concentration of spending on inpatient care appears to be attributable to the fact that the continuous length of stay of inpatients is high.

Most of the inpatients who stay in the hospital for a long time are elderly people who have difficulty living independently because they are left with physical disabilities after the completion of treatment during the acute stage of illness. Because there is a lack of alternative facilities for these elderly patients, this is called *social hospitalization.* In many cases, these long-term inpatients need long-term care, rather than actual medical treatment. How much of our valuable health care resources are taken up by these long-term inpatients whose need for medical treatment is limited? Is it perhaps possible that health care costs are higher in regions in which there are large numbers of long-term inpatients? Moreover, is it not true that increasing the supply of medical resources (the numbers of hospitals and hospital beds) will encourage long-term hospitalization, which in turn will generate higher health care costs?

In this section, we take the view that the existence of long-term hospitalization has a significant effect on the cost of health care for the elderly. Its effect on regional variations in health care expenditure, along with the effects that the regional supply of medical resources has on long-term hospitalization, are analyzed in this section from the point of view of the regional distribution of health care costs.

6.3.1   Explanation of the Data Set and the Definition of Long-Term Hospitalization

In the analysis of the concentration and continuation of health care expenditure discussed earlier, a new data set was created by combining two data sets, 1992 and 1993, with a common patient code among the insurance claims for health care for the elderly. Now we must obtain as much regional data as possible in order to analyze variations in regional health care costs. Thus, we discard the integrated two-year data in favor of the data for 1993 (twelve months) only.[7] (The original data consist of individual health care microdata for elderly people from twelve municipalities, but it was possible to consolidate the data for two consecutive years in only five prefectures.)

7. The data set used in this analysis consist of health care insurance claim data for the elderly, excluding the following microdata: (a) those who became eligible for health care for the elderly in the course of 1993; (b) those who lost their eligibility through death or other reasons during 1993; and (c) those who had no municipality address code. Excluding these, there are 1,286,559 items of microdata for eleven prefectures (77 medical zones and 765 municipalities) in the data set.

Next, we define long-term hospitalization as a period of three months (ninety days) or more. Inpatients staying for 180 days or more are, however, included when necessary. It should be noted that the number of long-term patients is probably underestimated because of the truncation of the data.[8] We cannot single out those who have been hospitalized three months or more among the inpatients in the first two months or the last two months of our twelve-month longitudinal data set.

6.3.2 Health Care Costs for Long-Term Inpatients

In section 6.2, the longitudinal data on two consecutive years of health care showed that health care costs were concentrated among a relatively small number of elderly patients with lengthy periods of hospitalization. In this section, we study the relationship between concentration and long-term hospitalization, as revealed by the data. (Although the data cover a period of only one year, they are based on a large number of samples.)

Table 6.13 shows the proportion of long-term inpatients generating high health care costs, and the proportion of long-term inpatient health care costs attributable to these patients. The table shows that 82.9 percent of the top 1 percent of high-cost patients were long-term inpatients staying ninety days or more. The share peaked at 88.3 percent for the top 3 percent, then fell to 82.6 percent for the top 5 percent and to 55.6 percent for the top 10 percent. The majority of patients in the top 5 percent were long-term inpatients. From a health care cost viewpoint, we can see that although the top 1 percent of high-cost elderly patients accounted for 11.3 percent of the total health care costs for the elderly, 82.9 percent of that expenditure was attributable to long-term inpatients staying ninety days or more. Similarly, the top 5 percent accounted for 36.0 percent of the total health care costs, but 83.9 percent of that figure was attributable to long-term inpatients. Furthermore, the top 10 percent accounted for more than half (52.1 percent) of health care costs; of this amount, 67.7 percent was attributable to health care costs for long-term inpatients. So, from the one-year health care cost data for 1993, we can also confirm that more than 80 percent of the top 5 percent of high-cost elderly patients' health care cost was attributable to long-term inpatients, and that these same patients accounted for more than 80 percent of the total expenditure on high-cost patients.

Next, we ascertain from table 6.14 the role of long-term hospitalization in the total cost of health care for the elderly. By looking at the health care cost shares in the three right-hand columns, we see that the cost of health

---

8. It was difficult to determine the effect of truncating data at both ends, but a Ministry of Health and Welfare patient survey showed, with respect to patients aged seventy or over, that 13.3 percent were hospitalized for three months or over, and 6.0 percent for six months or over. By contrast, in our data set the incidence of inpatients hospitalized for three months (90 days) or over was 5.8 percent, and for six months (180 days) or over, 3.4 percent.

Table 6.13   The Proportion of Long-Term Inpatients to Patients with High Health Care Costs

Patients with High Health Care Costs (share in total elderly enrollees)	Number of Patients			Patients with High Health Care Costs (share in total costs for the elderly)	Health Care Costs		
	Patients with High Health Care Costs	Inpatients Staying 90 Days or More	Inpatients Staying 180 Days or More		Patients with High Health Care Costs	Inpatients Staying 90 Days or More	Inpatients Staying 180 Days or More
Top 1%	100.0	82.9	69.8	11.3	100.0	82.9	69.6
Top 2%	100.0	88.2	75.1	19.1	100.0	87.2	74.1
Top 3%	100.0	88.3	73.4	25.7	100.0	87.6	73.1
Top 4%	100.0	86.3	68.5	31.3	100.0	86.3	69.7
Top 5%	100.0	82.6	61.8	36.0	100.0	83.9	65.1
Top 10%	100.0	55.6	34.2	52.1	100.0	67.7	47.5
Top 20%	100.0	28.9	17.1	68.8	100.0	51.8	35.9
Top 30%	100.0	19.3	11.4	78.9	100.0	45.2	31.4
Top 40%	100.0	14.5	8.6	86.0	100.0	41.5	28.8
Top 50%	100.0	11.6	6.9	91.3	100.0	39.1	27.1

Note: 12,286,559 observations in eleven prefectures were used from the insurance claim data for elderly health care (1993).

Table 6.14   Comparisons of Long-Term Inpatients and Other Enrollees

Prefecture	Share in the Number (%)			Average Health Care Costs per Enrollee in a Year (× 10,000 yen)			Share in Total Health Care Costs (%)		
	All Elderly Enrollees	Inpatients Staying 90 Days or More	Other Enrollees	All Elderly Enrollees	Inpatients Staying 90 Days or More	Other Enrollees	All Elderly Enrollees	Inpatients Staying 90 Days or More	Other Enrollees
Hokkaido	100.0	8.6	91.4	70.8	354.6	44.1	100.0	43.2	56.8
Aomori	100.0	6.6	93.4	49.6	275.4	33.6	100.0	36.7	63.3
Fukushima	100.0	4.4	95.6	44.5	300.3	32.8	100.0	29.6	70.4
Toyama	100.0	6.6	93.4	58.0	350.5	37.3	100.0	40.0	60.0
Ishikawa	100.0	7.5	92.5	62.5	334.7	40.5	100.0	40.0	60.0
Fukui	100.0	6.0	94.0	49.5	293.6	34.0	100.0	35.4	64.6
Shizuoka	100.0	3.2	96.8	42.9	339.1	33.2	100.0	25.0	75.0
Shiga	100.0	3.2	96.8	40.9	339.4	31.1	100.0	26.3	73.7
Wakayama	100.0	3.8	96.2	45.5	313.3	34.7	100.0	26.5	73.5
Okayama	100.0	5.9	94.1	53.0	319.0	36.3	100.0	35.6	64.4
Kochi	100.0	8.8	91.2	59.4	316.9	34.6	100.0	46.9	53.1
Average of eleven prefectures	100.0	5.8	94.2	53.0	326.8	36.2	100.0	35.7	64.3

care for long-term inpatients staying for ninety days or more accounts for 35.7 percent of the total cost of health care for the elderly. Thus, more than one-third of the cost of health care is spent on long-term inpatients who need comparatively little active medical treatment but much more long-term caretaking. Incidentally, there is a wide variation in these ratios from one prefecture to another. The cost of long-term inpatient health care accounts for more than 40 percent (the highest figures) in Kochi prefecture (46.9 percent) and Hokkaido (43.2 percent). The ratio is much smaller in Shizuoka prefecture (25.0 percent).

Why are there differences at a prefectural level in the share of health care costs attributable to long-term inpatients? In the 11 prefectures, the average cost of health care for a long-term inpatient is 3,268,000 yen, nine times higher than the figure of 362,000 yen for other elderly patients (columns [8] and [9] in the table). However, prefectural differences are surprisingly small and the difference between the figures is always less than 30 percent (2,754,000 yen in Aomori prefecture and 3,546,000 yen in Hokkaido). If this cannot be explained by the difference in per-patient health care costs, then the main reason for prefectural variations in the percentage share of health care costs for long-term inpatients (between 25 percent and 46.9 percent) must be the difference in numbers of long-term inpatients: In other words, the difference in the incidence of long-term hospitalization.

If we look at the percentage of long-term inpatients in the total of elderly patients (column [2]), although the average is 5.8 percent, the differences among prefectures vary widely between the high figures in Kochi (8.8 percent) and Hokkaido (8.6 percent) and the low ones in Shizuoka and Shiga (each at 3.2 percent). In other words, the figures confirm that the total long-term inpatient health care costs are high in prefectures with a large proportion of long-term inpatients.

Furthermore, in prefectures where the ratio of long-term inpatients is high, the average health care cost per elderly patient (column [4]) is also high. The scatter diagram in figure 6.5 confirms the relationship between the ratio of long-term inpatients and average health care costs. There is a strong positive correlation between the two, and the larger the number of long-term inpatients, the higher the average health care costs for the elderly become. From this, the possibility emerges that among the many reasons for the prefectural variations in health care costs for the elderly, the incidence of long-term hospitalization is a particularly valid one.

6.3.3   Long-Term Inpatients and the Distribution of Health Care Costs

We have now established that there are two effects of the incidence of long-term inpatients' staying ninety days or more. One is that the average health care cost rises significantly; the other is that regional variations in health care costs increase in direct proportion to the number of long-term inpatients. We examine this in more detail below.

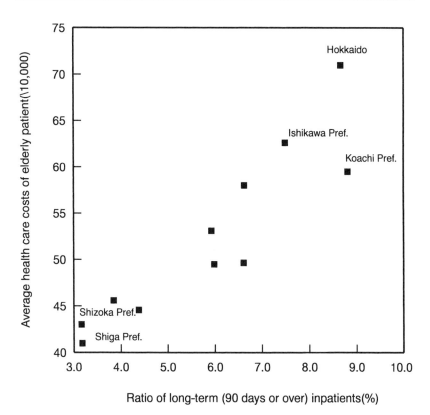

Fig. 6.5   Ratio of long-term inpatients to average health care cost of elderly patients (per prefecture)

First, however, let us consider what kind of regional medical units exist. In many cases, when discussing health care cost issues, a prefecture is taken as the unit of discussion. However, in terms of medical resources such as hospitals and hospital beds, there are many instances in which a medical zone is the unit of discussion. The number of medical zones depends to some extent on the area of the prefecture, but a prefecture is generally divided into several zones. From the viewpoint of a patient covered by National Health Insurance, the municipality should be considered the unit. We consider all three units in our analysis.

To establish the extent to which variations in health care costs can be increased by the incidence of long-term hospitalization, we compare the values of the total number of elderly people eligible for health care, including long-term inpatients, and the number of those eligible for health care, excluding long-term inpatients (table 6.15). The first and second rows show the values for microdata, whereas the third and fourth rows give the values at a prefectural level. The average prefectural health care cost per elderly

Table 6.15   Health Care Costs With and Without Long-term Inpatients in Different Aggregation Levels

	Number of Samples	Average Cost (yen)	Standard Deviation (yen)	Minimum Cost (yen)	Maximum Cost (yen)
Microdata					
All elderly enrollees	1,286,559	530,072	914,084	0	23,149,610
Excluding inpatients staying 90 days or more	1,212,069	361,803	502,682	0	16,335,410
Prefectural aggregation					
All elderly enrollees	11	524,150	93,340	409,179	708,435
Excluding inpatients staying 90 days or more	11	356,597	37,559	311,253	440,667
Medical-zone aggregation					
All elderly enrollees	77	533,358	129,172	331,559	817,414
Excluding inpatients staying 90 days or more	77	363,344	55,916	265,319	479,391
Municipality aggregation					
All elderly enrollees	765	526,564	144,255	244,774	1,118,971
Excluding inpatients staying 90 days or more	765	357,032	68,139	180,190	641,588

patient ranges from about 409,000 yen to about 708,000 yen, producing a standard deviation around 93,000 yen. If the long-term inpatients are excluded, however, the prefectural averages range from about 311,000 to about 441,000 yen, bringing the standard deviation down to around 38,000 yen. Thus, variations in health care costs for the elderly are relatively small when long-term hospitalization is excluded. If the element of long-term inpatient care could somehow be removed from the calculation of health care costs, the prefectural variations in such costs would automatically decrease.

Health care costs vary more widely between medical zones (rows [5] and [6] of the table) than between prefectures (rows [3] and [4]) and even more widely between municipalities (rows [7] and [8]). Our data set, which covers seventy-seven medical zones, shows that their average medical costs range between about 332,000 and 817,000 yen, the ratio of the maximum to the minimum being 2.5:1. If the element of long-term inpatient care is excluded, however, the costs range from about 265,000 to 479,000 yen, and the ratio falls to 1.8:1. For municipalities, the costs, including those of long-term inpatient care, range between about 245,000 and 1,119,000 yen, and the ratio rises to 4.6:1. Furthermore, this variation can be reduced to about 180,000 to 642,000 yen by excluding the cost of long-term inpatient care.

Thus, we can see that the distribution of average health care costs in medical zones and municipalities can be leveled to some extent by excluding expenditures on long-term inpatient care. To illustrate this visually, figures 6.6 and 6.7 show the changes in the frequency distribution. The upper graph shows the overall distribution including long-term hospitalization, and the lower graph shows the distribution when long-term hospitalization is excluded. In the upper graph, the distribution shows the right side (high-cost portion) extending farther because there are regions with high medical expenditures. It resembles a normal distribution more closely in the lower graph. Incidentally, the horizontal axis represents the annual health care costs in yen, and the vertical axis represents the relative frequency (percent).

6.3.4   Long-Term Inpatients and the Availability of Medical Resources

It is evident that long-term hospitalization not only pushes up the cost of health care for the elderly, but also that, because it distorts the distribution of health care costs, it influences regional variations in those costs. One of the reasons for these regional variations is that some regions have large numbers of long-term patients, while others have relatively few.

What are the reasons for these differing demands for long-term inpatient care? Starting from the premise that a market for health care for the elderly develops in each region, the elderly are consumers; hospitals, clinics, and other health care institutions are suppliers. (In Japan, it is more appro-

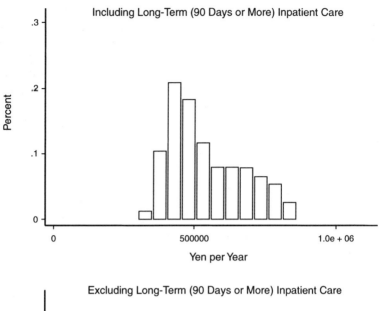

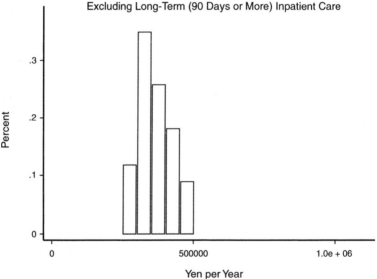

Fig. 6.6   Frequency distribution of average health care cost in fiscal 1993, by zone

priate to describe health care institutions, rather than individual doctors, as economic entities.)

Elderly consumers create a demand for health care as their health declines, but the extent of that demand is determined by such elements as age, sex, family circumstances, and so on. Since it is believed that the level of medical treatment demanded by an individual is a function of that person's financial status, the demand for health care may be considered to

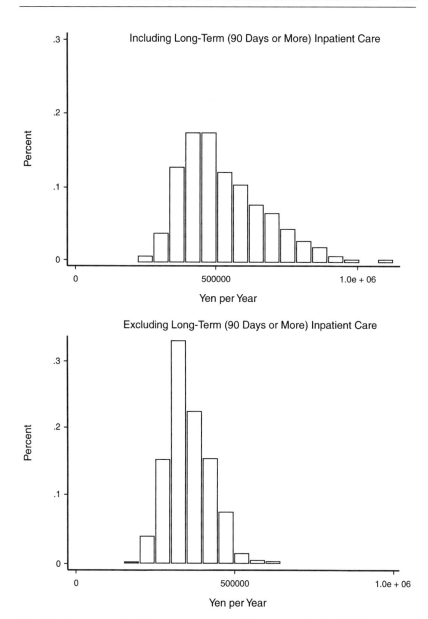

Fig. 6.7   Frequency distribution of average health care cost in fiscal 1993, by municipality

be an increasing function of the general level of income. However, if we consider that the possibility of declining health increases as the level of income diminishes, then the demand for health care can also be regarded as a decreasing function of the general level of income.

Health care institutions, on the other hand, provide services on a fixed-price basis. The government can restrict increases in the numbers of beds, but under the fee-for-service system, the institutions can provide unrestricted health care service to their patients. In regions where there are larger health care resources (numbers of doctors, health care institutions, beds) per capita, health care institutions have greater incentive to provide health care services in order to make a profit (supplier-induced demand hypothesis [Nishimura 1987]). The levels of incentive vary as a function not only of the availability of health care resources, but also of the degree of concentration.

According to American interpretations, the likelihood of oversupply diminishes as concentration decreases and the market becomes more competitive. This presupposes that prices are free to fluctuate in response to demand, a situation that does not necessarily apply in Japan. In fact, the opposite could be said to apply in Japan, where prices are fixed and the patient's own financial contribution is low. In other words, there is a tendency toward an oversupply with respect to health care services in regions in which there are of large numbers of medium-sized hospitals.

What about the demand for long-term hospitalization? If this demand is almost the same as that for health care, then the situation is almost the same as that of general health care services, in that demand is affected by individual and family circumstances. However, if we believe that patients with larger incomes are more likely to purchase health care services other than hospitalization, then the demand for long-term hospitalization should decrease as the level of patient income increases.

As to the provision of long-term hospitalization services, there is still a significant incentive for hospitals to accept elderly long-term inpatients, although the profit motive is considered to have diminished after Japan's Ministry of Health and Welfare introduced a system under which hospitalization charges decrease progressively as the period of hospitalization increases.

Recently, the fixed-price system was introduced. Under this system, a certain amount of remuneration is paid without the prescription of medicine or injections, if the capability of providing care is enhanced. Hence, accepting long-term inpatients leads to a stable operational basis for health care institutions. We can assume that health care institutions have an incentive to provide long-term hospitalization services to patients whose treatment at the acute stage has been completed.

What if the demand for long-term hospitalization and for caretaking are identical? The much higher demand than supply of caretaking leads to the rationing of services, rather than to the unreasonable creation of demand by health care institutions.

Whichever hypothesis is correct may be determined by taking into account the contribution by special nursing homes for the elderly—alternative institutions specializing in long-term care. If the levels of long-term hospitalization are lower in the regions with more of these special nursing homes, the first hypothesis applies. If the number of long-term hospitalizations remains the same when the number of special nursing homes increases somewhat, then the latter hypothesis that demand for caretaking exceeds the supply (total of the number of beds in health care institutions and special nursing home for the elderly) is valid.

6.3.5   Estimation of the Probability of Long-Term Hospitalization

The aim of this section is to determine whether the market hypothesis matches the reality, and to measure the extent to which the supply of health care influences the incidence of long-term hospitalization.

In the measurement, whether each elderly patient is (1) or is not (0) a long-term inpatient is defined as a dependent variable. Demand-side factors (patient attributes, income, etc.) and supply-side factors (density of health care resources, degree of market concentration, density of alternative care facilities, etc.), which were examined in the previous section, were defined as explanatory variables to explain the probability of long-term hospitalization.

Therefore, we use the estimation formula

$$Y = f(\text{Patient Attributes, Income, Density of Health Care Resources,}$$

$$\text{Degree of Market Concentration, Density of Alternative Care Facilities}),$$

where

$$Y = 1(\text{Long-term Inpatient}) \text{ and } 0 \text{ (Others)}.$$

In formulas such as this in which the dependent variable is 0/1, the logit model and the probit model typically are employed for estimation. Since it is easier to evaluate the estimation parameters, the logit model is used here.

Table 6.16 summarizes the variables used in the estimation. The dummy for long-term hospitalization, which is the dependent variable, will be 0 or 1, and the average value is 5.79 percent. The individual attributes used as demand factors are an average age of 77 and a male/female ratio of 40 percent to 60 percent. The share of subscribers to health insurance other than the National Health Insurance is 19.6 percent. Income is an individual attribute, but since individual income figures were not available, the average taxable income of the region (approximately 1,200,000 yen) was used as an alternative.

With regard to supply variables, three types of aggregate value were established for each market unit (the scale of the region). To indicate the density of health care resources, we used bed density (per capita number of beds) was used (the number of beds being the total in both clinics and hospitals). Doctor density is also frequently used as a variable, but in the case of long-term hospitalization, inpatient health care resources—partic-

Table 6.16   **Statistical Description of Variables**

Variables	Average	Standard Deviation	Minimum	Maximum
Microdata				
Long-term hospitalization				
Dummy[a]	0.0579	0.2336	0	1
Age	77.11	5.72	65	110
Male dummy	0.404	0.491	0	1
Non–National Health				
Insurance dummy	0.196	0.397	0	1
Prefectural aggregation data				
Number of beds[b]	110.1	23.8	75.0	146.8
Concentration index of beds[c]	0.011	0.005	0.003	0.02
Capacity of nursing homes for				
the elderly[d]	158.2	53.8	102.5	259.7
Taxable income[e]	1,261.2	198.0	889.5	1,530.5
Medical-zone aggregation data				
Number of beds[b]	109.6	34.9	10.7	236.8
Concentration index of beds[c]	0.070	0.065	0.020	0.554
Capacity of nursing homes for				
the elderly[d]	158.7	71.9	30.6	597.3
Taxable income[e]	1,246.2	229.6	728.8	1,614.2
Municipality aggregation data				
Number of beds[b]	106.4	83.1	0	2,670.8
Concentration index of beds[c]	0.336	0.333	0	1
Capacity of nursing homes for				
the elderly[d]	160.4	165.8	0	2,126.0
Taxable income[e]	1,232.4	258.2	573.5	1,886.2

[a]Length of stay in hospitals during the year (dummy variable: 180 or more = 1, less than 180 = 0).
[b]Number of hospital beds per 10,000 people.
[c]Herfindahl index.
[d]Capacity per 10,000 elderly patients aged sixty-five or above.
[e]Taxable income per capita (in thousands of yen).

ularly bed capacity—are considered to be more important. The Herfindahl index[9] for the number of beds is used to measure the degree of market concentration. The value of this index is between 0 and 1; the larger the figure, the higher the degree of concentration. The degree of bed density decreases as the market expands. At an average value, it gets higher in the order of prefectures, medical zones, and municipalities. The capacity of special nursing homes for the elderly is included as an alternative long-term hospitalization facility.

Table 6.17 shows the results. Number of beds, degrees of bed concentration, and capacity of special nursing homes for the elderly have significant

9. The Herfindahl index, which is defined by the following equation, indicates the degree of concentration or monopoly of suppliers in a market: $H = \sum_{i=1}^{n}[X_i/\sum_{i=1}^{n}X_i]^2$. In this analysis, X_i is the number of patients in i-th hospital in the given municipality.

Table 6.17   Estimation Results (logit model)

Explanatory variable	Prefectural Aggregation Data		Medical-Zone Aggregation Data		Municipality Aggregation Data	
	Parameter	z-value	Parameter	z-value	Parameter	z-value
Number of beds	0.01124	50.3	0.00640	48.3	0.00166	41.8
Bed concentration	−10.66006	−9.3	−2.46781	−27.4	−0.30137	−22.9
Capacity of nursing homes	0.00125	8.5	0.00147	24.3	0.00029	13.1
Taxable income	−0.00045	−15.6	−0.00038	−20.0	−0.00045	−27.1
Age	0.04821	78.3	0.04787	77.7	0.04725	76.8
Male dummy	−0.21385	−26.7	−0.21099	−26.3	−0.20295	−25.4
Non–National Health Insurance dummy	−0.02687	−2.6	−0.00803	−0.8	0.07355	7.5
Constant	−7.25689	−97.5	−6.78071	−114.6	−6.03846	−110.5
Pseudo R^2	0.027		0.0276		0.0174	

Notes: Dependent variable: Length of stay in hospitals during the year (dummy variable: 180 or more = 1, less than 180 = 0). 1,286,559 observations of eleven prefectures were used from the insurance claim data of elderly patients (1993). Those variables such as length of stay, age, male dummy, and non–National Health Insurance dummy are individual patient base, while the variables of the number of beds, bed concentration, capacity of nursing homes, and taxable income are aggregate values of each geographical boundary level of medical markets. Pseudo R^2 is $(1 − LI/LO)$ where LO is log-likelihood with only constant, and LI is log-likelihood when all explanatory variables are included in the calculation. If LI is the same as LO, it will be 0, and if it is a perfect prediction (LI = 0), then it will be 1.

explanatory power. The positive number of beds suggests that the larger the number of beds per capita, the higher the probability of long-term hospitalization. The negative degree of bed concentration shows that the probability of long-term hospitalization decreases as the degree of concentration gets higher. The positive capacity of nursing homes indicates that the probability of long-term hospitalization is higher in regions with more special nursing homes for the elderly. The hypothesis that the supply of long-term care services by special nursing homes for the elderly serves as an alternative to long-term hospitalization cannot be proved. As was mentioned earlier, one interpretation of this is that in the current situation, in which there is insufficient provision of specialist long-term care facilities such as nursing homes, both they and other health care facilities are providing long-term care services in regions where the demand for care is particularly high.

The estimation was based on the premise that there were three types of health care market (prefectures, medical zones, and municipalities). Overall statistical significance is highest in terms of the number of beds, degree of concentration, and capacity of special nursing homes for the elderly, in the medical zone. We conclude that the market for long-term hospitalization services is likely formed within medical zones.

Next, we evaluate the degree of effects by estimated parameters on the dependent variables using average values.[10] At the prefectural level, when the number of beds per 10,000 population is increased by one, the probability of average long-term hospitalization (5.79 percent) rises by 0.06 percent. Thus, a 10 percent increase in the bed density causes a 0.7 percent rise in the probability. The effect appears to be small. However, when this relationship is assumed to be constant, difference in bed density among prefectures (75.0 − 146.8 beds) may produce a maximum of 4.4 percent difference in the probability of the elderly's long-term hospitalization. As figure 6.4 shows, the effect of an increase in the number of long-term inpatients on health care costs is large, so the effects of the bed density cannot be ignored. A 10 percent change in bed density at the medical-zone level causes the probability of long-term hospitalization to increase by 0.38 percent, which is lower than at the prefectural level. However, since the variance in bed density is much larger (between 10.7 and 236.8) at the medical-zone level, the difference in bed density may produce a maximum of 7.9 percent difference in the probability of long-term hospitalization. The difference in the probability at the municipal level may reach as high as 24.2 percent.[11]

---

10. The changes in the probability P_i for the dependent variable Y to become 1 when the explanatory variable x_j changes is given by the formula $\partial P_i / \partial x_{ij} = \beta_j P_i (1 - P_i)$, where i and j are adscripts meaning observation and explanatory variables, respectively.

11. Since, in the logit model, the assessment of a parameter that is an average value cannot be applied at a point where it is far from the average value, the above applications to maximum and minimum values should be considered only as references.

When we look at the demand factors, income, age, and sex are all highly significant, except in the case of the non–National Health Insurance dummy, which has a low statistical significance. Moreover, the scale of the parameters at prefecture, medical zone, and municipality levels is stable. When trial estimations are made of the degree of influence of each variable, income has a clear negative effect, as expected, and a 100,000-yen increase in income reduces the long-term hospitalization probability by 0.2 percent. As for the effect of age, in an average sample age of seventy-seven, for each age increment of one year the long-term hospitalization probability increases by 0.26 percent. The probability of long-term hospitalization is 0.6 percent higher for males than for females.

From these estimation results, the following four points are evident:

1. Demand for long-term hospitalization (or long-term care service) forms a market within medical zones.

2. Long-term hospitalization increases when the number of beds per capita increases (when the number of beds increases by 10 percent at medical-zone level, the long-term hospitalization probability increases by 0.38 percent).

3. In areas with special large-capacity nursing homes for the elderly, the long-term hospitalization probability was also high.

4. As the long-term hospitalization probability increased with age (0.26 percent increase per year), the increase in the number of long-term inpatients reflected an increase in the numbers of late-stage elderly patients.

6.4   Conclusions

We have learned that more than 80 percent of high-cost elderly patients (top 5 percent) are long-term inpatients hospitalized for ninety days or more. One-third of the cost of health care for the elderly is devoted to such long-term hospitalization. Consequently, the difference in the incidence of long-term hospitalization is one of the main reasons for regional variations in health care costs. We also know that the probability of an elderly patient's becoming a long-term inpatient is high in areas where the number of beds per capita is high, and that the long-term hospitalization probability is high in areas where the capacity of special nursing homes for the elderly is large.

We conclude, therefore, that long-term hospitalization or care-oriented services explain the major part (over 80 percent) of high-cost elderly patients in the health care system in Japan, rather than any unforeseeable phenomena such as accidents, fatal diseases, or serious surgical operations. The health care costs associated with long-term hospitalization account for one-third of the total cost of health care for the elderly. It is interesting to note that expenditure on long-term care by Medicaid, the public health care insurance system for the elderly in the United States, accounted for 33 percent of the total expenditure in 1994, a figure almost identical to our own measurement. Because home-care charges are included in Medicaid's long-term care figures, we cannot compare the two directly, but it can be said that the cost of long-term care is very high in both countries. The important point here is that in the United States, long-term care is considered quite separately from acute care. In Japan, the same high level of human resources used at the acute stage is also employed in long-term care. It is apparent that this leads to a very considerable demand on such resources. It is important to define clearly the "care" aspect of health care, and to ensure that there is a "care" service in place to provide it.

Finally, there are more long-term hospitalizations in areas in which there are large numbers of beds in health care facilities, as well as in areas where the capacity of special nursing homes, which are formal long-term care service providers for the elderly, is large. This leads us to conclude that a care-service provision system, which combines health care facilities and special nursing homes for the elderly, exists in areas where there is a large demand for long-term hospitalization (that is, demand for long-term care). In order to establish whether rationing is occurring—because supply cannot catch up with a rapidly increasing care demand—a further detailed analysis, taking into consideration other care facilities and differences in family circumstances, is needed.

References

Gornick, M., A. McMillan, and J. Lubitz. 1993. A longitudinal perspective on patterns of Medicare payments. *Health Affairs* 12 (2): 140–50.
Niki, Ryu. 1990. *Empirical study on health care in modern Japan* [in Japanese]. Tokyo: Igaku Shoin.
Nishimura, Shuzo. 1987. Economic analysis of health care (in Japanese). Tokyo: Toyokeizai Shinposha.
Ogura, Seiritsu, and Reiko Suzuki. 1997. Physician supply and the demand for health care. Paper presented at Japan Econometric Society Meetings, 14–15 September, Tokyo.

7

The Effects of Demographic Change on Health and Medical Expenditures
A Simulation Analysis

Satoshi Nakanishi and Noriyoshi Nakayama

7.1 Introduction

In Japan, spending for medical care reached 25,790 billion yen in 1994. Between 1960 and 1994, medical expenditures grew at an annual rate of 12.3 percent, faster than the 10.1 percent annual growth of the gross domestic product (GDP) during the same period. As a result, medical expenditures as a percentage of GDP doubled, from 2.5 percent in 1960 to 5.4 percent in 1994. The largest average annual increases in medical spending occurred in the 1960s and 1970s (19.9 percent and 17.2 percent, respectively), while 1980 ushered in a period of relatively slow growth; from 1980 to 1994, medical expenditures grew at an average annual rate of only 5.5 percent (see fig. 7.1). Since the 1980s, the Japanese government's cost containment strategy, which limits reimbursement rates while increasing self-payments, has slowed the rate of growth. Nonetheless, in 1994 the average per capita medical cost for people aged sixty-five and over was 532,290 yen, 4.8 times higher than the per capita costs for those under sixty-five.

Demographic change was responsible for roughly one-fourth (26.8 percent) of the growth in medical costs between 1980 and 1990. In 1996 the proportion of the Japanese population aged sixty-five and over exceeded 15 percent. According to the United Nations definition, a society is an *aging society* when the ratio of the population aged sixty-five and over exceeds 7 percent, and is an *aged society* when this ratio exceeds 14 percent.

Satoshi Nakanishi passed away in May 2001. Prior to his death, he was associate professor of economics at Nihon Fukushi University. Noriyoshi Nakayama is associate professor of economics at the University of Marketing and Distribution Sciences.

The authors are grateful to Seiritsu Ogura for providing data on the future population. We would also like to thank David M. Cutler for his many helpful comments on an earlier draft.

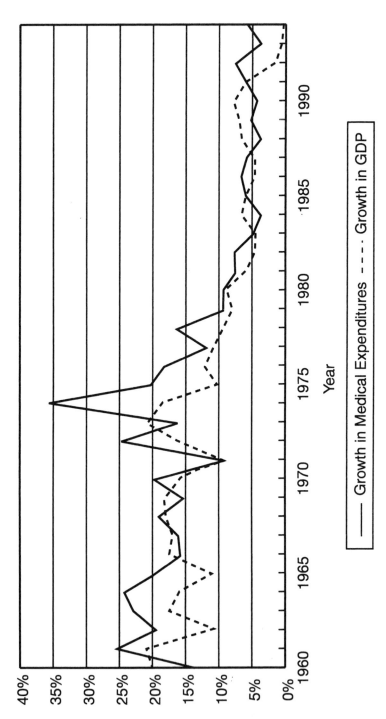

Fig. 7.1   Percent growth in medical care expenditures and GDP in Japan for fiscal years 1960–94
Sources: Kokumin Keizai Keisan Nenpō (Economic Planning Agency), and Kokumin Iryōhi (Ministry of Health and Welfare).

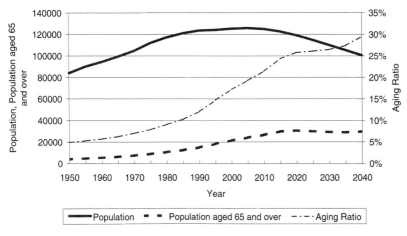

Fig. 7.2   Changes in Japanese population, population aged sixty-five and over, and aging ratio, 1950–2040
Sources: Jinkō Dōtai Chōsa (Ministry of Health and Welfare), and Ogura and Kurumisawa (1994).

Japanese society thus is already an aged society. Figure 7.2 illustrates the growth, and then decline, in Japan's total population, the population growth of those aged sixty-five and over, and the aging ratio (that is, the percentage of the population aged sixty-five and over) from 1950 to 2040. The total population is projected to peak around 2010, then to decrease gradually until 2040. The total over-sixty-five population will rise gradually between the 1990s and the 2010s, then remain almost constant after 2020. The aging ratio is expected to rise rapidly, however: In 1990 the aging ratio was 12 percent; in 2020 it will rise to 25.8 percent, and in 2040 it will reach 29.5 percent.

Since an aging population will likely result in sharp rises in medical expenditures, the Japanese government has been studying various proposals for dealing with this problem (e.g., raising the rate of self-payment). The purpose of this study is to analyze the effect of the aging of the population on the health sector and on the economy as a whole. We are concerned chiefly with (a) the effect of population aging on future medical care costs; (b) the effect of cost containment strategies on medical care expenditures; and (c) the extent to which licensing systems can or should be used to control the flow of new entrants into the medical profession.

Some of these issues have already been analyzed using macroeconometric models (Shakaihoshō-moderu-kaihatsu-kenkyūkai 1979; Hayashi et al. 1980; Hayashi, Kishi, and Mikami 1981; Nishina 1982; Kishi 1990; Inada et al. 1992). However, because these studies used annual data, their degrees of freedom are very limited. An alternative would be to use a simulation method, as Denton and Spencer (1975, 1983a,b, 1988) did in their examination of the relationship between the Canadian economy and the health care sector. In their model, household behavior depends on static demand theory; in ours, household behavior is formulated with a Grossman-type dynamic model (Grossman 1972).[1] This is a notable feature of our research: Until now, no study of the health care sector has used simulation methods and included a Grossman model.

The plan of the paper is as follows. First we estimate the parameters of several functions: the demand for health care and medical care services, consumption, government expenditures, exports, and imports. Then we provide an overview of the simulation model, report the results of the experiments, and finally provide a summary of our findings and briefly discuss the conclusions we draw from them.

7.2   Preliminary Estimation of the Simulation Model

7.2.1   Household Optimization Behavior

First we consider household behavior, which, as explained above, depends on the Grossman model in our model. In the early 1970s, Grossman (1972) turned to human capital theory to explain the demand for health. Medical care is, of course, different from other goods and services. Households do not gain utility from medical care services per se. Yet they do seek good health status and, therefore, demand medical care services as one of the inputs to produce it. When a person's health drops below a certain level, he or she dies. Because health lasts for more than one period and does not depreciate instantly, it may be regarded as a stock. Households make investments in health (their "stock") to compensate for its depreciation. In our model, such investments take the form of the purchase of medical care services, the demand for which derives from the health production function. This is the investment theory of demand for medical care proposed by Grossman. Adopting his model makes it possible to simulate not only changes in the demand for medical care but also changes in health status.

We formulate the maximization problem of a household as follows. A household maximizes the following intertemporal utility function subject to the following two constraints:

(1) $$\max U(t) = \int_0^T e^{-\rho t} [\alpha_0 e^{\eta_1 \, \mathrm{AGE}(t)} H(t)^{\alpha_1} + \beta_0 C(t)^{\beta_1}] dt \,,$$

(2)   subject to $$\dot{A}(t) = r(t)A(t) + w(t) - \gamma_0 p(t)^{\gamma_1} w(t)^{1-\gamma_1} I(t) - C(t)$$

(3) $$\dot{H}(t) = I(t) - \delta(t)H(t),$$

---

1. Wagstaff (1986, 1993) makes use of the Grossman model. Johansson and Lofgren (1995) have expanded the Grossman model theoretically.

where $A(t)$ is the stock of financial assets, $\dot{A}(t)$ is its rate of change over time, $C(t)$ is consumption of goods other than medical care services, $H(t)$ is health capital, $\dot{H}(t)$ is its rate of change over time, $I(t)$ is gross investment of health, $r(t)$ is the interest rate, $w(t)$ is wages, and $\delta(t)$ is the rate of depreciation of health. Furthermore, $p(t) = \theta(t)P_M(t)/P_C(t)$, $AGE(t) = POP65(t)/POP(t) \times 100$, where $\theta(t)$ is the self-payment rate, $P_M(t)$ is the price of medical care, $P_C(t)$ is the price of goods other than medical care services, $POP65(t)$ is the percentage of the population aged sixty-five and over, and $POP(t)$ is population.

Equation (2) shows a household's asset accumulation. A household produces a flow of health through an input of medical care and time. Therefore, the cost function of a flow of health is the function of the relative price of medical care services, wages, and gross investment in health capital. We specify the cost function as the third term on the right in equation (2). In equation (3), the household invests in health and accumulates health every year, but health is depreciated by $\delta(t)$. The rate of depreciation of health depends on the individual's age.

By solving this optimization problem, we derive the following conditions.

$$(4) \quad e^{-\rho t}\alpha_0 e^{\eta_1 AGE(t)}\alpha_1 H(t)^{\alpha_1 - 1} = \gamma_0 \lambda(t)p(t)^{\gamma_1}w(t)^{1-\gamma_1}$$

$$\left[-\gamma_1 \frac{\dot{p}(t)}{p(t)} - (1 - \gamma_1)\frac{\dot{w}(t)}{w(t)} + \delta(t) + r(t) \right]$$

$$(5) \quad -\rho + (\beta_1 - 1)\frac{\dot{C}(t)}{C(t)} = \frac{\dot{\lambda}(t)}{\lambda(t)}$$

Equation (4) shows the equilibrium condition of health capital. The marginal utility of the optimal stock of health capital equals the price of health capital. Equation (5) shows the equilibrium condition of goods other than medical services. With these conditions, we can derive the demand function for health and the demand function for goods other than medical care services. We can also obtain the derived demand equation for medical care services by using Shephard's lemma in the cost function of the flow of health. The demand equations are as follows:[2]

$$(6) \quad \ln H(t) = A_0 + \frac{\beta_1 - 1}{\alpha_1 - 1}\ln C(t) + \frac{\gamma_1}{\alpha_1 - 1}\ln p(t) + \frac{1 - \gamma_1}{\alpha_1 - 1}\ln w(t)$$

$$+ \frac{\delta_1 - \eta_1}{\alpha_1 - 1}AGE(t) + \frac{1}{\alpha_1 - 1}r(t),$$

---

2. The derivation of the demand equation for health, the demand equation for consumption goods other than medical services, and the derived demand for medical services are shown in the appendix in detail.

Table 7.1   **Estimation Results for Household Behavior**

	Coefficient	t-value
A_0	1.046	0.345
α_1	0.164	0.466
η_1	0.395	7.466
β_1	0.137	0.532
δ_1	0.035	4.544
B_0	0.237	0.422
C_0	0.003	0.232

$$(7) \quad \ln M(t) = B_0 + (\gamma_1 - 1)\ln p(t) + (1 - \gamma_1)\ln w(t) + \ln H(t)$$
$$+ \delta_1 \text{AGE}(t),$$

$$(8) \qquad \ln C(t) = C_0 + \ln C(t - 1) - \frac{1}{\beta_1 - 1}r(t).$$

We estimate equations (6), (7), and (8) using Japanese data from 1969 to 1994.[3] As we cannot observe health directly, we use the expected life expectancy at age 0 as the proxy of health. The demand equation for health, the demand equation for other goods, and the derived demand equation for medical care services are estimated by a two-stage nonlinear least squares procedure. Our estimation results are summarized in table 7.1.[4] Those results have the signs that we expected; however, some of the estimated parameters are not statistically significant.

7.2.2   Government Consumption Expenditures

We also need to estimate the government's consumption expenditures. Assuming that these expenditures are a function of GDP and the aging ratio, the government-expenditure equation is as follows:

$$\ln G(t) = \pi_0 + \pi_1 \ln Y(t) + \pi_2 \text{AGE}(t).$$

The estimation period is from 1955 to 1993 and the data sources are listed in note 4. The equations are estimated using ordinary least squares (OLS) techniques. We correct for serial correlation by allowing the residual to follow a first-order autoregressive process and estimate the equations using an iterated Cochrane-Orcutt procedure. Table 7.2 shows the estimation results for this equation.

3. We use another proxy of health other than life expectancy at age 0. We use the reciprocal of the crude death rate. However, the estimation result is almost the same as that of life expectancy at age 0.
4. We have obtained data from the following sources in order to estimate equations in the preliminary estimation section: Kokumin Keizai Keisan Nenpō (Economic Planning Agency), Keizai Tokei Nenpō (Bank of Japan), Kokumin Iryōhi (Ministry of Health and Welfare), and Jinkō Dōtai Chōsa (Ministry of Health and Welfare).

Table 7.2   **Estimation Results of Government Consumption Expenditures Equation**

	Coefficient	t-value
π_0	4.344	4.389
π_1	0.524	6.817
π_2	0.035	2.107
ρ	0.888	11.933
$\overline{R}^2$	0.994	

Table 7.3   **Estimation Results of Export Equation**

	Coefficient	t-value
ϕ_0	-146.73	-8.091
ϕ_1	-0.280	-2.075
ϕ_2	0.080	8.734
ρ	0.980	30.242
$\overline{R}^2$	0.995	

7.2.3   Export and Import Equations

Finally, we must estimate exports and imports. The equations are formulated as follows:

$$\ln EX(t) = \phi_0 + \phi_1 \ln\left[\frac{P_{EX}(t)}{P_{IM}(t)}\right] + \phi_2 YEAR$$

$$\ln IM(t) = \psi_0 + \psi_1 \ln Y(t) + \psi_2 \ln\left[\frac{P_{EX}(t)}{P_{IM}(t)}\right] + \psi_3 HSHARE + \psi_4 YEAR,$$

where EX is export, IM is import, P_{EX} is the price index of export goods, P_{IM} is the price index of import goods, HSHARE is the share of health sector to GDP, and YEAR is time trend. We introduce HSHARE into the import equation because we will investigate the effect of change in the industrial structure.

The estimation period is again 1955 to 1993, and the data sources are listed in note 4. Because of serial correlation, these equations are also estimated using an iterated Cochrane-Orcutt procedure. The estimation results for the export equation are shown in table 7.3 and those for the import equation in table 7.4. The sign of HSHARE is negative, which means that imports decrease when HSHARE rises.

Table 7.4   Estimation Results of Import Equation

	Coefficient	t-value
ψ_0	9.346	0.647
ψ_1	0.069	0.563
ψ_2	1.600	9.780
ψ_3	−0.022	−2.714
ψ_4	−0.010	−1.232
ρ	0.644	5.191
$\overline{R}^2$	0.993	

7.3   An Overview of the Simulation Model

Figure 7.3 provides a schematic representation of our model. The model has two producing sectors: a medical care services sector and a general economic sector. In the *general economic sector,* capital and general labor services (i.e., workers other than physicians and nurses) combine to produce Japan's aggregate output, minus the amount specifically associated with medical care. Nonmedical goods are absorbed by private consumption, government consumption, net exports, and physical investment. In this neoclassical macromodel, the supply of general output is predetermined by the input of labor and capital; savings (i.e., output minus consumption and net exports) automatically must equal physical investment, which, after allowing for depreciation, is added to the aggregate capital stock.

The *medical care service sector* uses capital and the labor services of physicians, nurses, and general workers. Production in both sectors requires combining capital and labor. The stock of capital is assumed to be homogeneous; that is, it can be freely transferred between sectors and earns its marginal product in both of them. General labor also moves freely between the two sectors, and its marginal product is the same in all uses. Physician and nurse services, of course, are relevant only within the medical care service sector.

The economic side of the model is neoclassical, so aggregate production is determined by supply in both the short and the long run. However, the allocation of production across sectors in each period depends on the interaction of supply and demand. On the supply side, labor and capital are drawn into productive activity in each sector to the extent that their rewards are equalized across sectors. Demand in the medical care service sector depends explicitly on the price to the ultimate consumer, wages, the demographic structure, and the demand for health. Higher demand, for example, will cause an increase in price, and hence supply, through the inflow of nonphysician labor and capital. When more resources are allocated to medical care, less output is produced in the general economy.

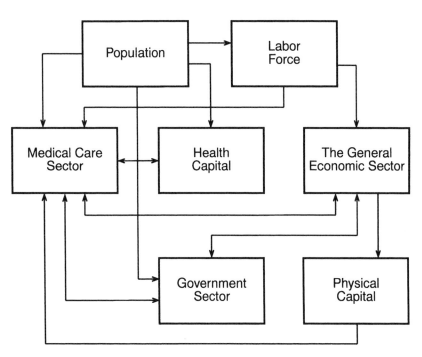

Fig. 7.3 Schematic outline of the population-economy medical care system

The government plays three possible roles in this model: spending (by claiming a share of the output of the general economy), controlling the number of licenses issued to physicians and nurses, and providing subsidies to reduce the private cost of medical care services. Through its subsidies, the government affects the spectral allocation of aggregate output.

We turn now to the components of the model. As shown in table 7.5, the equations are organized into four blocks. A subset of equations in block II (the medical care services sector) must be solved simultaneously; otherwise, the model is entirely recursive and can be solved sequentially.

7.3.1 Block I: Aggregate Economic Activity (equations [1–4])

This block tracks some basic economic aggregates: total labor force (L_t) and total output of the economy (Y_t), obtained by combining the two producing sectors (the medical care service sector, denoted by superscript 1, and the general economic sector, denoted by superscript 2); total capital stock, K_t (the undepreciated portion of last year's stock, plus new investment); and gross investment, I_t. Gross investment (equal to gross saving) is the portion of the economy's gross output not absorbed by current consumption and net export.

Table 7.5 **Equations for the Medical Care Macromodel**

I. Aggregate Economic Activity

1. $L_t = \sum_{i=1}^{2} \sum_{j=15}^{j\max} q_{ij} \overline{L}_{ijt} = L_t^1 + L_t^2$

2. $K_t = (1 - \varphi)K_{t-1} + I_{t-1}$

3. $Y_t = p_t Q_t^1 + Q_t^2$

4. $Y_t = p_t Q_t^1 + C_t + G_t + I_t + (\text{EX}_t - \text{IM}_t)$

II. Medical Care Service Sector

5. $M_t = \sum_{i=1}^{2} \sum_{j=25}^{j\max} q_{ij}^{\text{md}} \overline{M}_{ijt}$

6. $N_t = \sum_{i=22}^{i\max} q_i^{\text{nurs}} \overline{N}_{it}$

7. $\ln Q_t^1 = a_0 + \ln \text{POP}_t + \ln H_t + (\gamma_1 - 1)\ln p_t^o + (1 - \gamma_1)\ln(1 - \tau)w_t + \delta_1 \dfrac{\text{OLD}_t}{\text{POP}_t}$

8. $\ln Q_t^1 = \xi_0^1 + \xi_1^1 \ln K_t^1 + \xi_2^1 \ln L_t^1 + \xi_3^1 \ln M_t + (1 - \xi_1^1 - \xi_2^1 - \xi_3^1)\ln N_t$

9. $r_t^1 = \xi_1^1 \left(\dfrac{p_t Q_t^1}{K_t^1} \right) - \varphi = r_t$

10. $w_t^1 = \xi_2^1 \left(\dfrac{p_t Q_t^1}{L_t^1} \right) = w_t$

11. $w_t^{\text{md}} = \xi_3^1 \left(\dfrac{p_t Q_t^1}{M_t} \right)$

12. $w_t^{\text{nurs}} = \left(1 - \xi_1^1 - \xi_2^1 - \xi_3^1 \right)\left(\dfrac{p_t Q_t^1}{N_t} \right)$

13. $p_t Q_t^1 = r_t^1 K_t^1 + w_t^1 L_t^1 + w_t^{\text{md}} M_t + w_t^{\text{nurs}} N_t$

III. Health Capital Sector

14. $\ln H_t = b_0 + \dfrac{\beta_1 - 1}{\alpha_1 - 1}\ln C_t + \dfrac{\gamma_1}{\alpha_1 - 1}\ln p_t^o + \dfrac{1 - \gamma_1}{\alpha_1 - 1}\ln(1 - \tau)w_t$

$\qquad + \dfrac{\delta_1 - \eta_1}{\alpha_1 - 1}\dfrac{\text{OLD}_t}{\text{POP}_t} + \dfrac{1}{\alpha_1 - 1}r_t$

IV. General Economic Sector

15. $\ln C_t = \chi_0 + \ln C_{t-1} + \chi_1 r_t$

16. $\ln G_t = \ln \text{POP}_t + \sigma_0 + \sigma_1 \ln \dfrac{Y_t}{\text{POP}_t} + \sigma_2 \ln \dfrac{\text{OLD}_t}{\text{POP}_t}$

17. $\ln \text{EX}_t = \ln \text{POP}_t = \kappa_0 + \kappa_1 t$

18. $\ln \text{IM}_t = \ln \text{POP}_t + \upsilon_0 + \upsilon_1 \ln \dfrac{Y_t}{\text{POP}_t} + \upsilon_2 \dfrac{p_t Q_t^1}{Y_t}$

19. $\ln Q_t^2 = \zeta_0^2 + \zeta_1^2 \ln(K_t - K_t^1) + (1 - \zeta_1^2)\ln(L_t - L_t^1)$

20. $r_t^2 = \zeta_1^2 \left(\dfrac{Q_t^2}{(K_t - K_t^1)} \right) - \delta = r_t$

Table 7.5   (continued)

21. $w_t^2 = (1 - \zeta_1^2)\left(\dfrac{Q_t^2}{(L_t - L_t^1)}\right) = w_t$

Notes: C = annual private consumption; EX = annual gross export; G = annual government consumption; H = health capital; I = annual gross investment; IM = annual gross import; K = total stock of physical capital at beginning of year; K^1 = capital stock in medical service sector; K^2 = capital stock in general economic sector; L = total employed general labor force; $\bar{L}$ = nonphysician population; L^1 = general worker employed in medical sector; L^2 = general worker employed in general sector; M = employed physician; $\bar{M}$ = physician population; N = employed nurse; $\bar{N}$ = nurse population; OLD = population age sixty-five and over; p = relative price of a unit of medical care service; p^o = out-of-pocket price of a unit of medical care service; POP = total population; q = age-sex-specific labor employment rate for general workers; q^{md} = age-sex-specific labor employment rate for physicians; q^{nurs} = labor employment rate for nurses; Y = gross domestic product; Q^1 = gross product of the medical care service sector; Q^2 = gross product of the general economic sector; r = real interest rate; w = annual earnings of general worker; w^{md} = annual earnings of physician; w^{nurs} = annual earnings of nurse; α_1 = parameter of utility function about health; β_1 = parameter of utility function about consumption; γ_1 = parameter of cost function of health; η_1 = shift parameter of utility function for changing the degree of aging; δ_1 = parameter of health-capital depreciation rate for the degree of aging; a_0 = scale parameter of medical care demand function; b_0 = scale parameter of health demand function; c_0 = parameter of growth rate of private consumption per capita; ξ = parameter of production function in medical care service sector; ζ = parameter of production function in general economic sector; φ = annual rate of depreciation of physical capital; σ = parameter of government expenditure function; τ = overall rate of taxation applied to annual net income; κ = parameter of export function; υ = parameter of import function.

7.3.2   Block II: Medical-Care Service Sector (equations [5–13])

The employment level of physicians and nurses is determined on the supply side in this neoclassical model; the price adjustment assures the full employment of physicians and nurses. The labor supply of physicians and nurses is represented by equations (5) and (6); $\bar{M}$ and $\bar{N}$ represent the number of licensed persons, and q^{md} and q^{nurs} denote the labor force participation rate for medical specialists.

The demand for medical care and its supply are determined in this block. The demand function is presented in equation (7). The demand for medical care services depends on population; the optimal level of health capital; after-tax wage income (i.e., the opportunity cost of the time spent producing health capital), $(1 - \tau)w_t$; and the price of medical care services from the purchaser's point of view (out-of-pocket price), P_t^o. The production of services in equation (8) is equal to current production, which is based on the Cobb-Douglas production function, with inputs of capital, general labor, physician labor, and nurse labor. The supply function itself is implicit: It is derivable from the production function and other equations of block II. Under the assumption that physicians are price-takers and that other inputs receive the rates of return they would have received in the general economic sector, the price of medical care, the wage rates of physicians, the levels of all inputs, and the level (real) output of the sector are calculated by simultaneous solution of the system of nonlinear equations (7) through (13).

7.3.3   Block III: Health Capital Sector (equation [14])

The optimal level of health capital is determined in this block. The stock of health capital depends on per capita consumption, C_t, after-tax wage income, the degree of aging, the out-of-pocket price of medical care services, and on the real interest rate, r_t.

7.3.4   Block IV: General Economic Sector (equations [15–21])

The general economic sector produces the commodities used for general consumption, net export, and physical investment in the economy. Expenditure functions for the sector are presented in equations (15) to (18). Private consumption depends on lagged consumption, C_{t-1}, and on the real interest rate, r_t. Government expenditures are determined by per capita income, Y_t/POP_t, and by the population's age distribution. Net exports depend on the medical sector's income and its share of the total economy, $p_t Q_t^1/Y_t$.

An aggregate Cobb-Douglas production function is assumed in equation (19), the inputs being capital and general labor. The labor input is calculated in equation (1) by applying age-sex-specific participation to the male and female populations by single years of age. The wage rate, w_t^2, and the rates of return on capital, r_t^2, in this sector are determined under the assumption that factors of production receive their marginal products. The net rate of return on capital also serves as the (real) rate of interest in the economy as a whole, r_t.

7.4   Simulation Experiments and Results

To assess the impact of health policy on health status and medical expenditures, we have made a number of projections based on alternative assumptions about various parameters of the model. As noted, all projections start from labor-participation rates that are in keeping with the 1990 Japanese age-sex distribution. In addition, they start with data on the Japanese economic structure as it was in 1990: parameters of production function, scale parameters, depreciation rate of capital, and so on. The data on the future population are adopted from Ogura and Kurumisawa (1994).

7.4.1   Projection 1: Standard Simulation

Three assumptions underlie our first simulation of the dynamics of the population-medical macromodel: (a) The entrance rate of new physicians (aged twenty-five) does not change; (b) the entrance rate of new nurses

Table 7.6   **Standard Simulation Results**

Year	Medical Expenditures	Health Status	Medical Expenditures/ GDP	Doctor Income	Nurse Income	Others Income
1990	100.00	100.00	100.00	100.00	100.00	100.00
1995	198.79	108.05	149.08	183.45	172.54	134.65
2000	337.01	106.70	170.37	282.47	268.39	179.63
2005	502.13	99.84	212.97	403.12	382.43	235.88
2010	681.02	88.84	212.97	536.44	513.36	305.63
2015	875.54	75.23	234.26	685.85	665.53	388.98
2020	1,007.04	63.60	212.97	796.70	776.50	484.40
2025	1,070.94	54.09	191.67	850.98	847.09	590.58
2030	1,114.04	46.07	191.67	893.58	920.94	705.32
2035	1,169.81	39.47	170.37	961.15	1,024.72	820.81
2040	1,279.50	34.08	191.67	1,092.87	1,194.74	917.75

(aged twenty-one) does not change; and (c) the out-of-pocket price of medical care does not change. The results of this standard simulation are summarized in table 7.6.

In the year 2000, medical care expenditure will be 3.4 times its 1990 level; in 2010 it will be 6.8 times as much; in 2020, 10.1 times; in 2030, 11.1 times; and in 2040, 12.8 times. The forecast of the annual average growth rate of medical expenditure for the entire period is 4.3 percent. However, even though people will spend more for medical care in the future, aging will make them less healthy and the national health status will gradually decrease, reaching less than half its 1990 level by 2028. The share of medical expenditure in the whole economy (i.e., the GDP) will rise, reaching 10.8 percent in 2015, then gradually decline to 8.5 percent in 2040. During the simulation period, the wages of physicians will grow at 4.1 percent per annum, while the annual growth rate of wages for nurses and general workers will average 4.3 percent and 4.5 percent, respectively.

7.4.2   Projection 2: Cost-Containment Policy

How will the government's attempt to repress the growth rate of medical expenditures below the growth rate of GDP affect the medical care service sector, in particular the out-of-pocket price (self-payment) faced by health care users? Projection 2 simulates the change in these prices resulting from measures to contain medical expenditures; the results are summarized in table 7.7. Self-payment for medical care would have to increase to 1.83 times its 1990 level in 2017, then gradually decrease to 1.67 times that level in 2032, before rising again to 1.82 times the 1990 level in 2040. Figure 7.4 illustrates this transition.

The model also indicates that under a cost-containment policy, the de-

Table 7.7   Simulation Results of Cost-Containment Policy

Year	Medical Expenditures	Health Status	Self-Payment	Medical Expenditures/ GDP	Doctor Income	Nurse Income	Other Incor
1990	100.00	100.00	100.00	100.00	100.00	100.00	100.0
1995	138.13	98.36	123.97	106.48	127.52	119.93	134.3
2000	184.81	92.14	148.76	106.48	154.85	147.14	177.2
2005	236.14	84.09	165.29	106.48	189.52	179.80	229.7
2010	292.70	74.38	173.55	106.48	230.10	220.20	293.5
2015	354.98	63.20	181.82	106.48	277.61	269.38	368.9
2020	422.83	54.81	181.82	106.48	334.07	325.60	454.9
2025	493.75	48.48	173.55	106.48	392.46	390.67	550.9
2030	561.02	42.89	165.29	106.48	449.35	463.11	652.9
2035	610.22	37.78	165.29	106.48	500.68	533.79	752.1
2040	625.41	33.01	181.82	106.48	534.66	584.49	822.8

cline in national health status is more rapid than in the standard projection; the health indicator drops below half the 1990 level in 2025. Figure 7.5 compares the transition of health status under the two projections.

The annual growth rate of medical expenditures also decreases under cost containment, from 4.3 percent for the standard projection (Projection 1) to 3.6 percent (Projection 2). This comparison is shown in figure 7.6.

7.4.3   Projection 3: Increase in Medical Licenses

A rise in the market entrance rate for new physicians should, of course, decrease the annual growth rate of their wages. The number of medical licenses issued also affects productivity in the medical care sector and in the economy as a whole. In this projection, therefore, we investigate the effect of increasing the number of medical licenses by 25 percent above the 1990 level. The simulation results are summarized in table 7.8. Under this scenario, the annual growth rate of physician's wages over the period will be slower than in the standard case—3.5 percent, compared to 4.1 percent. Figure 7.7 presents a comparison of the relative wages of physicians and general workers in the above two cases; increasing the number of medical licenses issued suppresses the wage discrepancy between doctors and general workers. Although the demand for medical care does not change in this projection compared with the standard projection, the medical sector's share of GDP decreases, because a rise in the number of physicians releases many general workers from the medical care sector to the general economic sector. As the marginal productivity of physicians is greater than that of general workers in the medical care sector, increasing the supply of physicians encourages the production of goods and services in the general sector. This transition in the ratio of medical expenditure to GDP is presented in figure 7.8.

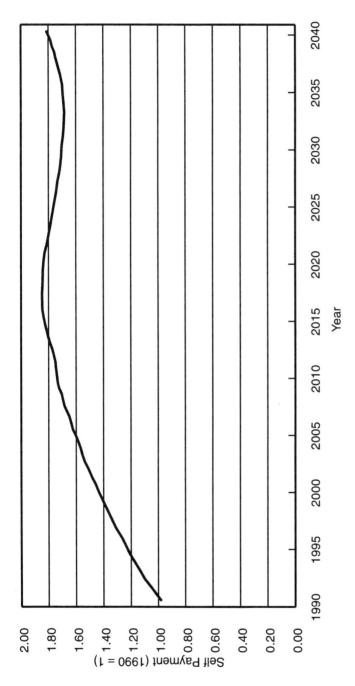

Fig. 7.4 The transition of self-payment

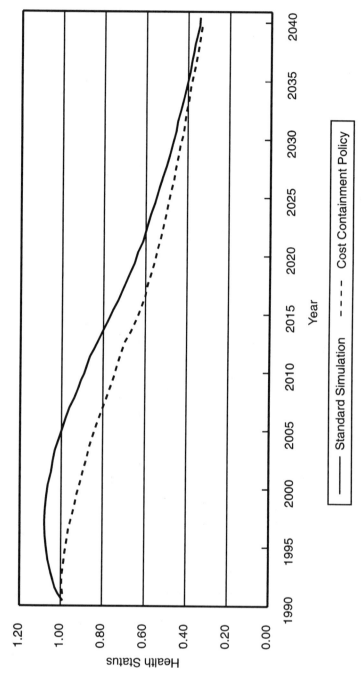

Fig. 7.5 Health status and cost-containment policy

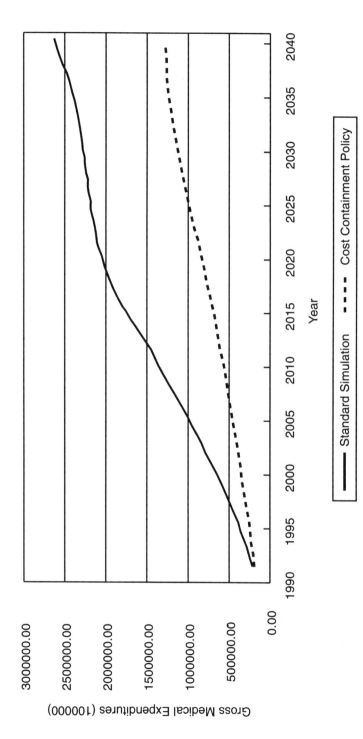

Fig. 7.6 Gross medical expenditures and cost-containment projections

Table 7.8   Simulation Results of Increasing the Number of Physician Licenses

Year	Medical Expenditures	Health Status	Medical Expenditures/ GDP	Doctor Income	Nurse Income	Others Income
1990	100.00	100.00	100.00	100.00	100.00	100.00
1995	197.34	108.09	149.08	176.22	170.95	134.64
2000	331.38	106.83	170.37	260.82	263.57	179.57
2005	488.95	100.06	191.67	362.62	373.46	235.68
2010	661.95	89.15	212.97	472.30	499.15	305.21
2015	848.24	75.59	212.97	592.58	644.79	388.24
2020	973.45	63.97	212.97	676.58	749.93	483.28
2025	1,031.10	54.44	191.67	709.69	815.38	588.99
2030	1,069.97	46.44	170.37	732.45	883.73	703.17
2035	1,120.72	39.83	170.37	775.96	980.85	817.86
2040	1,222.09	34.45	170.37	871.11	1,141.64	913.51

7.4.4   Projection 4: Increase in Nurse Licenses

Projection 4 looks at the effect on economic activity of increasing the ranks of nurses in the health care sector. The simulation results for increasing the number of nursing licenses issued are summarized in table 7.9. This action decreases the annual growth rate of nurses' wages as compared to the standard case (from 4.3 percent to 3.9 percent). Figure 7.9 illustrates the effect on the relative wages of nurses and general workers in the two cases; the wage discrepancy between them is reduced by increasing the number of nursing licenses. As in the preceding scenario, the demand for medical care remains unchanged but the share of medical expenditures in GDP is decreased compared to the standard case. This change is shown in figure 7.10.

7.5   Conclusions

In this study we constructed a model of the Japanese economy in order to analyze the effect of demographic changes and possible changes in health policy on the medical care sector and on the economy as a whole. Using the Grossman model of household behavior, we were able to derive the national demand for health, the demand for consumption goods, and the derived demand for medical services.

Our simulation shows that maintaining the present system of payment for health care as the population ages will result in medical care expenditures' growing at an average annual rate of 4.3 percent between 1991 and 2040. The share of medical expenditure in GDP will reach 10.8 percent in 2015, then gradually begin to decline. Moreover, even though people invest in their futures rather than their present medical care, their health status in the twenty-first century will be lower because of population aging.

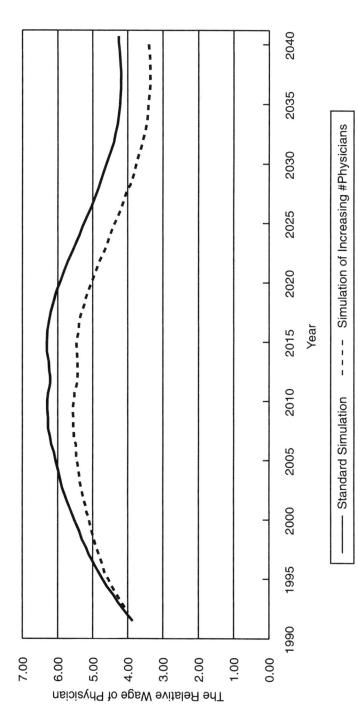

Fig. 7.7 Relative wage of physicians and increasing the number of licenses for physicians

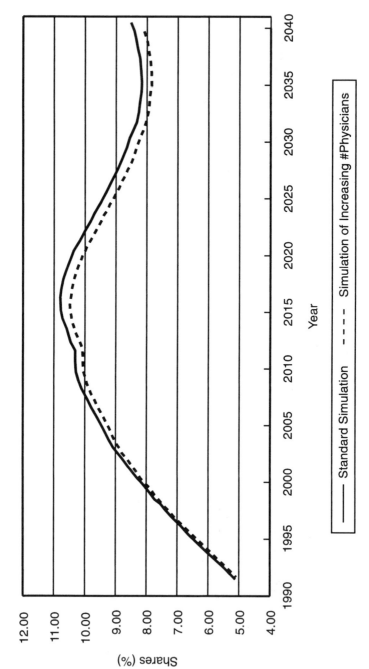

Fig. 7.8 Medical expenditures/GDP and increasing the number of licenses for physicians

Table 7.9   **Simulation Results of Increasing the Number of Nursing Licenses**

Year	Medical Expenditures	Health Status	Medical Expenditures/ GDP	Doctor Income	Nurse Income	Others Income
1990	100.00	100.00	100.00	100.00	100.00	100.00
1995	197.34	108.11	149.08	181.67	163.39	134.65
2000	331.39	106.88	170.37	278.17	246.13	179.55
2005	491.28	100.13	191.67	395.44	342.07	235.61
2010	667.18	89.25	212.97	524.55	448.86	305.04
2015	854.07	75.72	234.26	668.68	568.84	387.94
2020	979.59	64.12	212.97	774.48	648.49	482.80
2025	1,039.74	54.62	191.67	825.30	693.03	588.26
2030	1,078.51	46.40	170.37	865.29	741.16	702.05
2035	1,133.46	40.02	170.37	930.19	814.62	816.17
2040	1,239.14	34.65	170.37	1,058.31	942.04	910.87

Controlling medical expenditures through cost containment will require the Japanese people to accept both major increases in the rate of self-payment for medical care and a decline in national health status. Alternatively, increasing the supply of medical specialists would reduce the share of medical expenditure in the economy as a whole. Of course, taking this course would require Japan to raise its investment in the education of nurses and physicians.

Appendix
The Derivation of Demand Equations

We derive the demand function for health, the demand for other goods, and derived demand for medical services. We maximize the next utility function subject to constraints.

(A1) $U(t) = \int_0^T e^{-\rho t}[\alpha_0 e^{\eta_1 AGE(t)} H(t)^{\alpha_1} + \beta_0 C(t)^{\beta_1}]dt$

subject to

(A2) $\dot{A}(t) = r(t)A(t) + w(t) - \gamma_0 p(t)^{\gamma_1} w(t)^{1-\gamma_1} I(t) - C(t)$

(A3) $\dot{H}(t) = I(t) - \delta(t)H(t)$

Hamiltonian is

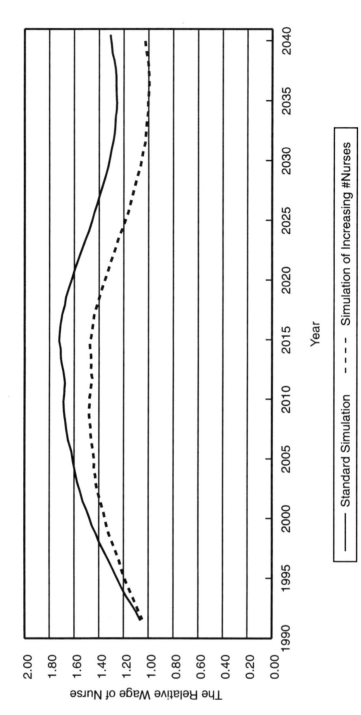

Fig. 7.9 The relative wages of nurses and increasing the number of licenses for nurses

—— Standard Simulation   - - - - Simulation of Increasing #Nurses

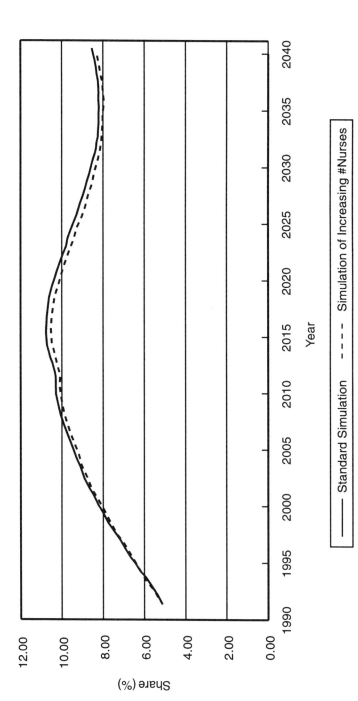

Fig. 7.10 Medical expenditures/GDP and increasing the number of licenses for nurses

Standard Simulation — — — — Simulation of Increasing #Nurses

(A4) $L(t) = e^{-\rho t}[\alpha_0 e^{\eta_1 AGE(t)} H(t)^{\alpha_1} + \beta_0 C(t)^{\beta_1}]$

$+ \lambda(t)[r(t)A(t) + w(t) - \gamma_0 p(t)^{\gamma_1} w(t)^{1-\gamma_1} I(t) - C(t)]$

$+ \mu(t)[I(t) - \delta(t)H(t)]$.

The following conditions are required to hold:

(A5) $\dfrac{\partial L(t)}{\partial I(t)} = -\lambda(t)\gamma_0 p(t)^{\gamma_1} w(t)^{1-\gamma_1} + \mu(t) = 0,$

(A6) $\dfrac{\partial L(t)}{\partial C(t)} = e^{-\rho t}\beta_0\beta_1 C(t)^{\beta_1-1} - \lambda(t) = 0,$

(A7) $\dfrac{\partial L(t)}{\partial A(t)} = -\dot{\lambda}(t) = r(t)\lambda(t),$

(A8) $\dfrac{\partial L(t)}{\partial H(t)} = -\dot{\mu}(t) = e^{-\rho t}\alpha_0 e^{\eta_1 AGE(t)}\alpha_1 H(t)^{\alpha_1-1} - \mu(t)\delta(t),$

(A9) $A(T)\lambda(T) = 0,$ and

(A10) $\mu(t)[H(T) - \overline{H}] = 0.$

From equation (A5),

(A11) $\mu(t) = \lambda(t)\gamma_0 p(t)^{\gamma_1} w(t)^{1-\gamma_1}.$

The derivative of equation (A11) is

(A12) $\dot{\mu}(t) = \gamma_0[\dot{\lambda}(t)p(t)^{\gamma_1} w(t)^{1-\gamma_1} + \lambda(t)\gamma_1 p(t)^{\gamma_1-1}\dot{p}(t)w(t)^{1-\gamma_1}$

$+ \lambda(t)p(t)^{\gamma_1}(1 - \gamma_1)w(t)^{-\gamma_1}\dot{w}(t)].$

Substituting equations (A7), (A8), and (A11) into (A12),

(A13) $e^{-\rho t}\alpha_0 e^{\eta_1 AGE(t)}\alpha_1 H(t)^{\alpha_1-1} = \gamma_0\lambda(t)p(t)^{\gamma_1} w(t)^{1-\gamma_1}$

$$\left[-\gamma_1\frac{\dot{p}(t)}{p(t)} - (1 - \gamma_1)\frac{\dot{w}(t)}{w(t)} + \delta(t) + r(t)\right].$$

From equation (A13), we can derive the demand function for health.

(A14) $\ln H(t) = A_0 + \dfrac{\beta_1 - 1}{\alpha_1 - 1}\ln C(t) + \dfrac{\gamma_1}{\alpha_1 - 1}\ln p(t) + \dfrac{1 - \gamma_1}{\alpha_1 - 1}\ln w(t)$

$+ \dfrac{\delta_1 - \eta_1}{\alpha_1 - 1} AGE(t) + \dfrac{1}{\alpha_1 - 1}r(t)$

We use the next equations in order to derive the demand function for health.

$$\ln\left\{\frac{\delta(t)e^{r(t)}}{[-\gamma_1\dot{p}(t)/p(t) \; - \; \gamma_2\dot{w}(t)/w(t) \; + \; \delta(t) \; + \; r(t)]e^{r(t)}}\right\} = 0$$

$$\ln\delta(t) = \delta_0 + \delta_1\text{AGE}(t)$$

From equation (A3) and the above two equations,

$$(A15) \qquad \ln I(t) = \ln[\dot{H}(t) + \delta(t)H(t)]$$

$$= \ln\left[\frac{\dot{H}(t)}{\delta(t)H(t)} + 1\right] + \ln\delta(t) + \ln H(t)$$

$$= \ln H(t) + \ln\delta(t).$$

From Shepherd's lemma,

$$(A16) \qquad \frac{\partial[p(t)^{\gamma_1}w(t)^{1-\gamma_1}I(t)]}{\partial p(t)} = M(t).$$

Therefore,

$$(A17) \qquad M(t) = \gamma_0\gamma_1 p(t)^{\gamma_1-1}w(t)^{1-\gamma_1}I(t).$$

From equations (A15) and (A16), we can derive the derived demand equation for medical services.

$$(A18) \quad \ln M(t) = B_0 + (\gamma_1 - 1)\ln p(t) + (1 + \gamma_1)\ln w(t) + \ln H(t)$$

$$+ \delta_1\text{AGE}(t)$$

Substituting equation (A6) into (A13)

$$(A19) \qquad e^{-\rho t}\beta_0\beta_1 C(t)^{\beta_1-1} = \lambda(t)$$

$$(A20) \qquad -\rho t + \ln\beta_0\beta_1 + (\beta_1 - 1)\ln C(t) = \ln\lambda(t)$$

$$(A21) \qquad -\rho + (\beta_1 - 1)\frac{\dot{C}(t)}{C(t)} = \frac{\dot{\lambda}(t)}{\lambda(t)}.$$

From equation (A21), we can derive the demand function for other goods.

$$(A22) \qquad \ln C(t) = C_0 + \ln C(t - 1) - \frac{1}{\beta_1 - 1}r(t)$$

References

Denton, F. T., and B. G. Spencer. 1975. Health care costs when the population changes. *Canadian Journal of Economics* 8 (1): 34–48.
———. 1983a. Population aging and future health costs in Canada. *Canadian Public Policy* 9 (2): 155–63.
———. 1983b. The sensitivity of health care costs to changes in population age structure. In *Economic resources for the elderly: Prospects for the future,* ed. C. Garvacz, 175–202. Boulder, Colo.: Westview Press.
———. 1988. Health care in the economic-demographic system: Macro-effects of market control, government intervention, and population change. *Southern Economic Journal* 55 (1): 37–56.
Grossman, M. 1972. On the concept of health capital and the demand for health. *Journal of Political Economy* 80 (2): 223–55.
Hayashi, H., H. Ichikawa, K. Baba, and I. Kishi. 1980. Estimation and analysis of the long-term social security model (in Japanese). *Quarterly of Social Security Research* 16 (2): 59–95.
Hayashi, H., I. Kishi, and F. Mikami. 1981. Simulation analysis of the long-term social security model (in Japanese). *Quarterly of Social Security Research* 17 (2): 222–49.
Inada, Y., K. Ogawa, M. Tamaoka, and I. Tokutsu. 1992. Econometric analysis of social security (in Japanese). *Quarterly of Social Security Research* 27 (4): 395–421.
Johansson, P., and K. Lofgren. 1995. Wealth from optimal health. *Journal of Health Economics* 14 (1): 65–79.
Kishi, I. 1990. Estimation of social security benefit by the long-term social security model (in Japanese). *Quarterly of Social Security Research* 25 (4): 364–78.
Nishina, T. 1982. An econometric analysis of the Japanese social security system with special emphasis on social medical insurance (in Japanese). *Economic Studies Quarterly* 33 (2): 168–82.
Ogura, S., and T. Kurumisawa. 1994. JCER projection of Japanese population up to year 2000 (in Japanese). *JECE Economic Journal* (27):77–101.
Shakaihoshō moderu kaihatsu kenkyūkai. 1979. *Econometrics of social security* (in Japanese). Tokyo: Ōkurashō Insatsukyoku.
Wagstaff, A. 1986. The demand for health: Some new empirical evidence. *Journal of Health Economics* 5 (3): 195–233.
———. 1993. The demand for health: An empirical reformulation of the Grossman model. *Health Economics* 2 (2): 189–98.

8

Choice among Employer-Provided Insurance Plans

Matthew J. Eichner

More choice has emerged as a politically palatable alternative to fundamental health care reform in the United States. After the 1980s brought explosive increases in the cost of providing coverage to employees, the elderly, and the indigent, there was widespread anticipation of some governmental reform of the health care market. Even before it became clear that such reform would not materialize, however, and with increasing momentum afterwards, firms sought to induce their employees to choose alternatives to the traditional fee-for-service plans that presented the insured, their providers, or both with better incentives to control costs.

The incentives offered by firms to accept these new alternatives have typically included expanded coverage and lower monthly premiums collected in the form of payroll deductions. So many employees now choose between a traditional fee-for-service plan with cost sharing and comparatively high payroll deductions, and one or more health maintenance organizations (HMOs) with no cost sharing and dramatically lower monthly payroll deductions. The HMOs use administrative or supply-side mechanisms to control the costs of providing care; they have even sought to entice workers in the automobile industry who are covered by a collective bargaining agreement that provides for health care without coinsurance or payroll deductions. The airwaves in Michigan are full of advertisements from these HMOs arguing that they best the traditional fee-for-service plans not only on price, which is irrelevant for this population, but also on quality control and on the speed and efficiency with which they provide care.

Matthew J. Eichner was professor of economics at the Columbia University Graduate School of Business when this work was completed. He is a faculty research fellow of the National Bureau of Economic Research.

The federal government, too, has seized on choice as a means to lower health care costs. The Medicare program has allowed a number of HMOs to sign up the elderly. In return for accepting administrative controls over provision of services, the elderly are offered an expanded basket of services, typically including such things as pharmaceuticals and well-care, and freedom from the bother of applying and then waiting for reimbursement from the Medicare system. As in the case of the automobile workers, the campaign to sign up this group has taken to the airwaves with commercial messages touting the advantages of each plan while showing pictures of happy, healthy senior citizens engaging in various outdoor activities.

While HMOs have been in the forefront of the health care reform movement, other alternatives to traditional fee-for-service coverage have also emerged. The Health Insurance Access and Portability Act of 1996, known also as the Kennedy-Kassebaum bill, authorizes a limited trial of catastrophic insurance. Instead of seeking to implement cost control through administrative mechanisms and essentially eliminating coinsurance, catastrophic insurance makes individuals behave as if they are spending their own money by, in most cases, forcing them to spend their own money. To provide the necessary liquidity to satisfy deductibles, which might be several thousand dollars, the Kennedy-Kassebaum bill also provides for a tax-favored savings account from which expenditures below the level of the deductible may be paid. This eliminates the tax advantages of low-deductible, high-premium insurance plans.

Under such systems, the issue of how individuals make choices about insurance is a critical one. There are two fundamental questions, the answers to which will determine the long-term prospects of a system incorporating a high degree of choice among insurance alternatives. First, adverse selection of sicker individuals into the more generous coverage options is of concern. The initial estimates of cost saving from managed care and other alternative arrangements surely is due at least in part to the fact that these schemes attract the healthiest segments of the covered population. There is reason to suspect, therefore, that the cost savings will disappear or at least diminish as the number of people, and the number of comparatively unhealthy people in particular, covered under the new alternatives increases. Equally important is the responsiveness of employees to the pricing of the various insurance options. For example, how much lower must premiums be before large numbers of covered individuals will accept greater levels of risk bearing.

This paper describes the choices made by employees of a firm that offers three different insurance options, which differ both in their generosity and their costs to the employee. Section 8.1 describes the claims data used in this analysis. Section 8.2 examines the options elected by employees when their firms shifted from offering what was essentially a single plan to the menu of three plans. Section 8.3 considers the relative prices of the different coverage options. Section 8.4 focuses on the apparent willingness of employees to bear greater risk in return for paying less for insurance. Section 8.5 describes the group of those employees who, after selecting initial coverage options, reconsider their choices and transfer into other plans. Section 8.6 concludes.

8.1   Claims Data

The data used in the following analysis consist of confidential MedStat claims records representing all expenditures incurred by a group of 16,930 firm employees and their dependents during the years 1989 through 1992. Each record represents a specific claim for a specific service on a specific date and indicates the identity of the individual receiving the service, the household to which he or she belongs, the plan under which the patient is covered, the diagnosis, the type of service, and the billed cost of care rendered. Basic demographic information, including the patient's age, gender, and location, is also included as part of each claim record. Claims data have an attractive property, in that individual plan enrollees are motivated to report every claim. At the same time, the firm paying the bill has an incentive to make sure that only legitimate claims are filed.

Two potential difficulties with the use of claims data must be addressed. First, only individuals who file claims are observed in the data. Aside from claims, there is no independent record of employment. Thus if an individual consumed no medical care during the three years of data available for each firm, he or she is invisible to the analysis described in this paper. This is not likely to be a large problem. Few individuals are so fortunate as to live three years without seeing a doctor either for preventive care or to address an acute condition. Figure 8.1 provides some descriptive evidence supporting this view. While large numbers of families appear in 1989 and 1990, by 1992 the new arrivals have slowed to a trickle. In a similar vein, the departure of an individual who leaves the firm during the three years covered by the data will not be detected. In this case, restricting the sample to employees aged twenty-five through fifty-five largely avoids the potential problem of retirees' vanishing from the panel.

A second concern involves the underreporting of claims that fall below the deductibles that apply to the various plans. Such behavior might result from individuals' believing that they would not, even with the claim, satisfy their annual deductibles. A significant degree of nonreporting would produce a discontinuity in the distribution of claims around the deductible. As shown in appendix figure 8A.1, on which the relevant deductible is indicated by a horizontal line, no such discontinuity is in fact present.

Beginning in 1990, the firm offers its employees a choice among three insurance plans with varying levels of premiums and benefits. Plan 1 features a comparatively high deductible and copayment percentage, while

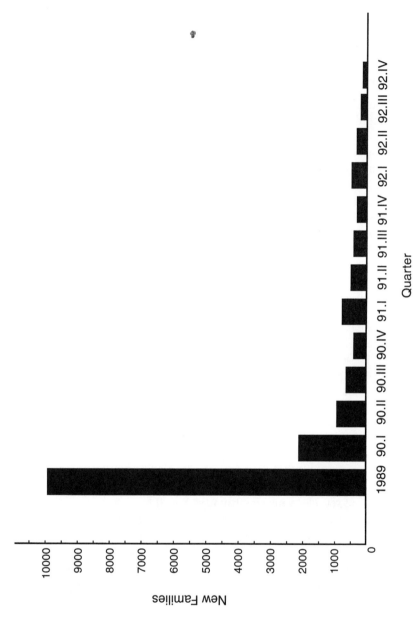

Fig. 8.1 New families appearing during each quarter

Table 8.1   **Plans Offered**

	Deductible ($)		Copayment (%)		Out-of-Pocket Limit ($)	
	Individual	Family	Individual	Family	Individual	Family
Plan 1	1,000	2,000	30	30	2,500	5,000
Plan 2	250	500	20	20	1,500	3,000
Plan 3	125	250	10	10	1,000	2,000

Source: Author's calculations from confidential MedStat claims data.

Table 8.2   **Demographic Characteristics by New Plan Chosen**

	Plan 1 (%)	Plan 2 (%)	Plan 3 (%)
Employee age			
25–34 Years	10.68	41.82	47.50
35–44 Years	13.16	39.32	47.51
45–55 Years	15.10	41.39	43.51
Employee gender			
Male	13.90	41.06	45.04
Female	10.83	40.73	48.44

Source: See table 8.1.

the provisions of plan 2 are typical of traditional fee-for-service options. Plan 3, with an individual annual deductible of only $125 and a copayment of 10 percent, is an option with particularly generous benefits. The exact provisions of each plan, for individual enrollees and employees with covered dependents, are shown in table 8.1. The table completely describes all differences among the three plans. Utilization review procedures for certain high-cost treatments and "carve-outs" for mental health, substance abuse, eyeglasses, and prescription drugs are the same across the three plans.

8.2   Initial Choice of Plan

At the start of 1990, the salaried employees of a Fortune 500 firm were required to elect new insurance coverage from a menu of three plans with varying employee contribution and reimbursement levels. Previously, all employees had essentially been covered under a single plan. In this section, I describe the characteristics of the employees who chose each of these options.

The basic demographics of those choosing each plan are shown in table 8.2. Somewhat surprising is the fact that the proportion of employees aged forty-five to fifty-five choosing plan 1, the high-deductible option, is actually greater than the proportion of employees in the younger age groups.

Table 8.3   Family Grouping by New Plan Chosen

	Plan 1 (%)	Plan 2 (%)	Plan 3 (%)
Employee only	18.72	35.05	46.23
Employee and spouse	9.85	46.95	43.20
Employee, spouse, and children	8.62	43.15	48.23
Employee and children	10.29	43.24	46.57

Source: See table 8.1.

A possible explanation may be that older employees tend to have higher asset balances, making the prospect of paying a deductible of $2,000 out of pocket during a year less daunting. Female employees are, on the whole, less likely to choose the high-deductible option. Enrollment in what the firm views as the base option, plan 2, remains at about 40 percent across all of the demographic groups. Table 8.3 shows the breakdown of enrollment decisions by family structure. Not surprisingly, those without families seem more likely to choose the high-deductible plan 1. As family size increases, the likelihood of electing this option falls.

Since the data include records from 1989, before the new system of three plans was introduced, it is possible to compare the spending in 1989 of those employees who elected each of the three options in 1990. Figure 8.2 does this by showing quintiles based on 1989 spending, and then looking at which plan employees in each of those quintiles chose in 1990. So, for example, about 17 percent of those who were in the lowest quintile in 1989 chose plan 1 in 1990. Generally, the proportion choosing plan 1 falls at the higher percentiles of the 1989 distribution, suggesting that individuals who spend more in 1989 are less likely to opt for the high-deductible plan in 1990. The individuals in the higher quintiles who do not choose plan 1 appear to opt for plan 2. Moving higher in the 1989 expenditure distribution, as plan 1 enrollment falls plan 2 enrollment rises. The proportion of individuals opting for the most generous plan does not appear to change appreciably across the 1989 expenditure distribution.

An ordered probit regression, relating 1990 plan choice to 1989 spending and the various demographic factors, confirms that controlling for all observables simultaneously does not appreciably alter the picture. The ordinal character of the dependent variable comes from the ranking of the plans in order of increasing generosity. Table 8.4 presents estimation results. The positive and significant coefficient on the indicators for 1989 expenditure quintile once again demonstrate that those individuals who spent more in 1989 chose more generous plans in 1990, even controlling for demographics and family structure. In addition, the positive coefficients on the indicator for spouse present and the indicator for spouse and children present suggest that an employee with a spouse was more likely

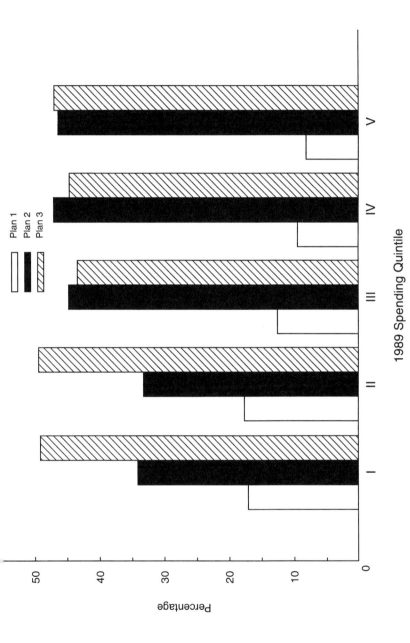

Fig. 8.2   1990 Plan choice by 1989 spending quintile

Table 8.4   **Ordered Probit Estimation of 1990 Plan Choice**

Second expenditure quintile in 1989	−0.0338
	(0.0284)
Third expenditure quintile in 1989	0.0831*
	(0.0292)
Fourth expenditure quintile in 1989	0.2154*
	(0.0305)
Fifth expenditure quintile 1989	0.2778*
	(0.0313)
Employee aged 25–35	0.0018
	(0.0363)
Employee aged 36–45	−0.0992*
	(0.0383)
Male employee	−0.2826*
	(0.0350)
Male employee aged 25–35	0.2239*
	(0.0454)
Male employee aged 36–45	0.2127*
	(0.0473)
Spouse present	0.0766*
	(0.0268)
Spouse and children present	0.1409*
	(0.0242)
Children (but not spouse) present	0.0560
	(0.0309)
First cut point	−0.9621
	(0.0373)
Second cut point	0.3317
	(0.0368)

Source: See table 8.1.

Notes: Specification also includes five location indicators. Sample size is 16,930. Standard errors are in parentheses.

*Significant at the 95 percent level.

to choose a more generous plan, and that an employee with both spouse and children was even more likely to elect such an option.

8.3   The Price of Insurance Coverage

The last section examined which employees chose the more generous coverage options. In this section I consider the price that employees pay, in the form of payroll deductions, for such a decision. I begin by considering the projections of the firm concerning the costs of the various insurance plans and then translate these expenditure projections into the relative costs to the employee.

Table 8.5 shows the projections prepared by the firm of the overall cost of the three coverage options. In other words, these figures reflect anticipated mean expenditure for family groups of each size under each of the

Table 8.5   **Projected and Actual Mean Expenditures, 1990–92**

	Projected ($)	1990 ($)	1991 ($)	1992 ($)	1990–92, annual average ($)
Plan 1					
Employee	1,890	874	1,136	1,245	1,109
		(270)	(310)	(504)	(217)
Employee and one dependent	3,590	1,860	1,850	3,138	2,367
		(240)	(213)	(506)	(211)
Employee and multiple dependents	5,190	4,370	3,253	5,052	4,380
		(587)	(445)	(1,810)	(713)
Plan 2					
Employee	2,200	1,362	1,770	1,660	1,654
		(152)	(217)	(166)	(104)
Employee and one dependent	4,200	3,467	3,046	3,371	3,364
		(252)	(176)	(264)	(135)
Employee and multiple dependents	6,090	5,382	4,734	4,846	5,137
		(125)	(279)	(297)	(165)
Plan 3					
Employee	2,460	2,154	2,504	2,045	2,240
		(143)	(185)	(140)	(90)
Employee and one dependent	4,720	5,081	4,946	4,366	4,841
		(460)	(478)	(431)	(269)
Employee and multiple dependents	6,650	6,266	6,575	5,610	6,094
		(348)	(468)	(355)	(221)

Source: See table 8.1.

plans. There are also some slight geographic adjustments in recognition of differences in cost across the six sites. While I will incorporate these in my calculations, the tables show only the price schedule for the largest site. In addition to the firm's estimates of costs, table 8.5 shows actual costs during each of the years covered by the data as well as the annual average over three years. The firm estimates correspond quite well to the actual costs for the more expensive plan and for the larger family groupings. For example, the firm estimates of average annual cost for plan 3 are $2,460, $4,720, and $6,650 for an employee alone, employee with a single dependent, and employee with multiple dependents, respectively. The corresponding actual mean costs for 1990 are $2,154, $5,081, and $6,266.

The estimates were less accurate for lower-cost employees, either those enrolled in plan 1 or those in plan 2 with few dependents. For these employees, the firm estimates tended to exceed the actual costs. For example, the projected mean expenditures for plan 1 were $1,890 for a employee alone, $3,590 for an employee with a single dependent, and $5,190 for an employee with multiple dependents. The actual average expenditures for 1990 were $874, $1,860, and $4,370. There are two possible explanations for these overly high estimates. Either the self-selection of healthy individuals into the low cost plans was greater than anticipated, or the incentive to spend less provided by the comparatively high deductible was more effective than anticipated.

The actual cost to the employee in payroll deductions of each of the three insurance options can be derived from these expenditure estimates. The firm follows an equal subsidy pricing rule, meaning that the firm provides the same dollar value of subsidy to its employees regardless of which plans they elect. The subsidy is set equal to 80 percent of the plan 2 average expenditure, so for an employee with no dependents, the subsidy is $440. For an employee with a single dependent, the firm contribution nearly doubles to $840, while an employee with multiple dependents receives a subsidy of $1,218. Table 8.6 shows the relative costs of the various coverage options after this equal-subsidy rule is implemented. The numbers in parentheses represent the percentage differences in payroll deductions for plans 1 and 3 relative to the base plan 2. Thus, plan 1 costs about 70 percent less than the base plan while plan 3 costs about 50 percent more.

These number still do not, however, reflect the true costs to employees. More generous plans bring, along with higher payroll deductions, lower deductibles and copayments. Deductibles are satisfied and copayments are made in after-tax dollars; yet the payroll deductions are essentially taken in pretax dollars. The firm provides employees a certain number of "benefit dollars" depending on salary. With these benefit dollars, an employee must purchase coverage through one of the three health insurance plans. The balance of these benefit dollars can then be used to purchase other insur-

Table 8.6   **Employee Cost by Plan and Family Grouping**

	Plan 1	Plan 2	Plan 3
Employee	$130 (−70%)	$440	$700 (59%)
Employee and one dependent	$230 (−73%)	$840	$1,360 (62%)
Employee and multiple dependents	$318 (−74%)	$1,218	$1,778 (46%)

Source: See table 8.1.

Table 8.7   **Employee After-Tax Cost by Plan and Family Grouping**

	Plan 1	Plan 2	Plan 3
Employee	$91 (−70%)	$308	$490 (59%)
Employee and one dependent	$161 (−73%)	$588	$952 (62%)
Employee and multiple dependents	$223 (−74%)	$853	$1,245 (46%)

Source: See table 8.1.

ance against death or disability, or they may be taken as salary, in which case they constitute taxable income. Therefore benefit dollars are essentially exchangeable against after-tax dollars in two different ways: They can be used to purchase a more comprehensive health insurance, thus reducing the coinsurance payments; and they may also be directly transformed into after-tax income. In either case, one of the benefit dollars can be traded against $1 - \tau$ after-tax dollars, where τ is the tax rate. For most of the calculations in this paper, I will assume τ to be 0.3 and convert the premiums on that basis into after-tax dollars. The resulting payroll deductions are shown in table 8.7.

8.4   Attitudes toward Risk

Thirteen percent of employees choose plan 1, 45 percent opt for plan 2, and the remaining 46 percent elect plan 3. Thus 45 percent pay about three times the plan 1 rate and 46 percent pay about five times the plan 1 rate to enroll in plan 3. This section examines these decisions. First, I look at the relation between premiums and reimbursements for employees electing plans 2 and 3 during the three years of data, and calculate the net cost of choosing the more generous coverage. Then I examine this issue in the expected utility framework, calculating the willingness to pay for expanded coverage under a set of admittedly rather restrictive assumptions.

Suppose that all employees who elected plans 2 and 3 in 1990 had instead chosen plan 1, and the money saved in payroll deductions was deposited in an account. Figure 8.3 shows the distribution of balances in these accounts after a three-year period. The mean balance is negative $57, suggesting that the average plan 2 and plan 3 enrollee in fact did better by choosing a more generous plan and paying the higher premiums. The median balance, however, is positive $277, so that over half of the plan 2 and plan 3 enrollees would end the period with more than that amount in their accounts. Once again assuming that 1989 expenditures may be used to control for differential health status, figure 8.4 makes clear that while the average employee saved by choosing plan 2 or plan 3, a substantial number of employees would have amassed more as plan 1 enrollees. About 65 percent of employees in the first two 1989 expenditure quintiles, for example, end the three-year period with a positive balance.

The analysis above, however, ignores at least two issues fundamental to the problem. First, a positive or negative balance is, in itself, inconclusive with regard to whether plan 1 represents a better choice than one of the more generous options. If there is at least a possibility of each employee's ending the three-year period with a negative balance, it is the employee's attitude toward risk that ultimately determines the optimal choice. A second, equally important issue relates to the fact that plan 1 not only costs less in premiums and pays less in reimbursements, but also offers a different schedule of incentives to which enrollees in the plan presumably respond. In fact, there is substantial evidence from experimental and nonexperimental research that the behavioral response to price incentives in the region relevant to these calculations—that is, in the part of the distribution between zero and several thousand dollars—is appreciable.[1]

To allow for both risk aversion and a behavioral response to the price of care requires a more structured approach to the problem. The first step in this analysis is to think about the out-of-pocket costs an employee is likely to face. As described in section 8.1 and shown in figure 8.5, the three plans offered by the firm each have different piece-wise linear price schedules, with kinks at the deductible and then again once the out-of-pocket maximum is reached. Each employee thus ends each year on one of the three segments. Ending the year on the first segment implies an out-of-pocket cost equal to expenditures. A family landing on the second segment pays the deductible plus the copayment rate times the difference between total expenditure and the deductible. Finally, the third segment is populated by those employees who have reached the out-of-pocket maximum and therefore pay no more than that amount.

I will begin by trying to model the probability that an employee with a

---

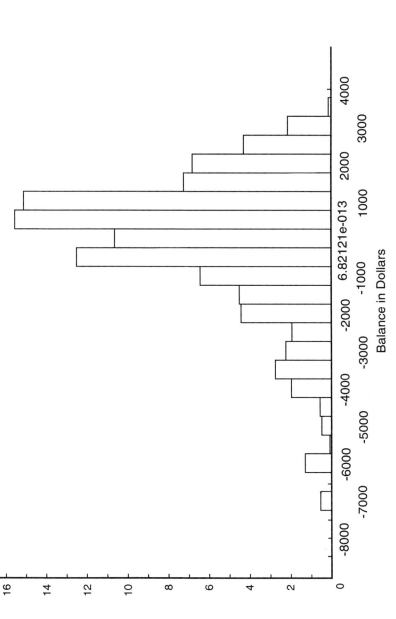

Fig. 8.3   Distribution of balance after three years

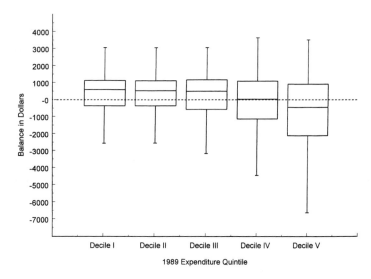

Fig. 8.4   Accumulation by 1989 expenditure quintile

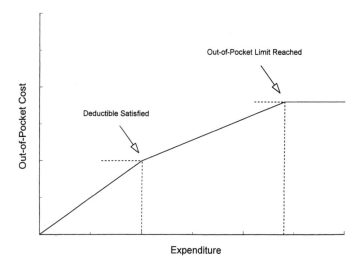

Fig. 8.5   Typical nonlinear price schedule

given age, gender, family grouping, and plan choice ends the year on one particular segment of the price schedule. This task is complicated by the fact that plan choice is surely correlated with unobservable health status. In order to separate the incentive effects of the plans from the self-selection behaviors of those who choose each plan, I will once again use 1989 expenditures as the means of controlling, however imperfectly, for differences in unobservable health status.

Once again, I will take advantage of the fact that the three segments have obvious rankings and use the ordered probit model. I perform the estimation by stacking all three years of data for those individuals who do not change plans during that time period and adding year effects to the specification. As shown in table 8.8, both the plan indicators and the 1989 expenditure-quintile indicators have the expected sign. The plan 1 indicator is negative and significant, suggesting that there is a plan 1 effect that tends to reduce expenditures. On the other hand, the positive and significant plan 3 effect captures the higher average spending under the more generous plan. The indicator for the second 1989 expenditure quintile is

Table 8.8	Ordered Probit Estimation of Price Schedule Segment	
	Second expenditure quintile in 1989	−0.0077
		(0.0195)
	Third expenditure quintile in 1989	0.1109*
		(0.0196)
	Fourth expenditure quintile in 1989	0.2790*
		(0.0204)
	Fifth expenditure quintile 1989	0.3776*
		(0.0209)
	Employee aged 25–35	−0.2597*
		(0.0244)
	Employee aged 36–45	−0.1250*
		(0.0257)
	Male employee	−0.0975*
		(0.0237)
	Male employee aged 25–35	0.0105
		(0.0307)
	Male employee aged 36–45	−0.0118
		(0.0318)
	Spouse present	0.2729*
		(0.0201)
	Single child present	0.1082*
		(0.0234)
	Multiple children present	0.3221*
		(0.0240)
	1991 indicator	−0.0825
		(0.0146)
	1992 indicator	−0.0825
		(0.0147)
	First cut point	−0.0989
		(0.0281)
	Second cut point	1.8670
		(0.0295)

Source: See table 8.1.

Notes: Specification also includes five location indicators. Sample size is 41,124. Standard errors are in parentheses.

*Significant at the 95 percent level.

Table 8.9   **Representative Probability Distributions**

		Below Deductible	Between Deductible and Limit	At or Above Out-of-Pocket Limit
Male age fifty, with spouse	Plan 1	0.5885	0.3972	0.0143
and children	Plan 2	0.2396	0.6563	0.1041
	Plan 3	0.2188	0.6642	0.1170
Male age thirty, without	Plan 1	0.8132	0.1847	0.0021
spouse	Plan 2	0.4506	0.5166	0.0327
	Plan 3	0.3242	0.6103	0.0655
Male age thirty-five, with	Plan 1	0.7145	0.2798	0.0057
spouse	Plan 2	0.3536	0.5905	0.0558
	Plan 3	0.2535	0.6502	0.0963

Source: See table 8.1

essentially zero while those for the higher quintiles are positive, increasing, and statistically significant.

Using the results of this estimation, it is possible to calculate a three-point distribution for persons with a particular set of characteristics. This distribution captures the likelihood of ending the year on each of the three segments: below the deductible, between the deductible and out-of-pocket limit, and above the out-of-pocket limit. Table 8.9 shows some representative probability distributions for persons in the third quintile in 1989, that is, for the median spender with a particular set of characteristics. Not surprisingly, the probability of being below the deductible is greatest for each of the representative families under plan 1, and the probability of being below the deductible is slightly greater for each employee under plan 2 than under plan 3. Family structure and age are important determinants of the distribution. The probability of being below the deductible under plan 1 is 23 percentage points greater for a single male aged thirty than for a married male aged fifty with children.

To use these probability distributions to calculate the willingness of employees to pay for more insurance coverage, I apply the standard expected utility framework developed as expounded by Arrow (1971). Suppose that $U(W)$ has a positive first derivative and negative second derivative, so as to represent the preferences of a risk-averse employee. Under a particular insurance plan, out-of-pocket losses are assumed to follow some distribution $f_L(1)$. Thus the expected utility can be written

$$U(M - L - P) = \int_L U(M - l - P) f_L(l) d,$$

where M is income and P is the premium associated with the particular insurance plan.

Suppose such a calculation is made for a particular insurance plan. One way to quantify the willingness to pay for an alternative is to find P^* such that

$$\int_{L^*} U(M - l^* - P^*)g_L^*(l^*)dl^* = \int_L U(M - l - P)f_L(l)dl,$$

where g_l is the density function describing the possible losses under the alternative plan. In other words, at what premium P^* is the utility the same under both plans?

Before I can make such a calculation, I need explicitly to recognize that the three-point distributions estimated above are only approximations to the continuous distributions. In order to calculate the premiums that leave the employees indifferent, I need to assign losses to each of the three mass points. I do this by assigning to each segment the mean loss for those employees located on the segment, conditional on plan choice and family grouping. The explicit form of the utility function I assume to be constant relative to risk aversion:

$$U(W) = \frac{W^{1-\rho}}{1 - \rho}.$$

Table 8.10 shows calculated and actual plan premiums for several representative employees. The utility function parameter ρ is set equal to 3.5, although the calculations are insensitive to other choices. The table reveals that plan 1 is available to all employees at a discount. In other words, the fifty-year-old male with a wife and children would be indifferent between

Table 8.10   **Premiums Calculated to Preserve Indifference with Plan 2**

Income		$30,000	$50,000	$70,000
	Plan 1	$379	$406	$417
		($223)	($223)	($223)
	Plan 2	($853)	($853)	($853)
Male age fifty, with spouse	Plan 3	$1,318	$1,309	$1,305
and children		($1,244)	($1,244)	($1,244)
	Plan 1	$228	$232	$234
		($91)	($91)	($91)
	Plan 2	($308)	($308)	($308)
Male age thirty, without	Plan 3	$407	$406	$406
spouse		($490)	($490)	($490)
	Plan 1	$243	$266	$275
		($161)	($161)	($161)
	Plan 2	($588)	($588)	($588)
Male age thirty-five, with	Plan 3	$888	$882	$880
spouse		($952)	($952)	($952)

Source: See table 8.1.

Note: Actual premiums in parentheses.

plans 1 and 2 if plan 1 were priced at $379. It is, in fact, available at the price of $223. Except for the fifty-year-old man with a wife and children, all employees pay more in premiums for the most generous option than the amount that the utility calculations suggest would leave them indifferent between plan 3 and plan 2. For example, the single male is indifferent between plans 2 and 3 if plan 3 can be had for $407. In fact, it is priced at $490.

8.5   Movement between Plans

Of the 19,930 employees in the sample, 3,224 are observed in more than one plan during the 1990–92 time period. In this section, I examine how these employees who switch plans differ in demographic characteristics and spending from those who remain in single plans during the three-year period.

Table 8.11 shows the observed transitions between plans. Over half of the movement consists of transfers from plan 3 to plan 2. Another 19 percent of those who switch move from plan 2 to plan 3. Movement into and out of plan 1 is much less common but more symmetrical.

Table 8.12 compares the demographic characteristics of employees who switch plans with the demographic characteristics of those who do not transfer during the 1990–92 period. With regard to age and gender, the switchers and stayers are essentially indistinguishable. However, employees with spouses and children are substantially more likely to switch plans than are single employees.

In spending patterns, the switchers and stayers are also dramatically different. Table 8.13 shows a series of censored regressions of log expenditures on an indicator for switching plans. The first column considers the relation between expenditures in 1990 and whether a transfer took place between 1990 and 1991. The positive and statistically significant coefficient of 2.03 suggests that those who switched plans spent about twice as much in 1990 as those who never switched plans. The second column tells

Table 8.11   **Movement between Plans**

New Plan	Plan 1	Plan 2	Plan 3
Old plan			
Plan 1	—	201	88
		(8.14%)	(3.56%)
Plan 2	229	—	486
	(9.28%)		(19.68)
Plan 3	107	1,358	—
	(4.33%)	(55.00%)	

Source: See table 8.1.

Table 8.12   Characteristics of Switchers and Stayers

	Stayers (%)	Switchers (%)
Age 25–34	41.60	38.09
Age 35–44	30.96	31.73
Age 45–55	27.44	30.18
Male	39.22	41.00
Employee only	38.99	23.95
Employee and spouse	18.17	19.73
Employee, spouse, and children	31.55	43.70
Employee and children (without spouse)	11.29	12.62

Source: See table 8.1.

a similar story with regard to 1991 expenditures and whether an employee chose a new plan in 1992. Individuals who switched plans spent more in their old plans during the year preceding the switch. The indicator in the specification shown in column (3) captures the effect on 1990 expenditures of a plan switch any time during the 1990–92 period. Once again, the coefficient is positive and statistically significant.

The fourth column of table 8.13 considers spending once an employee has entered a new plan. The positive and statistically significant coefficient on the indicator suggests that individuals also spend more after arriving in a new plan than do their colleagues who choose not to transfer. The fifth column reveals a similar picture for employees who transferred at the start of 1992. The specification in column (6) provides a backward look at spending and reveals that those who switched plans in either 1991 or 1992 spent over twice as much in 1992 as their colleagues who did not switch.

The final two columns show that the higher expenditures associated with plan-changers do trail off with time. The seventh column shows regression of 1990 expenditures on a indicator for having selected a new plan at the start of 1992. The eighth column similarly relates spending in 1992 with a change in plans at the start of 1991. In these last two regressions, the coefficient on the indicator is appreciably smaller, although still positive and significant.

8.6   Summary

This paper presents some basic evidence on how employees choose health insurance coverage from a menu of options. There is some evidence that they hesitate to choose low-deductible plans, even though these may be offered at a discount to a price that might leave them indifferent between the high-deductible plan and other, more generous coverage options. This conclusion, however, is based on adherence to a standard expected

Table 8.13   Expenditures and Movement between Plans

Dependent variable	Log expenditure 1990	Log expenditure 1991	Log expenditure 1990	Log expenditure 1991	Log Expenditure 1992	Log Expenditure 1992	Log Expenditure 1990	Log Expenditure 1992
Indicator	Transfer in 1991	Transfer in 1992	Transfer 1991 or 1992	Transfer in 1991	Transfer in 1992	Transfer in 1991 or 1992	Transfer in 1992	Transfer in 1991
Sample	Nonswitchers and switchers in 1991	Nonswitchers and switchers in 1992	All	Nonswitchers and switchers in 1991	Nonswitchers and switchers in 1992	All	Nonswitchers and switchers in 1992	Nonswitchers and switchers in 1991
Sample size	15,090	15,550	16,932	15,090	15,550	16,932	15,500	15,090
Age 25–34	−0.9547*	−0.9472*	−0.9669*	−1.0015*	−1.4304*	−1.5112*	−1.0870*	−1.6826*
	(0.1292)	(0.1418)	(0.1202)	(0.1476)	(0.1736)	(0.1674)	(0.1322)	(0.1971)
Age 35–44	−0.5396*	−0.4101*	−0.5111*	−0.4621*	−0.6170*	−0.7312*	−0.5615*	−0.7843*
	(0.1384)	(0.1522)	(0.1290)	(0.1580)	(0.1859)	(0.1792)	(0.1418)	(0.2104)
Male	−0.4217*	−0.1298	−0.3913*	−0.0953	−0.2264	−0.2927	−0.4279*	−0.3319
	(0.1292)	(0.1413)	(0.1199)	(0.1474)	(0.1722)	(0.1663)	(0.1316)	(0.1958)
Male, age 25–34	−0.3324*	−0.2399	−0.3428*	−0.2271	−0.1263	0.1874	−0.3296	−0.2249
	(0.1608)	(0.1761)	(0.1498)	(0.1834)	(0.2155)	(0.2084)	(0.1644)	(0.2448)
Male, age 35–44	−0.1475	−0.2809	−0.1977	−0.2753	−0.2478	−0.1168	−0.1938	−0.1782
	(0.1699)	(0.1862)	(0.1581)	(0.1938)	(0.2275)	(0.2197)	(0.1736)	(0.2582)
Spouse present	1.6035*	1.3648*	1.5446*	1.3955*	1.5833*	1.5788*	1.6463*	1.7761*
	(0.0702)	(0.0773)	(0.0656)	(0.0801)	(0.0946)	(0.0915)	(0.0721)	(0.1072)
Single child present	1.1624*	0.6710*	1.1271*	0.7056*	0.4583*	0.4981*	1.1804*	0.5682*
	(0.0828)	(0.0916)	(0.0775)	(0.0946)	(0.1121)	(0.1080)	(0.0853)	(0.1265)
Multiple children present	1.8257*	1.5705*	1.7933*	1.5961*	1.2131*	1.2214*	1.9096*	1.3758*
	(0.0834)	(0.0914)	(0.0774)	(0.0950)	(0.1116)	(0.1074)	(0.0853)	(0.1267)
Initially in Plan 1	−0.8905*	−1.0285*	−0.9333*	−0.9841*	−2.3894*	−2.1686*	−1.0308*	−2.4479*
	(0.1017)	(0.1155)	(0.0955)	(0.1162)	(0.1439)	(0.1351)	(0.1079)	(0.1585)
Initially in Plan 3	0.7571	0.7814*	0.6246*	0.8208*	−0.3677*	−0.1362*	0.7869*	0.3444*
	(0.0684)	(0.0752)	(0.0639)	(0.0780)	(0.0919)	(0.0887)	(0.0702)	(0.1039)
Indicator	2.0374*	2.4160*	1.1306*	2.5429*	3.8773*	2.6088*	0.4011*	0.8239*
	(0.1064)	(0.1039)	(0.0739)	(0.1208)	(0.1257)	(0.1020)	(0.0983)	(0.1635)
Constant	3.0450	3.0514	3.1266	2.9836	1.8374	1.6591	2.9125	1.0725

Source: See table 8.1.

Note: Regressions include six location indicators. Standard errors are in parentheses.

*Significant at the 95 percent level

utility approach, which might prove an inadequate framework for evaluating employee willingness to bear risk. In addition, the conclusions are no doubt sensitive to how one views the likelihood of persistent losses over a comparatively long time period. The probability of such outcomes can be assessed using the empirical approach taken by Eichner, McClellan, and Wise (1997). Applying this technique to the issue of plan choice is a future goal of this work.

In addition, the paper examines evidence concerning those employees who elect to change plans voluntarily. This group consists disproportionately of larger family groupings, which tend to move between the two more generous coverage options. Movement between plans seems to be associated with higher expenditures both before and after the move.

Appendix

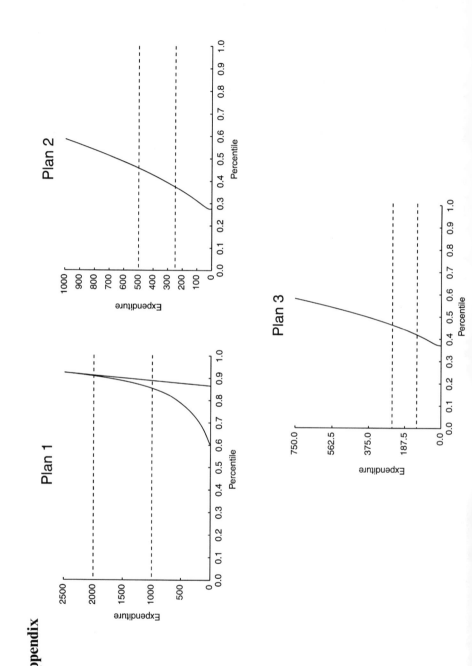

References

Arrow, Kenneth A. 1971. *Essays in the theory of risk bearing.* Chicago: Markham.
Eichner, Matthew J. 1996. Incentives, price expectations and medical expenditures. Mimeograph.
Eichner, Matthew J., Mark B. McClellan, and David A. Wise. 1997. Health expenditure persistence and the feasibility of medical savings accounts. In *Tax policy and the economy,* vol. 11, ed. J. Poterba, 92–128 MIT Press.
Newhouse, Joseph P. 1993. *Free for all: Lessons from the RAND health insurance experiment.* Cambridge: Harvard University Press.

9

Employees' Pension Benefits and the Labor Supply of Older Japanese Workers, 1980s–1990s

Yukiko Abe

9.1 Introduction

The population of Japan is aging rapidly. According to Ministry of Health and Welfare of Japan projections, the proportion of the population above the age of sixty-five years will reach about 25 percent by the year 2025. At the same time, the nation's social security benefits have increased substantially since the 1970s, and retirees now receive a generous tax deduction for pension income. Because the Japanese public pension program is organized as a pay-as-you-go system, and because the large cohort of baby boomers will retire early in the twenty-first century, the current benefit and tax structure soon will place a substantial burden on younger workers.[1]

In an attempt to reduce this burden, the Japanese government has instituted several modifications to the pension system. For example, whereas full social security benefits used to start at age sixty for men covered by the Employees' Pension program, reductions in benefits to be phased in

Yukiko Abe is associate professor at Asia University.

The author wishes to thank the Ministry of Labor of Japan for permission to use the microdata sets of the Survey on Employment Conditions of Older Persons (1983, 1988, and 1992) and the Japan Foundation Center for Global Partnership for financial support. She also thanks David Cutler, Yasushi Ohkusa, Atsushi Seike, David Wise, and participants in the National Bureau of Economic Research–Japan Center for Economic Research Conference on the Economics of Aging for their comments. Any errors in this paper are the sole responsibility of the author, as are the opinions expressed in it.

1. There are three major public pension programs in Japan. The Employees Pension insurance system (EP) covers workers in the private sector. Public-sector employees and private-school personnel are covered by mutual aid associations (MAAs) of several different types. The self-employed and farmers are covered by the National Pension (NP). Extensive discussions of the public pension system can be found in Ogura (1994) and Oguchi, Kimura, and Hatta (1996).

between 2001 and 2013 mean that men aged sixty to sixty-four and covered by Employee Pension insurance (EP) will receive smaller pensions.[2] Such reductions, as well as other changes in social security benefits and taxes, are likely to affect the number of older persons active in the labor market during the next few decades.

In the first section of this paper, therefore, I look at the recent employment history of Japanese men in this age group. Between the 1970s and the late 1980s their rate of participation in the labor market declined steadily; it rose in the early 1990s, then fell again between 1993 and 1996. Several economists (e.g., Seike and Shimada 1994) argue that the expansion of social security benefits in the 1970s is responsible for the decreasing employment rate for this group through the late 1980s. My initial focus on the subsequent rebound in paid employment of the early 1990s suggests several explanations for that rise. I then examine the effect on the labor supply of men aged sixty to sixty-four resulting from changes in the pension benefit scheme of the EP program. Throughout the paper I refer to workers sixty to sixty-four years old who have already applied for EP benefits and are therefore eligible to receive them as *EP eligibles;* people who are likely to qualify for EP benefits but have not yet applied for them are *potential EP eligibles.*[3]

In the past decade the Japanese government has cut pension benefits for working EP eligibles. In response to the criticism that such reductions distort labor supply of the elderly, the government several times has reformed the rules governing benefit reductions in an attempt to eliminate work disincentives. In the latter part of this paper, I examine the effect of these rule changes by comparing labor supply of older workers before and after the reform of the Employees' Pension Insurance Act (EPIA) instituted in 1989. The data I use come from the Survey on Employment Conditions of Older Persons (SECOP) for 1983, 1988, and 1992. Although EPIA reforms affect EP eligibles aged sixty to sixty-four, they do not apply to those aged sixty-five or older, nor to workers covered by non-EP public pension programs. I was therefore able to use the latter two groups as a control group for evaluating the response of EP eligibles to EPIA reform and its effect on the labor supply of men in this age group.

Even though regression estimates indicate that reductions in benefits that are related to earnings generally discourage labor supply of the

---

2. While nonworkers aged sixty to sixty-four stop making social security contributions, they will receive only the *proportional part* of the pension benefits (i.e., the amount proportional to their individual lifetime contributions). After age sixty-five, they will receive the *base part* (the standard pension amount received by all seniors) as well as the proportional part.

3. Application for determination of entitlement (*saitei*) by covered individuals (those who contributed to the EP before age sixty) is the necessary condition for receiving EP benefits. Based on this application, the benefit amount for the individual is calculated. Although the starting age for receiving EP benefits is sixty, many individuals covered by the program do not apply for EP benefits at that age.

affected group, the 1989 EPIA reforms do not seem to have significantly encouraged employment among men aged sixty to sixty-four.

According to several other studies comparing the earnings distribution of EP eligibles and EP noneligibles (Tachibanaki and Shimono 1994; Seike and Shimada 1994), EP eligibles avoid benefit reductions by adjusting their earnings.[4] However, while many of these studies suggest that reductions in benefits distort labor supply, none of the models used explicitly includes the institutional fact that benefit reductions apply only to EP eligibles who participate in EP at ages sixty to sixty-four. This fact has important implications for evaluations of the government's benefit reduction scheme, for the reasons outlined below.

There are several ways for working EP eligibles not to participate in EP, and thus to avoid benefit reductions. Employees' Pension benefits are cut only if the worker participates in EP through his or her current employer (i.e., pays the EP premium out of current earnings). In general, EP participation is required only when the following three conditions are all met: The worker is less than sixty-five years old, is employed in a private-sector establishment with more than five regular employees or in an incorporated enterprise of any number of employees, and works more hours than three-quarters of the regular employees in the same establishment. A worker who does not meet these qualifications—for example, by working outside the private sector, part-time, or in self-employment—does not have to participate in EP. Based on my analysis shown below, about 30 percent of working EP-eligible males choose to work under conditions in which EP participation is not required. This sizable proportion of nonparticipating, working EP eligibles suggests then that benefit reductions are likely to affect labor supply by making self-employment, part-time work, or public-sector employment more attractive to those who might otherwise choose to work full-time in the private sector.

Because benefit reduction is most likely to affect the likelihood of and the hours of private-sector employment, I analyze overall labor force participation and private-sector employment separately in this paper. This procedure contrasts sharply with that of previous studies, which either examine work-hours decisions without regard to choice of work mode or fail to distinguish among various kinds of work, even though benefit reduction has different implications for different work modes.

This paper is organized as follows. In section 9.2, I present an overview of the trend in the labor supply of Japanese men aged sixty to sixty-four. In section 9.3, I explain the EP benefit rule for active workers and review its history from the 1980s to the present. In section 9.4, I explain the Sur-

---

4. Seike and Shimada (1994) employ a labor supply model that incorporates selection bias. Ogawa (1997) studies labor force participation by using a binary choice model. Amemiya and Shimono (1989) use a nested logit model to examine workers' choices among full-time work, part-time work, and no work.

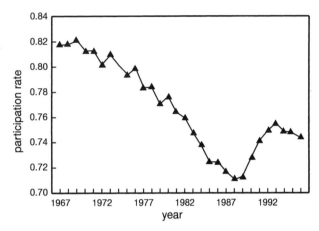

Fig. 9.1   Aggregate male labor force participation of men aged sixty to sixty-four
Source: Labor Force Survey, Statistical Bureau, Management and Coordination Agency, various years.

vey on Employment Conditions of Older Persons (SECOP, Konenreisha Shūgyō Jittai Chōsa), which is the data set used in this paper. In section 9.5, I explain the descriptive statistics of work-mode choice and hours. In section 9.6, estimates from a reduced-form analysis are presented. The paper concludes with a discussion of the policy implications of the findings.

9.2   Overview of the Labor Supply of Men Aged Sixty to Sixty-Four

Between 1967 and the late 1980s, the labor force participation of sixty- to sixty-four-year-old Japanese men decreased; it then increased until 1993 before again declining somewhat between 1993 and 1996. This transition is shown in figure 9.1. The first decline is often attributed to the expansion of public pension benefits during the same period (e.g., Seike 1993). Possible explanations for the rebound in employment from 1990 to 1993 include (a) increases in the mandatory retirement age and its spillover effects on older workers; (b) the government policy of subsidizing the hiring of older workers; (c) strong labor demand in the Japanese economy from the late 1980s to the early 1990s, and (d) reforms in EP benefit rules.[5]

All of these factors are likely to increase the private-sector employment of men aged sixty to sixty-four. In fact, as shown in figure 9.2, the proportion of private-sector employment (wage and salary workers, excluding those who work on a temporary basis) among men in this age group in-

---

5. The EP benefit rule adopted in 1995 is expected to be less distortionary than the ones that preceded it.

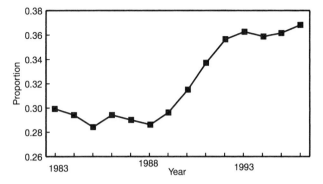

Fig. 9.2   Proportion of private-sector employment among men aged sixty to sixty-four
Source: Labor Force Survey, Statistical Bureau, Management and Coordination Agency, various years.
Note: The figure is (private-sector employed males aged sixty to sixty-four)/(total number of males aged sixty to sixty-four).

creased dramatically from 1988 to 1993 and continued to increase slightly until 1996. This rise occurred even though the overall labor force participation of the group declined between 1993 and 1996. The proportion of private-sector employment for men aged sixty to sixty-four rose from 30 percent in 1983 to 37 percent in 1996. The corresponding figures for the entire male population were 50 percent in 1983 and 53 percent in 1996; thus the increase in private-sector employment for the older group was higher than the economy-wide average.[6] It is quite possible that while the recession of the mid-1990s reduced the number of older workers employed, there were offsetting institutional forces that contributed to an overall increase.

9.2.1   Extension of the Mandatory Retirement Age

The first such force may have been raising the mandatory retirement age. In many firms the mandatory age of retirement was raised gradually during the 1980s and 1990s, as shown in table 9.1. Large firms tended to raise it earlier than small or medium-sized firms. In 1992, for example, 95.2 percent of firms with more than 5,000 employees had a mandatory retirement age of sixty. This figure was 67.5 percent for firms with thirty to ninety-nine employees in 1992 and 73.6 percent in 1995. Some analysts have suggested that this change causes people aged fifty-five to sixty to work more hours, and to be more likely to work full time.

---

6. The comparable figure for men aged fifty-five to fifty-nine increased even more dramatically, from 47 percent in 1983 to 63 percent in 1996. A large part of this increase was probably due to the rise in the mandatory retirement age.

Table 9.1   Distribution of Firms by Their Mandatory Retirement Age (percent)

	Below 55	55	56–59	60	Over 60
1980	0.2	39.5	20.1	36.5	3.2
1983	0.3	31.3	19.0	45.8	3.6
1985	0.1	27.0	17.4	51.0	4.4
1988	0.6	23.6	17.1	55.0	3.8
1992	0.2	11.5	11.7	71.4	5.2
1995	7.6		6.6	78.6	7.2

Source: Employment Management Survey (*Koyo Kanri Chōsa*).

9.2.2   Government Subsidies for Hiring Older Workers

The Japanese Ministry of Labor administers several programs to encourage companies to hire older workers. The programs include (a) a subsidy for introducing the practice of continuous employment for workers over age sixty-one (Keizoku Koyō Seido Donyū Shōrei-kin), (b) a subsidy for hiring a high proportion of older workers in the work force (Kōrei-sha Tasū Koyō Shōrei-kin), (c) a subsidy for introducing equipment suited to the needs of older workers (Kounenrei-sha Koyō Kankyō Seibi Shorei-kin), and (d) a subsidy for offering paid holidays to workers who use them to improve their employment skills in their old age (Kōrei-ki Shūgyō Junbi Shōrei-kin). These subsidies are provided to employers who introduce systems that increase or facilitate the hiring of older workers. Furthermore, hiring greater numbers of older workers may entitle employers to additional subsidies. For example, they may qualify to receive the Subsidy for Employment Development for Special Workers (Tokutei Kyūsyoku-sha Koyō Shōrei-kin) by using public job-placement offices to hire workers aged fifty-five or older. All of these subsidies are financed by the Employment Insurance Account (the Japanese equivalent of unemployment insurance).[7]

9.3   Benefit Reduction in Employees' Pension Insurance

Until the year 2000, EP eligibles began receiving benefits at age sixty; the starting age for receiving EP is scheduled to rise gradually between 2001 and 2013 (for men). Under the reformed rules, EP eligibles aged sixty to sixty-four, as explained in note 2, will receive only the part of the pension that is proportional to their lifetime EP contributions; they will not

7. In 1995, Employment Insurance started providing subsidies to older insured people who continue to work after age sixty (Kōrei-sha Koyō Keizoku Kyūfu). According to the *Annual Report on Employment Insurance* (Ministry of Labor 1995) the total amount paid through this system in 1995 was 10.9 billion yen (for seven months). The effect of this subsidy is not addressed in this paper, because the most recent data available are from 1992.

receive the base benefits until they reach age sixty-five (Ministry of Health and Welfare of Japan 1996).

Any model of the effect of EP benefit reduction on working beneficiaries must consider three decisions a covered person must make. The first, the application decision, is whether (and when) to apply for EP benefits sometime after the age of sixty. The second is the work-mode choice, since the benefit reduction scheme treats different types of jobs very differently. The final decision relates to the number of hours the worker chooses to work. The sequence of decisions described below is illustrated in figures 9.3 and 9.4.

9.3.1   Application Decision

As explained in note 3, application for determination of entitlement (*saitei*) by the covered individual is the necessary precondition for receiving EP benefits. A sizable proportion of qualified individuals (potential EP eligibles) does not file for EP benefits at age sixty. Based on a cross-sectional calculation from the 1992 Annual Report of the Social Insurance

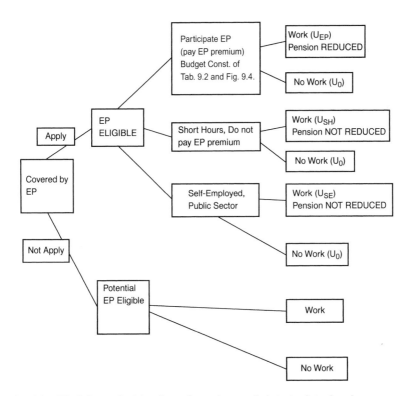

Fig. 9.3   Work-hours decision for male worker aged sixty to sixty-four by Employees' Pension

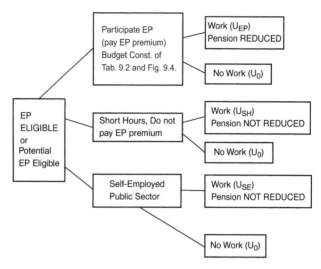

Fig. 9.4   Work-hours decision for Employees' Pension eligible or potential eligible male worker aged sixty to sixty-four

Agency, only about 57 percent of covered males apply at age sixty. About 21 percent apply between the ages of sixty-one and sixty-four, and most of the remainder apply at age sixty-five. Only 3 percent apply after age sixty-six.

The fact that less than 60 percent of covered individuals apply at the earliest possible age (sixty) is somewhat surprising. Because EP benefits are affected by the number of years a worker contributes to the program, some may want to increase their benefits by extending the period of contribution. Moreover, a delayed application does not cause a loss in cumulative benefits, because benefits for up to the five years preceding the application are paid once a worker's entitlement has been determined. Since most people file by the age of sixty-five, the only loss caused by a late application is the interest that workers could earn on the benefits due to them from the age of sixty.[8] It is likely that covered individuals who do not apply at age sixty face no liquidity constraints and choose to work. In that sense, the application decision and the decision to participate in the labor market are very closely related, and both should be treated as endogenous.

Although the SECOP data sets do not ask specifically about application status, the sample includes many male workers aged sixty to sixty-four who were employed in the private sector at age fifty-five (and so are likely

8. Because the past benefits paid at the time entitlement is determined (after age sixty) are the sum of past benefits, late application results in the loss of interest that might have accrued if the determination had taken place earlier. If a covered individual faces liquidity constraints after age sixty, therefore, it does not make sense to delay application.

to be covered by the EP) and who receive no EP benefits between sixty and sixty-four. Such individuals either have not filed the application for EP benefits or have filed but have incomes too high to receive benefits. The SECOP data sets do not allow me to distinguish between these two cases precisely. However, the number of people who can be put in either of these categories is much higher than the estimated number of those in the second category, which can be calculated by using the published data in the Annual Report of the Social Insurance Agency. This fact suggests that it is important to consider the possibility of nonapplication in analyzing the effects of benefit reductions on the labor supply of men in this age group.

9.3.2 Work-Mode and Hours Decisions

The second decision individuals must make concerns the mode and hours of work. As noted earlier, working EP eligibles aged sixty to sixty-four, who are wage or salary workers in the private sector and who work more hours than three-quarters of the firm's regular workers must participate in EP (i.e., must pay EP premiums out of their current earnings) until they reach age sixty-five. Under the EP benefit reduction scheme, the benefits received by EP an participant aged sixty to sixty-four depends on the level of employment income: An increase in employment income is "taxed" by a reduction in EP benefits.

The reduction rules for the years I analyze in this paper—1983, 1988, and 1992—are shown in table 9.2, which also explains the rule in effect after April 1995 under the reformed EPIA of 1994. Before 1995, there were many more "notches" in the budget constraints, which are likely to affect EP eligibles' decisions about the trade-off between consumption and leisure. There were four such notches until 1989, and eight between 1989 and 1995. Even after the 1994 reform, one notch still remained: the one at the margin between work and no work. Overall, from 1983 to 1995 the rule changed in the direction of encouraging participation in the labor force. The typical budget constraints in 1983, 1992, and 1995 are shown in figure 9.5.[9] The complicated benefit rule put into effect in 1992 increased disposable incomes in the intermediate range of the budget constraint compared with the situation before 1989. The 1994 reform eliminated most notches.

From 1986 to 2001, EP benefits are reduced for EP eligibles aged sixty to sixty-four, while those sixty-five or over receive full EP benefits regardless of their labor income.[10] However, until 1986, benefit reduction was

---

9. The graphs incorporate the following set of parameters: wage, 800 yen per hour; potential EP benefits, 180,000 yen per month; living with spouse, no dependents. Continuing to make contributions to EP between ages sixty and sixty-four increases future benefits, but this aspect is ignored in these figures.

10. Starting April of 2002, EP benefit reduction is going to be applied to EP eligibles aged sixty-five to sixty-nine, as well as those aged sixty to sixty-four.

Table 9.2   The Employee Pension Benefits Formula for Workers Aged Sixty to Sixty-four

1983 and 1988		1992		After April 1995	
Labor Income	Benefits	Labor Income	Benefits	Labor Income	Benefits
< 95	$0.8 \times B$	< 95	$0.8 \times B$	< $220 - 0.8 \times B$	$0.8 \times B$
95–130	$0.5 \times B$	95–114	$0.7 \times B$	$220 - 0.8 \times B$–340	$0.8 \times B - 0.5 \times [E - \max(0,220 - 0.8 \times B)]$
130–150	$0.2 \times B$	114–138	$0.6 \times B$	Over 340	$\max\{0.8 \times B - 0.5 \times [340 - \max(0,220 - 0.8 \times B)] - (E - 340), 0\}$
Over 150	0	138–165	$0.5 \times B$		
		165–185	$0.4 \times B$		
		185–210	$0.3 \times B$		
		210–250	$0.2 \times B$		
		Over 250	0		

Sources: Table prepared by the author based on Ministry of Health and Welfare of Japan (1995); Hattori (1996); Ministry of Health and Welfare of Japan and Social Insurance Agency (1987); Social Insurance Agency (various years).

Notes: Labor income is measured monthly in thousands of yen. The expressions in the Benefits column are the EP benefits for an individual with a corresponding amount of labor income, where B is the potential EP benefit, excluding the allowance for spouse and dependent children. The allowance for spouse and dependent children is paid as long as the base benefit is positive. The rule in 1992 was introduced in the Reform of Employee's Pension Insurance Act of 1989 and was in effect from December of 1989 to March of 1995. The rule after April 1995 was introduced in the EP Insurance Act of 1994.

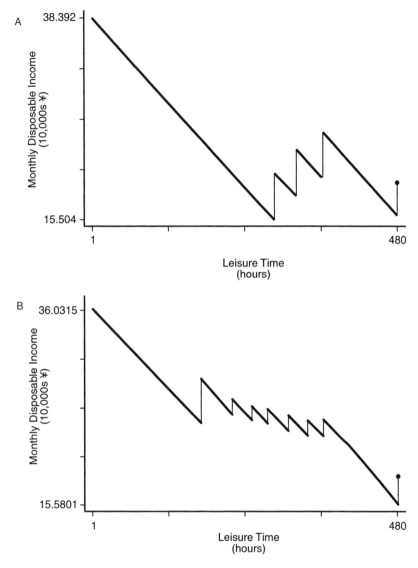

Fig. 9.5   **Budget constraint, with spouse (wage = 800 yen/hour): (*A*), 1983 and 1988; (*B*), 1992; (*C*), 1995**

also applied to those aged sixty-five or over. Before April 1986, EP benefits for those aged sixty-five or over with earnings of more than 160,000 yen (per month) were reduced by 20 percent. This rule was more generous than the one applied to workers sixty to sixty-four years old, who received no benefits at all for the same level of labor income. Thus the pre-1986

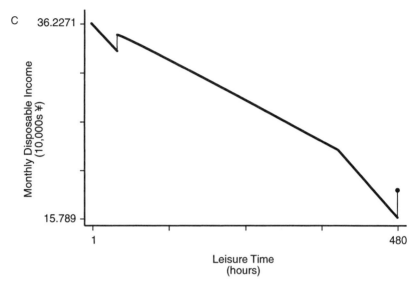

Fig. 9.5   (cont.)

rule seems likely to have encouraged work among men aged sixty-five or over, while discouraging it for those aged sixty to sixty-four.

The work-mode choices shown in figure 9.3 are (a) participating in EP, (b) working part time and not participating in EP, and (c) being self-employed and not participating in EP. In each work mode, a worker decides on working hours according to the budget constraint applicable to that particular mode. In the EP-participation mode, for example, the applicable budget constraint is shown in figure 9.5. In the part-time mode, limiting hours to less than three-quarters of those worked by regular workers produces no cut in benefits; in the self-employed mode, there are no benefit cuts at all. Employees' Pension eligibles aged sixty to sixty-four solve the problem in the following way. They first determine the maximum utility of each work-mode option, then compare the utilities and choose the mode that yields the highest utility. Since the budget constraints for different work modes are different, we need to identify each worker's chosen work mode.

The budget constraints applicable to potential EP eligibles are similar to those for EP eligibles. Assuming that covered individuals file their applications by age sixty-five, they can, as noted earlier, collect the benefits they would have received between the ages of sixty and sixty-four. The amount of benefits paid for those years will depend on the employment income earned. For example, if an individual's earnings at age sixty-two are positive, then the benefits corresponding to that year are cut based on the earnings of that time (at age sixty-two). Therefore, the amount the worker receives for past benefits after his or her entitlement is adjusted according to the labor income earned before filing the application. Thus, as far as choice of work mode and hours are concerned, EP eligibles and potential EP eligibles are in a similar situation.[11] For this reason, I consider them as one group when I analyze workers' labor-supply decisions, as illustrated in figures 9.3 and 9.4.

9.3.3 Identifying Chosen Decisions in the Data Set

The institutional structure discussed above must be incorporated into any model for analyzing the effects of the EP benefit reduction scheme. However, the SECOP data sets contain several ambiguities that make identifying the decisions made by individual workers difficult. First, the survey does not ask respondents whether they have already filed the application for EP benefits. Second, it does not ask whether they participate in EP. The question on current employment status does allow us to identify those who are currently self-employed or who work in other modes that do not require EP participation. It remains difficult, however, to identify the application status and EP-participation status of those employed in the private sector. The main reasons for the difficulty are that (a) part-time, private-sector workers may or may not participate in EP, and (b) EP benefits for high-income EP eligibles are cut to zero, so that these eligibles are indistinguishable from workers who are not EP eligible. There is some evidence that a sizable proportion of male part-time workers do not participate in EP, as the following analysis shows.

9.3.4 Evidence on Employees' Pension Participation

The administrative statistics of the Social Insurance Agency indicate how many EP eligibles actually receive reduced EP benefits. Until 1994, around 20 percent of male EP eligibles aged sixty to sixty-four (those who applied for EP benefits after age sixty) worked, participated in EP, and received reduced or zero benefits. That proportion rose to 28 percent in 1995, the year in which both the 1994 EPIA reform and Employment Insurance employment-continuation benefits for workers aged sixty to sixty-four were put into effect (see table 9.3).[12] These changes made working in the private sector more attractive for older people and so are likely to have increased EP participation among EP eligibles.

The figures, however, are much lower than the 1994 Labor Force Survey's proportion of private-sector employment, which was 36 percent. Since the data in the Labor Force Survey are based on the entire population and not on EP eligibles alone, part of the discrepancy may be attribut-

---

11. It is important to keep in mind that the *potential* EP eligibles are not included in some of the governmental statistics on EP eligibles.

12. Under the employment-continuation benefit, older workers who experience large wage decline can receive wage subsidy.

Table 9.3   **Employees' Pension Participation and Benefit Reduction among Those Eligible, Aged Sixty to Sixty-Four**

	EP Participation and Benefit Reduction	EP Participation and Benefit Reduction and Benefit > 0
1992	0.231	0.210
1993	0.224	0.203
1994	0.209	0.189
1995	0.284	0.227

Source: Numbers of EP eligibles (i.e., denominators) are from the Social Insurance Agency's annual report: the 1992 number is from the 1992 report (published in 1994); 1993 numbers, the 1995 report; 1994 numbers, the 1996 report; and 1995 numbers, the 1997 report. Numbers for EP participation and benefit reduction (i.e., numerators) are from Summary of the Social Insurance Policy (1995).

Notes: The figures are calculated as the number of those who received reduced benefits or zero benefits (due-to-the-means test) out of the total number of male EP eligibles aged sixty to sixty-four. The potential EP eligibles, who have not yet applied for EP benefits, are excluded from both the numerator and the denominator.

Basically, the EP benefit reduction applies only to workers sixty to sixty-four years old. However, there are rare cases in which people aged sixty-five or more face the benefit reduction, because of the transitional arrangements. Since the Social Insurance Agency does not publish the number of sixty- to sixty-four-year-old EP participants classified by sex, the numerator of the calculation for 1992–95 is slightly larger than the actual number of male EP participants in that age group.

able to differences in the labor supply behavior of EP eligibles and others. However, the differences also could be attributable to two other factors: (a) nonapplication to the EP by qualified individuals at age sixty, and (b) nonparticipation by EP eligibles who work part time. Potential EP eligibles are more likely to work than EP eligibles; thus the probability that EP eligibles work is likely to be lower than the one calculated for a group that also includes potential EP eligibles.[13] When EP eligibles work part time and choose not to participate in EP, neither they nor their employers are required to pay the EP premium. In addition, EP eligibles who work part time receive full benefits, but they lose the opportunity to increase their future EP benefits through a longer period of contribution.

The EP-participation decision may also be influenced by the worker's desire to participate in an employer-provided health insurance plan.[14]

13. Probability of working—that is, the ratio of the number of people who worked to the population as a whole—is used as one measure of labor supply in this paper. It differs from labor force participation, which includes unemployed workers in the numerator. The SECOP-IP questionnaire does not specifically ask people whether they have searched for jobs in a given period, which is part of the standard definition of unemployment.

14. There is a significant variation in the National Health Insurance premium across municipalities. Furthermore, employer-provided health insurance is more generous in benefits than National Health Insurance and allows the insured to cover family members at no additional cost. Therefore, if the National Health Insurance premium is high in an area or the

Table 9.4   **Proportion of Participation in Employees' Pension and Employer-
Provided Health Insurance**

	Short Hours	Long Hours
Male (%)		
1990	19.5	69.0
1995	36.5	79.0
Female (%)		
1990	24.8	71.9
1995	35.6	78.1

Source: Ministry of Labor (1992, 1997).

Since the criteria for participating in EP and participating in employer-provided health insurance are the same for those aged sixty-four or younger, it is difficult to enroll in an employer's health plan without also participating in EP. Thus a part-time worker who strongly prefers the employer-provided health insurance to the National Health Insurance might choose to participate in EP even though that requires payment of the EP premium and, possibly, reduces EP benefits.

Table 9.4 lists the summary statistics on EP participation and employer-based health insurance coverage from the Ministry of Labor's General Survey of Part-Time Workers (GSPTW) for 1990 and 1995 (see Ministry of Labor 1992, 1997). These statistics are calculated for part-time workers of all ages and not solely for the EP-eligible workers aged sixty to sixty-four.[15] In 1990, almost 20 percent of male workers who worked fewer hours than regular employees participated in EP and received health insurance provided by the employer; that figure increased to 37 percent in 1995. Furthermore, 20 to 30 percent of male part-time workers who worked as many hours as regular workers did not participate in EP. Although these figures are only indirect evidence of EP participation by male EP eligibles in the sixty- to sixty-four-year-old age group who work part time, they suggest that it is probably misleading to assume either that no part-time workers participate in EP or that all of them do.

9.4   Data Description

I turn now to an analysis of the EP benefit reduction scheme and its effect on the male labor supply of Japan, using the microdata sets of the Survey on Employment Conditions of Older Persons for 1983, 1988, and 1992. The SECOP consists of two surveys, one for individuals and the

worker has family members to insure, it makes more sense to participate in employer-provided health insurance.
15. As the survey questionnaire of GSPTW does not ask about the public pension under which an individual is covered, it is difficult to identify EP eligibles.

other for establishments.[16] The Individual Persons file (IP), a cross-sectional survey of individuals between the ages of fifty-five and sixty-nine, asks for detailed information on employment, labor income, pension type and amount received, nonlabor income, work history, and household characteristics.[17] The variables used in the analysis are explained below.[18]

9.4.1 Employees' Pension Eligibility

To analyze the effects of EP benefit reduction on labor supply, we need to identify the type of public pension covering each individual. The 1983 IP survey questionnaire asked respondents directly about their eligibility for a public pension. The questionnaires for 1988 and 1992, however, inquired about the amount of EP benefits received but did not ask specifically about eligibility. Obviously, those who received positive EP benefits were EP eligibles. The ambiguity arises from two other groups: The first group includes covered individuals who do not apply for EP benefits at age sixty but remain potential EP eligibles; the second group contains EP eligibles whose benefits are cut to zero because their labor income is too high (see table 9.2). According to the Annual Report of the Social Insurance Agency (1992), about 9 percent of EP eligibles who work and participate in EP receive no EP benefits for this second reason. As mentioned in the preceding section, the economic conditions for potential EP eligibles who work and for EP eligibles who receive zero benefits are similar, so I assume that both of them belong to the EP group. In the following discussion, therefore, I try to draw from the IP data set the combined number of potential EP eligibles and EP eligibles whose EP benefits are cut to zero.

There is no direct way to identify these two groups in the IP data set for 1988 and 1992. Therefore, following a procedure similar to the one employed by Ogawa (1997), I assume that a person with the following set of characteristics is an EP eligible, even though he received zero EP benefits: (a) He worked more than thirty-two hours per week; (b) his labor income

16. The establishment survey of the SECOP asks detailed questions about the number of older workers employed and the employment status of such workers in the organization.

17. Seike and Shimada (1994) based their analysis on the SECOP-IP data set for 1983; Tachibanaki and Shimono (1985) and Amemiya and Shimono (1989) used the data set for 1980; and Ogawa (1997) used 1983, 1988, and 1992 data sets.

18. In this study, I include people who answered no to the question "Were you an employee when you were 55?" This sample selection differs from that used by Seike and Yamada (1996), who included only those who answered yes to this question. Many individuals who answered no did in fact work at a later stage in life and, in 75 percent of such cases, they were self-employed. What is likely to have happened is that they became self-employed before age fifty-five and continued to be self-employed thereafter. Because the questionnaire asks whether the respondent was "an employee" at age fifty-five, some of the self-employed people may have answered no. Self-employed individuals can receive EP benefits if they participated in the EP sometime during their working lives. In fact, 16 percent of the sixty- to sixty-nine-year-old males who answered no to the question and were working at the times of the surveys received positive EP benefits.

was higher than the threshold at which EP benefits were reduced to zero; (c) he worked in the private sector as an employee at the time of the survey; (d) he worked in the private sector at age fifty-five; (e) he did not receive high benefits (more than 50,000 yen per month) from a Mutual Aid Association (MAA) pension program; and (f) he was between sixty and sixty-four years old. Criteria (a) and (c) ensure that the person makes EP contributions out of current labor income, which is a precondition for reductions in EP benefits. I assign a person who meets criteria (a), (c), (d), and (f) to the potential EP-eligible category if his receipts from all public pension programs are zero.[19] The idea behind this last condition is that if a person had claimed benefits from any of the public pension programs to which he contributed in the past, he probably would have applied for EP benefits as well.

The assignment of EP eligibility (including potential EP eligibility) in this way creates a sample EP group in which 15 percent of the observations receive zero benefits. This rather high proportion is understandable if it is caused by nonapplication.[20] Nonetheless, the procedure described above may cause one to classify someone who is unrelated to EP as an EP eligible or a potential EP eligible. For this reason, I base the analysis in this paper on two separate samples. Sample 1 includes all EP eligibles and potential EP eligibles as explained above. Sample 2 includes EP eligibles who receive positive EP benefits but excludes those who either (a) receive zero benefits because their labor income is too high, or (b) are potential EP eligibles who do not seem to have applied to EP benefits even though they are likely to have contributed to EP. Sample 1 might contain some non-EP individuals who are misclassified as EP eligibles (or potential EP eligibles). Sample 2 is likely to be free from classification errors but is a biased sample because it excludes those who endogenously choose to earn high income or choose not to apply for EP benefits.[21]

9.4.2 Pension Income

The IP questionnaire asks for the amount of pension benefits received by an individual from particular types of pension. The categories are EP (benefits given separately for working beneficiaries and others), National Pension (NP), Mutual Aid Association (MAA), company-provided pen-

---

19. The reasons for imposing conditions (a) and (c) for identifying potential EP eligibles are weak. I also experimented with a sample by dropping these conditions in assigning potential EP eligibles and found that some of the results are sensitive to such differences.

20. In fact, of those individuals I assigned to the nonapplication category, 33 percent are sixty years old and only 12 percent are sixty-four. (Note that I assigned only those aged sixty to sixty-four.) This pattern is consistent with the finding that more people finish their EP application as they get older.

21. Note that Sample 1 includes more workers than Sample 2 does. This is because men excluded from Sample 2 but included in Sample 1 are those who work. Sample 2 is a biased sample, but whether Sample 1 includes the "right" number of workers is not clear.

sions, and others (including private pensions purchased by the respondent). The EP benefits consist of the basic part and allowances for spouse and dependent children. The basic part is the sum of base benefits and the earnings related part. The amount of the latter is proportional to the individual's lifetime EP contributions. The allowances are not cut as labor income increases unless the benefits from the basic part become zero. When the worker's labor income hits the highest threshold for reduction (250,000 yen in 1992), the allowances for spouse and dependent children are eliminated. Since the amounts of the allowances for spouse and dependent children are not recorded in the data set, I base my analysis solely on the reported EP benefits for the basic part.[22]

The actual amount of pension received (asked in the IP survey) is not equal to the potential amount because the former is adjusted depending on labor income. Since the survey did not ask respondents how much they would receive if they were not working (potential EP benefits), that amount must be estimated. Ogawa (1997) developed the method to do this, which I have basically followed for determining the amount of an individual's potential EP benefits. For individuals whose labor income is high enough to cut EP benefits to zero, I have assigned a potential amount that is the mean value of nonworking individuals who receive EP benefits in full and have similar characteristics (in terms of birth year and occupation at age fifty-five or at retirement).

9.4.3   Weekly Hours

As the IP questionnaire asks separately about working hours per day and working days per week, I multiply the two figures to obtain hours of work per week. For a typical answer of eight hours per day and six days per week, I assign the number of weekly hours as forty-four, because one of the six working days is likely to be a half day. I eliminate weekly hours above seventy from the sample, since such figures are likely to be outliers for older workers.

9.4.4   Household Characteristics

The IP survey asked three questions related to household characteristics: (a) the number of people in the household, (b) the number of working individuals in the household, and (c) the respondent's main source of income. Following earlier researchers, I assume that respondents belong to one of the following five household categories: (a) *single,* one individual living alone; (b) *couple,* a two-person household in which the respondent is supported by himself or by his spouse; (c) *living with dependent children,*

---

22. It is difficult to arrive at any approximate figure for allowances without information on the characteristics that determine eligibility for allowances (e.g., age and/or income of spouse or children).

a household consisting of more than three individuals in which the respondent is self-supporting or is supported by his spouse; (d) *supported by children,* a household that consists of more than two individuals with the respondent is supported by his children; and (e) none of the above.

9.5   Descriptive Statistics from the SECOP-IP

The labor force participation statistics I cited earlier in the paper are based on the entire population of men aged sixty to sixty-four. The SECOP-IP data sets, however, allow me to compare the effects on labor supply of people covered by different public pension programs (in particular, EP and non-EP programs). As explained above, I use two samples to check for possible classification errors. Sample 1 includes EP eligibles and potential EP eligibles; Sample 2 excludes some of the EP eligibles and potential EP eligibles included in Sample 1.

Table 9.5 organizes the four measures of labor supply of men I derived from the SECOP-IP data according to the type of public pension received (EP and non-EP). For each age group the measures describe (a) the pro-

le 9.5   **Labor Supply of Men Aged Fifty-Five to Sixty-Five, 1983–92**

| | | $60 \leq$ Age ≤ 64 | | | Age ≥ 65 | |
	55 $\leq$ Age ≤ 59	EP (Sample 1)	EP (Sample 2)	NonEP	EP	NonEP
centage worked						
983	0.862	0.539	0.466	0.777	0.484	0.602
988	0.898	0.627	0.449	0.701	0.430	0.614
992	0.938	0.668	0.505	0.737	0.504	0.621
centage employed						
983	0.590	0.367	0.274	0.346	0.326	0.167
988	0.645	0.487	0.243	0.256	0.250	0.198
992	0.672	0.538	0.312	0.296	0.326	0.222
centage full-time						
983	0.779	0.419	0.327	0.601	0.364	0.408
988	0.781	0.484	0.238	0.444	0.252	0.369
992	0.861	0.545	0.321	0.495	0.301	0.387
erage weekly hours of working individuals						
1983	44.13	39.63	37.55	42.00	39.11	38.67
1988	43.47	39.34	32.44	37.11	33.80	35.87
1992	43.87	40.04	35.58	38.43	33.82	36.44

urce: Author's calculation from Survey on Employment Conditions of Older Persons (SECOP), 1983, 88, and 1992.

te: Sample 1 contains individuals who receive no EP benefits but are likely to be EP eligibles or tential EP eligibles; Sample 2 excludes them.

portion working, (b) the proportion employed in the private sector as wage or salary earners, (c) the proportion working full time (thirty-five hours or more per week), and (d) the average number of hours worked per week calculated among workers. I distinguish between the percentage of working and the percentage of those employed in the private sector because EP benefit reduction applies only to EP eligibles in the private sector. Reflecting the fact that the mandatory retirement age was raised from fifty-five to sixty, the proportion of men working in this age group increased between 1983 and 1992. For non-EP individuals sixty to sixty-four years old, the proportion decreased from 1983 to 1988 and then increased. For the combined group of EP eligibles and potential EP eligibles (Sample 1), the percentage working increased steadily from 1983 to 1992. On the other hand, the proportion of those working in the subsample of EP eligibles (Sample 2) decreased from 1983 to 1988 and then increased in 1992. In most categories, the number of hours worked decreased and then increased during this time period.

The 1983, 1988, and 1992 distributions of work hours for sixty- to sixty-four-year-old men, classified by public pension types (EP group includes potential EP eligibles), are shown in figures 9.6 to 9.11. The numbers for all groups and all years show the largest clusters of work hours at the points for no work and full-time work. The graphs indicate clearly that EP eligibles are less likely to work than others, but also that a larger proportion of EP eligibles worked in 1992 than before that time.

The Japanese government has recently adopted policies to shorten the maximum regular working hours of workers in the Japanese labor mar-

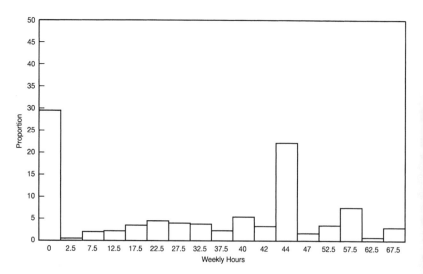

Fig. 9.6   Employees' Pension noneligible men, 1983

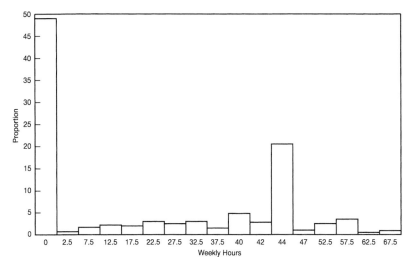

Fig. 9.7   Employees' Pension eligible men, 1983

ket.[23] Beginning in April 1997, the legal maximum was forty hours per week for all employers. According to the General Survey on Wages and Working Hours System of the Ministry of Labor (various years), the proportion of firms with regular work weeks of forty hours or less was 14.8 percent in 1980, versus 35 percent in 1992. The same trend is discernible in the proportion of firms with more than forty-four regular working hours, which declined from 54.6 percent in 1980 to 21.9 percent in 1992.[24] While the legal maximum on work hours applies to workers of all ages, this change in policy clearly has affected the hours-distribution of older workers. As shown in figures 9.8 through 9.11, the proportion of older workers working forty-four hours or more declined between 1988 and 1992 and the proportion of those working forty hours increased.

9.6   Reduced-Form Analysis of Male Labor Supply

I turn next to a reduced-form regression analysis of labor supply. The regression equation I estimate has the form

---

23. The restriction was first applied to large firms or growing industries and was later applied to smaller firms.

24. These figures are based on the weekly hours applied to most of a firm's employees. Increases in the number of part-time workers, therefore, are not likely to affect this figure even though that would make average hours of work smaller. The same figure weighted by the number of employees also appears in the survey; it shows a rise in the number of those working forty hours or less per week from 45.3 percent in 1980 to 67.4 percent in 1992.

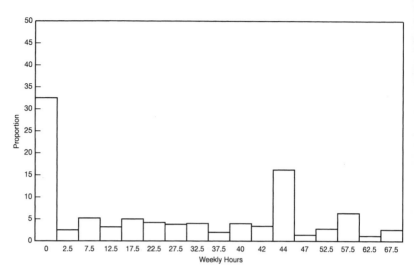

Fig. 9.8   Employees' Pension noneligible men, 1988

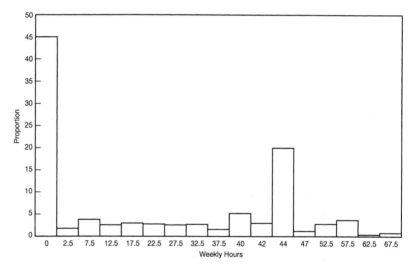

Fig. 9.9   Employees' Pension eligible men, 1988

$$(\text{Worked or Employed}) = \text{Probit}[\alpha_1(\text{Year Dummies})$$

$$+ \; \alpha_2(\text{Year Dummies} \times \text{Age60--64})$$

$$+ \; \alpha_3 \text{EP Eligibility} + \alpha_4(\text{EP Probability} \times \text{Age60--64})$$

$$+ \; \alpha_5(\text{EP Eligibility} \times \text{Age60--64} \times \text{Year Dummies})$$

$$+ \; \alpha_6(\text{EP Eligibility} \times \text{Age65over} \times \text{Year1983} + X] + \varepsilon,$$

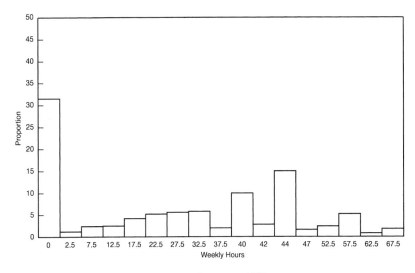

Fig. 9.10   Employees' Pension noneligible men, 1992

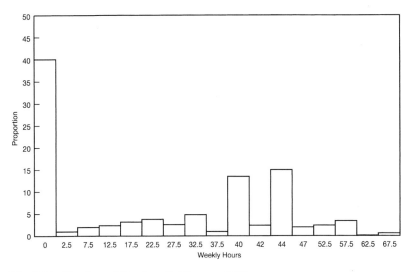

Fig. 9.11   Employees' Pension eligible men, 1992

$$\text{Log}(\text{Weekly Hours}) \ = \ \beta_1(\text{Year Dummies})$$
$$+ \ \beta_2(\text{Year Dummies} \ \times \ \text{Age60–64}) \ + \ \beta_3\text{EP Eligibility}$$
$$+ \ \beta_4(\text{EP Eligibility} \ \times \ \text{Age60–64})$$
$$+ \ \beta_5(\text{EP Eligibility} \ \times \ \text{Age60–64} \ \times \ \text{Year Dummies})$$
$$+ \ \beta_6(\text{EP Eligibility} \ \times \ \text{Age65over} \ \times \ \text{Year1983}) \ + \ X \ + \ \varepsilon.$$

The dependent variables are likelihood of working, likelihood of private-sector employment as a wage or salary earner, and weekly hours. Hours equations are estimated for each sample of workers or employees. The analysis of private-sector employment is included because EP benefits are cut only if an EP eligible works as a wage or salary earner in the private sector. Because the EP benefits formula for working beneficiaries changed in 1989, I was able to use the available data to compare labor supply outcomes before and after the policy change.

The summary statistics in table 9.5 show that the probability of working for EP eligibles aged sixty to sixty-four (the group affected by the policy change) increased from 1988 to 1992, although that probability rose for non-EP beneficiaries (i.e., the control group) as well. The interaction term of EP eligibility, age sixty to sixty-four, and the year dummy for 1992 reveals the effect of the policy change on EP eligibles (i.e., the treatment group). In addition, as noted earlier, in 1983 EP benefit reduction also applied to EP eligibles aged sixty-five or over, although the benefit schedule used was different from that applied to the sixty- to sixty-four-year-old group at any time. To extract the change in labor supply behavior by the group affected by the 1989 EPIA reform, I include a set of interaction terms of EP eligibility, age-category dummy, and year dummies. There are eleven such interaction terms. The set of control variables includes dummies for household characteristics, a dummy variable for having experienced mandatory retirement, a dummy for not being an employee at age fifty-five, a dummy for living in Tokyo, a health-status dummy, the amount of public pension received (the potential amount for EP eligibles), the amount of company pension receipt, a dummy variable for MAA pension beneficiaries, interaction terms of MAA and year dummies, and an interaction term of MAA and a dummy for having experienced mandatory retirement.

The regression sample consists of men aged sixty to sixty-nine. I do not include individuals aged fifty-five to fifty-nine because the information on their public pension status is not derivable from the data. (In any case, most of these people do not yet receive pension benefits.) I also exclude observations for individuals about whom information on any of the variables included in the regression analysis is missing.[25]

The descriptive statistics for the total sample are shown in table 9.6. First, using Sample 1 data, I estimate probit models for the decision to

---

25. An exception to this rule is treatment of a dummy for having experienced mandatory retirement. In the SECOP-IP questionnaire, anyone who answered no to the question "Were you an employee at age 55?" was not asked "Have you experienced mandatory retirement?" (see note 18). For these men, because the dummy for having experienced mandatory retirement is missing, I assign zero to the mandatory retirement dummy. I also include a dummy variable for nonemployment at age fifty-five for such individuals, to distinguish them from men who have not retired from career jobs.

Table 9.6   Descriptive Statistics of the Regression Sample

	Sample 1		Sample 2	
	Mean	S.D.	Mean	S.E.
Worked	0.622	0.485	0.588	0.492
Employed in the private sector	0.333	0.471	0.273	0.446
Full-time work (weekly hours > 35)	0.435	0.496	0.384	0.486
Weekly hours (worked = 1 only)	38.18	14.58	37.10	15.15
Log hourly wage (10,000 yen)	0.158	0.192	0.152	0.195
Ages 60–64	0.576	0.494	0.538	0.499
Single	0.038	0.190	0.038	0.191
Couple	0.346	0.476	0.344	0.475
With dependent children	0.441	0.497	0.430	0.495
Supported by children	0.114	0.317	0.122	0.328
Live in Tokyo	0.092	0.289	0.089	0.285
Executives	0.079	0.269	0.062	0.242
Self-employed	0.212	0.409	0.231	0.421
NonEP job[a]	0.065	0.247	0.071	0.257
Experienced mandatory retirement	0.418	0.493	0.426	0.495
Good health	0.677	0.468	0.662	0.473
EP eligible (inc. potential eligible)	0.513	0.500	0.469	0.499
EP × Age 60–64	0.284	0.451	0.220	0.414
EP × Age 60–64 × Year 1988	0.101	0.301	0.074	0.263
EP × Age 60–64 × Year 1992	0.131	0.337	0.096	0.294
MAA	0.202	0.401	0.219	0.414
MAA × Year 1988	0.064	0.245	0.070	0.255
MAA × Year 1992	0.077	0.266	0.084	0.277
MAA × experienced mandatory retirement	0.132	0.339	0.144	0.351
Public pension (10,000 yen)	11.28	8.83	10.79	8.86
Company pension (10,000 yen)	0.33	2.00	0.31	1.89
N	20,796		19,226	

Source: SECOP-IP data sets for 1983, 1988, and 1992.

Note: The sample consists of males aged 60 to 69. Hourly wage, the amount of public pension, and the amount of company pension are all deflated by CPI. For those who were not employed at age 55, value 0 is assigned to the mandatory retirement dummy.

[a] Self-employed jobs are excluded.

work and for private-sector employment, and linear regressions for weekly hours among workers (see table 9.7). Second, I estimate the same relationship using Sample 2 data (as shown in table 9.8). Here are my main findings.

1. The coefficient on a dummy of EP eligibility indicates that labor supply of EP eligibles and potential EP eligibles as a whole is not very different from that of other groups. However, EP eligibles aged sixty to sixty-four, who face benefit reductions if they work, are much less likely to work than other EP eligibles; the coefficient from Sample 2 suggests that they are 14 percent less likely to be employed in the private sector. Furthermore,

Table 9.7   **Reduced-Form Estimates of Male Labor Supply, 1983–92 (Sample 1)**

Dependent Variable	Decision to Work			Private-Sector Employment as Wage or Salary Earner		
	Worked	Marginal Probability	ln(weekly hours)	Employed	Marginal Probability	ln(weekly hours)
ln(hourly wage)	—	—	-0.301	—	—	-0.178
			(0.009)			(0.011)
Year 1988	0.084	0.031	-0.122	0.210	0.072	-0.092
	(0.064)		(0.033)	(0.076)		(0.043)
Year 1992	0.059	0.022	-0.036	0.252	0.086	-0.030
	(0.059)		(0.026)	(0.073)		(0.036)
Ages 60–64	0.312	0.115	0.090	0.426	0.140	0.116
	(0.055)		(0.020)	(0.062)		(0.029)
Ages 60–64 × Year 1988	-0.211	-0.079	-0.023	-0.286	-0.091	-0.170
	(0.079)		(0.037)	(0.088)		(0.051)
Ages 60–64 × Year 1992	-0.094	-0.035	-0.019	-0.216	-0.070	-0.112
	(0.077)		(0.031)	(0.084)		(0.044)
EP eligible	-0.111	-0.041	0.028	0.409	0.136	0.081
	(0.059)		(0.027)	(0.069)		(0.035)
EP eligible × Ages 60–64	-0.221	-0.083	-0.057	-0.347	-0.111	-0.075
	(0.081)		(0.033)	(0.086)		(0.038)
EP × Ages 60–64 × Year 1988	0.383	0.131	0.112	0.358	0.129	0.250
	(0.080)		(0.031)	(0.077)		(0.037)
EP × Ages 60–64 × Year 1992	0.419	0.142	0.087	0.389	0.140	0.127
	(0.078)		(0.027)	(0.074)		(0.032)
EP × Age ≥ 65 × Year 1988	-0.132	-0.049	-0.033	-0.400	-0.120	-0.032
	(0.083)		(0.044)	(0.094)		(0.055)
EP × Age ≥ 65 × Year 1992	0.137	0.049	-0.068	-0.152	-0.049	-0.108
	(0.077)		(0.037)	(0.088)		(0.046)
Single	0.562	0.179	0.150	0.820	0.312	0.203
	(0.073)		(0.049)	(0.081)		(0.059)
Couple	1.085	0.356	0.243	0.947	0.334	0.262
	(0.054)		(0.040)	(0.061)		

With dependent children	1.278	0.432	0.281	0.986	0.323	0.284
	(0.053)		(0.040)	(0.060)		(0.052)
Supported by children	0.131	0.047	−0.060	0.083	0.029	0.005
	(0.060)		(0.045)	(0.075)		(0.069)
Mandatory retirement	−0.614	−0.227	−0.163	−0.531	−0.173	−0.142
	(0.031)		(0.013)	(0.030)		(0.012)
Not an employee at age 55	−0.104	−0.039	0.093	−1.321	−0.352	0.011
	(0.032)		(0.016)	(0.036)		(0.025)
Live in Tokyo	0.193	0.069	0.088	0.239	0.085	0.036
	(0.040)		(0.015)	(0.038)		(0.016)
Good health	0.889	0.334	0.150	0.637	0.198	0.102
	(0.023)		(0.013)	(0.026)		(0.015)
Public pension amount	−0.035	−0.013	−0.003	−0.010	−0.003	−0.0003
	(0.002)		(0.0008)	(0.002)		(0.0008)
Company pension amount	−0.032	−0.012	−0.007	−0.013	−0.004	−0.0006
	(0.006)		(0.003)	(0.005)		(0.003)
MAA	−0.287	−0.109	−0.107	−0.241	−0.078	−0.117
	(0.057)		(0.025)	(0.063)		(0.037)
MAA × Year 1988	−0.146	−0.055	−0.067	−0.028	−0.009	0.105
	(0.069)		(0.035)	(0.071)		(0.045)
MAA × Year 1992	−0.086	−0.032	−0.046	−0.008	−0.003	0.041
	(0.069)		(0.030)	(0.068)		(0.039)
MAA × mandatory retirement	0.538	0.178	0.095	0.391	0.141	0.084
	(0.056)		(0.028)	(0.058)		(0.034)
N	20,679	—	12,771	20,679	—	6,683
R^2	—	—	0.33	—	—	0.16
Log-likelihood	−10618.23	—	—	−11544.35	—	—

Source: Author's calculation from SECOP-IP (Ministry of Labor 1983, 1988, 1992).

Notes: The columns for "marginal probability" correspond to the marginal increase in work probability when the explanatory variable changes its value by 1. For dummy variables, they are the difference of value 1 and value 0. For weekly hours equations, standard errors are corrected for heteroscedasticity. All regressions are weighted by the sampling weights.

Hours equations for working individuals also include three dummy variables for employment status (executives, self-employed, and jobs that do not require EP participation).

Dashes indicate that the corresponding variables are not used in the regression equation; or statistics for the corresponding regression are not applicable.

Table 9.8   Reduced-Form Estimates of Male Labor Supply, 1983–92 (Sample 2)

Dependent Variable	Decision to Work			Private-Sector Employment		
	Worked	Marginal Probability	Log(weekly hours)	Employed	Marginal Probability	Log(weekly hours)
Log(hourly wage)	—	—	−0.327 (0.009)	—	—	−0.248 (0.013)
Year 1988	0.067 (0.063)	0.026	−0.119 (0.033)	0.171 (0.074)	0.053	−0.086 (0.042)
Year 1992	0.055 (0.059)	0.021	−0.025 (0.026)	0.231 (0.071)	0.071	−0.018 (0.035)
Ages 60–64	0.314 (0.055)	0.120	0.095 (0.020)	0.418 (0.060)	0.124	0.125 (0.029)
Ages 60–64 × Year 1988	−0.211 (0.079)	−0.082	−0.028 (0.037)	−0.287 (0.085)	−0.081	−0.181 (0.050)
Ages 60–64 × Year 1992	−0.113 (0.076)	−0.043	−0.029 (0.031)	−0.238 (0.081)	−0.068	−0.127 (0.043)
EP eligible	−0.060 (0.059)	−0.023	0.081 (0.027)	0.439 (0.067)	0.134	0.125 (0.035)
EP eligible × Age 60–64	−0.371 (0.082)	−0.144	−0.128 (0.035)	−0.560 (0.086)	−0.148	−0.164 (0.041)
EP × Age 60–64 × Year 1988	0.189 (0.085)	0.070	−0.015 (0.038)	0.088 (0.085)	0.027	0.115 (0.046)
EP × Age 60–64 × Year 1992	0.251 (0.082)	0.092	0.018 (0.032)	0.185 (0.078)	0.059	0.034 (0.038)
EP × Age ≥ 65 × Year 1988	−0.100 (0.083)	−0.039	−0.216 (0.044)	−0.342 (0.091)	−0.092	−0.010 (0.055)
EP × Age ≥ 65 × Year 1992	0.159 (0.077)	0.059	−0.058 (0.037)	−0.113 (0.086)	−0.033	−0.096 (0.045)
Single	0.456 (0.077)	0.159	0.109 (0.053)	0.695 (0.085)	0.249	0.162 (0.064)
Couple	1.028 (0.056)	0.357	0.235 (0.041)	0.845 (0.063)	0.273	0.269 (0.06?)

	(1)	(2)	(3)	(4)	(5)	(6)
With dependent children	1.215 (0.056)	0.428	0.271 (0.041)	0.862 (0.062)	0.267	0.285 (0.054)
Supported by children	0.087 (0.062)	0.033	-0.093 (0.046)	0.013 (0.075)	0.004	-0.026 (0.071)
Mandatory retirement	-0.431 (0.035)	-0.165	-0.133 (0.016)	-0.288 (0.035)	-0.085	-0.115 (0.015)
Not an employee at age 55	0.016 (0.032)	0.006	0.104 (0.016)	-1.153 (0.037)	-0.283	0.061 (0.024)
Live in Tokyo	0.189 (0.042)	0.070	0.099 (0.017)	0.241 (0.040)	0.078	0.045 (0.020)
Good health	0.867 (0.024)	0.332	0.159 (0.014)	0.593 (0.027)	0.165	0.110 (0.018)
Public pension amount	-0.044 (0.002)	-0.017	-0.009 (0.001)	-0.021 (0.002)	-0.006	-0.006 (0.001)
Company pension amount	-0.046 (0.006)	-0.018	-0.015 (0.004)	-0.022 (0.006)	-0.007	-0.005 (0.004)
MAA	-0.147 (0.058)	-0.057	-0.052 (0.025)	-0.055 (0.062)	-0.016	-0.048 (0.037)
MAA × Year 1988	-0.090 (0.069)	-0.035	-0.032 (0.035)	0.063 (0.070)	0.019	0.137 (0.045)
MAA × Year 1992	-0.009 (0.066)	-0.004	-0.002 (0.030)	0.098 (0.067)	0.030	0.081 (0.038)
MAA × mandatory retirement	0.429 (0.057)	0.154	0.100 (0.029)	0.223 (0.059)	0.071	0.062 (0.035)
N	19,109	—	11,201	19,109	—	5,121
R^2	—	—	0.34	—	—	0.20
Log-likelihood	-9983.17	—	—	-9513.12	—	—

Source: Author's calculation from SECOP-IP (Ministry of Labor 1983, 1988, 1992).

Notes: The columns for "marginal probability" correspond to the marginal increase in work probability when the explanatory variable changes its value by 1. For dummy variables, they are the difference of value 1 and value 0. For weekly hours equations, standard errors are corrected for heteroscedasticity. All regressions are weighted by the sampling weights.

Hours equations for working individuals also include three dummy variables for employment status (executives, self-employed, and jobs that do not require EP participation).

when they do work, their weekly hours are shorter than those of other workers.

2. The coefficients on the interaction terms of EP eligibility, a dummy for age sixty to sixty-four, and year dummies (years 1988 and 1992) indicate that the probability of working and the probability of private-sector employment for EP eligibles aged sixty to sixty-four are higher for 1988 than for 1983 and continue to rise slightly from 1988 to 1992. The magnitude of these coefficients in Sample 1 (table 9.7) and Sample 2 (table 9.8) differ rather significantly, which makes it difficult to draw a general conclusion. Furthermore, the difference of the coefficients of (EP) $\times$ (age 60–64) $\times$ (Year 1988) and (EP) $\times$ (age 60–64) $\times$ (Year 1992) is statistically insignificant. The coefficients on these variables in weekly hours equations are generally positive but statistically insignificant. Although figures in table 9.5 indicate a large increase in the percentage of working and employed in the private sector among EP eligibles aged sixty to sixty-four between 1988 and 1992, other groups also increased their employment. Thus, the increases for EP eligibles aged sixty to sixty-four were not significantly larger than those of the control group. This finding suggests that the 1989 EPIA reform did not create a significant labor supply response.[26]

3. Older people living in single-person households or being supported by their children tend to work less than other groups do, while those with a spouse or dependent children are more likely to work. Workers who experienced mandatory retirement are also less likely to work. Those who answered "not an employee" at age fifty-five were not so much less likely to work than others, but they are much less likely to be employees: that is, many of them are self-employed (see notes 18 and 25). Good health is also an important factor for determining who works.

I estimate similar regression equations for a sample that excludes those aged sixty years old (results not shown). Because some men of this age have not yet retired from their career jobs, their behavior may be different from that of workers sixty-one to sixty-four years old. Since the mandatory retirement age has increased over time, excluding this group may provide a more accurate description of the labor supply of men in their early sixties. The general pattern of the coefficients for this group is similar to the ones shown in tables 9.7 and 9.8, with the following exceptions. First, the magnitude of the increase in labor supply of the EP group over time is estimated to be somewhat smaller than in Samples 1 and 2, and sometimes not significantly different from zero. Second, unlike the results in tables 9.7 and 9.8, the increase in labor supply of EP eligibles aged sixty-one to sixty-four between 1983 and 1988 is quite small (or insignificant) compared to the increase between 1988 and 1992.

---

26. In addition, the timing of the labor supply increase is somewhat at odds with that of the policy change, which took effect only in late 1989.

I also experiment with assigning a different rule for potential EP eligibles by dropping some of the conditions (see note 19). When I use the sample created in this way to do the same analysis as above, the coefficients on most variables have a pattern similar to those shown in tables 9.7 and 9.8. However, the coefficients on the interaction term of EP eligibility, the age sixty to sixty-four dummy, and the year dummies are somewhat sensitive to the assignment of EP eligibility. Therefore, the finding number 2 above is not as robust as the other two results.

In sum, EP benefit reduction does appear to discourage labor supply, although this tendency diminished somewhat between 1983 and 1992. It is not clear that the 1989 reform of EPIA evoked any large labor supply response among the affected group. After controlling for various characteristics, I find that the labor supply of EP eligibles aged sixty to sixty-four had already begun to increase before 1989. Moreover, there is some evidence that private-sector employment for this group continued to increase between 1988 and 1992.

9.7 Conclusions and Policy Implications

My analysis of the microdata for three points in time (1983, 1988, and 1992) yields three main findings about the effect of the 1989 EPIA reform on labor supply of Japan's elderly men. First, EP benefit reduction for working beneficiaries causes EP eligibles aged sixty to sixty-four to work less than others, suggesting that the benefit reduction scheme in fact depresses the labor supply. Second, based on the regression analysis, it is not clear that the 1989 EPIA reform (which raised the level of income at which benefit reduction took place) increased the labor supply of EP eligibles in that age group. Controlling for year effects and various personal characteristics, I find that labor supply of this group had already increased somewhat between 1983 and 1988, a time frame that does not coincide with the 1989 reform. Furthermore, labor supply of control groups also rose during the same period. Finally, I find that the coefficients of household characteristics, health status, and status for mandatory retirement have the expected sign. The analysis also points to the importance of modeling the pension-application decision and work-mode choice in evaluating any EP benefit reduction scheme.

The EP benefit reduction scheme is a kind of means test for pension benefits: By cutting benefits for those who have positive earnings, the government reduces expenditures while maintaining a stable income for older citizens (although seniors lose leisure time). Such a "growth approach" (i.e., one that increases the resources available for older people) is an attractive choice for an aging economy such as that of Japan, for two reasons. For one thing, older people are healthier than they used to be and so can often continue working into their sixties. For another, such an approach eases serious social concerns about the heavy burden placed on younger generations by increasing their contributions to public pension programs.

As a way to diminish these concerns, however, the current administrative rule for EP benefit reductions may have serious loopholes. Workers can avoid benefit reduction by choosing particular modes of work; those who successfully find such forms of employment can receive full benefits without paying EP premiums, even though they have positive labor income. Many such individuals receive benefits as high as those of nonworkers. On the other hand, those who choose to work full time in the private sector and participate in the EP receive reduced benefits and, furthermore, must continue to pay EP premiums.[27] Thus, horizontal equity among EP eligibles may be violated, depending on individuals' choices of work mode. Such loopholes may also have behavioral consequences, perhaps influencing workers in this age group to find jobs outside the private sector, to work only part time, or—because benefit reduction is severe within the same public pension program—to move across programs to avoid losing benefits. A more comprehensive means test might alleviate some of these inequities.

The analysis I performed was limited to the reduced-form regression. Since the EP benefit reduction scheme creates nonlinearities in the budget constraints in a critical fashion (as shown in panel C of fig. 9.5) a model to simulate the effects of alternative policies will require us to perform structural estimations.[28] I leave that task for future research.

References

Amemiya, T., and K. Shimono. 1989. An application of nested logit models to the labor supply of the elderly. *Economic Studies Quarterly* 40:14–22.
Hattori, E. (editor). 1996. *Nenkin no kiso-chisiki* (Basic knowledge on pension). Tokyo: Jiyū Kokumin Sha.
Ministry of Health and Welfare of Japan. 1995. *Nenkin to zaisei* (Pension and its financing). Tokyo: Hoken.
———. 1996. *Annual report on health and welfare 1994–1995*. Tokyo: Japan International Corporation of Welfare Services.
Ministry of Health and Welfare of Japan and Social Insurance Agency, eds. 1987.

27. Although future benefits are increased somewhat because of a longer period of contribution, such increases are usually quite modest.
28. The decision structure illustrated in figure 9.4 makes a structural analysis more complicated than the standard labor supply analysis under nonlinear budget constraints. Nevertheless, structural estimation would enable us to simulate the effects of such policy options as reforms in the EP benefit reduction scheme, use of a means tests for benefit determination, and elimination of the income tax deduction for pension benefits.

Kosei nenkin Hoken Hō kaisetsu (Guide to Employees' Pension Insurance Act). Tokyo: Shakai Hoken Hōki Kenkyūkai.

Ministry of Labor. 1983, 1988, 1992. Survey on employment conditions of older persons. Tokyo: Ministry of Labor.

———. 1992. General survey of part-time workers 1990. Ministry of Finance: Printing Bureau.

———. 1995. *Annual report on employment insurance.* Tokyo: Ministry of Labor.

———. 1997. General survey of part-time workers 1995. Ministry of Finance: Printing Bureau.

———. Various years. General survey on wages and working hours system. Tokyo: Ministry of Labor.

Ogawa, H. 1997. "Nenkin ga kōrei-sha no shūgyō koudou ni ataeru eikyū ni tuite" (Labor supply of the elderly and pension benefits). In *Nenkin seido kaikaku ga shūgyō intai koudou ni oyobosu eikyū ni kansuru kenkyū* (Research on pension reform on labor supply and retirement), 17–57. Tokyo: Japan Institute of Labor.

Oguchi, N., Y. Kimura, and T. Hatta. 1996. Redistribution effects of the Japanese public pension system. *Review of Social Policy* 5:25–52.

Ogura, S. 1994. The cost of aging: Public finance perspectives for Japan. In *Economics of aging in the United States and Japan: Economic trends,* ed. Y. Noguchi and D. Wise, 139–73. Chicago: University of Chicago Press.

Seike, A. 1993. *Kōrei-ka shakai no rōdō shijō* (Labor markets in an aged economy). Tokyo: Tōyō Keizai Shinpo Sha.

Seike, A., and H. Shimada. 1994. Social security benefits and the labor supply of the elderly in Japan. In *Economics of aging in the United States and Japan: Economic trends,* ed. Y. Noguchi and D. Wise, 43–61. Chicago: University of Chicago Press.

Seike, A., and A. Yamada. 1996. "Pension rich no jyoken" (The career job characteristics and pension status of older people). *Nihon Keizai Kenkyū* (JCER Economic Journal) 33:33–61.

Social Insurance Agency. Various years. *Annual report* (in Japanese). Tokyo: Social Insurance Agency.

Statistical Bureau, Management and Coordination Agency. Various years. Labor force survey.

Summary of the Social Insurance Policy. 1995. *Heisei-7-nendo shakai-hoken jigyō no gaiko.* Available at http://www1.mhlw.go.jp./houdou/0902/h0222–1.html.

Tachibanaki, T., and K. Shimono. 1985. Labor supply of the elderly: Their desires and realities about full-time jobs, part-time jobs, self-employed jobs or retirement. *Keizai Kenkyū* 36:239–50.

———. 1994. *Kojin chochiku to life cycle* (Personal saving and life cycle). Tokyo: Nihon Keizai Shimbun Sha.

The Motivations for Business Retirement Policies

Richard Woodbury

10.1 Introduction

Most traditional defined benefit pension plans in the United States encourage older workers to retire. For long-service employees, the financial incentive to retire often begins as young as age fifty-five. Essentially all pension plans encourage retirement by age sixty-five. The financial incentives in pension plans and their significant effects on retirement have been the subject of an established literature in economics.[1] Largely absent from the literature, however, is any clear analysis of why firms have designed pension plans this way. To the extent that firm motivations are addressed, a common theoretical assumption is that the incentives are deliberate business policy decisions designed to induce retirement among older workers who are paid more than their productive value.[2] However, this assumption is made without any evidence from the companies that have implemented the plans. It may also be true that firms are largely unaware of the complex financial incentives in their pension plans, and that they have designed

Richard Woodbury is associated with the program on aging at the National Bureau of Economic Research.

Financial support for this project was provided by the National Institute on Aging, the Japan Foundation Center for Global Partnership, and the National Bureau of Economic Research.

1. A good summary of this research is contained in Lumsdaine and Wise (1994).

2. The primary theoretical framework for this assumption derives from the literature on "implicit contracts." According to the theory, workers are paid less than their productive value at younger ages, and more than their productive value at older ages—creating an incentive for workers not to change jobs, and to work harder in anticipation of the future reward. Pensions then serve as a means of inducing retirement (or at least reducing the effective compensation) among those older workers who would otherwise be paid more than their productive value. See Lazear (1981).

their plans for completely different reasons. This study sets out to understand better the motivations of firms in designing pension plans, and why these motivations have resulted in plans that have the effect of encouraging early retirement.

The issue has particular importance in the context of current demographic trends. The average number of years spent in retirement has increased steadily, partly as a result of increasing life expectancy, and partly as a result of younger retirement ages. Between 1950 and 2000, labor force participation rates of older men dropped significantly—from 46 percent to 18 percent among men aged sixty-five and older, and from 87 percent to 68 percent among men between ages fifty-five and sixty-four. Among women, the large increase in labor force participation at younger ages is absent at older ages, suggesting the offsetting decision to retire earlier among women as well. The financial incentives in pension plans are an important factor affecting trends in retirement behavior, and inducing earlier retirement decisions. To the extent that these early retirement decisions are made based on distorted (or unintended) economic incentives, they may represent losses in both labor productivity and social welfare that will only grow larger as the population ages.

The study is based on the experience of twenty large U.S. corporations. The analysis draws in particular on a series of discussions about policy history and objectives with executives at each company, and a review of internal business documents relating to the design of the policies. In the case of some of the companies, several days were spent visiting the corporate headquarters, meeting with corporate personnel (including human resource executives, financial affairs executives, and employee benefits planners and administrators), and reading through business documents. Confidentiality of the companies and the executives participating in this study was critical in completing this research effectively, so that they would feel comfortable sharing internal business documents and discussing candidly their underlying business motivations.

The analysis identifies a number of objectives and motivations for the design of business retirement policies, including, in some cases, the desire for older workers to retire. In most cases, however, retirement incentives were either unintentional or secondary to the policy's central motivation. In general, the companies were much more concerned with providing competitive retirement policies (policies similar in structure and in value to those of their competitors in the labor market), and policies that adequately provided for the well-being of their retirees. The design and ongoing evaluation of the policies were targeted primarily toward monitoring the retirement policies offered by competitors, and assessing the adequacy of their own policies in satisfying (but not exceeding) the income replacement needs of their retirees.

10.2   The Retirement Policies at Twenty Companies

Twenty companies were selected to participate in this study. Although the twenty companies are not a random sample, they include companies from a variety of industries: financial services (four companies), high-technology manufacturing (four), other manufacturing (four), communications (two), retail sales (two), publishing (one), pharmaceuticals (one), consulting (one), and education (one). Their sizes ranged from 2,500 employees· to over 100,000 employees. Six of the companies employed between 2,500 and 5,000 workers; six employed between 5,000 and 20,000 workers; four employed between 20,000 and 40,000 workers; and four employed more than 40,000 workers. Nothing was known about the retirement policies used by these companies before their being selected to participate in the study.

Of the twenty companies, thirteen provided the same retirement benefits to all employees; five had two categories of employees, each with a different package of retirement benefits; and two had a large number of different employee groups, each with different retirement benefit programs. In both of the latter cases, however, one retirement benefit package applied to a majority of the company's employees. Thus, excluding the smaller benefit programs at companies with large numbers of different programs, twenty-five different retirement programs are represented in the sample.

All of the twenty-five employee groups participated in either a defined contribution (DC) plan or a defined benefit (DB) plan as their primary retirement income program. For twenty of the groups, the primary retirement income plan was a DB plan. For the other five groups, the primary retirement plan was a DC plan, although two of those five implemented their DC plans to replace older DB plans. Sixteen of the twenty employee groups with DB plans were also eligible for company contributions to a supplementary savings plan, usually with employers matching a specified percentage of each employee's contribution. Twenty of the twenty-five employee groups received postretirement medical benefits.

While the plans differ in detail, all of the DB plans encouraged retirement at older ages. The pension plan at company no. 20 illustrates the characteristics and complexity of the arrangements. The plan provided a "full" pension benefit of 1.5 percent of final average salary per year of service, less a Social Security offset of 1.5 percent of the Primary Insurance Amount per year of service. Employees could be credited with no more than thirty-five years of service; the Social Security offset could not exceed 50 percent of the Primary Insurance Amount; and final average salary was based on the highest five consecutive years. Employees could retire with this "full" pension amount at age sixty-five. With fifteen years of service, however, employees could retire with full benefits at age sixty-

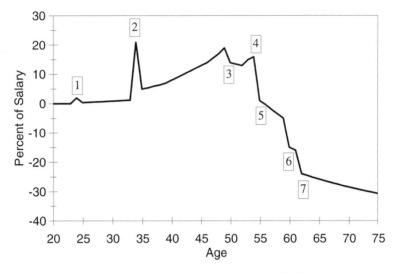

Fig. 10.1   Compensation value of pension plan, employee hired at age twenty

two, or with reduced benefits any time after age fifty. The reduction in the benefit rate for early retirement was 2 percent for each year between the ages of sixty and sixty-two, and 4 percent for each year between ages fifty and sixty. Thus, any employee hired by age thirty-five could retire with 56 percent of the normal pension formula at age fifty, 60 percent at age fifty-one, and so on, up to 96 percent at age sixty, 98 percent at age sixty-one, and 100 percent any time after age sixty-two.

The retirement incentives associated with DB plans are best illustrated by calculating the compensation value of the plan to employees at various ages. The compensation value of a plan is the incremental change in the present value of accrued future pension benefits that results from contin- ued work. The compensation value of the plan at company no. 20 is illus- trated in figure 10.1 for a hypothetical employee, with a standard wage history, hired at age twenty. The plan provisions cause numerous disconti- nuities in this compensation profile, represented at points (1) to (7) in this figure.

1. At age twenty-five, after five years of employment, the employee be- comes vested in the plan, and is credited with five years of service. The value of the pension is small, because of the lower salary early in a career.

2. At age thirty-five, after fifteen years of employment, the employee has accrued enough years of service to be eligible for the early retirement payment options. At this point, the employee can leave the company and still receive a pension at age fifty (the early retirement age), rather than at age sixty-five (the normal retirement age).

3. At age fifty, the employee can retire from the company and begin receiving his or her pension. At this point, continuing to work involves giving up a year of pension income, which partially offsets the increase in the future benefit rate that would be paid by continuing to work.

4. At age fifty-three, the maximum Social Security offset has been attained, so that continued work raises the future benefit without raising the future Social Security offset.

5. At age fifty-five, the maximum thirty-five years of service has been attained, so that continued work no longer increases the years of service credited toward the future pension.

6. At age sixty, the delayed retirement adjustment changes from 4 percent per year to 2 percent per year.

7. At age sixty-two, the delayed retirement adjustment is eliminated, as the employee is now eligible for the full pension. At this point, continued work involves giving up a year of pension income with no increase in years of service credited and no delayed retirement credit. For this employee, the value of the pension plan has dropped from about 15 percent of salary between ages forty-five and fifty-four to -25 percent after age sixty-two. This represents a sharp decline in total compensation that induces substantially more retirement than would occur with an age-neutral pension plan.

Although the plans differ in their details, each of the defined benefit plans provided by the employers in this sample had an economic structure broadly similar to that of the plan at company no. 20. Figure 10.2 illustrates the average compensation value of all of the DB pension plans in this sample. In figure 10.2, the calculations are based on three hypothetical employees with standard wage profiles, hired at ages twenty, thirty-five, and fifty, respectively.

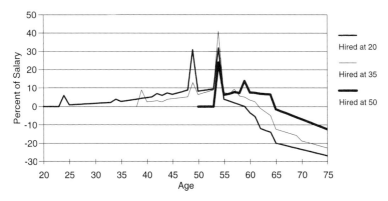

Fig. 10.2   Average compensation value of all pension plans, employees hired at ages twenty, thirty-five, and fifty

As shown, the average compensation value of the plans increases with age until workers are about fifty-five (a common age of early retirement eligibility), and then declines rapidly thereafter. The average compensation value of the plans becomes negative by age sixty for the very long service employee, by age sixty-two for the employee hired at age thirty-five, and by sixty-five for the employee hired at age fifty. Thereafter, the pension plan loses value, and thus represents a work-related cost rather than a work-related benefit. By age sixty-five, this cost is usually a significant percentage of one's salary.

Retirement incentives are also an implicit aspect of the postretirement medical plans, which were provided by fifteen of the twenty employers in the sample. These policies generally extended the employee's preretirement medical insurance through age sixty-five, and then provided a Medicare supplement policy after age sixty-five. Employees who had completed a minimum service requirement (usually ten years) were generally eligible to receive postretirement medical benefits if they remained employed through the early retirement age.

At companies that provide postretirement medical coverage, there is a sharp decline in the compensation value of firm health benefits, much like the decline in compensation value in pension plans. Firm health insurance benefits have a positive and increasing compensation value up to the early retirement age. (Their value increases due to increasing health risks as individuals age.) At the early retirement age, however, employees immediately accrue the full value of all future medical benefits. Thereafter, there is no compensation value in the plan, since medical benefits are provided regardless of employment status—so the incentive structure of such policies is to provide a large compensation reward for staying through the early retirement age, and then no compensation value thereafter. This decline in compensation value reinforces and increases the magnitudes of the incentive structures of the pension plans at most of the companies in this study.

In summary, the majority of the companies in this sample provided both DB pension plans and postretirement medical benefits, both of which have rapidly decreasing compensation values at older ages. It is not uncommon for the value of these benefits to change over a very short period, from a supplement of 20 percent or more of salary to a cost of 20 percent or more of salary. This induces substantially more retirement than would otherwise take place.

10.3   Retiree Welfare as a Company Objective

In discussing the design of their retirement policies, most of the executives participating in this study referred to "caring about retirees," "moral responsibility for retirees," "social responsibility for retirees," "social conscience," or some other expression of paternalistic company values. From the perspective of many executives, retirement benefits were viewed more as entitlements for retired employees than as compensation for working employees. The following comments and excerpts from company reports are representative of the views expressed by many of the company executives interviewed about their policies:

> We publicize our retirement plans extensively among our employees, so the cost of the policies has the best chance of paying off. But even if they don't pay off, and they probably don't, we feel it's our responsibility to provide the policies anyway. [Company no. 6] is very paternalistic. (Interview at company no. 6)
>
> In its role as a major corporation in our industrial society, [company no. 15] recognizes a responsibility and obligation to its employees to provide income for those years after an employee ceases active employment because of retirement. (Report from company no. 15)
>
> [Company no. 18's] new paternalism means: providing a safety net for retirees' needs. (Presentation slide at company no. 18)
>
> The retiree benefit programs . . . demonstrate [company no. 20's] continuing concern for the well-being of its retirees. (Report from company no. 20)

The practical application of paternalistic values in the design of pension plans is most clearly represented in the widespread use of explicit income replacement targets for retired employees. The idea behind income replacement targets is to identify the percentage of preretirement income that the company believes will provide an appropriate standard of living in retirement. The specificity of the income replacement targets varied across companies. Company no. 2 specified a postretirement income replacement target (including Social Security) of 55 percent of preretirement income for employees with at least thirty years of service. Company no. 4 had an income replacement target of 65–70 percent for employees with thirty years of service. Company no. 16 had an income replacement target of 75 to 80 percent for employees with twenty-five years of service. Company no. 19 had an income replacement target of 67 percent for employees with thirty-five years of service. Other income replacement targets, such as those shown in table 10.1, varied by income, marital status, and service tenure.

While the specific income replacement targets varied across companies and across groups of employees within companies, the important point is that companies adopted income replacement targets at all. Concerns about retirement standard of living, retiree welfare, and income replacement suggest a very different view of retirement benefits than as components of compensation designed to achieve labor market objectives for working employees.

Other aspects of company policy further demonstrate concern for retiree welfare. For example, many companies have implemented ad hoc increases in the pension payments of retirees to compensate them partially for in-

Table 10.1   **Income Replacement Targets**

	Income ($)	Single	Married
Company no. 20			
1980 report	6,500	.79	.86
	10,000	.73	.78
	15,000	.66	.71
	20,000	.61	.66
	30,000	.58	.60
	50,000	.51	.55
1989 report	20,000	.62	.82
	40,000	.56	.75
	80,000	.47	.63
	150,000	.46	.62
	300,000	.38	.50

	Pay Level	Full Career	Partial Career	Short Service
Company no. 18				
1977 report	Low	.74	.67	.56
	Medium	.61	.51	.39
	High	.45	.37	.29

creases in the cost of living. The additional expenses associated with ad hoc increases have been incurred, even though the companies have had no legal obligation to make them. The reason given for these benefit adjustments was that high inflation rates had placed a particular hardship on retirees, and that companies were concerned about the welfare of these retirees.

Concern for retiree welfare also motivated many of these firms to credit the years of service performed by employees *before* the implementation or improvement of a plan. Again, the motivation for this retroactive compensation seems based on a paternalistic concern for retiree welfare. A report outlining new pension benefits at company no. 15 clearly expresses this philosophy:

> It became obvious that the magnitude of the problem of prior service and its potential cost required detailed and careful analysis. . . . This Committee can see no valid reason, except possibly for cost, why the Philosophy and Objectives set forth should not apply to those persons who are nearing the end of their career as well as those just embarking on their careers. Thus, the improvement of benefits already accrued would not only seem a valid objective, but has an immediacy which dramatizes its importance.

Another policy decision made by most companies has been to provide (or at least subsidize) medical benefits for the spouses and dependents of retired (as well as active) employees. Again, these additional expenses were incurred even though there was no legal obligation to provide them. And again, concern (or responsibility) for employee and retiree welfare was the justification made by business executives. According to a report at company no. 20, "the benefit design reflects [company no. 20's] belief that it is the company's responsibility to provide protection for a retiree's dependents as well as for the retiree."

10.4 Paternalism and the Design of Retirement Policy

Having identified retiree welfare as a key motivating objective in the design of retirement policies, one then asks why the resulting policies have the effect of inducing retirement. This section provides some evidence on how these motivations were translated into policies with particular characteristics.

The typical business perspective on plan design had the following components:

1. Defined benefit plans, by providing an explicitly defined stream of retirement income, are thought to be more consistent with paternalistic company values than are DC plans, which have no future income assurances.

2. There is a sense that any employee who has committed a full career of service, as defined by years of employment, should be entitled to retire with the support of the company. Thus, a thirty-year employee, for example, should be entitled to health insurance and an adequate pension, whether he or she chooses to retire at age fifty-five or age seventy-five.

3. Pension payments should not be larger than what is necessary to maintain one's preretirement standard of living.

It turns out that these three motivating considerations have led to policies with implicit retirement incentives, even though the retirement incentives were not even considered when the policies were being implemented.

Among companies with DB plans, executives expressed the value of an assured level of retirement income that would enable career employees to retain their preretirement standards of living. The benefit formulas could be calibrated to any targeted level of income replacement. Formulas integrated with Social Security (like those used by most of the companies in this study) could be calibrated even more precisely to total income replacement objectives. For this reason, DB plans were often viewed as preferable to DC plans.

Of course, a company's choice of a DB plan (rather than a DC plan) need not imply an economic structure that encourages retirement. One could actuarially adjust the benefit rate to account for different retirement ages, so that the financial structure would be age neutral. However, this would lead to very different income replacement rates among those retiring at younger ages, as compared with those retiring at older ages. Either the early retirement benefit would be too low for career service employees whom the company wants to support fully in retirement; or the normal and late retirement benefits would be higher than what is considered an appropriate retirement pension. The resulting decisions about how to treat early and late retirees has led to pension plans with implicit retirement incentives such as those summarized in section 10.2. The following excerpts from company reports illustrate some of these concerns, including the decision to limit the years of service credited in many plans:

(a) With regard to age, we saw no rationale for maintaining that a 66 year old employee deserved a higher level of income replacement from the Company than a 65 year old with the same amount of credited service. (b) Specifically, it was felt that [company no. 15] should not allocate its resources to provide more than 100% replacement of pre-retirement disposable income.

This issue with regard to length of service greater than the full career benchmark is more complex inasmuch as one could maintain that employees with greater longevity are entitled to a greater level of income replacement solely because of that longevity. The Task Force's consensus, however, was that the proposed income replacement goals are a reasonable measurement of [company no. 15's] share of the total responsibility for providing post retirement income replacement. . . . It should not be necessary to spend money in order to provide levels of income replacement beyond these goals. For this reason, it was determined that a maximum limitation on the accumulation of credited service was needed to prevent the over-provision of benefits to those employees with service longer than the 30-year full career benchmark. (Report from company no. 15)

Studies show that if the pension benefit plus Social Security benefit exceeds more than 83 to 85 percent of final pay—[the] employee will have more after-tax dollars in retirement than while working. . . . [We are concerned] that future improvements in the pension plan will result in the sum of [company no. 7's] pension plan plus Social Security providing more than take home pay in some cases. (Slide at company no. 7)

The same way of thinking applies to postretirement medical benefits. Once an employee has had a service history long enough to become a responsibility of the company, then the full postretirement medical benefit has been provided, whether the individual chooses early, normal, or late retirement. Again, there is an implicit retirement incentive in this approach that has nothing to do with the paternalistic intent of the plan design.

In summary, companies expressed a great deal of concern for the well-being of their retired employees. This concern motivated the provision of retirement policies designed to provide an acceptable (but not excessive) standard of living to all long-service employees during their retirements, regardless of the age when retirement took place. Policies satisfying these paternalistic objectives implicitly contain retirement incentives, even though the incentives were not at all the primary motivation for the policy design.

10.5 Policy Competitiveness

Competitiveness was expressed as the other central motivation for the implementation and design of retirement policies at most companies. Companies spend considerable resources monitoring the retirement policies provided by competing employers and comparing those policies with their own. Benefits consultants assist companies in maintaining current information about the policies being provided by their competitors, and in making comparisons among the policies at different companies. In some cases, companies develop very explicit competitiveness targets much like the income replacement targets described above:

> We position pension benefits on the basis of comparative studies with major industries, and such comparisons are based upon current survey data. Market relationships based on these studies change over time and we need the ability to take into account such movements. (Report from company no. 7)
>
> Specifically, it is [company no. 9's] objective to provide retirement benefits to a typical employee . . . which places us at the 50th percentile of benefits payable from a large group of 250 U.S. based manufacturing companies. The income replacement of these benefit levels is higher for lower paid people than it is for higher paid people. (Report from company no. 9)
>
> An examination of the table in Appendix A will disclose that there is room for improvement in our competitive posture for normal retirement benefits. At the $70,000 income level, the Salaried Plan ranks 17th out of 38 companies, or in the lower end of the third quartile. The income replacement level exactly matches the mean. [Company no. 15] ranks 22nd, or at the bottom of the second quartile at the $30,000 income level and 35th—well within the lowest quartile—at the $15,000 income level. (Report from company no. 15)

Desired Competitive Position (quartile ranking relative to competing companies)					
	Retirement or Termination Age				
Years of Service	65	62	55	45	35
35	1st	1st	1st	—	—
25	1st	1st	Median	3rd	—
18	Median	Median	Median	3rd	—
10	4th	4th	4th	4th	4th
(Report from company no. 18)					

> The retiree benefit program is designed to be generally competitive within the . . . industry. (Report from company no. 20)

The implication of these concerns is that company policies tend to evolve together. Because each company is continually monitoring the policies of competitors in the labor market, there is a strong tendency to create policies with a similar structure and a similar value. Considering this in historical context, the leading large companies in the United States established retirement plans thinking largely about retirement security for their career-service employees. This approach then became the model from which other companies needed to compete. Thus, many more companies subsequently implemented traditional DB pension plans, not because of their retirement incentive effects, nor because of their concern for retiree welfare, but because it became the standard for major U.S. employers.

The development of retirement plans at companies no. 2 and no. 8 supports this perspective. Both companies began with no retirement benefits and with a comparatively young labor force. According to executives at each company, as workers got older, they became more interested in retirement and, consequently, more interested in retirement benefits. Observing the retirement benefits provided to employees at other companies, employees at companies no. 2 and no. 8 began to request similar benefits for themselves. Responding to these requests, company no. 8 implemented a DB plan in the mid-1970s, and company no. 2 implemented a similar plan in the late 1970s. The plans were selected because they were similar to those offered by other large employers. Since both companies were expanding rapidly during this period, inducing retirement was almost certainly not the motivation for the plan design. According to executives at these companies, there were no specific objectives in designing their pension plans other than to satisfy their older workers by offering a standard plan.

In some cases, companies have revised their policies to provide larger early retirement incentives, not because they have wanted to encourage earlier retirement, but because they have wanted to remain competitive. An executive at company no. 19, for example, suggested that his company was considering a revision to the pension plan for this exact purpose:

> We have a program that asks for employee recommendations about the business. It's a program called "[company no. 19] listens." Lately, we have had a lot of requests for larger early retirement benefits. Employees are pointing out other companies that have more generous early retirement benefits, and they think [company no. 19] ought to have those benefits, too.

In summary, many companies choose their retirement policies to be similar in structure and in value to the retirement plans offered by competing companies. Defined benefit pension plans and postretirement medical plans have historically been the standard for large employers in the United

States. Over time, many companies have implemented similar plans. In almost every case, the incentive effects of the policies have been irrelevant to their design.

10.6   The Role of Work and Retirement Incentives

The interviews conducted at each of the twenty companies in this study generally began with a deliberately broad inquiry about the history of the plans, the motivations and objectives of the plans, and the reasons for their particular plan-design decisions. Much later in the interviews, after fully exploring the issues raised by company executives independently, the topic of work and retirement incentives was introduced explicitly. Inducing retirement was almost never suggested as a plan motivation during the open-ended parts of the interviews. Reactions to the idea that the plans might encourage retirement varied considerably—first, in the extent to which the incentives were even recognized, and second, in the extent to which they were considered a desirable outcome of the policies. Those most familiar with the incentive effects of the plans were at companies that had implemented temporary early retirement incentive plans (window plans) as a means of downsizing their total employment.

Overall, companies expressed varying degrees of recognition and attributed varying levels of importance to the work and retirement incentives associated with their policies. In reference to retirement before the normal retirement age and before Social Security eligibility, it was quite common for executives to discount the importance of retirement incentives. At company no. 2, it was suggested that there were no particular retirement incentives in the policies, because "most people can't afford to retire before they become eligible for Social Security and Medicare." At company no. 9, it was suggested that "retirement incentives and the trend toward earlier retirement are a non-issue here." An executive at company no. 18 recognized—"mathematically"—that the company's pension plan made less than actuarially fair increases in the pension benefits of employees delaying retirement after the early retirement age; this executive argued that few employees could afford to retire before Social Security eligibility, so that the mathematical calculation was not relevant to retirement behavior at company no. 18. At company no. 20, a plan report stated that "the benefit design encourages early retirement" and that "the full availability of medical benefits in early retirement further encourages early retirement," yet an executive at the company discounted the importance of early retirement because "people can not afford to live on their company benefits alone."

A comment from the top human-resource executive at company no. 9 is representative of the way most business executives viewed the financial characteristics of their plans. The comment was made after the person heard an economic explanation of how pension accrual varies with age:

The company's labor cost doesn't change when a person reaches age fifty-five or age sixty-two. The cost of the pension plan gets averaged out over all employees. We look at it in a very aggregate way. . . . Your argument might be right, technically, but it's not how we do it at [company no. 9].

The tendency to look at the *aggregate* cost of the retirement plans per employee (or the cost as a percentage of payroll) was evident at most companies. None of the companies interviewed had calculated the accrual pattern of future retirement benefits (the compensation value of the plans) for individual employees, as has been done extensively in economics studies. Thus, the views executives offered about retirement incentives were quite general, rather than quantitatively specific.

In reference to retirement incentives after the normal retirement age, most executives did acknowledge that their policies (along with public retirement policies) probably encouraged retirement, and that this was probably a desirable outcome. While inducing retirement was not considered a key motivation for the design of the policies, most executives were not unsatisfied with the overall retirement behavior of their labor forces.

The extent to which retirement at older ages was viewed as desirable varied across companies and, frequently, across executives within companies. For example, in a series of interviews at company no. 15, one executive argued that it is good for workers and good for the company if people retire between ages fifty-five and sixty, two other executives argued that the company was essentially indifferent to when workers retire; and a fourth executive was referenced arguing that it would be best if workers never retired. While the interviews at most companies elicited less diversity of opinion, the tone in which opinions were expressed was similar at most companies. They were offered as just that—opinions. They were neither company decisions nor company policies, but individual executives thinking through the desirability of retirement at older ages, and offering their personal judgments. Both the diversity of opinion and the tone in which opinions were offered reinforce the idea that influencing retirement behavior was not a primary motivation for the policy design.

Numerous opinions were expressed on the desirability of retirement, many of which parallel reasoning used in the economics literature. Some suggested that salary increases over a working career have resulted in older workers' being paid more than their productive value. In many cases, younger workers were thought to be as effective or almost as effective as older workers, but at a lower cost. Some executives also suggested that the productivity of labor declines at older ages. Company no. 1 suggested that older workers do not cope well with change. Company no. 5 suggested that one major class of its employees needs a great deal of energy to do their jobs well, and that older employees often lack this energy. Companies no. 6 and no. 7 suggested that many of their employees are engaged in physically demanding jobs that are too strenuous for older employees. An executive at company no. 15 suggested that workers become less flexible, less energetic, and less knowledgeable about new skills and techniques as they age.

In addition to these arguments about individual compensation patterns and productivity patterns, some executives argued that the business environment benefits from retirement. According to an executive at company no. 14, the morale, retention, motivation, and productivity of younger workers depends on their having opportunities for advancement, and retirements create these opportunities. According to an executive at company no. 15, the regular turnover of older workers also enables companies to hire new workers with new skills and new ideas, the steady flow of which is essential for a productive business environment.

A number of executives also offered some good explanations for why retirement incentives should be applied through retirement benefits rather than through wage reductions or layoffs. For example, age discrimination laws prevent the use of layoffs, terminations, or wage reductions that disproportionately affect older people. By contrast, retirement benefits are praised as corporate generosity. According to an executive at company no. 6, "Cutting the wages of older people would be bloody. . . . Layoffs create ill will. . . . Generous retirement benefits create good will."

It is clear that every company has some older employees that they would prefer to keep employed for many years in the future, and other older employees that they wish had retired years earlier; but it is essentially impossible to apply compensation arrangements selectively to some employees and not others. Executives at companies no. 1 and no. 16 suggested the use of retirement policies as a device for screening older workers. Unproductive employees are then eliminated (retired) permanently, while productive employees are hired back on an hourly or consulting basis (at no cost to their ongoing pension benefits). While all employees are *eligible* to participate in the hire-back programs at these companies, only the productive older workers are *encouraged* to participate.

These interviews give one the sense that company executives were generally satisfied with a compensation system that leads to retirement at older ages. The precise age-specific incentive structure of the plans was rarely if ever considered in the design of the plans—but their role in inducing retirement was not inconsistent with what companies seemed to view as desirable to business dynamics.

10.7 Retirement Incentives and Downsizing

The few companies that referred to retirement incentives as a relevant policy motivation tended to have declining or changing employment needs. After declining sales, changes in production technology, or changes in product composition, some companies want to reduce the number of active employees on their payrolls, or to encourage greater turnover among employees with unneeded skills. Inducing retirement among older workers has been an important alternative to layoffs in achieving these workforce management objectives. The reasons suggested for using retirement incentives, rather than layoffs, relate to their public acceptance. Early retirement benefits are viewed as acceptable and even generous, whereas layoffs are viewed as unpleasant and insensitive to employees.

Unlike the permanent retirement policies discussed above, window plans are quite explicitly designed to encourage retirement among older workers. A report at company no. 15, for example, includes the following justification for a window plan at one of its divisions:

> The proposed voluntary early retirement incentive program is part of a plan developed by [division] to produce a downsized, more efficient organization. This plan was developed due to a 42% decline in net after-tax profits from 1983 to the 1985 midyear estimate, a decline which has been attributed to industry overcapacity and severe price competition.

Because window plans are explicitly designed to induce retirement, executives at companies that have used window plans have gained a great deal more appreciation for the capacity of retirement policies to influence retirement behavior. Thus, when these executives discussed the motivations for their retirement policies—broadly defined—they were more likely to include retirement incentives as a relevant policy motivation. What is different about these companies is the greater awareness and appreciation of the retirement incentives that already existed in their regular retirement policies, rather than any differences in the original motivations for their policies.

The experiences of companies no. 5 and no. 7 exemplify both the role of retirement policies in the transition process and the resulting appreciation for retirement policy incentives. Both companies experienced major technological innovations in their production techniques. Because of these innovations, the skills of most of their workers were no longer necessary in the production process, and the total number of workers needed was smaller.

At company no. 5, the decline in employment needs was almost entirely among the unionized workers. This presented a particular challenge for management at company no. 5, since the unions placed a high value on job security. The challenge was compounded because different unions had claims on different parts of the production process. If union 1 had a claim on production process A, then no non–union 1 employees were allowed to contribute to process A, and no union 1 employees were allowed to do anything but process A. Because of the priorities and strengths of the unions, neither layoffs nor retraining were as attractive to the company as retirement incentives. Executives believed that it would be less costly for the company to fund enormous retirement incentives rather than to fight the unions. Thus, a considerable portion of company no. 5's downsizing was accomplished through window plans, many of which provided almost as much money for retiring as for working.

> There was a big technological change in the . . . industry, and we had to negotiate automation with the unions. At the same time, the unions wanted a lifetime job guarantee. So retirement incentives have been a very important part of our retirement policies. (Interview at company no. 5)

Company no. 7 also used a window plan to facilitate its transition to a lower level of employment. In addition, company no. 7 implemented new "permanent" pension plans for management and nonmanagement employees. What is particularly interesting about the experience of company no. 7 is its explicit reference to retirement incentives in the design of the new permanent plans. According to an executive at company no. 7, the new pension plans were deliberately designed to require periodic updates, partly so that the company could respond to changing business conditions. Specifically, benefit values were set at fixed dollar amounts that depreciated in real terms over time. Plan updates could be implemented deliberately at times when management would like more retirement to occur. Part of the effectiveness of this approach resulted from changes in employee expectations. Since the updates became a standard and well-understood provision of the plans, many employees learned to defer retirement until just after a plan update. This provided an even greater ability for company no. 7 to retain employees by deferring a plan update or to encourage retirement by implementing a plan update.

For some companies, retirement incentives have provided an important alternative to layoffs in reducing employment and encouraging worker turnover. Moreover, the increasing use of window plans has increased the awareness among business executives of the capacity for retirement policies to influence retirement behavior.

10.8   Plans without Retirement Incentives

A few of the companies participating in this study diverged from the "standard" approach to retirement policy. Companies no. 1, 3, 10, 11, and 17 had no retirement incentives in their pension plans for at least one category of employees. Defined contribution pension plans were the primary retirement policy for these employee groups. Two themes characterize the explanations for the plan design at these companies. First, these companies tended to prefer the immediate distribution of employee benefits, rather than deferred distribution. Second, the employee relations strategy used by these companies was more often oriented toward performance and productivity monitoring rather than paternalistic support.

Immediate distribution was considered valuable from the perspective of both employer and employee. According to executives at these companies, a retirement account that is denominated and maintained for each employee individually is more tangible during the employee's working years than is a future pension entitlement. The employee can see that a particular asset has been set aside in his or her name and for personal use in retirement. This tangibility creates a greater sense of wealth or value to the employee than the value conveyed by a defined benefit plan. The popularity of primary DC plans was emphasized at all of the companies offering them.

The financial predictability of DC plans was another factor suggested among employers choosing them. An executive at company no. 11, for example, argued that the certain cost associated with DC plans enabled more accurate cost monitoring, and thus better business decisions. At company no. 17, it was suggested that the company had very little physical or financial capital, and thus could not afford to assume any large financial risks. Defined benefit plans have an implicit risk to the company, since the company is obligated to pay a defined pension amount regardless of the investment performance of the pension fund.

While it is impossible to generalize about the characteristics of companies choosing one approach or the other in this small sample, the choice of a DB or DC approach seems to be associated with a broader choice of employee relations strategy. Some companies motivate workers through direct productivity incentives, carefully monitoring employee performance, and rewarding high productivity. These companies tend to like DC plans with no future promises. Other companies motivate workers indirectly through expressions of paternalistic support. These companies tend to like DB plans and postretirement medical plans that are designed to insure the long-term well-being of long-service employees. Executives at two companies referred directly to these differences in strategy.

> Some industries, like the chemical industry, are very gentlemanly. Other industries, like the high-tech industry, are dog-eat-dog. (Interview at company no. 2)
>
> Different companies use different strategies in their relationship to employees. IBM uses a soft approach, trying to elicit good worker morale by never firing workers. [Company no. 11] uses a performance-oriented approach in which unprofitable divisions are rapidly changed. (Interview at company no. 11)

At the companies choosing DC plans, productivity monitoring on the employee and business-unit levels was suggested as a critical ongoing aspect of employment. At company no. 1, it was only the commissioned employees who participated in the DC plan, and their entire compensation was based on productivity. At companies no. 3, 11, and 17, annual wage adjustments were based on careful and detailed worker performance analyses; workers receiving poor evaluations were routinely terminated. At company no. 11, unprofitable subdivisions of the company were quickly redesigned or closed. Companies following this aggressive, performance-oriented strategy considered their retirement benefits as components of current compensation for worker productivity. The immediate distribution and certain cost of DC plans make them more consistent with a performance-oriented approach.

While this study includes too few companies to draw any systematic conclusions about the determinants of policy variability across companies, the interviews suggest that many policy decisions are not carefully conceived, and are, to a significant extent, arbitrary. Based on the few companies participating in this study, the idiosyncratic preferences of chief executive officers (CEOs) seems to dominate any observable company characteristics. Although no CEOs were interviewed for this study, discussion with other executives suggests the overwhelming influence of CEOs at many companies, and the apparent arbitrariness of many of the decisions made.

> We boil up ideas, but the Chairman comes through with the tablet. . . . Top management just likes defined benefit plans. They think defined benefit plans are what retirement policy should be. They have a perception that this is what [company no. 6] owes its retirees. (Interview at company no. 6)
>
> Most companies don't have any great philosophy. Senior management just likes a defined benefit plan. They think it's "right." (Interview at company no. 8)
>
> [The CEO] started this company and we hear a lot of stories about when the company was small: how people gave up a lot, and how we owe them for it. He believes that we should take care of retired employees. (Interview at company no. 18)
>
> I don't know about other companies, but this CEO is involved in everything. . . . We'll take a proposal to him. He'll ask us 500 different questions about it, and then he'll tell us what he wants. We have no idea what he will decide until we present a proposal. (Interview at company no. 20)
>
> The top managers are older and that has a big influence. They weigh retirement more heavily than a typical worker, and that affects their policy decisions. (Interview at company no. 2)

In summary, companies that appear quite similar can have very different retirement policies, and these differences in policy may not be explained by differences in observed company characteristics. Moreover, because of the many competing factors influencing retirement policy decisions, executives making these decisions can find a reasonable justification for just about any policy selected. In the end, it appears that the idiosyncratic judgments of individual executives guide at least part of retirement policy design.

10.9   A Case Study

One of the companies in the sample conducted a particularly comprehensive evaluation of its pension plans over the period of this study. What is interesting about this case study is the company's explicit objective to design a pension plan that is "neutral relative to the age at which retirement occurs," and the company's subsequent development of a policy proposal that contains retirement incentives anyway.

The policy evaluation was implemented because of a concern among company executives that the value of the benefits from the DB plan and the supplementary savings plans were lower than the values of comparable benefits offered by competing employers. To address these competitive deficiencies, a special committee was appointed to evaluate the then-current policies and to develop a new policy proposal. Two philosophies dominated the evaluation process. First, the company wanted a retirement policy that adequately supported the retirement income needs of retirees. Second, the company wanted a retirement policy that was competitive with those offered by competing employers. A great deal of the committee's time was spent evaluating the relative importance of these two philosophies.

Initially, the primary motivation of the committee was to develop a new policy that would adequately support the needs of retired employees. According to executives at the company, the importance of these company values dated back to the founding of the company, and to the founder's belief that employees should be treated as family. As in past policy evaluations, the company established a series of income replacement targets, calibrated to enable "full career" employees to maintain their preretirement standards of living. The company then compared the replacement rates of the current plans with the target replacement rates. This retirement needs analysis was conducted in some detail, with calculations made for employees with different salary levels, different service histories, and different retirement ages. The primary conclusion of this analysis was that the company's existing policies fell significantly short of their income replacement targets.

As the evaluation process progressed, the company's interest in designing a policy to satisfy retiree needs lost some of its importance, because members of the committee noted the diversity of the company's labor force and the wide variation in retirement needs across employees—and, thus, the inability of the company to choose one right retirement policy (or income replacement rate) for every employee.

> The company cannot determine the retirement cash needs of employees since each individual's situation is different. This has been caused by changed workforce demographics, such as the prevalence of dual wage-earner families. Therefore, the company should not base the design of

its retirement programs on the perceived retirement cash needs of an "average" employee. (Presentation slide)

In its place, the company adopted a retirement policy strategy based more heavily on competitiveness in the labor market, and on flexibility to meet a diversity of employee needs:

The company recognizes employees' responsibility to set their own retirement objectives. The company will help employees achieve their objectives by providing automatic and elective retirement benefits as well as education. The value of benefits received by employees and the resulting cost to the company will be driven mainly by competitive positioning and the extent to which employees utilize elective benefits. (Presentation slide)

Thus, competitive positioning became the most important criterion motivating the policy design, and a group of thirty competing employers was selected for comparison. The existing retirement policy was carefully ranked relative to those of the competing companies. The primary conclusion of this competitive analysis was that the company's current retirement policies ranked very low relative to the policies offered by competing employers.

While competitive positioning became the most important policy objective, the committee developed a number of other criteria on which their retirement plans should be evaluated. The final set of objectives included competitiveness objectives, financial objectives, employee education objectives, workforce planning objectives, and employee relations objectives. These are summarized in table 10.2, using language adopted by the committee for a presentation to senior management. Note that under its "Workforce Planning Objectives" the company explicitly referred to a policy that is "neutral relative to the age at which retirement occurs."

These objectives were formally approved by senior management, and the committee was then directed to develop a retirement policy proposal based on these objectives. The committee proposal included a new DB pension plan, and the addition of employer matching provisions to the supplementary savings plan. Figure 10.3 shows the compensation values of the proposed pension plan, by age.

The new plan clearly was not age neutral. According to an executive who worked extensively on the plan evaluation, "there were competing objectives and other objectives were weighed more heavily." In the end, by far the most important factor motivating the policy proposal at this company was a desire to be competitive in the labor market—it had been the competitive deficiency in the existing policy that inspired a policy evaluation in the first place. Then, to address this competitive deficiency, a policy was designed with a similar structure and a similar value to the policies offered by competing companies. Despite the decision to move away from

Table 10.2   Retirement Policy Objectives

Competitiveness Objectives: The aggregate position of the company's retirement programs should be average; the company should value longer service more than higher age; retirement benefits should be independent of hierarchy . . .

Financial Objectives for the Company: Retirement benefits programs must be affordable to the company; provide the company with a predictable financial cost; and provide retirement benefits in the most cost-effective manner.

Financial Objectives for Employees: Provide employees with a predictable financial benefit to help them plan savings for their retirement; provide retirement benefits in the most cost-effective manner to employees; provide retirement benefits with an acceptable level of investment and inflation risk.

Employee Eduction Objectives: The company has a responsibility to ensure that employees understand that they are responsible for planning for their retirement; to provide opportunities for employee education so that they are able to plan for their retirement; to provide a comprehensive set of tools to enable employees to plan for their retirement.

Workforce Planning Objectives: Plan design should be neutral relative to the age at which retirement occurs, but should be flexible to react to business and changing workforce requirements. Plan design must support recruitment and retention of employees with desired skill mix; plan design must support the recruitment of skilled senior employees.

Employee Relations Objectives: Employees believe that the company's retirement programs are valuable, competitive, equitable. Employees believe that the company helps them prepare for retirement.

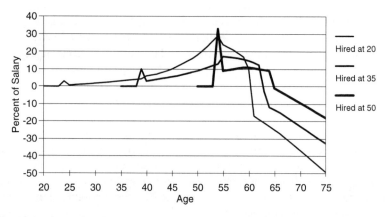

Fig. 10.3   Compensation value of new pension plan, employees hired at ages twenty, thirty-five, and fifty

explicitly paternalistic policy objectives, several executives on the policy review committee emphasized retiree welfare as a long-standing priority of their CEO and as the second-most important motivation in the final plan design. The presence or absence of retirement incentives was a third tier of concern in the evaluation process, and was eventually outweighed by other policy priorities.

10.10   Retirement Policy in Transition

Many of the companies participating in this study evaluated or changed one or more aspects of their retirement policies around the time of the study. First, two companies replaced their DB plans with DC plans, and several others increased their contributions to supplementary retirement saving plans. Second, several companies with DB plans raised the ages of early and normal retirement, and implemented larger decreases in the benefits of those choosing early retirement. Third, several companies eliminated, decreased the value of, or at least questioned the provision of post-retirement medical benefits. Table 10.3 lists the policy changes or proposed changes by these companies.

Together, these changes are suggestive of a trend toward policies with fewer early retirement incentives. This results partly from the increasing use of DC plans and other retirement saving plans, relative to that of traditional DB pension plans; partly from increases in the age of eligibility for

Table 10.3   **Changes in Retirement Policies**

Changes in Defined Contribution Plans	
Company no. 2	Raised company matching rate from 25 to 50 percent.
Company no. 3	Terminated defined benefit plan and implemented defined contribution plan.
Company no. 11	Terminated defined benefit plan and implemented defined contribution plan.
Company no. 12	Raised matching rate from 67 to 75 percent for management. Raised matching rate from 50 to 60 percent for nonmanagement.
Company no. 18	Considered implementation of 25 percent company match.
Changes in Defined Benefit Plans	
Company no. 1	Raised minimum age for full pension from 60 to 62. Reduction factor increased from 3 to 5 percent per year.
Company no. 3	Terminated defined benefit plan and implemented defined contribution plan.
Company no. 11	Terminated defined benefit plan and implemented defined contribution plan.
Company no. 12	Raised minimum age for full pension from 55 to 60.
Company no. 18	Considered reduction factor of about 6 percent, instead of graded (3.33 percent and 6.67 percent); and raising normal retirement age from sixty-five to sixty-seven (with Social Security), and early retirement age from fifty-five to fifty-seven.
Changes in Post-Retirement Medical Plans	
Company no. 1	Raised employee share of premium.
Company no. 4	Raised employee share of premium.
Company no. 14	Eliminated plan.
Company no. 20	Raised employee share of premium.

early and normal benefits within the traditional plans; and partly from the decreasing prevalence of postretirement medical benefits.

The consistent explanation for increasing provision of DC and supplementary saving plans was related to their popularity among employees and to the need to remain competitive with other employers who were offering these benefits. An additional explanation for terminating the DB plan at company no. 3 was to gain access to the surplus assets in the pension fund. Other managers of DB plans referred to the growing legal and administrative costs of DB plans in complying with new regulations, and their decreasing desirability for that reason.

At the companies that changed the provisions of their DB plans, inducing employees to defer retirement until older ages has been an important motivation. There was a particular concern at some companies that fewer younger workers would be available in the future to fill the positions currently held by older workers. Though applicable to only a few companies, these comments were the most direct evidence of retirement incentives' having a significant role in policy reform.

The consistent explanations for reductions in postretirement medical benefits was their increasing cost, based on increasing health care costs generally, and the increasing ratio of retirees to employees at most companies.

Overall, the change in the age demographics of the U.S. population seems particularly important in inspiring current trends. At one time, paternalistic retirement policies were inexpensive. Companies could support retirees without a large expenditure of resources because there were many more working employees than retired employees, and because retired employees had shorter life expectancies. Indeed, the employee-relations advantages of being a "caring" company almost certainly exceeded the cost of paternalistic programs. The increasing older population, and the increasing cost of retirement programs, have inspired a growing number of companies to reevaluate their traditional paternalistic values.

A number of companies referred to these changing priorities and, at the same time, to the significant impediments to policy reform. This suggests that the current trend away from DB plans and postretirement medical plans is likely to continue into the future, though the pace of change may continue to be gradual.

> The old plan was a remnant of a different era in retirement planning. When the defined benefit plan was implemented, there was no such thing as a 401(k) plan, and defined benefit plans were considered state of the art. In addition, defined benefit plans were satisfactory to employees at that time, because very few other companies offered defined contribution plans. (Interview at company no. 3)
>
> A lot of companies are locked-in to their existing plans. If they could start again, they would choose defined contribution plans, but they al-

ready have defined benefit plans that are too costly to terminate. First, hourly employees are very suspicious of changes, particularly the "cancellation" or "termination" of a pension plan. Second, defined benefit plans are one of the main selling points used by unions to attract union membership. Unions claim that their protection of defined benefit plans assures that workers will have a decent retirement income. (Interview at company no. 11)

Do you want to convince employees that they are better off without the type of pension plans they are used to, and without the type of plan that is offered by the competitors? Do you want to renegotiate the new retirement plan with thirty unions? Do you want to pay the legal and administrative costs associated with terminating the existing plan, and setting up the new plan? Do you want to figure out how to comply with all of the government regulations associated with terminations? . . . As long as no one is complaining about the current plan, it just isn't worth trying to change it. (Interview at company no. 9)

10.11   Summary and Discussion

At fourteen of the twenty companies in this study, all employees participated in a retirement policy with incentives to retire at particular ages. At another three of the companies, some categories of employees participated in a retirement policy with incentives to retire at particular ages. Only three companies had retirement policies that did not encourage the retirement of older workers. Despite the widespread use of policies that encourage retirement, the main finding of this study is that retirement incentives are typically not a central motivation for the policy design.

Two motivations have dominated the past design of business retirement policies—concern about retiree welfare, and concern about competitiveness in the labor market. A great deal of the current structure of business retirement policies is based on a history of paternalistic company values. Many executives indicated that their companies had the responsibility to insure the well-being of retired employees and, because of this responsibility, many executives viewed their retirement policies more as entitlements or welfare for retired employees than as compensation for working employees. This view of retirement policies is reflected in pension plans and post-retirement medical plans designed to support the needs of retired employees.

The effect of these company values on the economic structure of retirement policies is to encourage retirement. The benefits of those retiring early cannot be reduced too dramatically, or early retirees will be unable to maintain their preretirement standards of living. Similarly, the benefits of those retiring late need not be increased, since their preretirement standards of living can be maintained with normal benefit levels. Thus the retirement policies have an economic structure that encourages retirement, even though retirement incentives were not a central motivation in their design.

Business concerns about competitiveness in the labor market have had the effect of spreading these traditional policies more widely through the business community. In order to be competitive, companies have chosen policies with similar structures and similar values to those offered by competing employers. Thus companies without strong paternalistic values have been driven by competitive pressures to implement policies with the same economic structures. Whether the policies at a company were motivated more by a concern for retiree welfare or more by a concern for competitiveness in the labor market, the same policies with the same economic structures and the same retirement incentives have been chosen. In either case, it was not the retirement incentives that motivated the policy design.

A study by Siegel (1990) reaches many of the same conclusions made in this study. Siegel's study focuses on the retirement policy decisions that have been made by companies that terminated their DB pension plans in order to remove excess assets from overfunded pension accounts. This was a particularly interesting sample, because these companies were in the position to design and implement new policies with any economic structure.

According to Siegel's study, approximately 20 percent of companies terminating their DB plans in 1987 and 1988 replaced the terminated plans with DC plans. This is consistent with the idea of a gradual transition in plan design. Most of the other companies apparently implemented plans identical to those that had been terminated. For both the companies restoring DB plans and the companies replacing their terminated plans with DC plans, Siegel finds that retirement incentives (or their absence) were not a motivating factor in the company's decision. According to Siegel:

> Not a single person mentioned retirement incentives in any aspect of the discussion. All of the firms in this sample cancelled their plans because they wanted to recoup excess assets. Almost all firms that chose defined benefit plans replaced with mirror plans. Reasons that they gave for their decision included appeasing alarmed workers, providing for long-term employees sufficiently, inertia, and their ability to save money with riskier investments. Treasurers who chose defined contribution did so because employees appreciate more knowledge and control over their assets, cash flow management is easier, and administrative costs are lessened. Again, not a single interviewee mentioned incentives for retirement as an influence on their decision.

Siegel's conclusions are much the same as those reported in this study. Even though most large companies have retirement policies that encourage retirement among older workers, these retirement incentives were not a primary motivation for the policy design.

Given the loss in productive activity caused by retirement in the United States, it is potentially worrisome that businesses do not consider the effects of their policies on retirement behavior more carefully. At the same time, however, there are increasing indications that companies that are dissatisfied with the retirement behavior of their workers are looking toward their retirement policies as potential instruments for changing that behavior.

The idea that pensions are deliberately designed to encourage retirement is not supported by this study. However, as the population continues to age, and as retirement policies consume an even larger percentage of corporate payrolls, businesses are likely to focus much more attention on the retirement behavior of their workers and, consequently, on the relationships between retirement policies and retirement behavior. Indeed, this same study conducted in 2020, when the baby-boom generation is retiring in record numbers, is likely to reach some very different conclusions about the key motivations for retirement policy decisions of the future.

References

Lazear, Edward. 1981. Agency, earnings profiles, productivity, and hours restrictions. *American Economic Review* 71 (4): 606–20.

Lumsdaine, Robin, and David Wise. 1994. Aging and labor force participation: A review of trends and explanations. In *Aging in the United States and Japan,* ed. Y. Noguchi and D. Wise, 7–41. Chicago: University of Chicago Press.

Siegel, Adam. 1990. The choice of pension provision: Economic theory versus managerial reality. Undergraduate thesis, Harvard University, Department of Economics.

Promotion, Incentives, and Wages

Toshiaki Tachibanaki and Tetsuya Maruyama

11.1 Introduction

In many advanced countries, there is a growing interest in the relationship between incentive pay and careers in organizations, and in particular between incentive pay and promotion on the hierarchical ladder. There are two main reasons for this: First, theoretical economists in general are interested in firms, contracts, incentives, performance, and the like. Second, a number of surveys on wages, positions, performance, and other features of individual employees have become available recently. These surveys enable economists to conduct rigorous empirical studies more efficiently than aggregate data did.

This paper investigates the story of Japanese firm experience with incentive pay. Since both the aging of the Japanese population and the slower growth rate of Japanese firms force those firms to reduce the cost of labor (by decreasing the total wage cost), the system must not reduce the work incentives of employees who may see a decrease in their average wages.

In Japan it has been understood that the average labor productivity of manual (blue-collar) workers is quite high, while that of nonmanual (white-collar) workers is considerably lower than it is in other industrialized nations. There are several convincing reasons for this belief. First, team production is common among manual workers in manufacturing, and such a system is apt to increase labor productivity because neither strong leadership nor excellent contribution by a single person is required. In other words, among manual workers everyone is motivated to raise the average productivity. Second, nonmanufacturing industries in which the majority

Toshiaki Tachibanaki is professor of economics at Kyoto University. Tetsuya Maruyama is a graduate student of economics at the University of Pennsylvania.

of workers are white-collar exhibit lower labor productivity; that implies that the average labor productivity of white-collar workers is lower than that of blue-collar workers. Third, leadership, individual contributions, and the workers' skills are all crucial in determining productivity of white-collar workers who are engaged in complicated jobs. Fourth, compressed wage dispersion among workers and a seniority-based promotion system, two representative features of the industrial relations system in Japan, are relevant for manual workers, but not suitable for white-collar workers.[1] This study examines whether that latter statement is true for white-collar workers.

11.2 Theoretical and Empirical Facts on Incentives and Careers

Two important articles focusing on the United States deal with the relationship between incentive pay and careers in organizations (Gibbons 1997; Prendergast 1999). This section therefore relates strictly to the experience of Japan. In particular, we ask, "Does pay vary with performance, and do incentives matter, particularly for white-collar workers?"

Two important earlier studies investigated the issues of insurance, contracts, and incentives in Japan: Mitani (1998) and Ito and Teruyuma (1998). It is useful to summarize their findings here. Mitani investigated the positive and the negative effects of the incentive for wages and promotion on employees in terms of individual and firm performance. Workers who are fond of risk-taking, and who clearly understand the relationship between incentive and performance, are affected positively; workers who are risk averse and who do not appreciate the effect of incentives on their performance are affected negatively. Mitani found that the Japanese incentive system was at an optimal level, balancing the positive and the negative effects perfectly.

Ito and Teruyuma (1998) were concerned with the economic effect of job tenure on wages and promotion. They found that no single theory could explain this relationship perfectly. These two studies were important, however, because they were the first attempts (at least for Japan) to depart from human capital as the sole background theory for explaining wage differentials.[2]

Job tenure in Japan has a particularly strong effect on the determination of wages and promotion. Wages increase almost proportionately with job tenure in the firm and decrease after a certain point.[3] The influence of job tenure also has been examined in the determination of promotion along

---

1. See Lazear (1989) about the implication of compressed wage dispersion.
2. The theory of human capital had been dominant in Japan for a long time, although some dissatisfaction with it has been addressed (e.g., Ishikawa 1992; Tachibanaki 1996).
3. Many empirical studies have attempted to determine the role of tenure in the determination of wages. See, for example, Mincer and Higuchi (1988) and Tachibanaki (1996).

the hierarchical ladder in organizations. This effect of job tenure on wages and promotion is called the *seniority rule* in Japan, and is one of the most important institutional features in industrial relations.

Currently there is a shift of interest in the role of job tenure from wages to promotion. There are two conflicting views on the questions "Who is promoted?" and "What are the main criteria for the determination of promotion?" The first view gives the role of job tenure (seniority) and the performance of the individual employee almost equal significance.[4] The second view emphasizes the performance of the individual employee over seniority.[5]

Of course, promotion rates differ by industry and depend on the growth rate of the firm. Tomita (1992) looks at bank, while Ohtake (1995) and Ariga and his coauthors (1997) study electric firms which have considerably higher growth rates in their sales and their employment.[6] Promotion policies also differ among the particular firms, even in the same industry and with similar growth rates. Matsushige (1998) shows that seniority plays a very important role for those with ten to thirteen years of job tenure, even in one very large electric company with a growth rate that is only moderate. In that firm, no one is promoted before accumulating those ten to thirteen years of tenure.

Our data cover various industries. Thus, we can avoid the effect of a specific industry's experience on the results. Also, the data include different rates of firm growth, although we consider only larger firms.

One interesting question is the role of education in promotion rates. It may be a signaling effect, in the sense that only university graduates will be promoted and non–university graduates will have a very slim chance of promotion. This is particularly true in larger firms (see, e.g., Tachibanaki 1996). There is also the issue of "what university he or she graduated from." Academic credentials, that is, the name of the university, matter to a considerable extent in the determination of promotion.[7] In sum, education plays a special role in promotions, particularly in Japan.

Some natural questions arise after these issues are examined. First, what is the effect of position or promotion on wage increases? How are wages distributed among workers who are promoted to higher positions versus those who are not? Second, do early promotions or quick wage increases better induce higher motivation and work incentives, and thus raise individual productivity? Which is more influential in determining workers' in-

4. Tomita (1992) is a typical example of this view.
5. See Ohtake (1995), Ariga, Ohkusa, and Brunello (1997), Bruderl, Diekman, and Preisendörfer (1991), and Baker, Gibbs, and Holmstrom (1994a,b) for the United States; they find a "fast track" or "serial correlation" in promotion rates.
6. See also Ohashi and Matsushige (1994) for the effect of firm growth rate on promotion.
7. See, for example, Tachibanaki (1998a) and Ohashi (1998). This also can be interpreted in the framework of favoritism, as in Prendergast and Topel (1996).

centives, position or remuneration? Third, how do different positions on the hierarchical ladder affect incentives?

11.3 Model Specification

This section presents three basic models that describe the relationship of promotions and wages. The three models are presented in the appendix.

Model I shows the relationship between promotion and incentive. In particular, it gets at whether a promotion raises a worker's incentive, expressed as EFFORT. Put more simply, does an employee who has been successful in his career (promoted to a higher position) work hard and efficiently, or simply respond to higher incentives? Of course, there is the possibility of the inverse causality, in which a highly motivated and hardworking employee is more likely to be promoted. Both questions are posed in Model I.

Model II considers a similar problem. The crucial difference, however, is that it investigates the relationship between incentives and wages rather than between promotion and incentives. The difference between promotion and wages in terms of their effect on effort (incentives) can be estimated by comparing the empirical results of Model I and Model II.

It is likely that these three variables—promotion, incentive, and wages—are jointly determined. In other words, they may be endogenous. Therefore, Model III is a simultaneous equation model. Both Model I and Model II are also simultaneous equations models, despite the fact that they have only two endogenous variables, respectively.

One important feature of this study is the discrete nature of several of the endogenous variables. Typically, promotion is defined by zero (not promoted) or one (promoted). This discrete nature must be considered with a simultaneous equation framework.

Finally, we adopt a large number of exogenous (independent) variables in estimating these models. These include not only demographic variables for each employee, such as education, job tenure, and the like, but also several subjective evaluations and preferences for promotion and the incentives of each employee. These subjective variables are expected to answer the following questions: "What variables are influential?" and, "What variables are not important in the determination of the relationship among promotion, incentive, and wages?"

11.4 Data and Institutional Features

The data used in this study come from a survey conducted in 1993 of white-collar employees in five large firms: an automobile manufacturer, an electronics manufacturing company, a chemical firm, an electric power company, and a department store. The sample includes not only managerial and administrative employees (who were promoted) but also employees who were not promoted. In total, 2,100 questionnaires were sent to employees, and there were 1,816 responses. The high response rate, 86.5 percent, was achieved because both the firms and the labor unions helped us greatly.

It is useful to describe several institutional features that govern the promotional system in large firms in Japan in order to understand the empirical results. First, seniority (job tenure) has been quite important in determining the promotions to certain positions, and is still important in some industries.[8]

Second, strict promotion proceeds vertically, from ordinary worker (not promoted), to section head (kakari-cho), to department head (kacho), to director (bucho), and finally to executive (torishimariyaku). In many cases, deputy positions serve as preparation for department heads and directors. A section is the smallest employee unit, consisting of roughly two to five members. A department is the intermediate unit, consisting of roughly five to thirty members. A directorate is the largest unit, consisting of roughly twenty to one hundred or even more members. The number of members in each section, department, and directorate differs considerably from firm to firm.

Third, several types of department heads have no subordinates. In other words, they have only the titles without any supervisory tasks. Nevertheless, they are treated almost exactly like department heads with regard to qualifications and grades, which determine wage payments. In many cases, they work as specialists rather than managers.

Why would firms establish department heads who do not have any subordinates? First, the aging trend in the population plus the slower growth rate of firms has reduced the available number of department head positions. In other words, firms are unable to promote a large number of employees to department heads unless there are changes in firms' hierarchical structures. Second, employees who have not been promoted to department heads for those reasons may lose their incentive to work because of their lower wages and a lower degree of responsibility. Third, the seniority system, which guarantees promotion of all employees to department head, may ensure a good working environment within the firm. Finally, there are several important and specialized jobs that can be done without subordinates, and there is an increasing trend toward these jobs in many firms. These four conditions have encouraged firms to create the position of department head with no subordinates. Employees are entitled to be called department heads, and they receive nearly the same amount of wages as those department heads who do have subordinates.

8. See for example, Tachibanaki (1982) for earlier studies that showed the importance of seniority.

11.5 Empirical Results

Tables 11.1 through 11.12 present the estimated results for the three models. Many of the tables include two or three estimated results separated from those for the full samples. These estimates are according to position in the hierarchical ladder of a firm, and are done for all employees, employees who are section heads or higher (thus being promoted to department head), and employees who are department heads or higher (being promoted to director or deputy director). These distinctions are quite important, because the positions are crucial in determining promotion possibility, incentives, and wages. When there are several endogenous variables in the model, the two-stage least squares (2SLS) method is applied. When one of the dependent variables is defined discretely, special methods, such as the two-step Heckman method, are undertaken in addition to the 2SLS.

Table 11.1 shows the estimated effort function calculated by the ordi-

Table 11.1   **Model I, Estimated Effort Function (OLS)**

	Coefficient (A)	Coefficient (B)
Constant	2.729**	2.911**
	(0.144)	(0.262)
STD	0.157*	0.086
	(0.085)	(0.133)
SAWD	−0.569**	−0.632**
	(0.083)	(0.135)
WVARD	−0.208	−0.111
	(0.128)	(0.199)
OPD	−0.208	0.218
	(0.128)	(0.139)
AGRD	0.148*	0.048
	(0.084)	(0.217)
PROSD	0.001	0.264**
	(0.122)	(0.142)
PNOTICED	−0.007	−0.005
	(0.098)	(0.173)
PVARD	0.016	−0.105
	(0.100)	(0.198)
PROM	0.063	−0.175
	(0.084)	(0.164)
$\bar{R}^2$	0.177	0.157

Source: Data are from Tachibanaki and Maruyama (1993).

Notes: See appendix for an explanation of variables. Figures in parentheses are standard errors. For sample A, samples are restricted to employees who occupy section head positions or higher. The number of observations is 352. For sample B, samples are restricted to employees who occupy department head positions or higher. The number of observations is 150.

**Significant at the 5 percent level.

*Significant at the 10 percent level.

nary least squares (OLS) method. It addresses whether promotion to higher positions increases effort (provides incentives) among white-collar employees. Table 11.2 shows the promotion function estimated by the probit method. Since these tables do not take into account the simultaneity property, we discuss them only briefly. The estimated results, nevertheless, reveal several interesting points.

First, the effect of promotion on incentive for effort is statistically insignificant in both samples. Put simply, promoted employees do not feel a strong incentive for effort. This is somewhat surprising, because it is contrary to common beliefs, and because employers expect that promoted employees will be highly motivated.

Second, job tenure or the number of years before reaching section head is positive and significant for promotion to department head, while it is negative and significant or statistically insignificant for promotion to director or deputy director. This distinction suggests that the seniority system works, at least for the promotion to department heads, while it does not work for further promotions.

Third, the number of job sections in which a worker is placed before being promoted to department head is positive and significant for promotion to department head. Thus, capable employees who are promoted to very high positions change their sections more frequently than others. This is consistent with the understanding in Japan that employers try to assign capable white-collar employees to many different job sections in order to provide them with an opportunity to learn a wide range of business activities in the firm. This is called a *wide career pattern* (see Kioke 1991).

Tables 11.3 through 11.5 present the estimated results taking into consideration the simultaneity property. Tables 11.3 and 11.4 are based on Lee's method, while table 11.5 is based on Heckman's two-step method. Tables 11.3 and 11.4 indicate that the constant term is significantly higher for employees who are promoted to department head (sample A in table 11.3) than for employees who are not promoted (sample A in table 11.4). Thus, promoted employees show higher effort than nonpromoted employees. The results using Heckman's method also support this observation because PROS (the inverse Mills ratio) is positive and significant. It is interesting to note, however, that the estimated result for promotion to director or deputy director is not consistent with the above finding. Perhaps this is because those positions, which are higher than department head, are normally occupied by very capable and ambitious people. Therefore, it is hard to believe that they have different incentive efforts or motivations; everyone in very high positions is well motivated.

Several noteworthy observations regarding the effect of each explanatory variable on the incentive effort follow. The effect of wage satisfaction (SAWD) is negative on incentive effort, while the effect of the future promotion prospective (PROSD) is positive. The former suggests that wages do not have any effect, while the latter implies that when employees feel

	Coefficient (A)	Coefficient (B)
Constant	−11.337**	−8.079
	(3.040)	(5.521)
TENU	0.394**	0.211
	(0.188)	(0.354)
PCAR	−0.079	−0.464**
	(0.110)	(0.205)
TENU2	0.000	−0.002
	(0.004)	(0.006)
PCAR2	−0.008*	0.007
	(0.004)	(0.005)
IND	0.117	0.119
	(0.087)	(0.117)
OUTD	0.115	0.266**
	(0.070)	(0.093)
SHUKO	0.181	0.595
	(0.341)	(0.488)
EDUD	2.346**	0.734
	(0.830)	(0.614)
F1D	−0.892	—
	(0.592)	
F2D	0.076	−0.214
	(0.534)	(0.687)
F3D	0.344	0.030
	(1.446)	(0.528)
F4D	−0.805	−0.620
	(0.574)	(0.983)
AGE	0.124	0.195
	(0.113)	(0.171)
SEXD	0.047	−4.153
	(0.989)	(3.060)
PHD	−0.684**	−0.267
	(0.321)	(0.501)
STD	0.846**	−0.161
	(0.243)	(0.419)
SAWD	−0.238	−0.514
	(0.272)	(0.433)
WVARD	−1.517**	−1.657**
	(0.472)	(0.729)
OPD	−0.157	−0.723
	(0.238)	(0.445)
AGRD	−0.293	−0.099
	(0.342)	(0.624)
PNOTICED	0.292	0.888
	(0.282)	(0.615)
PROSD	0.560**	1.175**
	(0.263)	(0.513)
PVARD	−0.705**	0.778
	(0.325)	(0.685)
Log-likelihood	−92.5	−34.3

Table 11.2   Model I, Estimated Promotion Function (probit)

Source: Data are from Tachibanaki and Maruyama (1993).
Notes: See table 11.1.

Table 11.3   Model I, Estimated Effort Function (Lee's method), for
                Promoted Employees

	Coefficient (A)	Coefficient (B)
Constant	2.995**	2.476**
	(0.220)	(0.917)
STD	0.095	0.002
	(0.110)	(0.352)
SAWD	−0.507**	−0.317
	(0.113)	(0.338)
WVARD	−0.267	0.077
	(0.168)	(0.476)
OPD	0.294**	0.584*
	(0.116)	(0.341)
AGRD	−0.040	0.114
	(0.178)	(0.496)
PROSD	0.216*	0.026
	(0.111)	(0.505)
PNOTICED	−0.068	−0.401
	(0.145)	(0.644)
PVARD	−0.068	0.343
	(0.150)	(0.804)
PROS	0.116	−0.112
	(0.141)	(0.329)
$\bar{R}^2$	0.160	−0.053

Source: Data are from Tachibanaki and Maruyama (1993).
Notes: See table 11.1.

that there is a good chance of future promotion they show a strong incentive for effort.

Second, the effect of both wage differentials (WVARD) and differentiation in promotion (PVARD) among colleagues employed in the same year is not statistically significant. However, the effect of the propensity to promote (OPD) and of the satisfaction with wage payment (STD) are positive on effort incentive for samples who have been promoted to section head and on those competing for department head. The latter finding suggests that the effect on effort incentive differs according to one's hierarchical position. This is also confirmed by the significantly positive effect of the recognition of promotion possibility among workers (PNOTICED) on effort incentive for samples who have been promoted to section head and for those competing for department head, and by the significantly negative effect of the same variable for samples who have been already promoted to department head.

In summary, the effect of wages is significant only for samples who so far have not been promoted. The effect of satisfaction with wages, however, is significantly negative for all samples. The effect of the recognition of

Table 11.4   Model I, Estimated Effort Function (Lee's method), for Nonpromoted Employees

	Coefficient (A)	Coefficient (B)
Constant	2.616**	2.962**
	(0.206)	(0.287)
STD	0.157	0.075
	(0.141)	(0.152)
SAWD	−0.619**	−0.690**
	(0.125)	(0.157)
WVARD	−0.136	−0.162
	(0.201)	(0.235)
OPD	−0.007	0.123
	(0.128)	(0.159)
AGRD	0.078	0.035
	(0.167)	(0.250)
PROSD	0.361**	0.275*
	(0.125)	(0.163)
PNOTICED	0.092	0.042
	(0.136)	(0.184)
PVARD	0.027	−0.114
	(0.136)	(0.215)
PROS	0.281**	0.068
	(0.136)	(0.249)
$\bar{R}^2$	0.216	0.174

Source: Data are from Tachibanaki and Maruyama (1993).

Notes: See appendix for an explanation of variables. Figures in parentheses are standard errors. For sample A, samples are restricted to employees who are not promoted to section head. For sample B, samples are restricted to employees who are not promoted to department head.

**Significant at the 5 percent level.
*Significant at the 10 percent level.

promotion possibility is positive for samples of those in lower positions, while it is negative for samples of those in higher positions. This is consistent with the fact that the number of explanatory variables that are statistically significant on effort incentive decreases when we look at employees who have been promoted to very high positions. This reflects the decreasing role of the incentive mechanism in competition for very high positions. In other words, the incentive mechanism works best for competition within the range of lower positions.

Tables 11.6 through 11.10 show the estimated results for Model II, for both effort incentive functions and wage functions. They are estimated by OLS as well as 2SLS. The distinction between OLS results and 2SLS results gets at whether it is useful to consider the nature of the endogeneity in terms of effort and wages. We find that the effect of wages on effort is statistically significant for the total sample, but not for samples of those

Table 11.5   Model I, Estimated Effort Function (Heckman two-step), for
                    Promoted Employees

	Coefficient (A)	Coefficient (B)
Constant	2.703**	2.906**
	(0.144)	(0.264)
STD	0.126	0.087
	(0.086)	(0.133)
SAWD	−0.576**	−0.632**
	(0.083)	(0.135)
WVARD	−0.215*	−0.109
	(0.128)	(0.200)
OPD	0.154*	0.217
	(0.084)	(0.139)
AGRD	0.019	0.047
	(0.122)	(0.218)
PROSD	0.241**	0.272*
	(0.082)	(0.150)
PNOTICED	−0.027	−0.001
	(0.098)	(0.174)
PVARD	−0.002	−0.100
	(0.100)	(0.201)
PROS	0.195*	−0.203
	(0.106)	(0.219)
$\bar{R}^2$	0.183	0.154

Source: Data are from Tachibanaki and Maruyama (1993).

Notes: See appendix for an explanation of variables. Figures in parentheses are standard errors. For sample A, samples are restricted to employees who occupy the position of section head or higher. The number of observations is 352. For sample B, samples are restricted to employees who occupy the position of department head or higher. The number of observations is 150.

**Significant at the 5 percent level.

*Significant at the 10 percent level.

who have been promoted to section head and positions higher than section head, such as department head and director. This is true even in the case of the 2SLS method. Therefore, we conclude that when all white-collar employees are considered, wages have an influence on effort and incentive. When only promoted employees are considered, wages have no influence.

The effect of incentive effort on wages is not statistically significant for either OLS or 2SLS results, implying that having a strong effort incentive does not increase the wage payment. Nor do wages decrease when an employee has a strong effort incentive. This implies that wages are not affected by employees' effort level. Still, a strong effort incentive leads to a higher probability of promotion in the lower range of hierarchical positions. Thus, effort is important for promotion in early stages of careers but not important for wages. However, wages are affected by the hierarchical posi-

Table 11.6   Model II, Estimated Effort Function (OLS)

	Coefficient (A)	Coefficient (B)	Coefficient (C)
Constant	0.814**	2.116*	2.549
	(0.414)	(1.094)	(2.204)
OPD	0.013	0.116	0.221
	(0.051)	(0.086)	(0.143)
SAWD	−0.668**	−0.580**	−0.635**
	(0.051)	(0.089)	(0.145)
WVARD	−0.128	−0.189	−0.131
	(0.086)	(0.130)	(0.199)
PROSD	0.306**	0.243**	0.197
	(0.054)	(0.082)	(0.137)
STD	0.245**	0.134	0.001
	(0.061)	(0.092)	(0.146)
PVARD	0.178**	0.021	−0.046
	(0.055)	(0.104)	(0.173)
PNOTICED	0.052	0.004	−0.116
	(0.055)	(0.098)	(0.202)
WAGE	0.266**	0.103	0.063
	(0.067)	(0.166)	(0.324)
$\bar{R}^2$	0.238	0.165	0.134

Source: Data are from Tachibanaki and Maruyama (1993).

Notes: See appendix for an explanation of variables. Figures in parentheses are standard errors. For sample A, all samples are included. The number of observations is 1,037. For sample B, samples are restricted to employees who occupy the position of section head or higher. The number of observations is 337. For sample C, samples are restricted to employees who occupy the position of department head or higher. The number of observations is 147.
**Significant at the 5 percent level.
*Significant at the 10 percent level.

tions. In other words, promoted employees receive considerably higher wages than nonpromoted employees. Therefore, effort is important in order to receive higher wages through the indirect effect of promotion, although the direct effect of effort on wages is negligible.

The overall result, in terms of both the number of statistically significant coefficients and the closeness of fit, is excellent for the wage functions. The wage model, which investigates how wages are differentiated by hierarchical position and incentive, is explained fairly well by this specification.

The position variables (POSIT) are statistically significant for all equations, implying that the effect of hierarchical position is always positive regardless of the sample of white-collar workers. In other words, employers pay significantly higher wages to employees who occupy significantly higher positions. Tachibanaki (1996) concluded that hierarchical positions had the strongest effect on wage differentials among employees. The effect of job tenure, shown by both a linear term and its square term, is strongly significant, suggesting that the shape of the wage-tenure profile is convex.

Table 11.7   **Model II, Estimated Wage Function (OLS)**

	Coefficient (A)	Coefficient (B)	Coefficient (C)
Constant	4.937**	5.384**	5.253**
	(0.083)	(0.128)	(0.219)
POSIT	0.079**	0.121**	0.114**
	(0.015)	(0.018)	(0.033)
TENU	0.049**	0.036**	0.065**
	(0.005)	(0.008)	(0.014)
TENU2	−0.001**	−0.001**	−0.001**
	(0.000)	(0.000)	(0.000)
PHD	−0.014	n.a.	n.a.
	(0.020)		
AGE	0.015**	0.009**	0.010
	(0.003)	(0.005)	(0.008)
EDUD	0.233**	0.172**	0.089
	(0.030)	(0.034)	(0.055)
SEXD	0.299**	0.205**	0.063
	(0.035)	(0.054)	(0.088)
F1D	−0.082**	−0.043	n.a.
	(0.031)	(0.03)	
F2D	−0.013	−0.055*	−0.022
	(0.031)	(0.030)	(0.044)
F3D	−0.101**	−0.139**	−0.127**
	(0.029)	(0.022)	(0.032)
F4D	0.005	0.113**	0.088**
	(0.029)	(0.026)	(0.041)
EFFORT	0.010	0.012	0.010
	(0.009)	(0.010)	(0.014)
$\bar{R}^2$	0.616	0.729	0.579

Source: Data are from Tachibanaki and Maruyama (1993).
Notes: See table 11.6. n.a. = not available.

The effect of job tenure on wages also is statistically significant even for employees who occupy higher positions (samples B and C). It was anticipated before we launched this exercise that wages would be unaffected by job tenure for employees who were promoted to higher positions, because the other factors would be more significant than the job-tenure effect for these promoted employees. This turned out to be wrong. However, the estimated R^2 is considerably lower for sample C, those who occupy very high positions. Other factors, or unobserved factors, such as the employee's contribution to the firm, an assessment of the employee's performance, and so on, may contribute to wage differentials even among employees who occupy very high positions.

The effect of job tenure on wages is a controversial subject in many countries. Some authors believe that unobserved heterogeneity of employees reduces the effect of job tenure on wages, while other authors do not

Table 11.8   Model II, Estimated Effort Function (2SLS)

	Coefficient (A)	Coefficient (B)	Coefficient (C)
Constant	−0.126	2.974**	4.744*
	(0.567)	(1.277)	(2.768)
OPD	−0.016	0.0113	0.214
	(0.312)	(0.086)	(0.143)
SAWD	−0.676**	−0.559**	−0.583**
	(0.051)	(0.090)	(0.151)
WVARD	0.216	−0.186	−0.128
	(0.086)	(0.131)	(0.199)
PROSD	0.284**	0.250**	0.223
	(0.055)	(0.082)	(0.139)
STD	0.237**	0.144	0.000
	(0.061)	(0.092)	(0.145)
PVARD	0.127*	0.037	−0.093
	(0.059)	(0.104)	(0.202)
PNOTICED	0.038	0.007	−0.043
	(0.055)	(0.098)	(0.173)
WAGE	0.419**	−0.028	−0.262
	(0.092)	(0.194)	(0.408)
$\bar{R}^2$	0.242	0.164	0.142

Source: Data are from Tachibanaki and Maruyama (1993).
Notes: See table 11.6.

believe it.[9] Our study proposes that job tenure has a positive effect (with statistical significance) on the wage growth, even after controlling for both job positions and effort incentive, although we do not propose that its effect is smaller than is popularly believed.

Our calculation suggests that the wage increase due to promotion to department head is equivalent to the one due to having four years' job tenure. The comparable figure for promotion to director is two years' job tenure. Our calculation implies that promotion to department head increases wage payment drastically. Since employees know this, they struggle to obtain the position of department head, and it is regarded as a symbol of promotion, power, or prestige by many employees (as Tachibanaki 1998b concludes).

The effect of age on wages is also positive except for employees who are department heads or higher (sample C). As Ohta and Tachibanaki (1997) propose, the effect of age and job tenure on wages should be clearly distinguished, at least in Japan, with respect to its economic interpretation as well as its statistical estimation. The effect of age has some relation to the

9. In the United States, we can raise Abraham and Farber (1987) and Altonji and Shakotko (1987) for the former, and Topel (1991) for the latter. Brunello and Ariga (1995), Genda (1997), and Genda and Yee (1997) are useful for Japan and (South) Korea, respectively.

Table 11.9   Model II, Estimated Wage Function (2SLS)

	Coefficient (A)	Coefficient (B)	Coefficient (C)
Constant	4.942**	5.415**	5.399**
	(0.091)	(0.143)	(0.245)
POSIT	0.079**	0.122**	0.125**
	(0.015)	(0.018)	(0.035)
TENU	0.049**	0.036**	0.064**
	(0.005)	(0.008)	(0.014)
TENU2	−0.001**	−0.001**	−0.001**
	(0.000)	(0.000)	(0.000)
PHD	−0.014	—	—
	(0.020)		
AGE	0.015**	0.009*	0.011
	(0.003)	(0.005)	(0.008)
EDUD	0.233**	0.168**	0.063
	(0.030)	(0.035)	(0.060)
SEXD	0.299**	0.206**	0.059
	(0.035)	(0.054)	(0.087)
F1D	−0.083**	−0.044	—
	(0.032)	(0.031)	
F2D	−0.013	−0.053*	−0.007
	(0.032)	(0.030)	(0.046)
F3D	−0.102**	−0.137**	−0.115**
	(0.029)	(0.022)	(0.033)
F4D	0.003	0.108**	0.083**
	(0.031)	(0.028)	(0.041)
EFFORT	0.008	0.002	−0.029
	(0.022)	(0.024)	(0.037)
$\bar{R}^2$	0.616	0.727	0.580

Source: Data are from Tachibanaki and Maruyama (1993).
Notes: See table 11.6.

life cycle of employees. For example, the older the employee, the more necessary is his or her income. Still, employers do not take into consideration this life-cycle aspect for employees who have been promoted to very high positions.

The effect of education (EDUD) and sex (SEXD) are not statistically significant for department heads and higher (sample C), while they are significant for employees who have not been promoted to very high positions.

We conclude that there are several unobservable factors that affect the determination of wages for employees who have been promoted to department head. Which variables or factors are influential in the determination of wages for employees who occupy very high positions will be a subject of future research.

Tables 11.10 through 11.12 present the estimated results for Model III

Table 11.10   **Model III, Estimated Effort Function (2SLS)**

	Coefficient (A)	Coefficient (B)	Coefficient (C)
Constant	1.715	5.276**	4.119
	(1.116)	(2.163)	(3.233)
OPD	0.026	0.116	0.213
	(0.051)	(0.086)	(0.143)
SAWD	−0.671**	−0.519**	−0.594**
	(0.051)	(0.095)	(0.154)
WVARD	0.114	−0.209	−0.120
	(0.086)	(0.132)	(0.200)
PROSD	0.239**	0.213**	0.269*
	(0.058)	(0.087)	(0.161)
STD	0.198**	0.109	0.006
	(0.064)	(0.096)	(0.146)
PVARD	0.084	0.032	−0.069
	(0.061)	(0.105)	(0.207)
PNOTICED	0.029	−0.027	−0.024
	(0.055)	(0.102)	(0.177)
WAGE	0.119	−0.413	−0.118
	(0.181)	(0.351)	(0.542)
POSIT	0.191**	0.203	−0.194
	(0.091)	(0.156)	(0.371)
$\bar{R}^2$	0.246	0.166	0.138

Source: Data are from Tachibanaki and Maruyama (1993).
Notes: See table 11.6.

Table 11.11   **Model III, Estimated Position Function (2SLS)**

	Coefficient (A)	Coefficient (B)	Coefficient (C)
Constant	−2.148**	−2.062**	0.204
	(0.112)	(0.263)	(0.416)
TENU	0.136**	0.145**	0.067**
	(0.008)	(0.0172)	(0.029)
TENU2	−0.002**	−0.001**	−0.001
	(0.000)	(0.000)	(0.001)
EDUD	0.843**	0.956**	0.600**
	(0.050)	(0.072)	(0.099)
EFFORT	0.295**	0.311**	0.123*
	(0.043)	(0.062)	(0.070)
$\bar{R}^2$	0.550	0.561	0.259

Source: Data are from Tachibanaki and Maruyama (1993).
Notes: See table 11.6.

Table 11.12   Model III, Estimated Wage Function (2SLS)

	Coefficient (A)	Coefficient (B)	Coefficient (C)
Constant	5.290**	5.672**	5.140**
	(0.159)	(0.158)	(0.212)
TENU	0.038**	0.020**	0.054**
	(0.007)	(0.010)	(0.014)
TENU2	−0.001**	−0.000*	−0.001**
	(0.000)	(0.000)	(0.000)
PHD	−0.018	0.010	0.014
	(0.020)	(0.020)	(0.030)
AGE	0.008**	0.003	0.003
	(0.005)	(0.006)	(0.008)
EDUD	0.143**	0.060	−0.054
	(0.048)	(0.053)	(0.065)
SEXD	0.291**	0.228**	0.177*
	(0.035)	(0.056)	(0.090)
F1D	−0.032	0.008	0.089
	(0.038)	(0.034)	(0.056)
F2D	0.051	−0.013	0.023
	(0.041)	(0.024)	(0.046)
F3D	−0.108**	0.153**	−0.084**
	(0.029)	(0.032)	(0.036)
F4D	0.043	0.153**	0.139**
	(0.033)	(0.032)	(0.044)
POSIT	0.214**	0.267**	0.390**
	(0.057)	(0.054)	(0.080)
$\overline{R}^2$	0.611	0.709	0.609

Source: Data are from Tachibanaki and Maruyama (1993).
Notes: See table 11.6.

based on the 2SLS method. There are three endogenous variables, EFFORT, WAGE, and PROMOTION, and many exogenous variables. Since Model III is essentially a combined version of Model I and Model II, we do not discuss it in detail here. It simply intends to find the casual relationship among hierarchical position, effort incentive, and wages. Another important feature of tables 11.10 through 11.12 is that the model is estimated for separate samples—total sample, employees who have been promoted to section head and higher, and employees who have been promoted to department head and higher—as in the previous tables.

In tables 11.10 through 11.12, the estimated results are best for "all samples," and inferior when samples are restricted to employees who occupy higher positions. This was also true in Models I and II and implies that while the theoretical framework adopted in this study is supported for all samples, it is not supported for samples of those who occupy very high positions. It is likely that there are several unobservable variables for these samples, such as contribution to the firm, the firm's performance in profits or sales, and so on.

Further, the principal causality proceeds in the following way: position → effort incentive → wages. Position and effort affect each other, but wages have no effect on them except for samples of those who have not been promoted yet.

11.6   Who Is Promoted?

The previous sections presented several models and estimated their parameters empirically. However, the results did not show who is promoted, and on what criteria. This section is concerned with that question, although the method of investigation is descriptive.

We use the same data source, including questions such as "What are the reasons or criteria for the determination of promotion to department head and director?" The questionnaire is based on self-assessment of white-collar employees regarding the issue of promotion.

Table 11.13 shows the most important, second most important, and third most important criteria for promotion to department head and director, respectively. For promotion to department head, the most important criterion is the performance evaluation of an individual employee. The next most important is age and job tenure, followed by education. As for the second set of important criteria, age and job tenure are the highest, followed by performance evaluation and a manager's "pull." For the third set, managerial pull and personal character were about the same in importance.

For promotion to director, the most important criteria are the performance evaluation of an individual employee and managerial pull. They are virtually equal. Performance evaluation is less important for promotion to director than for promotion to department head. Of secondary importance are managerial pull and performance evaluation, which rank almost the same. Personal character is also fairly important. For the third set, personal character is the highest—much higher than the other criteria in the third set.

The discussion of promotion in Japanese firms may be summarized as follows: Before being promoted to department head, it is crucial to have excellent performance in business and to reveal one's capability and productivity to colleagues and managers. Since the effects of age and job tenure are quite important, too, even an extremely capable employee who shows excellent performance cannot expect to be promoted extremely rapidly. At the same time, even a less capable employee, or one with inferior performance in business, can be promoted up to a certain limited level, although more slowly. The record of an employee's performance during his or her career is documented, however, and it is certainly used as information for future promotion possibility.

Table 11.13   Criteria for the Determination of Promotion to Department Head and Director (percent)

	(A)	(B)	(C)	(D)	(E)	(F)	Not Available	Total
To Department Heads								
(1) Most important	**40.9**	20.0	12.1	2.4	18.0	3.5	3.1	1816
(2) Second-most important	20.5	**27.8**	22.4	7.4	9.2	8.6	4.1	1816
(3) Third-most important	16.7	14.9	**22.9**	8.3	10.5	21.5	5.2	1816
To Director								
(1) Most important	**34.1**	6.3	33.3	0.3	16.1	6.4	3.5	1816
(2) Second-most important	22.4	14.0	**26.3**	3.4	11.8	17.6	4.6	1816
(3) Third-most important	17.5	17.6	17.8	3.5	10.2	**27.2**	6.2	1816

Source: Data are from Tachibanaki and Maruyama (1993).

Notes: Boldface signifies the largest share for each row. Column A represents the performance evaluation of each individual employee. Column B represents age and job tenure. Column C represents the pull of managers who occupy superior positions than employees. Column D represents the result of the examination. Column E represents education (both the level of schooling and the name of the university). Column F represents personal character.

After being promoted to department head, the information on past and current performance in business determines the possibility of promotion to deputy director and director. At the same time, pull by superior managers becomes important at this stage. "Pull" is a mysterious element in the following senses: First, it may be equivalent to favoritism, as (for example) among relatives, graduates of the same university, or those with the same personal likes and dislikes. Second, an extremely powerful and influential manager is likely first to pick and then to recommend a capable subordinate for a higher position. Third, a much less capable employee, one with inferior performance, cannot be a candidate for the influence of managerial pull because the use of this influence would be judged unfair for such a person. Thus, pull may be called "luck" in some sense. Finally, good personal character matters to a certain extent.[10]

11.7 Concluding Remarks

This study investigated the relationship among promotion, effort incentive, and wages. Individual observations on white-collar workers in several large Japanese firms were used to investigate this issue. We obtained the following findings.

First, the employee's position on the hierarchical ladder is crucial in understanding the relationship among promotion, effort incentive, and wages. The effect of wages on effort is important for employees early in their careers or before being promoted. The higher the wage payment, the higher the effort from these employees. However, the crucial variable that increases effort for employees in mid-career is promotion prospective as measured by, for example, better performance in business. In the samples of workers promoted to department-head level, there is no incentive mechanism that works. In other words, neither prospective promotion nor wages affects the effort of employees who occupy very high positions. Unobservable factors, possibly including managerial pull (or luck) are important for these employees in terms of their promotion incentive.

Next, effort can be increased only for employees who are early in their careers, or are lower on the hierarchical ladder. There are several methods to increase the incentive for these employees: showing an explicit or implicit sign of the prospect of early promotion; providing frequent internal transfers among different sections; or using information on the employee's capability and sharing it among other employees who are in very early career stages. One important reason why the effort incentive mechanism works only for employees in early careers, or lower on the hierarchical ladder, is that employees who have been promoted quickly to higher posi-

10. Tachibanaki (1998a) investigated promotions to the highest positions, namely to top executive (board member), and presented several useful observations.

tions have already shown their excellent performance and capability, and thus they are highly motivated in any case.

Our estimated wage functions worked well even for white-collar employees. We confirmed the role of hierarchical positions in wage differentials in this study. In particular, we found that the level of wages jumps considerably when an employee is promoted to department head.

We also found age and job tenure to be effective for the determination of both the promotion possibility and wages. For the former, age and job tenure were secondarily important to employees early in their careers, following performance evaluation. For wages, the effect of job tenure was prevalent even after controlling for the simultaneous presence of hierarchical position and job tenure.

Finally, what determines promotion, or how to select promoted employees, differs according to the position. In other words, the decision-making variables are different for promotion to department head versus promotion to director. Very simply speaking, performance evaluation of an individual employee and job tenure matter for department head positions, whereas performance evaluation and managerial pull perhaps matter for the position of director.

What are the implications for human resource management in view of the recent aging trend in the Japanese population and the slower growth rate of firms in Japan? It is essential for firms to reduce the cost of labor and, at the same time, to raise productivity of employees by increasing their incentives. Competition among employees, in particular younger and not-yet-promoted employees, is desirable to achieve such a goal. Competition in terms of merit, evaluated by the contribution and performance of each individual employee, is likely to distinguish between capable employees and less capable ones in their early careers. Quicker promotions for more capable employees and wider wage differentials among employees are unavoidable.

Appendix

List of Variables

EFFORT: Work effort compared with job requirements
    4: contribution to the firm higher than required
    3: contribution to the firm somewhat higher than required
    2: contribution to the firm almost equivalent to requirements
    1: needs somewhat higher effort
    0: needs higher effort

PROM (or PROD): A dummy variable for promotion
   1: promoted
   0: not promoted

WAGE: Natural log of annual wage

OPD: A dummy variable for propensity to promote
   1: strong propensity
   2: no propensity

SAWD: Own evaluation of wage compared with contribution to the firm
   1: wage is higher than contribution
   0: otherwise

WVARD: Wage differentials among colleagues who were employed in the same year
   1: wide differential
   0: small or no differential

PROSD: A dummy variable for prospect of promotion
   1: expecting to be promoted to director
   0: otherwise

STD: Satisfaction with wage payment
   1: satisfied
   0: otherwise

PVARD: A dummy variable for whether promotion is differentiated among colleagues who were employed in the same year
   1: yes
   0: no

AGRD: Propensity to compete with other people
   1: yes
   0: no

PNOTICED: A dummy variable for whether promotion possibility is easily recognized among workers
   1: yes
   0: no

TENU: Job tenure (TENU2 is its squared form)

PCAR: Years toward section head (PCAR2 is its squared form) for samples of section heads and higher positions. Years towards department head for samples of department heads and higher positions.

AGE: Age

SEXD: A dummy variable for sex
   1: male
   0: female

EDUD: A dummy variable for university education
  1: university
  0: otherwise

PHD: A dummy variable for specialty in university education
  1: law and economics
  0: otherwise

IND: The number of changes in job section before promotion to section head

OUTD: The number of changes in job section before promotion to department head

SHUKO: A dummy variable for temporary work in the subsidiary firm
  1: yes
  2: otherwise

BUKAD: A dummy variable for whether an individual department head has subordinates
  1: yes
  2: no

F1D–F4D: Dummy variables for particular firms

POSIT: Variables for positions
  3: higher than deputy director
  2: division head
  1: section head
  0: otherwise

Model Specification

Model I
  EFFORT = X + **PROM**
  PROM = Z + EFFORT
  X, Z: exogenous variables;

Model II
  EFFORT = X + WAGE
  WAGE = Y + EFFORT
  X, Y: exogenous variables;

Model III
  EFFORT = X + **PROM** + WAGE
  WAGE = Y + **PROM**
  PROM = Z + EFFORT
  X, Y, Z: exogenous variables;

where EFFORT may be interpreted as incentive, and **PROM** signifies promotion possibility where it is defined discretely in some cases. Boldface implies the possibility of such a discrete nature. WAGE is the annual wage payment.

References

Abraham, K. G., and H. S. Farber. 1987. Job duration, seniority, and earnings. *American Economic Review* 77:278–97.
Altonji, J. S., and R. A. Shakotko. 1987. Do earnings rise with job seniority? *Review of Economic Studies* 69:437–59.
Ariga, K., Y. Ohkusa, and G. Brunello. 1997. Fast track: Is it in the genes? The promotion policy of a large Japanese firm. *Kyoto Institute of Economic Research.* Discussion Paper no. 452.
Baker, G., R. Gibbs, and B. Holmstrom. 1994a. The internal economics of the firm: Evidence from personal data. *Quarterly Journal of Economics* 109:881–919.
———. 1994b. The wage policy of a firm. *Quarterly Journal of Economics* 109: 492–525.
Baker, G., R. Gibbs, and K. J. Murphy. 1994. Subjective performance measures in optimal incentive contracts. *Quarterly Journal of Economics* 109:1125–56.
Becker, G. 1962. *Human capital.* New York, NY: Columbia University Press.
Bruderl, J., A. Diekman, and P. Preisendörfer. 1991. Patterns of intraorganizational mobility: Tournament models, path dependency, and early promotion effects. *Social Science Research* 20:197–216.
Brunello, G., and K. Ariga. 1995. Is the tenure-earning curve really steeper in Japan? A re-examination based on U.K.-Japan comparison. In *The structure of the Japanese economy,* ed. M. Okabe, 109–34. London: Macmillan.
Carmichael, L. 1983. Firm-specific human capital and promotion ladders. *Bell Journal of Economics* 14:251–58.
Genda, Y. 1997. Japan. In *Wage differentials: An international comparison,* ed. T. Tachibanaki, chap. 2. London: Macmillan.
Genda, Y., and S. Y. Yee. 1997. Wage determination and labour turnover in Korea. In *Wage differentials: An international comparison,* ed. T. Tachibanaki, chap. 3. London: Macmillan.
Gibbons, R. 1997. Incentives and careers in organizations. In *Advances in economic theory and econometrics,* ed. D. Kreps and K. Wallis, 1–37. New York: Cambridge University Press.
Harris, M., and B. Holmstrom. 1982. A theory of wage dynamics. *Review of Economic Studies* 49:315–33.
Hashimoto, M. 1981. Firm-specific human capital as a shared investment. *American Economic Review* 71:475–81.
Holmstrom, B. 1979. Moral hazard in teams. *Bell Journal of Economics* 13:324–40.
Ishikawa, T. 1992. *Distribution in income and wealth* (in Japanese). Tokyo: Iwanami-shoten.
Ito, H., and H. Teruyama. 1998. Effort incentive: Evidence from Japanese data. In *Who runs Japanese business?* ed. T. Tachibanaki, chap. 6. London: Elgar.
Koike, K. 1991. *Economics of jobs* (in Japanese). Tokyo: Toyokeizai-shimposha.
Lazear, E. 1979. Why is there mandatory retirement? *Journal of Political Economy* 87:1261–84.

———. 1989. Pay equality and industrial politics. *Journal of Political Economy* 97:561–80.

Matsushige, T. 1998. White-collar careers in a large electronics company. In *Who runs Japanese business?* ed. T. Tachibanaki, chap. 7. London: Elgar.

Mincer, J., and Y. Higuchi. 1988. Wage structures and labour turnover in the United States and Japan. *Journal of the Japanese and International Economies* 2:97–133.

Mitani, N. 1998. Work incentive of white-collars in wages and promotion. In *Who runs Japanese business?* ed. T. Tachibanaki, chap. 5. London: Elgar.

Murphy, K. J. 1986. Incentives, learning and compensation: A theoretical and empirical investigation of managerial labor contracts. *Rand Journal of Economics* 17:59–76.

Ohashi, I. 1998. The name of the university matters? In *Who runs Japanese business?* ed. T. Tachibanaki, chap. 8. London: Elgar.

Ohashi, I., and T. Matsushige. 1994. The growth of the firm and promotions in the Japanese seniority system. In *Labour market and economic performance: Europe, Japan and the U.S.A.* ed. T. Tachibanaki, 131–54. London: Macmillan.

Ohta, S., and T. Tachibanaki. 1997. Job tenure versus age: Their effects on wages, and the implication of consumption for wages. In *Internal labour market incentives and employment,* ed. I. Ohashi and T. Tachibanaki, chap. 3. London: Macmillan.

Ohtake, F. 1995. The determinants of promotion: The effects of length of tenure and performance evaluation (in Japanese). *Keizai Kenkyu* 46:241–48.

Prendergast, C. 1999. Provision of incentives in firms. *Journal of Economic Literature* 37:7–63.

Prendergast, C., and R. H. Topel. 1996. Favoritism in organizations. *Journal of Political Economy* 104:958–78.

Tachibanaki, T. 1982. Further results on Japanese wage differentials: Nenko wages, hierarchical positions, bonuses and working hours. *International Economic Review* 33:447–61.

———. 1987. The determination of the promotion process in organizations and of earnings differentials. *Journal of Economic Behaviour and Organizations* 8:603–16.

———. 1996. *Wage determination and distribution in Japan.* Oxford, England: Clarendon.

———, ed. 1997. *Wage differentials: An international comparison.* London: Macmillan.

———. 1998a. Roads towards top executive positions (board members) and their management goals. In *Who runs Japanese business?* ed. T. Tachibanaki, chap. 2. London: Elgar.

———, ed. 1998b. *Who runs Japanese business?* London: Elgar.

Tachibanaki, T., and T. Maruyama. 1993. Survey of white collar employees. Tokyo: Research Institute for Advancement of Living Standards (RIALS).

Tomita, Y. 1992. System of promotion: An influence of assessment and job tenure. In *Assessment, promotion and wage determination* (in Japanese), ed. T. Tachibanaki, 49–65. Tokyo: Yuhikaku.

Topel, R. 1991. Specific capital, mobility and earnings: Earnings rise with job seniority. *Journal of Political Economy* 99:145–76.

What Went Wrong with the
1991–92 Official Population
Projection of Japan?

Seiritsu Ogura

12.1 Introduction

The track records of the last two official Japanese population projections have been very poor, judging from the accuracy of the figures for new births (fig. 12.1). Every five years, the National Institute of Population Research, which is now the National Institute of Social Security and Population Research, prepares three different sets of projections based on middle, high, and low fertility assumptions. The projection based on the middle fertility assumption is treated as the official population projection for Japan. This projection is linked almost automatically to many long-term plans the government prepares, from Public Pensions Projections to Energy Projections, and hence any sizeable error in the projection seriously affects resource allocation over time and income distribution across generations.

The 1986 projection, for instance, predicted a recovery of the Total Fertility Rate (TFR) to 1.86 but ended up overestimating 1991 births by almost 300,000. In fact, TFR dropped from 1.72 in 1986 to 1.51 in 1991. In spite of this experience, in the 1991–92 projection, demographers at the Institute again predicted a recovery in TFR beginning in 1995. At this time, however, there is no sign of the predicted recovery and, in fact, TFR continued to slip by another 0.1 during the five-year period. Thus, the projection ended up overestimating 1996 births by more than 120,000, and the

Seiritsu Ogura is professor of economics at Hosei University.

The author wishes to thank Professor Yutaka Kosai, Mr. Richard Woodbury, and Professor David Cutler for helpful comments and Tamotsu Kadoda for capable assistance in computation. This research was supported by grants from the Abe Foundation and a faculty research development grant from Hosei University.

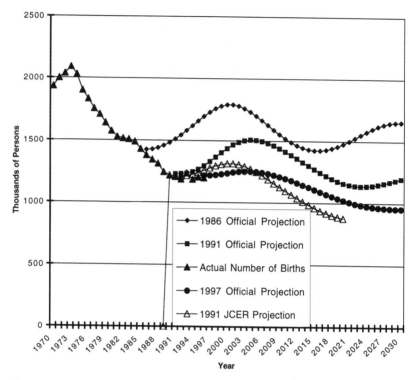

Fig. 12.1   Actual number of live births and official population projection in Japan

gap between projected and actual figures would have reached almost a quarter of a million early in the twenty-first century. Because all the Japanese social insurance programs are essentially income transfer mechanisms between the old and the young generations, these optimistic fertility assumptions allowed the government to understate the burdens on future generations very substantially. In a sense, these optimistic fertility projections also allowed the government to adopt a long series of ad hoc measures to solve only the immediate crises, without addressing the problems that occur in the long run.

From the purely technical point of view, to be sure, the 1991–92 projection was an innovative one. As we will see in detail shortly, it tried to estimate age-specific fertility rates of female cohorts by fitting their records to a class of special statistical distribution functions. This procedure allowed fertility behavior to be represented by a small number of parameters, which can be used to predict future fertility for this cohort as well as for future generations. Thus armed, the projection confidently declared that the observed decline in the fertility rate of Japanese women had been a temporary phenomenon resulting from delayed marriage and childbearing, and that both would end by the mid-1990s, raising TFR to where it was in the middle of 1980s.

Unfortunately, this attempt to introduce rigorous science into the population projection rather than inventing fertility rates out of thin air was not very successful in terms of its outcome; it seems to have been abandoned in the latest projection. In fact, in the 1997 projection (which was made public in January 1997), the projection of fertility rates is based on marriage rates and the marital fertility rates of recent cohorts, as I had done in the last two Japan Center for Economic Research (JCER) population projections. Because marriages precede births by many years, and given substantial information on the marriage behavior of a cohort, one using the information should be able to predict the future course of the number of births by the cohort far more precisely than by, say, using their age alone.

This paper attempts to show the following: The government demographers failed in their 1991–92 projection because there was a fundamental flaw in their methodology. In fact, if we apply the same methodology in the 1997 projection, there is hardly any need to change their 1991–92 projection. Thus, their methodologically "correct" projection will continue to diverge from reality for another five years, when they are scheduled for another projection.

The rest of this paper is constructed as follows. In section 12.2, I present the formal demographic model used in the 1991–92 projection and report my own estimation results using new data made available since 1992. In section 12.3, I formulate a marriage/birth model and explore the possibility of misspecification as a source of the government model's sensitivity to truncation. In section 12.4, I formulate the age distribution of marital fertility rates and report my estimation results. In section 12.5, I look at significant changes in the marital behavior of Japanese women that took place in the last twenty years. In section 12.6, I analyze the causes of the drop in the fertility rates observed among three different cohorts, almost five years apart. In section 12.7, I provide concluding remarks.

12.2 Official 1992 Projection Model: Direct Estimation of Birth Rates

In the Japanese official population projection of 1992, the probability distribution of giving birth to a child of a particular order (first child, second child, etc.) in a female cohort is fitted to an incomplete log-gamma distribution function. Although it is not usually treated in introductory statistics, a complete log-gamma probability distribution that seems to be popular among demographers and sociologists (e.g., Coale 1971; Coale and McNeil 1972; Kaneko 1991) can be written as

$$(1) \qquad g(x) = \frac{1}{\beta^{\alpha}\Gamma(\alpha)}|\mu|\exp\left\{\alpha\mu(x - u) - \frac{1}{\beta}\exp[\mu(x - u)]\right\},$$

with four distribution parameters (α, β, μ, u). Multiplying this function by a positive factor, C, which is less than 1, generates the incomplete log-gamma distribution function. Kaneko (1993), for instance, presents the distribution function used for the official population projection (Kenkyusho 1992) as

$$(2) \quad h(x) = \frac{C|\lambda|}{b\Gamma(\lambda^{-2})}\left(\frac{1}{\lambda^2}\right)^{\lambda^{-2}} \exp\left\{\frac{1}{\lambda}\left(\frac{x-u}{b}\right) - \frac{1}{\lambda^2}\exp\left[\lambda\left(\frac{x-u}{b}\right)\right]\right\}.$$

In equation (2), C is the incompleteness factor, which we shall ignore for the moment. By comparing equations (1) and (2), we can conclude initially that the parameters in these two expressions are related in the following manner:

$$(3) \qquad\qquad\qquad \alpha = \frac{1}{\lambda^2},$$

$$(4) \qquad\qquad\qquad \beta = \lambda^2,$$

$$(5) \qquad\qquad\qquad \mu = \frac{\lambda}{b}.$$

Second, I find that equation (2) imposes a restriction on the parameters of equation (1) such that

$$(6) \qquad\qquad\qquad \alpha\beta = 1,$$

where $\alpha\beta$ is equal to the mean of the gamma variable in the original gamma distribution. Thus equation (2) is equivalent to

$$(2') \quad g(x; a, \mu, u) = \frac{\alpha^\alpha}{\Gamma(\alpha)}|\mu|\exp\{\alpha\mu(x-u) - \alpha\exp[\mu(x-u)]\}$$

in my notation.

Finally, I define a new distribution function $f(x)$ obtained by multiplying equation (1) by a positive constant factor C that is smaller than 1, namely,

$$(7) \qquad\qquad h(x) = Cg(x; \alpha, \mu, u).$$

The cumulative distribution function for h is then defined by

$$(8) \qquad\qquad H(x) = \int_0^x h(\tau; a, \mu, u)dt = CG(x),$$

where $G(x)$ is the cumulative distribution function for g, or

$$(9) \qquad\qquad G(x) = \int_0^x g(\tau; a, \mu, u)dt.$$

Kaneko (1993) provides a fairly detailed account of how estimates of the parameters for different cohorts were obtained. He applied a standard probability model in a multinomial distribution, where the probability of giving birth at age i, denoted by P_i, is defined as

$$(10) \qquad P(i) = H(i) - H(i - 1).$$

Now, suppose a cohort has accumulated complete data regarding the number of births at each age between fifteen and forty-nine, $(m_{16}, m_{16}, \ldots, m_{49})$. Because the probability of such a sequence of events taking place is

$$(11) \qquad L = P(15)^{m_{15}} \cdot P(16)^{m_{16}} \cdots P(i)^{m_i} \cdots P(49)^{m_{49}},$$

the parameters of an incomplete gamma distribution function for this cohort must be set in such a way as to maximize this joint probability, L.

12.2.1 A Formulation Involving Right-Censored Data

If one insists on using only the cohort data with completed birth data, however, then the latest cohort available for obtaining distribution parameters for the last official projection (1991–92) would have been the cohort born in 1941. In estimating the degree of structural changes taking place, even the data from this cohort will have very limited value. As a practical matter, therefore, we have to find a way to extract information from those cohorts that are still in the middle of their child-bearing ages. One way to do so is to apply the same principle as above but allow for the possibility of right-censoring.[1]

Suppose that the age-specific birthrate data for a first child are available up to the age $x - 1$ for a particular cohort. Then a woman in this cohort either has already given birth to a child at some age between fifteen and $x - 1$, or she has not yet given birth by age $x - 1$. Suppose the proportion of women in the second group in the cohort is given by $S(x)$. The probability of observing a woman having a child between ages fifteen and $x - 1$ is given by

$$(12a) \qquad P(15)^{m_{15}} \cdot P(16)^{m_{16}} \cdots P(x - 1)^{m_{x-1}},$$

while the probability of observing $S(x)$ women not yet having a child is given by

$$(12b) \qquad \left[1 - \sum_{i=15}^{x-1} P(i) \right]^{S(x)}.$$

The product of these two probabilities gives the probability of the observed experience. Accordingly, the log-likelihood function is given by

$$(13) \qquad \ln L = \sum_{i=15}^{x-1} m_i \ln P(i) + S(x) \ln \left[1 - \sum_{i=15}^{x-1} P(i) \right].$$

---

1. I do not consider, however, using the left-censored data.

Since all the $P(i)$s are constructed by equation (10) from a log-gamma distribution function, they are functions of the parameters of the original log-gamma distribution function. Denoting a particular parameter of the log-gamma distribution function by θ, we can estimate its value by maximizing equation (13) with respect to θ. The first-order condition for maximization is given by

$$(14) \quad \frac{\partial \ln L}{\partial \theta} = \sum_{i=15}^{x-1} \frac{m_i}{P(i;\theta)} \frac{\partial P(i;\theta)}{\partial \theta} - \frac{S(x)}{1 - \sum_{i=15}^{x-1} P(i;\theta)} \sum_{i=15}^{x-1} \frac{\partial P(i;\theta)}{\partial \theta} = 0.$$

12.2.2   Updating the 1991–92 Estimation

Using the age-specific fertility rate of Japanese women born between 1950 and 1966, and considering their first, second, and third children, I estimate the five parameters of the incomplete log-gamma distribution functions. The fertility data used in the estimation are annual data from 1979 to 1994. The likelihood function is first maximized analytically with respect to Cs to yield a concentrated log-likelihood function, which is then optimized with respect to α, β, μ, and u using a Gauss-Newton method with a Berndt, Hall, Hall, and Hausman (BHHH) method for Hessian matrices. For computer software, I used GAUSS. The results are shown in tables 12.1 through 12.3 for selected years.

There are three possible sources of difference between my results and those obtained by the government demographers as a part of the previous official population projection. First, in my computation, I added data for three years (1992 to 1994) in the truncated estimation. Second, there are minor differences in the fertility data used, because I constructed my own data rather than using the cohort fertility data published by the National Institute of Population Research.[2] Third, the government's 1991–92 projection involves an error correction function on top of the estimated theoretical distribution, which I decided to skip because they perform, in my judgment, merely cosmetic adjustments to augment its goodness of fit.

The results of these updated estimations are summarized as follows:

1. According to table 12.1, the estimated completed fertility rate with respect to the first child seems to have come down from 0.90 of the cohort born in 1950 to around 0.81 of that born in 1960. The completed fertility rate seems to stay slightly below 0.8, but it seems to bounce back to 0.84 for those born in 1965. In any case, the official projection assumed the value of 0.821 as the long-run equilibrium value, and it seems to have been more or less appropriate.

---

2. This is done so that I can compare the results with another method, which I will explain later.

Table 12.1   Estimated Parameters for the Age–Specific First Child Fertility Rate (incomplete log-gamma function), by Birth Year

	1950	1955	1960	1961	1962	1963	1964	1965
α	1.4698	2.2380	3.4161	4.2767	3.6792	4.6745	4.5118	3.5082
β	0.2384	0.3474	0.2718	0.2646	0.3200	0.4038	0.4329	0.3504
μ	−0.2832	−0.2037	−0.1577	−0.1372	−0.1428	−0.1217	−0.1164	−0.1199
u	20.7266	23.8383	25.2534	26.7872	27.1037	31.4160	32.2879	28.7668
C	0.8991	0.8750	0.8143	0.7998	0.7928	0.7787	0.7844	0.8345
Likelihood	−2.6660	−2.7111	−2.5831	−2.5318	−2.4555	−2.3458	−2.1896	−1.9978
FOC								
α	−0.00382	0.00010	−0.00010	−0.00010	0.01073	−0.00009	−0.00006	−0.00003
β	−0.10808	−0.00006	0.00007	0.00010	0.12348	0.00010	0.00010	0.00010
μ	0.04461	−0.00006	−0.00002	−0.00007	0.05385	−0.00010	−0.00009	−0.00005
u	0.00191	0.00000	0.00000	0.00000	−0.00574	0.00000	−0.00001	0.00000

Source: All tables are based on author's estimation, as described in the text.

2. According to table 12.2, for the second child the story is similar to that for the first child. The estimated completed fertility rate with respect to the second child seems to have come down from 0.78 for the cohort born in 1950 to around 0.69 for that born in 1960. The official projection used the value of 0.685 as the long-run equilibrium. Again, a recovery seems to be taking place after the 1963 cohort, and for the 1965 cohort, fertility is projected to be 0.77.

3. The change in the fertility rate for a third child, on the other hand, seems to have followed a very different pattern (see table 12.3). The estimated completed fertility rate with respect to the third child was 0.26 for the 1950 cohort and reached 0.29 for the 1957 cohort. After a slight decline, it seems to be picking up again, reaching 0.32 for the 1965 cohort. The official projection used the value of 0.2510 as the long-run equilibrium, which seems to be rather modest.

Thus, if the government demographers had carried out the identical estimation of completed fertility rates in 1997 for the 1964 cohort, they should have obtained 0.8 for the first child, 0.69 for the second child, and 0.30 for the third child. Furthermore, they should have shown the fertility rates rising in more recent cohorts. There seems to be no reason for them to lower the long-run TFR of 1.8 assumed in the 1991–92 projection. In the 1997 population projection, however, the government did lower the long-run TFR level to 1.6, which is an admission of the general failure of the procedure used in 1991–92 projection.

12.3   The Implications of Conditioning Births to Marriages

In Japan, in contrast to most of the other developed countries, an overwhelming majority of births still take place within marriages, particularly in first marriages. Because marriages precede births by many years, it is natural to expect that one should be better able to forecast the number of future births by explicitly using information on marriages. One way to do this is to treat all the women in a given cohort who have married at a given age as a homogeneous group, because there seems to be a very stable (nonlinear) relationship between the number of years married and childbearing behavior.

Suppose that the probability is denoted by

$$(15) \qquad \pi(s, k - s),$$

for a k-year-old woman who has been married for s years, to give a birth to a child of any given order. Here $k - s$ denotes the age at which she was married, which will be referred to as her marital age. (I ignore the possibility of divorce here.) Suppose also that there are $M(k - s)$ women at age k (or, in the same cohort) who were married at age $(k - s)$. In this birth order, the expected number of births from these women is given by

Table 12.2   Estimated Parameters for the Age-Specific Second Child Fertility Rate (incomplete log-gamma function), by Birth Year

	1950	1955	1960	1961	1962	1963	1964	1965
α	3.3370	3.9881	3.4645	3.8341	3.1418	3.1103	3.0436	2.9690
β	0.3010	0.2848	0.2894	0.2826	0.2954	0.2923	0.2813	0.2805
μ	-0.1721	-0.1488	-0.1523	-0.1393	-0.1447	-0.1362	-0.1267	-0.1191
u	27.4225	28.7419	28.2974	29.0294	28.1339	28.2849	28.3510	28.6731
C	0.7770	0.7605	0.6932	0.6819	0.6819	0.6894	0.7215	0.7658
Likelihood	-2.5745	-2.5616	-2.2618	-2.1423	-1.9759	-1.7758	-1.5314	-1.2692
FOC								
α	0.000705	-0.000268	-0.000326	-0.000206	-0.000170	-0.000077	0.000034	0.000026
β	0.000361	-0.000867	0.000437	0.000336	0.000084	-0.000282	0.000437	0.000096
μ	-0.000117	0.000600	-0.000983	-0.000965	-0.000997	-0.000630	0.000831	0.000936
u	-0.000019	0.000037	-0.000019	-0.000013	-0.000004	0.000011	-0.000016	-0.000003

Source: See table 12.1.

Table 12.3   Estimated Parameters for the Age-Specific Third Child Fertility Rate (incomplete log-gamma function), by Birth Year

	1950	1955	1960	1961	1962	1963	1964	1965
α	3.2266	3.8397	3.4810	3.4253	2.9392	3.0554	3.0323	2.5283
β	0.2672	0.2678	0.2839	0.2639	0.2759	0.2623	0.2477	0.2671
μ	−0.1609	−0.1448	−0.1365	−0.1302	−0.1303	−0.1211	−0.1124	−0.1155
u	28.9391	30.6122	30.9929	30.5911	30.1550	30.3962	30.3123	30.0219
C	0.2569	0.2881	0.2793	0.2797	0.2883	0.2943	0.3079	0.3221
Likelihood	−1.2605	−1.3376	−1.0233	−0.8961	−0.7559	−0.6111	−0.4689	−0.3444
FOC								
α	−0.0008	−0.0005	−0.0001	0.0000	0.0000	0.0000	0.0000	0.0000
β	−0.0008	0.0009	−0.0001	0.0007	0.0000	−0.0002	−0.0001	0.0006
μ	−0.0004	−0.0001	−0.0010	0.0008	−0.0004	−0.0007	0.0005	0.0010
u	0.0000	0.0000	0.0000	0.0000	0.0000	0.0000	0.0000	0.0000

Source: See table 12.1.

(16) $$\pi(s,k - s)M(k - s).$$

I assume that the lowest age of marriage is fifteen and the maximum age of reproduction is fifty. Assuming that it takes a year to give birth to a child after marriage, in equation (16), k goes from 16 to 50 and there will be $(k - 16)$ possible values of s. The expected number of births from women at age k, or $B(k)$, can be obtained as the sum of equation (16) over these $(k - 16)$ possible values of s; or

(17) $$B(k) = \sum_{s=1}^{k-16} \pi(s,k - s)M(k - s).$$

Equation (17) points to the source of the fundamental problem in the direct approach in the official 1991–92 projection. To see this more clearly, for the moment, we can take $M(k - s)$ as weights for $\pi(s, k - s)$. Let us denote the relevant characteristics of women who married at age $(k - s)$ by ω_{k-s}. We emphasize this by rewriting equation (17) as

(18) $$B(k) = \sum_{s=1}^{k-16} \pi(s,k - s,\omega_{k-s})M(k - s).$$

Thus, when we estimate an age-specific distribution function using the birthrate data up to age k, we implicitly take into account in the process all the relevant characteristics up to $k - 1$, or the information set at age k is given by

(19) $$I(k) = (\omega_{15},\omega_{16},\ldots,\omega_{k-1}; M_{15},M_{16},\ldots,M_{k-1}),$$

as far as this cohort is concerned.

In the next year, when data on $B(k + 1)$ become available,

(20) $$I(k + 1) = (\omega_{15},\omega_{16},\ldots,\omega_{k-1},\omega_{k}; M_{15},M_{16},\ldots,M_{k-1},M_{k}),$$

will be used for the estimation. However, it is not immediately clear how important this additional information can be in obtaining the correct parameters of the distribution. I have conducted experiments by controlling the last data used in the estimation, and have found that in the cohorts born after 1960, the estimated parameters, particularly C, are generally very sensitive to the addition of new data. In some cases, adding even a year's data completely changed the value of their s. A number of factors can contribute to this phenomenon; for instance,

1. *Misspecification problem.* If the $\pi(s, k - s)$s are not generated by an identical exponential distribution function, then the resulting age-specific distribution is no longer a log-gamma function as specified earlier. In such a case, the model is misspecified and the parameters are not consistent; hence, they may be unstable as more data are added (see appendix).

2. *Heterogeneity problem.* A cohort may not be very homogeneous.

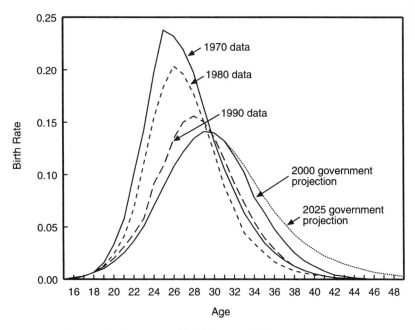

Fig. 12.2   Changes in the age-specific birthrates of Japanese women

Those married later may be very different from those married younger. Furthermore, those married later may be making choices under a very different set of circumstances from those of individuals who married younger. Heterogeneity thus may result in considerable and complex differences in the timing of having children after marriage that may not be captured by the very limited number of parameters in a log-gamma distribution function.

3. *Truncation and log-gamma variable.* Since the value of the log-gamma variable is defined from negative infinity to positive infinity, I may be getting distributions that technically fit well with the existing data but that have too much area in the truncated region to be consistent with human behavior. Such an example can be found in the 1992 official projection, in which women in their late forties are supposed to be giving birth almost as often as women in their late thirties today (fig. 12.2).

12.4   Estimation of Marital Fertility Functions

12.4.1   Beta Distribution Specification

In order to implement the fertility-rate projection on the basis of equation (17), we have to estimate both age distribution functions of marital fertility rates conditioned on marital ages, or $(k - s)$, and age distribution functions of first marriages, or $m(k - s)$. For the former, I have selected incomplete beta distribution functions, and for the latter, incomplete log-gamma functions. A beta distribution is defined as

(21) $$f(x) = \frac{\Gamma(\alpha + \beta)}{\Gamma(\alpha)\Gamma(\beta)} x^{\alpha-1}(1 - x)^{\beta-1}, \quad 0 < x < 1.$$

The mean and the variance of this distribution are given by

(22) $$\mu = \frac{\alpha}{\alpha + \beta};$$

(23) $$\sigma^2 = \frac{\alpha\beta}{(\alpha + \beta + 1)(\alpha + \beta)^2}.$$

Thus, given β, a larger α moves the mode of the distribution to the right, and makes the mountain taller. Proportional increases in both α and β do not change the location of the mode in terms of the horizontal axis, but make the mountain taller and steeper as they reduce the variance. Although a beta function is not nearly as flexible as a log-gamma function given by equation (1), its domain is between 0 and 1, and it will not give us a phantom baby boom in women in their forties or fifties (as the government's projection does).

We must account for the possibility of women's not having children of that particular order or higher, and hence, I have added an incompleteness factor, C_M, to the beta distribution function. Thus, for each age of marriage in a cohort, the distribution of marital fertility rate is assumed to be given by

(24) $$f(x) = C_M \frac{\Gamma(\alpha + \beta)}{\Gamma(\alpha)\Gamma(\beta)} x^{\alpha-1}(1 - x)^{\beta-1}, \quad 0 < x < 1,$$

where the unit interval starts at the age of marriage and ends at age fifty. I again have accounted for the right-censoring problem by constructing a log-likelihood function similar to equation (15); I then optimize the likelihood function with respect to C_M and transform it into a concentrated likelihood function.

12.4.2   Data Problems

Underreporting

Marital fertility-rate data for each cohort have been computed from the vital statistics table on the number of first marriages for each woman's age and the cross-tabulation of the mother's age and the number of years married for each order of birth. The latter figures (seem to) include the births from couples who had started living together without formally reporting their marriages, but who decided to report just before the birth of a child. As a result, in some marital age groups, there are more first children born than the number of first marriages reported. Another possible explanation for this phenomenon could be the ignored second and third marriages, because I focused only on first marriages to economize the estimation. It is clear that second marriages will soon become an important factor that should not be ignored in the analysis of birth rates.

In order to deal with this problem in the simplest possible way, I multiplied all the first marriages by a factor of 1.25 in the denominator of marital fertility rate. This factor was chosen because, prior to this adjustment, the highest cumulative marital fertility rate was recorded at 1.21 by those born in 1950 and married at age thirty. Thus, the marital fertility rates I actually used are about 25 percent smaller than the ratio of the number of children born and the number of first marriages in all marital age groups.

Similarly, I noticed some women giving birth to second or third children within a year of their marriages; most of these women are presumably married for the second or the third time. In figure 12.3, I show the age distribution of the marital fertility rate for the third child among those married at age thirty-three for three different cohorts. Clearly, this seems to be constructed as a composite of two different curves: one a downward-sloping curve and the other a single-peaked curve. In order to capture such reproductive behavior, I have assumed that the distribution function is a sum of a beta distribution function and an exponential distribution function, given by

$$(25) \quad f(x) = C_M \frac{\Gamma(\alpha + \beta)}{\Gamma(\alpha)\Gamma(\beta)} x^{\alpha-1}(1 - x)^{\beta-1} + C_K \delta \exp(-\delta x), \quad 0 < x < 1.$$

Censoring

Because Vital Statistics did not begin to publish the mother's age and the years married for each order of birth until 1979, my computation is limited to cohorts and their subgroups for which there is no left-censoring. Thus I have limited the exercise to groups of women on whom I have complete birth records starting from the first year of marriage and up to year 1994. If I were to estimate equation (25) for each cohort, because I have five parameters (namely, α, β, δ, C_M, C_K) to estimate, I would need at least six or seven observations for each cohort. The marital fertility data of cohorts that fall short of this requirement would not be used in the estimation at all. In order to avoid throwing out these data, I have assumed the values of α, β, and δ are common for all cohorts, but that the values of C_M and C_k vary across cohorts, and have used all the available data.

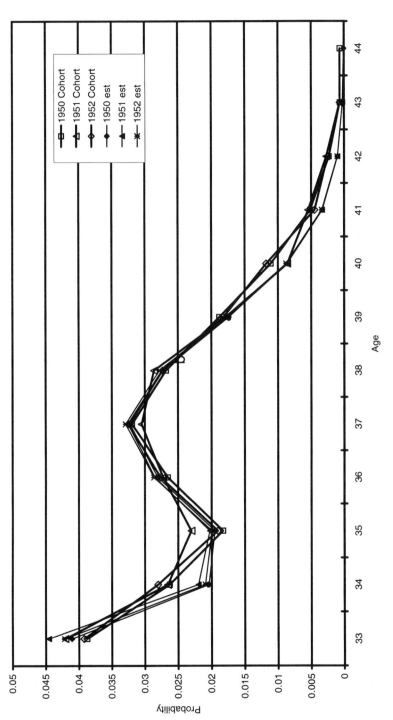

Fig. 12.3 Age distribution of third child fertility of women who married at age thirty-three (1950, 1951, and 1952 cohorts)

The actual estimation was carried out in two steps. In the first step, I estimated one set $(\hat{\alpha}, \hat{\beta}, \hat{\delta}, \hat{C}_M, \hat{C}_k)$ by the maximum-likelihood method using all the available data. In the second step, by keeping the same values of $(\hat{\alpha}, \hat{\beta}, \hat{\delta})$, I estimated (C_M, C_k) for each cohort using only the data belonging to the cohort.

Cross-Cohort Comparisons of Marital Fertility Rates

Estimation result. The result of my estimation is summarized in tables 12.4 through 12.6, where only the sums of C_M and C_k are reported. The blank spaces in the tables represent the absence of estimates. There are two large blank areas in these tables: one in the upper-left region and the other in lower-right region. The upper-left blank region reflects the left censoring problem; that is, prior to 1979, the necessary data for estimation are not available as far as these groups are concerned. If earlier data on the marriage and childbearing behaviors are made available by the government, then the blank space in this region can be eliminated. Most of the second region, however, is attributable to the combination of the birth year and marital age that are yet to come. As such, they can never be filled in completely.

Estimation of the completed marital fertility rates. In order to construct estimates of completed fertility rates for the cohorts, we need a complete set of estimated marital fertility functions for all marital ages, and we must somehow fill the blank spaces in tables 12.4 through 12.6. To fill these spaces, I have taken a simple shortcut: For each order of birth, I take the log value of the estimated Cs, regress them on age-married, age-married squared, and age-married cubed, and cross terms with age-married (raised to the third power) and with birth year, age, and birth year dummies. More specifically, for a woman born in year j who was married at age k, the completed marital fertility rate for her sth-order child $C_{k,j}(s)$ is

$$(26) \qquad \ln C_{k,j}(s) = \alpha + \sum_{r=1}^{3} \beta_r(s) \times k^r + \sum_{r=1}^{3} \lambda_r(s) \times j \cdot k^r$$

$$+ \sum_{j=1950}^{1964} \delta_j(s) \text{Dummy}_j + \varepsilon_{k,j}(s),$$

where Dummy$_j$ is a dummy variable for the cohort born in year j.

As far as the first- and second-child fertility rates are concerned, this specification has shown a good fit. For the first child, as the marital age approaches forty, the completed fertility drops sharply. As for the second child, a sharp drop occurs at the marital age of thirty-five. For the third child, however, the coefficient of the cubed age term turns out to be positive, and the fertility rate does not fall to zero as the marital age increases. Thus, for the third child I have dropped the third-power terms altogether and estimated parameters of the following function:

Table 12.4   **First Child Marital Fertility Rate**

	18	19	20	21	22	23	24	25	26	27
1950										
1951										
1952										0.922
1953									0.927	0.946
1954								0.855	0.943	0.910
1955							0.789	0.859	0.911	0.892
1956						0.719	0.809	0.847	0.899	0.913
1957					0.682	0.727	0.764	0.827	0.884	0.887
1958				0.693	0.634	0.655	0.656	0.702	0.743	0.793
1959			0.627	0.667	0.678	0.701	0.762	0.829	0.812	0.918
1960		0.699	0.639	0.660	0.667	0.702	0.759	0.793	0.834	0.869
1961	0.710	0.705	0.630	0.656	0.682	0.711	0.728	0.805	0.784	0.829
1962	0.708	0.701	0.624	0.652	0.669	0.684	0.738	0.771	0.790	0.831
1963	0.710	0.688	0.645	0.665	0.676	0.695	0.711	0.738	0.793	0.772
1964	0.687	0.697	0.663	0.636	0.674	0.671	0.692	0.728	0.749	0.741

(continued)

Table 12.4 (continued)

1950	28	29	30	31	32	33	34	35	36	37	38
1950		0.908	0.968	0.919	0.863	0.862	0.845	0.785	0.759	0.602	0.540
1951	0.962	0.915	0.954	0.907	0.908	0.871	0.839	0.792	0.757	0.588	0.597
1952	0.976	0.878	0.961	0.943	0.910	0.833	0.828	0.786	0.693	0.628	0.594
1953	0.950	0.874	0.952	0.952	0.868	0.856	0.804	0.755	0.762	0.632	0.576
1954	0.937	0.884	0.965	0.883	0.880	0.845	0.790	0.764	0.619	0.620	
1955	0.956	0.873	0.922	0.915	0.859	0.796	0.782	0.757	0.712		
1956	0.946	0.852	0.953	0.886	0.820	0.798	0.778	0.774			
1957	0.914	0.851	0.897	0.847	0.845	0.794	0.796				
1958	0.878	0.869	0.833	0.854	0.872	0.856					
1959	0.882	0.828	0.883	0.860	0.863						
1960	0.831	0.842	0.880	0.902							
1961	0.841	0.788	0.895								
1962	0.786	0.754									
1963	0.757										

Source: See table 12.1.

Table 12.5

Second Child Marital Fertility Rate

	18	19	20	21	22	23	24	25	26	27	28
1950											
1951											0.694
1952										0.767	0.720
1953									0.791	0.779	0.704
1954								0.759	0.801	0.757	0.694
1955							0.707	0.769	0.775	0.751	0.714
1956						0.646	0.722	0.737	0.769	0.755	0.696
1957					0.611	0.650	0.677	0.721	0.762	0.736	0.666
1958				0.577	0.617	0.630	0.663	0.715	0.738	0.691	0.653
1959		0.547	0.518	0.585	0.610	0.620	0.672	0.710	0.697	0.675	0.614
1960		0.542	0.508	0.571	0.595	0.615	0.661	0.667	0.691	0.635	0.594
1961	0.529	0.549	0.526	0.562	0.602	0.619	0.630	0.658	0.640	0.603	0.607
1962	0.521	0.531	0.514	0.561	0.601	0.582	0.615	0.614	0.609	0.584	0.550
1963	0.509	0.546	0.528	0.571	0.584	0.584	0.580	0.590	0.590	0.520	0.540
1964	0.503		0.537	0.559	0.575	0.547	0.555	0.579	0.541	0.457	0.460

(continued)

Table 12.5   (continued)

	29	30	31	32	33	34	35	36	37
1950	0.656	0.629	0.552	0.497	0.435	0.365	0.279	0.221	0.135
1951	0.652	0.623	0.536	0.508	0.415	0.371	0.311	0.230	0.100
1952	0.646	0.620	0.558	0.491	0.427	0.351	0.284	0.193	0.110
1953	0.640	0.632	0.540	0.482	0.433	0.341	0.269	0.206	0.098
1954	0.656	0.626	0.519	0.478	0.395	0.321	0.290	0.198	0.082
1955	0.642	0.596	0.539	0.458	0.402	0.348	0.281	0.176	0.073
1956	0.621	0.608	0.487	0.426	0.406	0.334	0.278	0.182	
1957	0.615	0.561	0.493	0.461	0.375	0.314	0.234		
1958	0.573	0.550	0.501	0.419	0.359	0.283			
1959	0.553	0.557	0.458	0.390	0.344				
1960	0.557	0.523	0.445	0.382					
1961	0.511	0.499	0.425						
1962	0.494	0.474							
1963	0.454								

Source: See table 12.1.

Table 12.6   **Third Child Marital Fertility Rate**

	18	19	20	21	22	23	24	25	26	27
1950										
1951										
1952										0.269
1953									0.280	0.282
1954								0.281	0.292	0.280
1955							0.264	0.287	0.282	0.276
1956						0.263	0.271	0.272	0.280	0.278
1957					0.249	0.270	0.258	0.268	0.273	0.270
1958				0.242	0.253	0.259	0.250	0.260	0.263	0.253
1959			0.226	0.250	0.248	0.256	0.251	0.257	0.245	0.251
1960		0.234	0.225	0.241	0.239	0.256	0.243	0.232	0.239	0.242
1961	0.238	0.224	0.230	0.238	0.246	0.228	0.226	0.220	0.229	0.229
1962	0.221	0.217	0.228	0.230	0.232	0.217	0.215	0.211	0.219	0.179
1963	0.215	0.217	0.218	0.216	0.231	0.204	0.210	0.207	0.177	0.148
1964	0.213	0.220	0.210	0.201	0.224	0.202	0.201	0.167	0.132	0.163

(*continued*)

Table 12.6   (continued)

	28	29	30	31	32	33	34	35	36	37	38
1950		0.234	0.234	0.207	0.209	0.199	0.188	0.173	0.156	0.158	0.154
1951	0.254	0.244	0.235	0.228	0.223	0.206	0.203	0.176	0.186	0.148	0.166
1952	0.263	0.239	0.243	0.224	0.222	0.204	0.203	0.188	0.164	0.155	0.166
1953	0.260	0.243	0.246	0.227	0.220	0.200	0.190	0.167	0.176	0.166	0.155
1954	0.261	0.251	0.249	0.219	0.217	0.202	0.180	0.167	0.160	0.159	0.178
1955	0.265	0.241	0.227	0.220	0.202	0.183	0.163	0.158	0.138	0.132	
1956	0.268	0.232	0.230	0.207	0.192	0.186	0.156	0.155	0.113		
1957	0.251	0.228	0.209	0.194	0.181	0.163	0.142	0.136			
1958	0.246	0.210	0.204	0.187	0.174	0.148	0.142				
1959	0.246	0.190	0.185	0.160	0.141	0.126					
1960	0.239	0.179	0.160	0.130	0.157						
1961	0.135	0.112	0.123								
1962	0.104	0.138									
1963	0.095										

Source: See table 12.1.

$$(27) \qquad \ln C_{k,j}(3) = \alpha + \sum_{r=1}^{2} \beta_r(3) \times k^r + \sum_{r=1}^{2} \lambda_r(3) \times j \cdot k^r$$

$$+ \sum_{j=1950}^{1964} \delta_j(3)\text{Dummy}_j + \varepsilon_{k,j}(3),$$

where the number 3 in the parenthesis indicates that the relevant parameters are for the third child.

The results of this estimation for each birth-order/cohort/marital age are shown in tables 12.7 through 12.9. They indicate that the sharpest drop in fertility occurred (or is occurring) with the third child, and in particular, in the 1964 cohort; women marrying at age thirty-five or above are essentially not expected to produce a third child. For three cohorts (1955, 1960, and 1964), the shapes of the estimated C_{kj} function are shown in figures 12.4 through 12.6. In the same figures, I have added the point estimates of the completed fertility rates of each cohort. There are substantial differences in the goodness of fit among these three cohorts, because the cohort dummies alone have absorbed the differences across cohorts.

12.5 Age Distribution of First Marriages

In equation (17), the number of births from a given cohort in a given year is obtained as the sum of the products of the marital fertility rate and the number of women in all the groups, which consist of women who married at the same age for the first time. Thus, I need to obtain estimates of the age distribution of marriages for respective cohorts. For this purpose, I have followed the demographers' tradition and fitted incomplete log-gamma functions using maximum likelihood estimation.

The first marriage rates have been computed by combining the census data with the Vital Statistics data. Here I have experienced relatively little difficulty in obtaining reasonably good estimates of the actual age distributions by maximum likelihood method. The estimated parameters are shown in table 12.10. By comparing the age distribution data of first marriages with the estimated distributions, even for cohorts born after 1960, the estimated log-gamma distributions seem to fit the data relatively well, in spite of a substantial right-censoring problem (fig. 12.7).

A very substantial drop has been occurring in the lifetime probability of a Japanese woman's experiencing first marriage. Between the two cohorts born in 1950 and in 1965, I observe a 10 percentage point decline. The decline in the rate between the 1950 and 1957 cohorts, however, is hardly noticeable, and the decline between the 1957 and 1960 cohorts is relatively mild. The rapid decline seems to have taken place in the 1960 cohort, whose probability of getting married in the first half of their twenties is only half that of their predecessors. Although in subsequent cohorts the probability of marriage in the few years after age twenty-seven has

Table 12.7   Estimated First Child Completed Marital Fertility Rate, by Birth Year and Marital Age

	18	19	20	21	22	23	24	25	26
1950	0.807	0.785	0.775	0.775	0.783	0.796	0.815	0.836	0.858
1951	0.817	0.796	0.787	0.787	0.796	0.810	0.830	0.852	0.875
1952	0.810	0.790	0.782	0.783	0.792	0.808	0.827	0.850	0.873
1953	0.803	0.784	0.777	0.779	0.789	0.805	0.825	0.848	0.872
1954	0.778	0.760	0.754	0.757	0.768	0.784	0.804	0.827	0.850
1955	0.767	0.751	0.746	0.750	0.761	0.777	0.798	0.821	0.845
1956	0.752	0.737	0.733	0.738	0.749	0.766	0.787	0.810	0.834
1957	0.728	0.715	0.711	0.716	0.728	0.746	0.767	0.790	0.813
1958	0.675	0.663	0.661	0.666	0.678	0.694	0.715	0.737	0.759
1959	0.701	0.689	0.687	0.694	0.707	0.725	0.746	0.770	0.793
1960	0.689	0.679	0.678	0.685	0.698	0.717	0.738	0.762	0.786
1961	0.676	0.667	0.666	0.674	0.688	0.707	0.729	0.753	0.776
1962	0.666	0.658	0.659	0.667	0.681	0.700	0.723	0.747	0.771
1963	0.661	0.653	0.654	0.663	0.678	0.698	0.721	0.745	0.769
1964	0.648	0.642	0.644	0.653	0.668	0.688	0.711	0.736	0.760

	27	28	29	30	31	32	33	34	35	36	37
1950	0.879	0.898	0.910	0.915	0.910	0.893	0.862	0.818	0.760	0.691	0.612
1951	0.897	0.915	0.928	0.933	0.927	0.909	0.877	0.831	0.771	0.699	0.618
1952	0.895	0.914	0.927	0.932	0.925	0.907	0.874	0.827	0.766	0.693	0.612
1953	0.895	0.913	0.926	0.930	0.924	0.904	0.871	0.823	0.761	0.688	0.605
1954	0.873	0.891	0.903	0.907	0.900	0.881	0.847	0.800	0.739	0.666	0.585
1955	0.867	0.886	0.898	0.902	0.894	0.874	0.840	0.792	0.730	0.657	0.576
1956	0.857	0.875	0.887	0.890	0.882	0.862	0.827	0.779	0.717	0.644	0.564
1957	0.835	0.853	0.865	0.868	0.860	0.839	0.805	0.757	0.696	0.624	0.545
1958	0.780	0.796	0.807	0.810	0.802	0.782	0.749	0.704	0.646	0.578	0.503
1959	0.815	0.833	0.844	0.847	0.838	0.817	0.782	0.733	0.672	0.600	0.522
1960	0.808	0.825	0.837	0.839	0.830	0.808	0.773	0.724	0.662	0.591	0.512
1961	0.798	0.816	0.827	0.828	0.819	0.797	0.761	0.712	0.651	0.579	0.501
1962	0.793	0.810	0.821	0.822	0.813	0.790	0.754	0.705	0.643	0.571	0.493
1963	0.792	0.809	0.820	0.821	0.811	0.788	0.751	0.701	0.638	0.566	0.488
1964	0.782	0.800	0.810	0.811	0.801	0.787	0.741	0.690	0.628	0.556	0.478

(continued)

Table 12.7 (continued)

	38	39	40	41	42	43	44	45	46	47	48	49	50
1950	0.528	0.442	0.358	0.280	0.211	0.153	0.107	0.071	0.045	0.028	0.016	0.009	0.004
1951	0.532	0.444	0.358	0.280	0.210	0.152	0.105	0.070	0.044	0.027	0.015	0.008	0.004
1952	0.525	0.437	0.352	0.273	0.205	0.147	0.102	0.067	0.042	0.025	0.014	0.008	0.004
1953	0.518	0.430	0.345	0.267	0.199	0.143	0.098	0.064	0.040	0.024	0.014	0.007	0.004
1954	0.499	0.413	0.331	0.255	0.190	0.135	0.092	0.060	0.038	0.022	0.012	0.007	0.003
1955	0.491	0.405	0.323	0.248	0.184	0.131	0.089	0.058	0.036	0.021	0.012	0.006	0.003
1956	0.479	0.394	0.313	0.240	0.177	0.125	0.085	0.055	0.034	0.020	0.011	0.006	0.003
1957	0.461	0.378	0.300	0.229	0.168	0.118	0.080	0.051	0.031	0.018	0.010	0.005	0.003
1958	0.426	0.348	0.275	0.209	0.153	0.107	0.072	0.046	0.028	0.016	0.009	0.005	0.002
1959	0.440	0.359	0.283	0.214	0.156	0.109	0.073	0.046	0.028	0.016	0.009	0.004	0.002
1960	0.431	0.350	0.275	0.208	0.151	0.105	0.070	0.044	0.027	0.015	0.008	0.004	0.002
1961	0.420	0.341	0.267	0.201	0.145	0.101	0.066	0.042	0.025	0.014	0.008	0.004	0.002
1962	0.413	0.334	0.260	0.195	0.141	0.097	0.064	0.040	0.024	0.013	0.007	0.004	0.002
1963	0.407	0.328	0.255	0.191	0.137	0.094	0.061	0.038	0.023	0.013	0.007	0.003	0.002
1964	0.398	0.320	0.248	0.185	0.132	0.090	0.059	0.036	0.021	0.012	0.006	0.003	0.001

Source: See table 12.1.

Table 12.8   Estimated Second Child Completed Marital Fertility Rate, by Birth Year and Marital Age

	18	19	20	21	22	23	24	25	26	27	28	29	30	31	32	33
1950	0.366	0.404	0.446	0.492	0.540	0.587	0.632	0.670	0.698	0.713	0.710	0.689	0.648	0.590	0.517	0.436
1951	0.381	0.418	0.460	0.505	0.551	0.596	0.639	0.674	0.699	0.710	0.705	0.681	0.638	0.579	0.506	0.425
1952	0.402	0.439	0.480	0.524	0.569	0.613	0.654	0.686	0.709	0.717	0.708	0.681	0.636	0.575	0.501	0.420
1953	0.425	0.462	0.503	0.546	0.590	0.632	0.670	0.701	0.720	0.725	0.713	0.683	0.636	0.572	0.497	0.415
1954	0.457	0.494	0.534	0.577	0.620	0.662	0.698	0.726	0.743	0.745	0.729	0.696	0.645	0.578	0.501	0.417
1955	0.479	0.515	0.555	0.596	0.638	0.677	0.710	0.735	0.749	0.747	0.729	0.692	0.639	0.571	0.493	0.409
1956	0.485	0.519	0.556	0.595	0.633	0.668	0.698	0.719	0.729	0.724	0.703	0.665	0.612	0.545	0.469	0.388
1957	0.493	0.525	0.559	0.595	0.630	0.662	0.688	0.705	0.711	0.704	0.680	0.641	0.587	0.521	0.447	0.369
1958	0.498	0.527	0.559	0.591	0.623	0.651	0.674	0.687	0.690	0.679	0.654	0.614	0.560	0.495	0.423	0.348
1959	0.502	0.529	0.558	0.588	0.616	0.641	0.659	0.670	0.669	0.656	0.629	0.588	0.534	0.471	0.401	0.329
1960	0.508	0.532	0.558	0.585	0.610	0.631	0.646	0.653	0.649	0.634	0.605	0.563	0.510	0.448	0.380	0.311
1961	0.513	0.534	0.558	0.581	0.603	0.621	0.633	0.637	0.630	0.612	0.582	0.539	0.486	0.426	0.360	0.294
1962	0.511	0.530	0.550	0.571	0.589	0.603	0.612	0.612	0.603	0.583	0.552	0.510	0.458	0.399	0.337	0.274
1963	0.508	0.524	0.542	0.559	0.574	0.585	0.590	0.588	0.576	0.555	0.523	0.481	0.430	0.374	0.314	0.255
1964	0.509	0.523	0.537	0.551	0.563	0.571	0.574	0.569	0.555	0.532	0.499	0.457	0.408	0.353	0.296	0.239

(*continued*)

Table 12.8   (continued)

	34	35	36	37	38	39	40	41	42	43	44	45	46	47	48	49	50
1950	0.352	0.272	0.199	0.139	0.092	0.057	0.033	0.018	0.009	0.004	0.002	0.001	0.000	0.000	0.000	0.000	0.000
1951	0.343	0.264	0.193	0.134	0.088	0.055	0.032	0.018	0.009	0.004	0.002	0.001	0.000	0.000	0.000	0.000	0.000
1952	0.337	0.259	0.189	0.132	0.087	0.054	0.031	0.017	0.009	0.004	0.002	0.001	0.000	0.000	0.000	0.000	0.000
1953	0.333	0.255	0.186	0.129	0.085	0.053	0.031	0.017	0.009	0.004	0.002	0.001	0.000	0.000	0.000	0.000	0.000
1954	0.333	0.255	0.186	0.129	0.085	0.052	0.031	0.017	0.009	0.004	0.002	0.001	0.000	0.000	0.000	0.000	0.000
1955	0.326	0.249	0.181	0.125	0.082	0.051	0.030	0.016	0.008	0.004	0.002	0.001	0.000	0.000	0.000	0.000	0.000
1956	0.309	0.235	0.171	0.118	0.077	0.048	0.028	0.015	0.008	0.004	0.002	0.001	0.000	0.000	0.000	0.000	0.000
1957	0.293	0.222	0.161	0.111	0.073	0.045	0.026	0.014	0.007	0.004	0.002	0.001	0.000	0.000	0.000	0.000	0.000
1958	0.276	0.209	0.151	0.104	0.068	0.042	0.025	0.014	0.007	0.003	0.002	0.001	0.000	0.000	0.000	0.000	0.000
1959	0.260	0.196	0.142	0.098	0.064	0.040	0.023	0.013	0.007	0.003	0.001	0.001	0.000	0.000	0.000	0.000	0.000
1960	0.245	0.185	0.133	0.092	0.060	0.037	0.022	0.012	0.006	0.003	0.001	0.001	0.000	0.000	0.000	0.000	0.000
1961	0.231	0.174	0.125	0.086	0.056	0.035	0.020	0.011	0.006	0.003	0.001	0.001	0.000	0.000	0.000	0.000	0.000
1962	0.215	0.161	0.116	0.079	0.052	0.032	0.019	0.010	0.005	0.003	0.001	0.001	0.000	0.000	0.000	0.000	0.000
1963	0.199	0.149	0.107	0.073	0.048	0.029	0.017	0.010	0.005	0.002	0.001	0.000	0.000	0.000	0.000	0.000	0.000
1964	0.186	0.139	0.100	0.068	0.044	0.027	0.016	0.009	0.005	0.002	0.001	0.000	0.000	0.000	0.000	0.000	0.000

Source: See table 12.1.

Table 12.9   Estimated Third Child Completed Marital Fertility Rate, by Birth Year and Marital Age

	18	19	20	21	22	23	24	25	26	27	28	29	30	31	32	33
1950	0.115	0.128	0.141	0.154	0.167	0.178	0.188	0.197	0.204	0.209	0.212	0.212	0.211	0.207	0.201	0.193
1951	0.140	0.155	0.169	0.183	0.196	0.208	0.218	0.226	0.232	0.235	0.236	0.235	0.230	0.224	0.215	0.204
1952	0.160	0.176	0.192	0.206	0.219	0.230	0.239	0.246	0.250	0.251	0.249	0.245	0.238	0.228	0.217	0.204
1953	0.181	0.198	0.214	0.228	0.241	0.251	0.258	0.263	0.265	0.264	0.259	0.252	0.242	0.230	0.216	0.200
1954	0.198	0.215	0.231	0.244	0.256	0.264	0.270	0.273	0.272	0.268	0.261	0.251	0.239	0.224	0.208	0.191
1955	0.206	0.222	0.236	0.249	0.258	0.265	0.268	0.268	0.265	0.259	0.249	0.237	0.223	0.207	0.190	0.172
1956	0.221	0.237	0.251	0.261	0.269	0.274	0.275	0.273	0.267	0.258	0.246	0.232	0.216	0.198	0.180	0.161
1957	0.225	0.240	0.252	0.260	0.266	0.269	0.267	0.263	0.255	0.244	0.230	0.215	0.198	0.180	0.161	0.142
1958	0.232	0.245	0.255	0.262	0.266	0.266	0.263	0.256	0.246	0.233	0.218	0.201	0.183	0.164	0.146	0.127
1959	0.232	0.243	0.251	0.257	0.258	0.256	0.251	0.242	0.230	0.216	0.200	0.183	0.165	0.146	0.128	0.111
1960	0.231	0.240	0.247	0.250	0.250	0.246	0.239	0.228	0.215	0.200	0.183	0.166	0.148	0.130	0.112	0.096
1961	0.225	0.232	0.237	0.238	0.236	0.230	0.222	0.210	0.196	0.181	0.164	0.147	0.129	0.112	0.096	0.081
1962	0.220	0.227	0.230	0.229	0.225	0.218	0.208	0.195	0.181	0.165	0.148	0.131	0.114	0.098	0.083	0.069
1963	0.222	0.226	0.228	0.226	0.220	0.211	0.200	0.186	0.171	0.154	0.137	0.120	0.103	0.088	0.073	0.061
1964	0.212	0.216	0.215	0.212	0.205	0.195	0.183	0.169	0.153	0.137	0.121	0.105	0.089	0.075	0.062	0.050

(continued)

Table 12.9   (continued)

	34	35	36	37	38	39	40	41	42	43	44	45	46	47	48	49	50
1950	0.184	0.173	0.161	0.149	0.136	0.122	0.109	0.097	0.085	0.073	0.063	0.053	0.044	0.037	0.030	0.025	0.020
1951	0.192	0.178	0.164	0.149	0.134	0.119	0.105	0.092	0.079	0.067	0.057	0.047	0.039	0.032	0.026	0.020	0.016
1952	0.189	0.173	0.157	0.141	0.125	0.110	0.095	0.082	0.069	0.058	0.048	0.040	0.032	0.026	0.020	0.016	0.012
1953	0.184	0.166	0.149	0.132	0.116	0.100	0.085	0.072	0.060	0.050	0.041	0.033	0.026	0.021	0.016	0.012	0.009
1954	0.173	0.154	0.137	0.119	0.103	0.088	0.074	0.062	0.051	0.041	0.033	0.026	0.021	0.016	0.012	0.009	0.007
1955	0.154	0.136	0.119	0.102	0.087	0.073	0.061	0.050	0.040	0.032	0.026	0.020	0.015	0.012	0.009	0.007	0.005
1956	0.142	0.124	0.107	0.091	0.076	0.063	0.052	0.042	0.033	0.026	0.020	0.016	0.012	0.009	0.007	0.005	0.003
1957	0.124	0.107	0.091	0.076	0.063	0.052	0.042	0.033	0.026	0.020	0.016	0.012	0.009	0.006	0.005	0.003	0.002
1958	0.110	0.093	0.078	0.065	0.053	0.043	0.034	0.027	0.021	0.016	0.012	0.009	0.006	0.005	0.003	0.002	0.002
1959	0.094	0.079	0.066	0.054	0.043	0.034	0.027	0.021	0.016	0.012	0.009	0.006	0.005	0.003	0.002	0.002	0.001
1960	0.081	0.067	0.055	0.044	0.035	0.027	0.021	0.016	0.012	0.009	0.007	0.005	0.003	0.002	0.002	0.001	0.001
1961	0.067	0.055	0.045	0.035	0.028	0.021	0.016	0.012	0.009	0.007	0.005	0.003	0.002	0.002	0.001	0.001	0.000
1962	0.057	0.046	0.037	0.029	0.022	0.017	0.013	0.009	0.007	0.005	0.003	0.002	0.002	0.001	0.001	0.000	0.000
1963	0.049	0.039	0.031	0.024	0.018	0.014	0.010	0.007	0.005	0.004	0.003	0.002	0.001	0.001	0.001	0.000	0.000
1964	0.040	0.032	0.025	0.019	0.014	0.011	0.008	0.005	0.004	0.003	0.002	0.001	0.001	0.001	0.000	0.000	0.000

Source: See table 12.1.

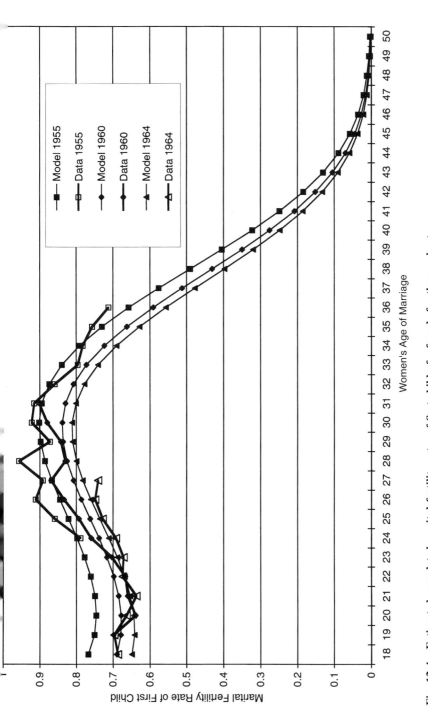

Fig. 12.4 Estimated completed marital-fertility rates of first child of a female for three cohorts

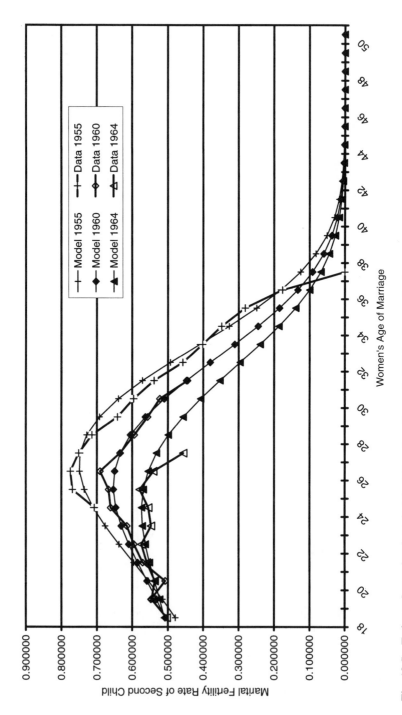

Fig. 12.5 Estimated completed marital-fertility rates of second child for three cohorts

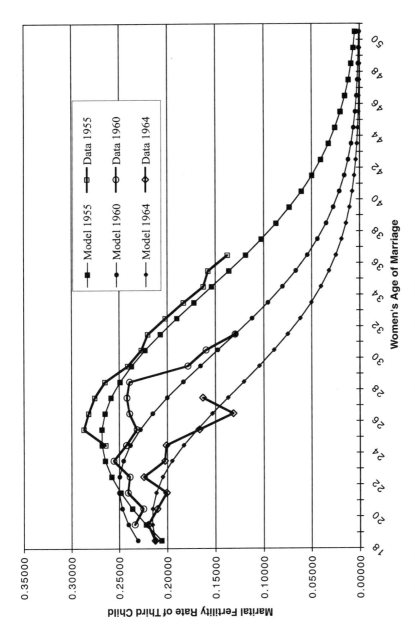

Fig. 12.6   Estimated completed marital-fertility rates of third child for three cohorts

Table 12.10   **Estimated Parameters of Age Distribution Function of First Marriage (incomplete log-gamma function), by Birth Year**

	1950	1955	1960	1961	1962	1963	1964	1965
α	1.0740	1.6386	2.5796	3.1566	3.8334	4.8363	5.5960	5.8053
β	0.4990	0.4648	0.2774	0.2966	0.3416	0.4719	0.3452	0.4461
μ	-0.3746	-0.2687	-0.2085	-0.1842	-0.1644	-0.1432	-0.1293	-0.1233
u	21.4220	22.6289	22.6800	24.0757	26.2199	30.5007	30.0440	32.8875
C	0.8771	0.8623	0.8352	0.8242	0.8114	0.7909	0.7822	0.7796
Likelihood	-2.5812	-2.6236	-2.5429	-2.5120	-2.4601	-2.3767	-2.2639	-2.1043
FOC								
α	0.000003	-0.000062	-0.000094	-0.000099	-0.000100	-0.000096	-0.000097	-0.000098
β	-0.000100	0.000099	0.000094	0.000047	0.000096	0.000099	0.000043	0.000061
μ	0.000052	-0.000074	-0.000090	-0.000093	-0.000036	-0.000069	-0.000444	-0.000048
u	0.000019	-0.000012	-0.000005	-0.000003	-0.000005	-0.000007	-0.000002	-0.000003

Source: See table 12.1.

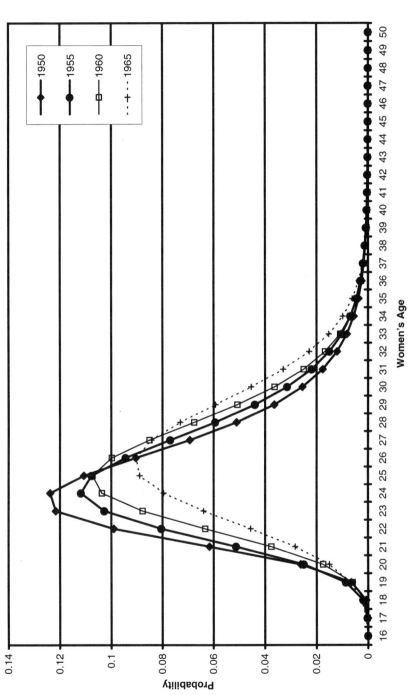

Fig. 12.7 Estimated age distribution functions of marriage probability of Japanese females by birth years

increased by a few percentage points, this increase does not seem to extend beyond the first half of the thirties. In the 1991–92 projection, it was assumed implicitly that the 1960 cohorts would complete the structural adjustment in childbearing behavior. My estimation suggests that in the next five cohorts the lifetime probability of first marriage declined by 7 percentage points.

12.6   Analyzing the Sources of the Decline in Fertility Rates

In my notation, for a woman born in year j married at age k, $C_{kj}(s)$ gives the expected number of children of the order s in her lifetime. Thus, as far as the children of order s are concerned, the completed fertility of a woman born in year j is obtained as the weighted sum of $C_{kj}(s)$'s, or

$$(28) \qquad \hat{C}(s) = \sum_{k=15}^{49} C_{k,j}(s) \cdot m(k),$$

where k stands for the age at first marriage. Using equation (28), in table 12.11 I have computed the fertility rates of each cohort between 1950 and 1964 for their first three children.

According to the table, the completed fertility rate shows a consistent decline for the first child, with the birth year of the woman. For the second and the third child, however, the fertility rates seem to rise until 1954 and then decline. The latter is not an actual phenomenon, but is a problem caused by insufficient information in my "extrapolation" method[3] when cohorts are considerably heterogeneous. For women born in 1950, for example, I began my observation of their reproductive behavior only for age twenty-nine, which is probably too late to start observations even for the second child in those days. In contrast, for cohorts born after 1955, my extrapolation should be far more reliable, since for the 1955 cohort, the observation started at age twenty-four. Thus, 1955 should serve as a good starting point for comparative analysis. If I concentrate on cohorts born after 1955, I notice a general decline in fertility rates between the 1955 and 1960 cohorts. The estimated fertility rates have dropped by almost 0.1 for each order of birth, a drop of at least 0.3 in the TFR.

Has the drop in TFR been brought about by changes in marriage rates or by changes in marital fertility rates? In order to answer this question, I computed the hypothetical completed fertility rates using the estimated marriage-rate function of the 1955 cohort. The differences between these hypothetical fertility rates and those in table 12.12 are attributable solely to changes in marital behavior between the 1955 cohort and the previous cohort.

For instance, for the 1955 cohort, the sum of the completed fertilities of

---

3. Needless to say, this problem will be solved once the relevant data prior to 1979 are made public.

Table 12.11   **Estimated Fertility Rates of First Three Children of a Female Born after 1950**

	First Three Children	First Child	Second Child	Third Child
1950	1.785	0.909	0.670	0.206
1951	1.823	0.920	0.669	0.234
1952	1.840	0.912	0.676	0.251
1953	1.876	0.914	0.693	0.269
1954	1.916	0.904	0.730	0.282
1955	1.875	0.881	0.724	0.270
1956	1.859	0.873	0.711	0.275
1957	1.832	0.861	0.705	0.266
1958	1.697	0.781	0.667	0.250
1959	1.702	0.817	0.649	0.236
1960	1.637	0.797	0.622	0.218
1961	1.570	0.778	0.596	0.196
1962	1.501	0.761	0.562	0.178
1963	1.427	0.741	0.523	0.164
1964	1.363	0.725	0.495	0.144

Source: See table 12.1.

Table 12.12   **Hypothetical Fertility Rates of Women Born after 1950 with Marital Behavior of 1955 Cohort**

	First Three Children	First Child	Second Child	Third Child
1950	1.766	0.899	0.663	0.204
1951	1.815	0.916	0.666	0.233
1952	1.842	0.913	0.677	0.251
1953	1.869	0.911	0.691	0.268
1954	1.879	0.887	0.716	0.276
1955	1.875	0.881	0.724	0.270
1956	1.851	0.869	0.708	0.274
1957	1.804	0.846	0.694	0.264
1958	1.721	0.788	0.676	0.257
1959	1.725	0.823	0.659	0.243
1960	1.687	0.815	0.643	0.229
1961	1.642	0.804	0.627	0.211
1962	1.598	0.797	0.604	0.197
1963	1.563	0.795	0.580	0.188
1964	1.517	0.785	0.562	0.171

Source: See table 12.1.

the first three birth orders that I have estimated is 1.875, whereas for the 1954 cohort it was 1.916. Thus, the total change is −0.041. If I had applied the estimated marriage-rate function of the 1954 cohort to the 1955 cohort, the sum of the three fertility rates would have been 1.913 instead of 1.875. In other words, if the marriage behavior remained unchanged, the sum of the fertilities would have changed only very slightly (or 1.913 − 1.916 = −0.003, to be exact). Thus the remainder of the change (namely 1.875 − 1.913 = −0.038) is attributable to changes in marital fertility rates.

The same analysis is repeated for cohorts born between 1955 and 1964, and the results are shown in table 12.12. The results suggest that, of a 0.55 drop in the sum of these three fertility rates, changes in marital behavior explain −0.19, while changes in marital fertility rates account for −0.36.

12.7 Concluding Remarks

It should be clear by now why the last official population projection failed. In an attempt to estimate directly the age-specific fertility rate distribution, the projection assumed a priori the stability of parameters beyond the 1960 cohort, probably the last cohort for which demographers were able to obtain stable distribution parameters. This is equivalent to assuming that this cohort would complete the behavioral changes in childbearing for Japanese women. Instead, it took another five cohorts for this happen and, in the meantime, lifetime marital rates dropped by 15 percentage points.

In the new population projection announced in January 1997, the government forecasters again have predicted that TFR will recover to 1.6 by the end of the second decade of the next century. On this point, I have only two things to say. First, the TFR for the latest cohort (those born in 1964) that I was able to estimate stands at slightly above 1.4, or about the current TFR of all Japanese women, because fertility rates attributable to a birth order higher than three add very little. Thus, the present Japanese women's TFR is at its equilibrium level, not at a transitory or disequilibrium low level as government demographers have argued.

Furthermore, there is no inherent demographic mechanism for a rebound in fertility rates to occur. In fact, the lifetime rates that I used to derive the expected completed fertility rates are based on the estimated dynamic behavioral equations of childbearing. Hence, I have already taken dynamic adjustment behaviors into account. As far as I know, there are no demographic grounds for a fertility rebound to occur, but there are very strong economic grounds for expecting another drop to take place. Since the labor force is expected to decline at the rate of almost one percent a year starting early in the next century, female labor is expected to fill part of the shortage. This will mean better employment opportunities and better pay for women, raising the opportunity costs of having children even further. In Tokyo, TFR stands at about 1.1, and we should not be surprised to see the national TFR drop to that level.

What does this all mean in terms of our (or our children's) lives in the twenty-first century? First of all, if one limits the analysis to the first quarter of the century, differences in the TFR matter very little. This is true of pay-as-you-go public pension program costs or of public health insurance costs. The difference will show up in the second quarter of the century. Second, the difference in these costs is substantial. The new population projection is equivalent to the government's officially admitting that the costs of these programs have been underestimated by at least 20 percent. As I suspect, even their new projection turns out to be too optimistic. If no rebound occurs, the per capita costs of these programs will increase by at least another 10 percent. It is clear that the time has come to begin reengineering the fundamental frameworks of our social insurance programs, particularly their financing mechanisms, rather than putting more money into the terminal care of these programs.

Appendix
Source of Instability in the Estimated Parameters

Let us explore the source of the instability in the estimated parameters as more data are added. Collecting the terms in equation (14), and noting

$$S(x) = 1 - \sum_{\tau=15}^{x-1} m_\tau,$$

we obtain the first-order condition

(14′) $$\sum_{\tau=15}^{x-1} \left[\frac{m_\tau}{P(\tau;\theta)} - \frac{1 - \sum_{\tau=15}^{x-1} m_\tau}{1 - \sum_{\tau=15}^{x-1} P(\tau;\theta)} \right] \frac{\partial P(\tau;\theta)}{\partial \theta} = 0.$$

Let us define the theoretical probability of not giving birth of the child of that order by $P(51;\theta)$, or the probability of giving birth at age fifty-one. Similarly, if the proportion of women not giving birth to a child is given by m_{51}, we have

(15′) $$1 - \sum_{\tau=15}^{x-1} P(\tau;\theta) = \sum_{\tau=x}^{51} P(\tau;\theta)$$

$$1 - \sum_{\tau=15}^{x-1} m_\tau = \sum_{\tau=x}^{51} m_\tau.$$

Furthermore, the optimality condition (14′) with respect to C is particularly simple and is given by

(16′) $$\sum_{\tau=x}^{51} m_\tau = \sum_{\tau=x}^{51} P(\tau;\theta).$$

For the rest of the parameters of log-gamma distribution function, (14′) can be written as

$$(17') \quad \Psi_\theta(x - 1; \hat{\theta}) = \sum_{\tau=15}^{x-1} \frac{m_\tau}{P(\tau; \hat{\theta})} \frac{\partial P(\tau; \hat{\theta})}{\partial \theta} - \left[\frac{\sum\limits_{x}^{51} m_\tau}{\sum\limits_{x}^{51} P(\tau; \hat{\theta})} \right] \sum_{\tau=15}^{x-1} \frac{\partial P(\tau; \hat{\theta})}{\partial \theta}$$

$$= \sum_{\tau=15}^{x-1} \frac{m_\tau}{P(\tau; \hat{\theta})} \frac{\partial P(\tau; \hat{\theta})}{\partial \theta} - \sum_{\tau=15}^{x-1} \frac{\partial P(\tau; \hat{\theta})}{\partial \theta} = 0.$$

Moreover, the sum of all the possibilities including $P(51; \theta)$ is always equal to one, regardless of the value of θ; hence we have

$$(18') \qquad \sum_{\tau=15}^{51} \frac{\partial P(\tau; \theta)}{\partial \theta} = 0.$$

Therefore, equation (17′) implies θ

$$(19') \quad \Psi_\theta(x - 1; \hat{\theta}) = \sum_{\tau=15}^{x-1} \frac{m_\tau}{P(\tau; \hat{\theta})} \frac{\partial P(\tau; \hat{\theta})}{\partial \theta} + \sum_{\tau=x}^{51} \frac{\partial P(\tau; \hat{\theta})}{\partial \theta} = 0.$$

Adding the fertility data at age x, the optimality condition is given by

$$(20') \qquad \Psi_\theta(x; \tilde{\theta}) = \sum_{\tau=15}^{x} \frac{m_\tau}{P(\tau; \tilde{\theta})} \frac{\partial P(\tau; \tilde{\theta})}{\partial \theta} + \sum_{\tau=x+1}^{51} \frac{\partial P(\tau; \tilde{\theta})}{\partial \theta} = 0.$$

If the right-hand side of the equation is evaluated at the previous optimal value $\hat{\theta}$,

$$(21') \qquad \Psi_\theta(x; \hat{\theta}) = \left[\sum_{\tau=15}^{x-1} \frac{m_\tau}{P(\tau; \hat{\theta})} \frac{\partial P(\tau; \hat{\theta})}{\partial \theta} + \sum_{\tau=x}^{51} \frac{\partial P(\tau; \hat{\theta})}{\partial \theta} \right]$$

$$+ \left[\frac{m_x}{P(x; \hat{\theta})} - 1 \right] \frac{\partial P(x; \hat{\theta})}{\partial \theta},$$

and we obtain the dynamic equation

$$(22') \qquad \Psi_\theta(x; \hat{\theta}) = \Psi_\theta(x - 1; \hat{\theta}) + \left[\frac{m_x}{P(x; \hat{\theta})} - 1 \right] \frac{\partial P(x; \hat{\theta})}{\partial \theta}.$$

It is clear from equation (22′) that the estimated parameters are consistent even when one truncates samples provided that the fertility data at every age have been generated by the theoretical distribution. If the sample size gets arbitrarily large for every t, we have

$$m_t \to P(t; \theta),$$

and, from equation (22′), at every age x, we should have

$$\lim_{n\to\infty} \Psi(x - 1;\theta) = \lim_{n\to\infty} \Psi(x;\theta) = 0.$$

Ordinarily, if we have one million observations, the law of large numbers should work to give us this condition. If, on the other hand, the estimated parameters remain unstable, it is most likely that the fertility data have not been generated by that particular theoretical distribution.

The source of the instability is the second term of equation (22′). The larger the divergence of the new fertility data at age x, or m_x, and the estimated fertility rate $P(x;\hat{\theta})$ using the data up to age $(x - 1)$, the absolute value of the coefficient in the second term,

$$\frac{m_x}{P(x;\hat{\theta})} - 1,$$

will be larger, and the revision of the estimated parameters will be larger.

References

Coale, A. J. 1971. Age patterns of marriage. *Population Studies* 25 (2): 193–214.

Coale, A. J., and D. R. McNeil. 1972. The distribution of age of the frequency of first marriage in a female cohort. *Journal of the American Statistical Association* 67 (340): 743–49.

Kaneko, Ryuichi. 1991. "Shokon kateino jinkoga kuteki bunseki" (A demographic analysis of first marriage process). *Jinkogaku Kenkyu* 47:3–27. Koseisho Jinko Mondai Kenkyusho (Institute of Population Problems, Ministry of Health and Welfare).

———. 1993. "Nenrei betsu shusseiritsu no shourai suikei sisutemu" (A projection system for future age-specific fertility rates). *Jinkogaku Kenkyu* 49:17–38. Koseisho Jinko Mondai Kenkyusho (Institute of Population Problems, Ministry of Health and Welfare).

Kenkyusho, Koseisho Jinkomondai, ed. 1992. *Nihonno shorai suikei jinko: Heisei 4 nen 9 gatu suikei* (Population projections for Japan: 1991–2090). Kosei Tokei Kyokai.

Contributors

Yukiko Abe
Faculty of Economics
Asia University
5-24-10, Sakai, Musashino-shi
Tokyo 180-8629
Japan

Seki Asano
Faculty of Economics
Tokyo Metropolitan University
1-1 Minami-Osawa
Hachioji, Tokyo, 192-0397
Japan

David M. Cutler
Department of Economics
Harvard University
Cambridge, MA 02138

Matthew J. Eichner
Columbia Business School
Uris Hall
3022 Broadway
New York, NY 10027

Tetsuya Maruyama
Graduate School of Economics
University of Pennsylvania
160 McNeil Building
3718 Locust Walk
Philadelphia, PA 19104

Satoshi Nakanishi
Department of Economics
Nihon Fukushi University
Okuda Mihama-cho
Chita-gum, Aichi 470-3295
Japan

Noriyoshi Nakayama
Department of Finance
University of Marketing &
    Distribution Sciences
3-1, Gakuen-nishi-machi, Nishi-ku
Kobe, Hyogo 651-2188
Japan

Seiritsu Ogura
Faculty of Economics
Hosei University
4342, Aihara-machi
Machida-shi, Tokyo 194-02
Japan

James M. Poterba
Department of Economics
Massachusetts Institute of Technology
50 Memorial Drive
Cambridge, MA 02142

Makoto Saito
Graduate School of Economics
Hitotsubashi University
2-1 Naka, Kunitachi
Tokyo 186-8601
Japan

Andrew A. Samwick
Department of Economics
6106 Rockefeller Hall
Dartmouth College
Hanover, NH 03755-3514

Reiko Suzuki
Japan Center for Economic Research
2-6-1, Nihonbashi-Kayabacho
Chuo-ku, Tokyo 103-0025
Japan

Toshiaki Tachibanaki
Faculty of Economics
Kyoto Institute of Economic Research
Kyoto University
Yoshida-Honmachi, Sakyo-ku
Kyoto 606-8500
Japan

Steven F. Venti
Department of Economics
6106 Rockefeller Hall
Dartmouth College
Hanover, NH 03755

David A. Wise
John F. Kennedy School of
 Government
Harvard University
79 John F. Kennedy Street
Cambridge, MA 02138

Richard Woodbury
MCPR
89 Main Street
Yarmouth, ME 04096

Author Index

405

Subject Index

Adverse selection: in choices for health care plans, 13–14, 16, 183; in third wave of health care reform, 12, 169

Altruism: as motive for intergenerational transfer, 149–66; tested against life-cycle hypothesis, 149–54

Asset accumulation: attitudes toward, 50–59; life-cycle model assumptions, 100

Asset allocation: financial, 77–91; portfolio choice, 66–77; to prepare for risks, 105

Assets: business, 97, 99; financial assets as share of total, 91–92; in lifetime earnings deciles, 30–33; post-retirement in Japan, 106–7; real estate, 94–97

Choice: for employee health care plans, 15, 249; evidence for choice of health insurance, 16, 250; in Japanese Employees' Pension system, 278–87; in Medicare program, 15, 250; of private annuity or public life insurance, 107–11, 113–26; saving attributed to, 26–27, 38–47, 57–59; for saving toward retirement, 3–4, 26–27. *See also* Retirement policies of firms

Choice of health insurance: demographic characteristics of, 253–56; plan switching, 266–69; risk- and price-related, 256–66

Competition: in firms' retirement policies, 19–20, 317–19; in third wave of health care reform, 12

Consumption: age and cohort effects in Japan on, 156–58; age and cohort effects in United Kingdom on, 156, 161–62; age and cohort effects in United States on, 156, 159–60; age and cohort effects on, 9–10, 137–46; cross-age distribution in Japan, 139–41; cross-age distribution in United Kingdom, 139, 143–44; cross-age distribution in United States, 139, 142; evolution of cross-age distribution, 136–37; intergenerational distribution of, 9

Data sources: for analysis of Japan's Employee Pension benefits, 274, 276, 285, 287–88; for cross-age consumption distribution analysis, 137–39; for dispersion of wealth accumulation analysis, 28–30, 59–60; for distribution in Japan of health care costs, 188–89; MedStat claims records, 251; Nikkei Radar Survey (RADAR), 105, 111; promotion, incentives, and wages analysis in Japan, 338–39

Debt: ownership and share for financial, 91, 93–94; ownership and share of real estate, 94–98

Economic growth: consumption distribution with, 9, 139–44

Elderly people, Japan: distribution of health care costs for, 188–205; as long-